ABIDJAN USA

AFRICAN EXPRESSIVE CULTURES

Patrick McNaughton, *editor*

Associate Editors
Catherine M. Cole
Barbara G. Hoffman
Eileen Julien
Kassim Koné
D. A. Masolo
Elisha Renne
Zoë Strother

ABIDJAN USA

Music, Dance, and Mobility in the Lives of Four Ivorian Immigrants

Daniel B. Reed

Indiana University Press

Bloomington and Indianapolis

This book is a publication of

Indiana University Press
Office of Scholarly Publishing
Herman B Wells Library 350
1320 East 10th Street
Bloomington, Indiana 47405 USA

iupress.indiana.edu

© 2016 by Daniel B. Reed

All rights reserved

No part of this book may be reproduced or utilized in any form or by any means, electronic or mechanical, including photocopying and recording, or by any information storage and retrieval system, without permission in writing from the publisher. The Association of American University Presses' Resolution on Permissions constitutes the only exception to this prohibition.

The paper used in this publication meets the minimum requirements of the American National Standard for Information Sciences—Permanence of Paper for Printed Library Materials, ANSI Z39.48-1992.

Manufactured in the United States of America

Library of Congress Cataloging-in-Publication Data

Names: Reed, Daniel B. (Daniel Boyce), author.
Title: Abidjan USA : music, dance, and mobility in the lives of four Ivorian immigrants / Daniel B. Reed.
Other titles: African expressive cultures.
Description: Bloomington ; Indianapolis : Indiana University Press, 2016. | Series: African expressive cultures
Identifiers: LCCN 2016026920 (print) | LCCN 2016028421 (ebook) | ISBN 9780253022219 (cloth : alk. paper) | ISBN 9780253022295 (pbk. : alk. paper) | ISBN 9780253022363 (ebook)
Subjects: LCSH: Ivoirians—United States—Music—History and criticism. | Music—Côte d'Ivoire—History and criticism.
Classification: LCC ML3760.6 .R44 2016 (print) | LCC ML3760.6 (ebook) | DDC 780.89/96668—dc23
LC record available at https://lccn.loc.gov/2016026920

1 2 3 4 5   21 20 19 18 17 16

We must never forget . . . that migrants, rather than simply being a statistic, are first of all persons who have names, faces, and individual stories.

—Pope Francis, April 16, 2016

Contents

Ethnomusicology Multimedia Website — *ix*
Preface: A Confluence of Beginnings — *xiii*
Acknowledgments — *xxiii*
Notes on Language — *xxvii*

Part I. Program Notes

1. Introduction: Abidjan USA — 3
2. "Ballet" as Nexus of Discourses — 33

Part II. Stages and Stories

Act I. Vado Diomande

3. *Kekene*: The Performance of Oneness in NYC — 75
4. "If You Aren't Careful, You Don't Know Where You Will End Up!": Vado Diomande and Transcendence — 91

Act II. Samba Diallo

5. "Culture Brings Everybody Together": Samba Diallo's *Ayoka* — 129
6. "I'm Happy Because I'm Different": Samba Diallo and Exceptionalism — 141

Act III. Sogbety Diomande

7. "You Know You're in a Different Country": Sogbety Diomande's West African Drum and Dance — 181
8. "When You're in a New Context, You Try Things That Work in That Context": Sogbety Diomande and Adaptability — 192

Act IV. Dr. Djo Bi Irie Simon

9 "Open Village": An Ivorian Wedding in an Indiana Cornfield — 227

10 "Everyone Is a Cook, but He's a Chef!": Dr. Djo Bi and Innovation — 243

Part III. Finale

11 Thoughts on the Way Out — 279

Glossary — 285
Notes — 291
Bibliography — 299
Index — 309

Ethnomusicology Multimedia Website

Guide to Online Media Examples

Each audio, video, or still image example listed is associated with specific passages in this book and each has been assigned a unique persistent uniform resource locator, or PURL, which identifies it on the Ethnomusicology Multimedia website.[1] In the text, a PURL number in parentheses functions like a citation—for example, "(PURL 3.1)" means chapter 3, first example.

To access all media, first create a free account on the website (which requires reading and electronically signing a license agreement) and sign in. There are two ways to access and play back the examples. Search "Daniel B. Reed" to be taken to a page with information about the book as well as a playlist of all media examples. To access a specific example, enter its six-digit PURL, which is located at the end of the full PURL address (see the next section). The page that comes up contains that example as well as a full playlist. In the electronic edition, simply click on the PURL address for each media example to be taken directly to it.

List of PURLs

Chapter 2

PURL 2.1 | Mask spirit Gue Pelou leads the Lotus Parade in Bloomington, Indiana, 2006. Gathering of drummers and crowd.
http://purl.dlib.indiana.edu/iudl/em/HsuReed/910226

PURL 2.2 | Mask spirit Gue Pelou leads the Lotus Parade in Bloomington, Indiana, 2006. Transnationalism on parade.
http://purl.dlib.indiana.edu/iudl/em/HsuReed/910227

PURL 2.3 | Mask spirit Gue Pelou performs at the Lotus Festival in Bloomington, Indiana, 2006. Drummers play while the crowd awaits Gue Pelou.
http://purl.dlib.indiana.edu/iudl/em/HsuReed/910228

PURL 2.4 | Mask spirit Gue Pelou performs at the Lotus Festival in Bloomington, Indiana, 2006. Two manifestations of Gue Pelou arrive and perform.
http://purl.dlib.indiana.edu/iudl/em/HsuReed/910229

PURL 2.5 | Mask spirit Gue Pelou performs at the Lotus Festival in Bloomington, Indiana, 2006. Two manifestations of Gue Pelou lead a parade through downtown.
http://purl.dlib.indiana.edu/iudl/em/HsuReed/910230

PURL 2.6 | Mask spirit Gue Pelou performs at the Lotus Festival in Bloomington, Indiana, 2006. Gue Pelou's final performance at Walnut and 6th Streets.
http://purl.dlib.indiana.edu/iudl/em/HsuReed/910231

Chapter 3

PURL 3.1 | "History of Mahou Masks" in New York City, 2010. Introduction.
http://purl.dlib.indiana.edu/iudl/em/HsuReed/910217

PURL 3.2 | "History of Mahou Masks" in New York City, 2010. Song "Tama diani ne we" (You must go to a good place).
http://purl.dlib.indiana.edu/iudl/em/HsuReed/910218

PURL 3.3 | "History of Mahou Masks" in New York City, 2010. Interethnicity in the song "Ma lo ma ge ka Daloa."
http://purl.dlib.indiana.edu/iudl/em/HsuReed/910219

Chapter 5

PURL 5.1 | Samba Diallo's *Ayoka* in Smyrna, Georgia, 2010. Dance with Mau song and Mau stilt mask spirit, both accompanied by the *kuku* rhythm.
http://purl.dlib.indiana.edu/iudl/em/HsuReed/910220

PURL 5.2 | Samba Diallo's *Ayoka* in Smyrna, Georgia, 2010. Guro mask Zauli dancing to the *zauli* rhythm."
http://purl.dlib.indiana.edu/iudl/em/HsuReed/910222

PURL 5.3 | Samba Diallo's *Ayoka* in Smyrna, Georgia, 2010. Ensemble and solo dances and drum breaks to the *kuku* rhythm.
http://purl.dlib.indiana.edu/iudl/em/HsuReed/910221

PURL 5.4 | Samba Diallo's *Ayoka* in Smyrna, Georgia, 2010. Samba Diallo's speech and final dance party.
http://purl.dlib.indiana.edu/iudl/em/HsuReed/910223

Chapter 7

PURL 7.1a | Sogbety Diomande at the 2008 Lotus Festival in Bloomington. Stilt mask spirit Gue Pelou, introduction.
http://purl.dlib.indiana.edu/iudl/em/HsuReed/910252

PURL 7.1b | Sogbety Diomande at the 2008 Lotus Festival in Bloomington. Stilt mask spirit Gue Pelou, benedictions.
http://purl.dlib.indiana.edu/iudl/em/HsuReed/910253

PURL 7.2 | Sogbety Diomande at the 2008 Lotus Festival in Bloomington. Vado Diomande's song and dance with *jembe* solos.
http://purl.dlib.indiana.edu/iudl/em/HsuReed/910249

PURL 7.3 | Sogbety Diomande at the 2008 Lotus Festival in Bloomington. Sogbety Diomande on *baade* drum.
http://purl.dlib.indiana.edu/iudl/em/HsuReed/910251

PURL 7.4 | Sogbety Diomande at the 2008 Lotus Festival in Bloomington. Guinean mask Soli Wule.
http://purl.dlib.indiana.edu/iudl/em/HsuReed/910250

Chapter 9

PURL 9.1 | Djo Bi's wedding near St. Bernice, Indiana, 2008. Friday night informal music making with drum breaks.
http://purl.dlib.indiana.edu/iudl/em/HsuReed/910233

PURL 9.2 | Djo Bi's wedding's near St. Bernice, Indiana, 2008. Friday night informal music making with guitar, *jembe*, and voice.
http://purl.dlib.indiana.edu/iudl/em/HsuReed/910234

PURL 9.3 | Djo Bi's wedding near St. Bernice, Indiana, 2008. Friday night informal music making with guitar, *jembe*, and Guro two-part singing.
http://purl.dlib.indiana.edu/iudl/em/HsuReed/910235

PURL 9.4 | Djo Bi's wedding near St. Bernice, Indiana, 2008. Saturday morning rehearsal for the formal wedding ceremony with Gue Pelou rhythms.
http://purl.dlib.indiana.edu/iudl/em/HsuReed/910236

PURL 9.5 | Djo Bi's wedding near St. Bernice, Indiana, 2008. Saturday morning rehearsal for the formal wedding ceremony with the *bolohi* rhythm.
http://purl.dlib.indiana.edu/iudl/em/HsuReed/910238

PURL 9.6 | Djo Bi's wedding near St. Bernice, Indiana, 2008. Formal wedding ceremony I: Gue Pelou encircles the site.
http://purl.dlib.indiana.edu/iudl/em/HsuReed/910239

PURL 9.7 | Djo Bi's wedding near St. Bernice, Indiana, 2008. Formal wedding ceremony II: Gue Pelou's benediction and song.
http://purl.dlib.indiana.edu/iudl/em/HsuReed/910241

PURL 9.8 | Djo Bi's wedding near St. Bernice, Indiana, 2008. Formal wedding ceremony III: wedding party procession.
http://purl.dlib.indiana.edu/iudl/em/HsuReed/910244

PURL 9.9 | Djo Bi's wedding near St. Bernice, Indiana, 2008. Formal wedding ceremony V: United Nations Band.
http://purl.dlib.indiana.edu/iudl/em/HsuReed/910242

PURL 9.10 | Djo Bi's wedding near St. Bernice, Indiana, 2008. Formal wedding ceremony VII: Guro mask Zauli dancing.
http://purl.dlib.indiana.edu/iudl/em/HsuReed/910246

PURL 9.11 | Djo Bi's wedding near St. Bernice, Indiana, 2008. Formal wedding ceremony VI: Gue Pelou's second appearance.
http://purl.dlib.indiana.edu/iudl/em/HsuReed/910245

PURL 9.12 | Djo Bi's wedding near St. Bernice, Indiana, 2008. Formal wedding ceremony IV: the bride and groom dance.
http://purl.dlib.indiana.edu/iudl/em/HsuReed/910243

PURL 9.13 | Djo Bi's wedding near St. Bernice, Indiana, 2008. Afternoon informal music and dance following the ceremony.
http://purl.dlib.indiana.edu/iudl/em/HsuReed/910247

PURL 9.14 | Djo Bi's wedding near St. Bernice, Indiana, 2008. Evening informal music and dance following the formal ceremony.
http://purl.dlib.indiana.edu/iudl/em/HsuReed/910248

Chapter 10

PURL 10.1 | Djo Bi and his band Asafo at the Bluebird in Bloomington, Indiana, 2009. Song "Bolohi."
http://purl.dlib.indiana.edu/iudl/em/HsuReed/910232

Preface: A Confluence of Beginnings

Beginnings. "let us go back to the dawn of time," began the narrator, his voice booming from huge PA speakers echoing in the mass expanse of Pyramid Stadium on the shores of the Mississippi River in Memphis, Tennessee. The lights dimmed, highlighting an enormous backdrop featuring a sixty-foot-tall "tribal mask"[2]; a rain forest environment, including elephants, hippos, crocodiles, and colorful birds; a village of thatched-roof huts on one side and several contemporary buildings on the other—the only reference to a "modern" Africa, incongruous and misplaced. Suspense building, the lights slowly faded in hues of soft reds and oranges, suggesting a sunrise. "In the beginning," continued the narrator, as live elephants and Ivorians in grass skirts roamed the stage. First heard—the *boing-boing* of a musical bow. Then drums as dozens of dancers began mingling with mask spirits on stilts. From the sides of the stage, enveloping the Ivorian sounds, trumpets announced the opening phrase of Straus's *Also Sprach Zarathustra*, a sonic representation of sunrise (Glass 2015) and "the development of the human race from its origin" that was popularized in "The Dawn of Man" section of Stanley Kubrick's *2001: A Space Odyssey* (Jacobson 2013). Thus began the central event of the 1994 Memphis in May Festival, which that year featured Côte d'Ivoire.

The performance was a military-style "tattoo." Ostensibly designed to showcase the featured country of the 1994 festival, this grand spectacle brought together over one hundred performers from Côte d'Ivoire with at least a dozen other ensembles (see figure P.1). Joining the Ivorians were no fewer than five choirs—the Memphis Symphony Chorus, the Perfect Praise Community Gospel Choir, the Roxie Gunter Singers, Bibleway House of Prayer, and the March On Choir—organized for the twenty-fifth anniversary of the assassination of Dr. Martin Luther King, Jr. But that was not all. Also performing were seven or eight huge instrumental ensembles (there were so many that I lost track): the US Army Harold Trumpets, the Pipes and Drums of the Canadian Scottish Regiment, the North Coast Pipe Band, the Rosa Fort High School Band, and several bands from the US Navy.

Threading together these myriad musical ensembles and styles was a narrative, read aloud, entitled "The Evolution of African Music into Modern American Music." For just the first twenty minutes of the two-hour display, over one

xiii

Figure P.1 May 1994, Memphis in May Tattoo at Pyramid Stadium in Memphis, Tennessee.

hundred performers flown all the way from West Africa allegedly to represent Ivorian music and dance traditions were instead framed in someone else's discourse, (mis)representing them as primal homo sapiens from the dawn of time— "modern America's" evolutionary forebears. No matter that the majority of the Ivorians were cosmopolitan city dwellers, every bit as modern as any Memphis man or woman at that late twentieth-century moment in time.[3]

Beginnings. Among those Ivorian performers in Memphis were two men who were not on the plane when it left Memphis to return to Abidjan. Separately and unknown to the other, both Vado Diomande and Samba Diallo "disappeared," each choosing a strategic instant to fade into the crowds in downtown Memphis. Vado and Samba, at great risk, chose to stay rather than return with the entourage, thus beginning their lives as Ivorian immigrant performers in the United States.

Another performer in the 1994 Memphis in May Festival, fourteen-year-old mask dancer Sogbety Diomande, noticed his uncle Vado missing as he boarded the return flight to Côte d'Ivoire, only later learning why. In 1997 Sogbety (thanks to Vado) found his name among those of a few Ivorian musicians and dancers invited to perform with a New York City–based Ivorian troupe called the Mask Dance Company. Sogbety accepted, and this time he stayed. Also accepting the invitation was a brilliant Ivorian drummer named Dr. Djo Bi; like Sogbety, he chose not to return when his one-year visa expired. Directly or indirectly, Memphis in May, where late twentieth-century Ivorians were made to represent the beginnings of the human race and its music, served as a gateway for the four artists featured in this book to begin new lives as Africans in America representing Africa on stage.

Beginnings. A graduate student in ethnomusicology, folklore, and African studies, I spent early 1994 planning for my first research trip to Côte d'Ivoire. My advisor, Ruth Stone, put me in touch with Ivorian ethnomusicologists Paul Dagri and Adépo Yapo, with whom I shared correspondence and phone calls to prepare for my summer fieldwork. In what was to be our final conversation before my trip, Adépo casually mentioned that he and many other Ivorians in the elite circles of performers, scholars, and politicians in the country's arts and culture world would be in Memphis just before my departure. Excited by this serendipitous turn of events, I called my Ivorian friend Emmanuel Yankey, and we climbed into my old Datsun and drove six hours from Bloomington, Indiana, to Memphis, where I met many people who would prove to be important contacts in Côte d'Ivoire. Moreover, in Memphis I experienced for the first time live performances of Ivorian music and masks, beginning a twenty-two year career researching, teaching, and writing on these subjects.

Beginnings. Fast-forward twelve years, to 2006. I have lived in Côte d'Ivoire and I have written a book, an online multimedia resource, and numerous articles and book chapters on Dan music and masks (Reed 2014, 2012, 2011, 2009, 2008, 2005, 2005, 2004, 2003, 2001). Following a stint at the University of North Carolina at Greensboro, I have returned to Bloomington for a position at my alma mater. One afternoon in my office, I found a message on my phone. It was my father calling from my hometown of Mansfield, Ohio. Dad ran an outdoor school that in the summer months occasionally rented out buildings for various events. That day a woman from Mansfield, Melanie Seaman, had arrived at the school with a gentleman from Africa, hoping to produce an "African Music Festival."

As they talked, Dad started to make connections. Côte d'Ivoire. Drumming. Stilt masks. "This reminds me of what my son does," he said. While his visitors waited in his office, Dad called me, and, sure enough, he was right. This new resident of my hometown, a small, rust belt city in north central Ohio, was from just north of where I had lived in Côte d'Ivoire and identified as Mau—neighbors to the north of the Dan ethnic group, with whom I had lived and conducted field research—who practice some of the same mask and music traditions I had spent several years studying. His name: Sogbety Diomande.

The next thing I knew, I had been invited to give a talk at a festival featuring Ivorian music and masks at my dad's school. At the festival, I met Sogbety, his uncle Vado, then in early recovery from anthrax, and many others, including Samba Diallo who, while walking with me on a path between classes, casually took my hand and asked me to come to Atlanta to study his life and work. Thus, in the little Ohio city where my life began, so began the research for this book on Ivorian immigrant performers.

Fast forward again, to 2008. By this point, I have been on sabbatical and fully engaged in field research for this book. I sat with Vado Diomande in his apartment in Harlem, conducting my second interview with this elder statesman of the American community of Ivorian immigrant performers. Discussing his life story, we bounced around through time. Suddenly he mentioned Memphis. "You were there in 1994?" I asked, eyes wide with astonishment over this apparent coincidence.

I thought back to those opening moments of Memphis in May. I recalled that my jaw had tightened and my stomach had become mildly queasy. That those contemporary human beings—some of whom I now considered friends—had been framed as primitives in someone else's social evolutionary discourse had pained me. I remembered sitting in the stadium perplexed, thinking about the politics of representation and the power to define. I remembered wondering what the performers thought about this experience. Finally, fourteen years later, I had the opportunity to ask.

DANIEL REED (DR): Do you remember Memphis in May in 1994 . . . How was it? Did you like that show?

VADO DIOMANDE (VD): Yes, yes, but . . . it was too short. . . . All four masks had to dance in five minutes. . . . So the show was rather long but . . . Côte d'Ivoire was short. Elephants walked around—did you see that?

DR: Yes.

VD: That was the first time I saw elephants walking like that.

And this was supposed to represent him, I thought.

DR: Did you understand the story that they told during the show?

VD: No I didn't really understand that. . . . What did they say? You know at that moment I didn't really understand English. In any case, I didn't understand what they said.[4]

Discourses collide, abrasively. Unwittingly, Vado had represented someone else's discourse of Africa, making me think of Anna Tsing's "frictions" in her ethnography of global connections (Tsing 2005). I now have seen Vado perform on numerous occasions when he *did* have agency and the power to define and represent what he chose. But even in those instances, there was friction—abrasive contact in attempts to connect. Competing, incompatible discourses. Contact-induced tensions. But as Tsing argues, in moments of friction—when contrasting materials rub against each other—heat is produced, light appears. Each is fundamentally altered by its contact with the other. Things change. Frictions are uncomfortable, but frictions are connections.

This is the America where African immigrants in the late twentieth and early twenty-first centuries have come. A country in which slavery is a distant cultural memory, even Jim Crow laws have long been abolished, and an African American with an African name has been elected president of a "multicultural" nation. And yet racist discourse persists in numerous forms, discourse based on a profoundly racist history. In 2014 events in Ferguson, Missouri, unleashed fierce debates over the persistence of institutionalized racism and racial profiling, with resulting protests thrusting civil rights for people of African descent back into the national spotlight. Increasingly diverse, thanks in part to exponential increases in the rates of immigration, the twenty-first-century United States remains a country in which a person of African descent, considered a fraction of a human being, was once bought and sold; a country where, throughout the colonial era and beyond, Africa was regularly represented as the "dark continent" (Wallace 2005; Reed 2002; Reed 1993, 76ff); a world in which even scientific discourse once defined Africans as an apelike "separate and unequal branch of the human family" (Lindfors 2014, 3–4) and categorized Africa as "primitive" in contrast to the dynamic, civilized, modern "West" (see Mudimbe 1988); a nation that still imagines itself as a modern Now, with Africa playing its Past (Ebron 2002, 19).

Dominant colonialist discourses about Africa, evident in everything from travel writing to early anthropology to popular media during the colonial era (see Mudimbe 1988) feed representations of Africa that continue to abound in popular culture. Garuba and Himmelman (2012) offer Hollywood as a case in point:

> Representations of Africa in these films work on a referencing system of citations in which the present image builds on a previous, always already known image of Africa . . . of adventures or safaris . . . of savagery and sexuality, cannibalism and concupiscence, drumming and dancing, and so on; in short, depictions that show an excess of physicality and primitive passion. (16)

This system of African representational referents was itself built on visual stereotypes propagated by "African show business in the West in the nineteenth and early twentieth centuries . . . in which African peoples were represented . . . in person, in pictures, or in parodies"; world's fairs and other such entertainments generated "a long history of the reification of derogatory racial concepts" (Lindfors 2014, 8–9). Such representations, ostensibly about "the African gnosis of Europe" were in fact at least as much about "the invention of Europe" (Erlmann 1999, 8).

The 1994 Memphis In May Festival stands as evidence that colonial-era discourses about Africa and Africans were present in 1994 America—the context in which the individuals whose stories this book tells began arriving. "The Evolution of African Music into Modern American Music" evokes Edward Said's critique of Western hegemonic thinking that claims the right to represent the Other through discourses of difference (discussed in Ebron 2002, 2; cf. Agawu 2003). The "knowledge" implied in the discourse of "The Evolution of African Music . . ." is inextricably tied to and results from hegemonic power, the power to define Africa as Other, Different, Primitive, Our Past, and Musical (Said 1978; Ebron 2002; Agawu 2003).[5]

Americans have been fed such representations of African music for so long now that it is no wonder that urban, worldly immigrants such as Vado, Samba, Sogbety, and Djo Bi, during my research for this book (2006–2014), regularly encountered expectations that they grew up beating drums and swinging from trees. Although in performed and spoken discourse they have forcefully offered counternarratives of the reality of life in contemporary Africa, aspects of ballet discourse nonetheless can potentially be creatively (mis)interpreted to support primitivist discourses of Africa. Drumming, dancing, mask spirits, and village scenery might evoke such imaginaries of Africa, despite the fact that the most common drum, the *jembe*, in its present transnationally known form is in fact a mid-twentieth-century invention of industrialized African cities; despite the fact that a dancer like Samba Diallo spends more time promoting his Afrofit exercise program than he does performing "ethnic" dance; despite the fact that sacred stilt masks dance in Manhattan jazz clubs and tour with tap dancers. Ballet, though created through a dynamic process and characterized by a dizzying array of difference, can be misinterpreted as the essence of African purity.

But the stereotype of primitiveness is but one of many preconceptions about Africa and African music that predate the arrival in the 1990s of Vado, Samba, Sogbety, and Djo Bi in the United States. Some preconceptions create contexts for clashes and friction; others make space for transcending difference, for bringing people together; still others bring both friction and transcendence at once. At the same time, expectations based on historical precedents and preestablished discourse offer immigrant performers opportunities to engage an international marketplace and enact personal agency to meet their own goals (cf. Flaig 2010, 80; Schauert 2015, 10). The widespread popularity of the *jembe* and representations of Africa promoted by early tours of Guinea's national dance troupes, although they necessitated adaptation by these four men, also created opportunities for them to make money (e.g., drum repair, classes, performances) and innovate (e.g., connecting with people of many musical backgrounds who could relate to and identify with African music via shared interest in the *jembe*). Examining Ivorian immigrant performers' engagement with such competing discourses is an exercise in what Steven Feld calls "the politics of con/disjunction" (Feld 2012, 7).

Ballet in reality, and like any genre, is a social field ripe not just for communication but also for the strategic pursuit of goals. Through ballet, contemporary Ivorian immigrants forge connections with others who share their experience based on an identity as powerful for immigrants in America as is ethnicity for the inhabitants of rural Côte d'Ivoire. Through ballet performers transform themselves into migrant laborers in the transnational marketplace of the staged representation of Africa. Ballet, like the visible tip of an island, is what American audiences see when these four artists take the stage, but it also runs much deeper in their lives; it is inextricably intertwined with their stories of migration from Abidjan to America.

The stories in this book offer individual, ethnographically grounded perspectives on life in an interconnected world—where transnational economic and political networks interlay transnationally circulating discourses such as globalization, the New African Diaspora, and cosmopolitanism. They reveal the lives of people immersed in movement across oceans and across stages, figurative and actual. These stories illuminate lives in which music, dance, and transnational mobility intertwine, so much so that understandings of story and staged performance are mutually informative. They portray the lives of people for whom music and dance are fundamental to their beings to the extent that to understand their performances is to understand their humanity. These are stories in which great opportunity and profound difficulty, celebratory communion and sorrowful disconnection, economic betterment and bitter hardship coexist. They uncover the complexities of the lives of turn-of-the-century immigrants inhabiting multiple worlds simultaneously, at turns understood and unrecognized. Embodied on stage and in stories of four Ivorian immigrants are life experiences that represent the complexities of interconnection and disconnection in their mobile, transnational lives.

The 1994 Memphis in May Festival ended as it began: with a Western art music piece evoking an evolutionary dawn. "The famous American composer Aaron Copland," announced the narrator, "wrote a fanfare which seems to typify the ascent of man, the 'Fanfare for the Common Man.'" Framing the performance with works intended to evoke evolution by great composers of the Western world only served to underscore the Enlightenment era–inspired social evolutionary frame in which the Ivorian performers were placed. The Beginning was Straus's beginning; the End, Copland's end, the story of human evolution told with tone poem soundtrack.

Just before the Copland, a grand finale brought all dozen or so ensembles together for a "rousing rendition" of "I Got Rhythm," the famous song by George Gershwin, who was known for his incorporation of African American musical elements in his compositions. I have nothing against Gershwin, and yet the use of his song in the tattoo stands as further evidence of a colonialist discourse. Just as Gershwin used African American musical aesthetics as raw material for his compositions, the creators of the tattoo used their Ivorian guests to represent their idea of Africa in their own story. A colonial model—Africa as source of raw goods to be converted by westerners into things of value.

It is not lost on me that, as author of a book about the lives of Africans, I am in a position similar to that of Gershwin and the creators of the tattoo (see Agawu 2003). In recontextualizing something of people's lives, I create my own story based on discourses of the academy—an undeniable exercise of power made possible by the privilege of access to education, grants, expensive equipment, and the luxury to spend vast periods of time doing fieldwork, reading, thinking, and writing. Still, my hope is that by using the tools of ethnography I tip the balance a bit more in the direction of my research consultants' own life stories. Relying on their life stories and their performances, cointerpreted with them through feedback interviews and casual conversations, and engaging them in conversation about their own promotional materials and methods and their struggles and successes as immigrant artists, I do not pretend that I have no mediating role, nor do I deny the authority etymologically and politically embedded in the word *author*. Still, ethnography tells me to be aware of my role in this work, to reflect on it, even as my goal is to help the reader better understand the lives of four individuals.

If the book succeeds, readers will know something of these four men and, through them, something of the experience of late twentieth- through early twenty-first-century migration, a new diaspora, the relationships of Africans to their music and dance, and their encounters with American conceptions of African music in their lives as immigrant artists. The nation that my four consultants now inhabit is one in which fear-based, anti-immigrant political discourse has become increasingly common, finally reaching a xenophobic, fever pitch in the presidential primary election campaign of 2016. Leading presidential contenders have proposed to ban all Muslims from entering the country and to deport millions of illegal immigrants. These reactionary proposals have been made against the backdrop of the crisis in the European Union, where, in 2015 alone, over a million migrants fleeing wars and/or poverty in Africa and the Middle East sought asylum, resulting in a humanitarian crisis on a scale not seen in Europe since World War II (International Organization for Migration 2016). Also in 2015, an estimated 3,771 migrants died trying to cross the Mediterranean from Africa (ibid.). My hope is that the stories of Vado, Samba, Sogbety and Dr. Djo Bi will humanize the issue of immigration, offering a counter-narrative to the loud isolationist and xenophobic voices currently reigning in their adopted home.

Postscript: Punctuation Politics

Abidjan USA is a name that describes the transnationally interconnected nature of Ivorian immigrant performers' lives. Intentionally, the title of this book is *not Abidjan, USA*—with a comma that could connote a neocolonial, hegemonic relationship (Abidjan *within*, *part of*, or even *owned by* the United States). Nor is it *Abidjan-USA*—the hyphen suggesting too strong a connection, not placing one within the domain of the other but blending them into one entity. As interconnected as my consultants' lives are, they still construct their world not as a single, unified space but as multiple spaces. No punctuation at all places *Abidjan* and *USA* in an ambiguous relationship, juxtaposed but not in a clearly defined manner. Punctuation defines relationships between words; leaving it aside, I wish to represent a world where in people's experience continents, nations, cities, states, regions, towns, and villages at turns blend and clash, interweave and collide, integrate yet seem more separate than ever before.

Why not two countries, then: *Côte d'Ivoire USA*? With *Abidjan USA*, I mean to represent unevenness—like immigration pathways from African cities to multiple destinations that are one way only—to get at the ambiguity of governmental geographic entities and borders in today's transnational world. Diaspora does not spell the end of nation or city or region; in people's experience, these entities are as real as ever but ambiguously related and blurred. Just as the ballet stage simultaneously interweaves and reifies ethnicity, the national and the transnational, *Abidjan USA* suggests a world in which difference is not dissolved but reconfigured, reimagined.

Acknowledgments

A RESEARCH PROJECT that has spanned nearly a decade, this ethnography has been anything but a solo venture; rather, it has been created through a collaborative process involving the support of many people and organizations. Of course, my most profound thanks goes to Samba Diallo, Dr. Djo Bi Irie Simon and Harmony Harris, Sogbety Diomande and Melanie Seaman, and Vado and Lisa Diomande for inviting me into their homes, their performances, and their lives. All of them have devoted countless hours to this project, and I cannot thank them enough. Barika barika barika! I ni baaraji! Merci mille fois, mes amis.

Many others in the community of Ivorian immigrants and friends also contributed substantially to this research, especially Moha Dosso, Papa Diarra, Blaise Zekalo, Hamidou Kovogui, Aristide, and Tra Bi Lizzie; also Clarice Toa, Marylese Burton, Kierno Diabate, Yahya Kamate, Euphrasie Gohoun, Mamadou Dahoue, Seguenon Kone, Bi Bo Ti, Gogoua Richard, Pablo Dembele, Justin Kafando, Papa Titos Sompa, Zagbo Martin, and Gao Bi. And to Jennifer Vincent, I offer enormous thanks for making first contact.

Several others played important roles during my research. Thanks to Lee Williams and the Lotus Festival for booking my Ivorian friends; Major Sir Michael Parker for locating his personal archives and generously sharing documents and photographs; former Memphis in May director Cynthia Ham for helping me track down people and materials; Alain Tailly, Director of the Centre National des Arts et de la Culture (CNAC) in Abidjan; and Paul Dagri for his help with archival research at the CNAC. Thanks also to Ron Reed for thinking to call when Sogbety first dropped by; Deb Reed for the trailer writing retreat and many meals for the family; Andy Reed for videotaping the parade; Edie Reed for persistent support; and Tim Reed for persistent smiles and music.

Many colleagues have provided constructive feedback on this research. Much gratitude goes to Alex Perullo and Eric Charry for their thoughtful comments and suggestions on an early draft. I offer thanks to many colleagues at Indiana University, especially those who make up my scholarly communities in the Department of Folklore and Ethnomusicology and the African Studies Program, for their inspiration and support. Colleagues at IU and elsewhere who have offered particularly useful ideas and comments on portions of this research include Kay Kaufman Shelemay, Patty Tang, Ruth Stone, Marvin Sterling, Portia Maultsby, Sue Tuohy, Javier Leon, David McDonald, Patrick McNaughton, Maria Grosz-Ngate, Mellonee Burnim, Beth Buggenhagen, Susan Gagliardi, Lisa

Homann, Ulrike Meinhof, and Denis Constant-Martin. I thank Ingrid Monson and Carol Muller for encouragement and letters of support, the whole gang at the 2011 NEH Summer Institute at Wesleyan for feedback and fun, and Anne-Marie Bouttiaux and Henry Glassie, each for kind words and the gift of a book.

For stimulating feedback that greatly enriched this research as it developed, I thank Indiana University graduate students, many of whom are now colleagues at other institutions, including Austin Okigbo, Juan Eduardo Wolf, Gillian Richards Greaves, Rebekah Moore, Colleen Haas, Angela Scharfenberger, Bernard Woma, Shaun Williams, Cullen Strawn, Hsin-wen Hsu, Cari Friesen, Oliver Shao, Paul Schauert, Jude Orakwe, and especially Jason Nguyen, whose "sensibilities" concept is fundamental to my analysis. Alan Burdette, Mike Casey, Anthony Guest-Scott, and Juan Eduardo Wolf helped me think through the complicated process of managing a born-digital archival collection.

Research assistants Paul Schauert, Hsin-wen Hsu, and Heather McFarland played vital roles over the course of this project, and they deserve much credit for its success. Hsin-wen in particular was invaluable in assisting the creation of the online Ethnomusicology Multimedia resource. Clara Henderson helped in many ways large and small, from talking through research problems to preparing grant applications to being a wonderful neighbor and friend. I thank Andrew Albrecht for his Ethnomusicology Multimedia technical support, Diane Goldstein and John McDowell for letters, Eberhard Fischer and Lorenz Homberger for providing my first opportunity to present this research in Europe, and Sheri Sherrill and Michelle Bright for helping manage the finances of this project.

At Indiana University Press, I have had the great fortune to work yet again with editor Dee Mortensen, whose commitment to helping scholarly manuscripts reach their fullest potential has brought her much deserved recognition and many awards. Thanks Dee, for everything. Thanks also to Rachel Rosolina, Mollie Ables, and the rest of the team Dee assembled to bring this work to fruition.

For their financial support of this project, I acknowledge and thank the following units and programs at Indiana University: the Office of the Vice President for Research for a New Frontiers in the Arts and Humanities Grant (2008) and a Collaborative Research and Creative Activity Fellowship (2012); the Office of the Vice Provost for Research for a Summer Faculty Fellowship (2014) and a Grant-in-Aid of Research (2016); and the College of Arts and Sciences for a College Arts and Humanities Institute Fellowship (2009).

Finally, to my family I offer gratitude beyond what words can describe. My wife Christy True played many significant roles in this research. She accompanied me on field trips to Atlanta, New York, Ohio, and in our home state of Indiana. She took wonderful photographs, some of which are in this book. She helped with meals and general hospitality on occasions when our Ivorian friends were in Bloomington. Amiable and adaptable, she often accompanied me to interviews and performances, immediately connecting with my consultants and helping us all create deeper and more meaningful social bonds. When early on in this research I received a life-altering medical diagnosis, she remained steadfast and ever supportive, helping me recenter again and again when my health issues challenged my ability to balance the stresses and strains of interweaving a long-term field research project with daily life. My children Zoë, Adrian, Jessica, and Connor also have helped tremendously during this long process, often reminding me to prioritize what matters most when I most needed it. They have endured my many trips away for field research, writing retreats, and conferences and lectures as the book took form. They generously opened our home to strangers, allowing them to become friends. They have grown up during the research and writing of this book, and I wish for them a future in which the love, joy, insight, and inspiration they have given me is returned a million-fold. To all of you, and to Christy, I dedicate this book with all my heart. Je vous aime beaucoup.

Notes on Language

Because it deals with ballet and immigration, both contexts in which ethnic interaction and interweaving of traditions from many groups occur, this book includes a number of Ivorian and other West African words. Choosing orthographic characters and spelling for even a single African language is often complex and always political. Many words in common usage in Ivorian ballet circles are spelled using French as their basis. Ivorians generally favor French spellings for everything from ethnic group names to personal names to names of rhythms/dances and musical instruments. West African linguists and other ethnographers, however, have created orthographic systems and characters specific to individual languages and/or language groups both to accurately represent sounds and to avoid reifying colonial logics and systems in such representations. Having studied northern and to a lesser degree southern Mande languages, I am familiar with and ultimately favor using African language–specific orthographies, and yet (1) I lack the expertise in many of the languages represented in this book to do so effectively for all of them, and (2) using non-French spellings and characters, oddly enough given that they are not used by my consultants, has the effect of "correcting" my consultants' spelling, which feels neither ethnographically sound nor ethically comfortable. Ultimately, there is no perfect solution and so I have devised a compromise.

First, in most cases in which a word appears regularly in print spelled a certain way, I conform to that spelling. Thus, geographic terms, such as village, town, and city names, are spelled as they are on most maps, using French spellings for sounds such as \u\ ("ou" in "**Tou**finga,") and \e\ ("é" in "Ségu**é**la"). Likewise, I spell consultants' names as they write them (Diomande, Diallo, Djo, etc.). However, for most other words I default to symbols from the International Phonetic Alphabet (IPA), which, as a standard system, promotes accuracy of phonetic legibility and provides orthographic characters for sounds that do not exist in English. Therefore, in ethnic group names, \u\ ("u" in "r**u**le") represents "u" in "Ma**u**" or "G**u**ro" and \e\ ("ay" in "ray") represents "e" as in Bau**le**. Instrument names include symbols such as "ɗ" to indicate a voiced dental/alveolar implosive as in "ɓaaɗe."

Given the range of languages and sounds in this book, and the fact that I am using the IPA system, I do not include a complete key to symbols and sounds. Instead, I refer readers to the IPA's website, which offers charts of symbols and audio examples.[6]

ABIDJAN USA

PART I
PROGRAM NOTES

1 Introduction
Abidjan USA

ABIDJAN USA. Not a place in the sense of a physical location. While there are pockets of immigrants from Côte d'Ivoire in certain neighborhoods in cities such as New York and Atlanta, there is no geographical equivalent of a Chinatown or a Little Italy. Rather, Abidjan USA is dispersed and in motion. It is New York and Atlanta; St. Louis and Orlando; Mansfield, Ohio, and Scottsburg, Indiana. And it is Abidjan and smaller cities, towns, and villages in Côte d'Ivoire. Abidjan USA is a concept that becomes physically manifest—a place—when US-based Ivorians enact who they are on stage, from the Kennedy Center to Disney World to rural Ohio school gymnasiums. Abidjan USA becomes realized socially when one immigrant finds a gig of sufficient pay to hire his friends, reuniting on stage individual performers who live across the Eastern United States. Their community, in other words, is physically constituted primarily in performance. Abidjan USA is embodied in the everyday, transnational life experience of Ivorians in the United States, on cell phones and social media, on planes and on stage, through ritual sacrifices and remittances to families back home. In the life stories and performances of drummers and dancers such as Vado Diomande of New York City; Samba Diallo of Atlanta; Sogbety Diomande of Mansfield, Ohio; and Dr. Djo Bi Irie Simon of Clinton, Indiana—the four individuals at the center of this book—Abidjan USA becomes realized.

This ethnography, which integrates individual life stories with the study of performance, seeks to understand the mobile lives of musicians, dancers, and mask performers from Côte d'Ivoire living in the United States. I have found that music and dance performances, being transportable, fluid, and adaptable, serve as an effective arena for the analysis of human migration (see Shelemay 2006). Life story reveals resonances between performative transformations and shifting circumstances in performers' mobile lives. Immigrant performers occupy multiple spaces simultaneously: as members of an immigrant community dispersed across the United States, they are unmoored from their place of origin and deeply engaged in its symbolic representation to North American audiences. Yet, unlike Africans who in earlier times were brought forcibly to the Americas, recently arrived Ivorian immigrants are not disconnected from their homeland; rather, they are transnational, in motion between continents, constantly in communication with Ivorians at home and around the world.

Metaphorically characterizing this book's approach to understanding the lives of Vado, Samba, Sogbety, and Djo Bi, performance is the visible tip of an island, the surface that one can see above the water, and life story is the foundation below, generally not visible or known to the American public. The book dances on the surface and then dives into the water to circumnavigate each island's base. A sustained, deep exploration finds that the land mass descending from each island eventually ascends, ultimately jutting back into view as another land mass, maybe another island or even a continent. A deep dive yields a truth beneath the surface that the seeming isolation of individual land masses is illusory; in reality they are interconnected. The water[1] surrounding the land is in constant motion; its daily tides render visible shorelines ever changing as unceasing waves change the shape of the land beneath the surface. The land itself appears permanent and fixed,[2] but, again, geology tells us of molten fluidity and tectonic plates always in motion. Performance becomes a visual and audible means of access for understanding the human experience of turn-of-the-century transnational labor practices and the pursuit of financial security in the fluid and unstable arena of contemporary immigration.

Immigration to wealthy nations has grown dramatically in recent decades, the exponential increase of Africans coming to the United States being a case in point.[3] While there is a growing social sciences literature on African immigration and the so-called New African Diaspora (e.g., Okpewho and Nzegwu 2009; Konadu-Agyemang, Takyi, and Arthur 2006; Stoller 2002; Arthur, Takougang and Owusu 2012), less has been written about African immigrant lives from a humanist perspective.[4] How can a study of music and dance performance help us understand the African immigrant experience? What can a study of individual immigrants' life stories teach us about the experience of twenty-first century immigration more broadly? How can performance and life story help us understand immigrants' social worlds, including their interactions with each other, with families back in Africa, and with other "diasporic" communities in the United States?

This ethnography focuses primarily on four immigrant performers' lives from the perspective of concrete, empirical, lived experience. How, for example, did people from a former French colony in West Africa end up at a wedding on a rural farm on the Indiana-Illinois border in the early twenty-first century, playing music and dancing in ways suggesting they were a regularly performing group when, in fact, many had not seen one another in years? And what can an analysis of the wedding's form and performance teach us about human experience in an increasingly mobile world?

Neither the Ivorians' immigration stories nor their performance practices can be understood without reference to ballet. Understanding ballet necessitates telling a history of newly independent Africans using staged performance to toss aside the chains of colonial rule and colonial mentality and seeking recognition not as colonial subjects but as African players on the global stage.[5] Like Eleni Bizas in her study of Senegalese *sabar* dance classes in New York and Dakar, I offer a locally grounded ethnographic perspective on theoretical discussions about "social life and the movement of people and cultural forms in an increasingly interconnected[6] world" (Bizas 2014, 127).

Music, Dance, Mobilities

Movement, a central feature of human life throughout history, has intensified, multiplied, and increased in frequency and velocity in the past quarter-century. Human movement is not democratically distributed among contemporary global citizens any more than is the movement of capital—the single most critical impetus to movement of people themselves. The powerful have the means to stay put and move money; those without means move in pursuit of money. Diaspora as a concept applies not to "those who are in place" Oliver Shao, personal communication) but only to those whose circumstances either force them (e.g., the "old" African Diaspora) or compel them (most in the "new" African Diaspora) to move. As actors embracing opportunities to improve their lot in life, Ivorian immigrant performers' mobility follows the disparities of global political economic networks (cf. Bizas 2014, 5). They draw on ballet training to provide a skill set that prepares them to move into a transnational labor market, a market in which discourses on the representation of Africa on stage, generated through a history rooted in mid-twentieth-century African ballet tours, create economic opportunities for early twenty-first-century performers to transform performance into labor.

The use of performance for economic gain in transnational economic and discursive networks is a theme that the individuals in this book share with many African performing artists, as represented in several recent ethnographies. Over a decade ago, anthropologist Paulla Ebron urged scholars to pay attention to links between aesthetic practice and economic production, "particularly in relation to the economic importance of self-consciously cultural activities" (Ebron 2002, 20). Following a line of inquiry similar to the one in this project, Ebron asks, "How has the art of *jeliya* become an object of economic and aesthetic value during the post-independence years in the Gambia?" (ibid; cf. Tang 2012). Debra Klein asserts that *Yoruba bata* performers overcome inequalities in global economic relations through diligent networking, creating and managing strategic collaborations with promoters, agents, academics, and others, thus "sustaining their careers and names as traditional artists" (2007, xxciii). While Klein's analytical lens focuses on the human actors who actively create "global connections" (her agency-centered antidote to "globalization"), Nadia Kiwan and Ulrike Meinhof's "transcultural capital" zeros in on not just *who* but also *what* is being exchanged in the nation- and continent-crossing activities of migrant artists. Building on Pierre Bourdieu, Kiwan and Meinhof's model combines cultural capital, such as artistic skills brought from the country of origin, with social capital, meaning the social networks that artists use to connect to the markets in which they can transform their cultural capital into economic opportunity (Kiwan and Meinhof 2011, 8–9). For Ivorian immigrant performers, ballet serves both as cultural *and* social capital—the artistic resource and the network, like a fraternity of sorts, linking the dispersed community of performers across transnational space.

Like hiplife musicians in Ghana, my four consultants transform "various kinds of value—aesthetic, moral, linguistic, and economic" (Shipley 2013, 4). That is, their cultural and aesthetic practice—language, clothing, music, dance, beliefs (religious, such as those surrounding sacred masks; social/ideological/moral, such as those propagating universalism, unity, multiculturalism, and/or tolerance) are transformed into labor and product.[7] Alex Perullo's research analyzes Tanzanian popular music both as "works" and as "commodities," the former to emphasize the creativity and enjoyment of expressive forms, the latter to get at their vital role as means of financial gain (Perullo 2011, x–xi). With Perullo, I see the artists with whom I work as innovative agents of "creative practice" (ibid., x) in all of their endeavors, from choreography to publicity.

Ivorian immigrant artists' stories and shows also provide answers to anthropologist Jesse Shipley's question about Ghanaian hiplife stars: "How does an artist as entrepreneur convert musical labor into fame and economic value?" (2013, 198). Shipley continues, "Underlying the work of transnational musicians . . . are profound shifts in broader dynamics of labor and value and how African youths reimagine dispersed communities of affiliation through musical labor" (201). While my four consultants no longer identify as "youths" (though all four of them *would have* done so in the earlier years of their engagement of the transnational labor market) and they, unlike the subjects of Shipley's research, are not involved primarily in popular music production and commodification, their stories echo Shipley's pronouncements. Shifts in the broader transnational economy and in global capital networks of the past few decades—from changes in immigration codes in the global North to relaxed trade laws in new liberal economic policies—have opened up opportunities for savvy individuals from former colonies to market aesthetic practice as labor.

But while Shipley argues that hiplife artists "reimagine dispersed communities of affiliation," this book shows my consultants not just reimagining but also *actively creating* new communities. Ballet itself operates as one such affiliation—one that crosses national borders, continents, and oceans to unite performers who share training and experience in this form. Shipley's hiplife artists use "mediating digital technologies, text messaging, entertainment websites, and rapid filesharing" to remake Ghanaian national affiliation "into an increasingly transnational musical culture" (2013, 232). Likewise, from the stage to the internet to cell phones to Western Union to dreams, my four consultants refashion Ivorian national identities into transnational affiliations that transcend geographical space. Again, the performance stage is that visible tip of an island that runs deep and wide, beyond its apparent terrestrial boundaries; it is a dynamic space whose apparent solidity is illusory.

Diasporans? Cosmopolitans? Scholars? Sensibilities and the Politics of Naming

As I began writing this book, I became bothered by a disconnect: familiar with a fast-growing literature on the "New African Diaspora" and familiar with characterizations, based on trait lists, of the people this literature so labeled, and finally noting that Vado Diomande, Samba Diallo, Sogbety Diomande, and Dr. Djo Bi Irie Simon all fit this characterization like a glove, I was struck that I could not recall a single occasion on which I had heard any of them self-identify as part of *any* kind of diaspora, new or old. Increasingly disturbed by this disconnect, I decided, six years into the research, to do something about it. I called up the elder of the group, Vado Diomande, and his wife Lisa on Skype. By this time, I felt I knew both Vado and Lisa very well. Because I had spent so much time with them face to face and had even done a previous Skype interview with Vado, I felt confident in our ability to communicate easily through computer webcams. I decided to abandon my normal practice of carefully avoiding the superimposition of terminology and related epistemologies and instead favoring those of my consultants. What I needed now was to ask a very specific question that I would not have deemed appropriate to ask earlier in the research. I wanted to plant a term in Vado's mind and see how he would react. So I asked Vado a very leading question:

DANIEL REED (DR): Do you know the word *diaspora*?

VADO DIOMANDE (VD): I don't understand [it]. I can't define it.

DR: So *diaspora* is not a word that you use?

VD: No.

I then defined both *diaspora* and *New African Diaspora*. I told him about the copious literature on the New African Diaspora and that I recognize him in it. He smiled. Passionately I continued:

DR: I don't want to use words to represent you that you don't feel represent you. . . . Should I use the word *immigrant*? What do you think about this diaspora idea now that I've talked about it? What do you think?

He laughed and threw the question back at me:

VD: What do *you* think?

DR: What do *I* think?

VD: Yeah, what do you think is going to be good for you?

DR: Well there are two things that matter here. The most important one is that I don't want to misrepresent you. I want the way that I write about you . . . I want you to read it and say, "Yes, that's me." But I also have to talk to my scholarly community.

Then Lisa Diomande weighed in. Actually, it was more of a jumping in with a huge splash, a cannonball:

LISA DIOMANDE: First, define "scholar."

DR: That's a good question. For me, Vado, you are a scholar. I am a particular kind of scholar, but you are a particular kind of scholar. I'm your student. So, a scholar is somebody who has studied something in depth for years. If anybody is a scholar, Vado Diomande is.

LD: So maybe that's the word you're looking for.

DR: He's a scholar. I like that.

We all laughed. We then returned to the original question, and Vado told me that, based on what I had said, he is both an immigrant and diasporan—either word would be fine with him.

DR: I appreciate your flexibility, Vado, in letting me use the words that I feel work best.

He laughed.

DR: You don't really care, do you?

VD: About what?

DR: About these words.

VD: No, say anything!

Lots of laughter.

In this conversation, I received a response more complex and nuanced than the question I initially asked. With wisdom and humor, Vado, with the aid of Lisa, had questioned my epistemologies. On some level, I felt I had been given permission to connect his story to diaspora literature, but I also felt more committed than ever to represent him in terms of his own making. I remained reluctant to identify my four friends with any label that they themselves did not use or recognize, but I was still convinced of the importance of their stories to scholarly conversations.

While I deliberated, I recalled yet another reason I was reluctant to adopt the label of *diaspora*: my fear that this admittedly loaded word would color my perspective in unproductive ways. Calling a group's displacement a *diaspora* privileges a very particular (usually academic) discursive understanding of movement, and might obscure other types of social formations that might be more meaningful to the people in my study. If I employed this term, I thought, would the very act of using it crowd out other ways of defining and understanding movement? Would I be favoring and normalizing *diaspora* when that term might not reflect the way my Ivorian consultants see themselves?

Fortunately for me, in my Music, Immigration and Diaspora seminar at Indiana University in 2013, graduate student Jason Nguyen, in a paper on dispersed Vietnamese communities, addressed this same problem and proposed what I found to be a theoretically innovative solution. Nguyen advocates the use of a nonsubstantive conceptualization of diaspora, arguing that using *diasporic* as a modifier,[8] especially when applied not to people but to behavior such as artistic expression, is less reductive. He resolves the problem by locating the diasporic not in human groups but in performed expressions of identity that feature "diasporic sensibilities" (J. Nguyen, personal communication, 2013). This allows him to make room for other identities and focuses the lens squarely on the place diaspora actually lives: in its performative expression (cf. Hall 2008; Butler 1999).

With these correctives in hand, I decided to make a space for the concept of diaspora in this research project. Not only do I want scholars studying the construction of diaspora to confront the stories of my consultants; I also want them to take stock of performance and its value as a meeting site for multiple discourses. I want them to encounter the polysemous power of performance, its importance in reflecting on the old and negotiating the new, its inherent dynamism, its efficacy as representation. I want to engage diaspora scholars with my consultants' stories and performance stages. Following Nguyen, I want to confront them with the notion of diaspora not as a label for human beings but as an interpretive frame for certain human behaviors. As ethnomusicologist Portia Maultsby, a specialist in African Diaspora music, insisted in a conversation with me after a public lecture I presented: "You have to use the word *diaspora*. If not, it's a missed opportunity to advance thinking on the topic." So in this work I consider the lives of the four men I have studied in relationship to the literature on the New African Diaspora, although I take pains not to *label* them as diasporic. Rather, I cautiously invoke the "New African Diaspora" as one interpretive frame for the analysis of their stories and shows.

Diaspora?

Invoking diaspora as an interpretive frame raises the question of what it is in the first place. However, defining *diaspora* is difficult, particularly given the expansions of meaning the term has undergone during the last couple of decades. Indeed, at points it has seemed almost as if *everything* can be a diaspora in scholarly discourse (Toloyan 2012, 4; see also Slobin 2012; Cohen 2008, xv). There is the phenomenon "out there" of people moving in particular ways; there are ways people think about that movement, talk about it, and define it; there is diaspora as theory in scholarly discourse, where it is conceptually extended to cover movements of things other than people (such as media or musical instruments). And I am only just getting started. Essential, however, to any defensible model of diaspora is that it is *constructed*; that is, it does not exist independent of people thinking about it as such. It is in naming certain dispersions of people *disaporas* that the construction is realized. In fact, the very idea of an African Diaspora is itself a construction; while Africans have been dispersed for centuries, the understanding of that dispersal as an African Diaspora was created only in 1964, when historian George Shepperson first used the term at a Pan-Africanist conference in Dar es Salaam (Toloyan 2012, 6).

James Clifford argues against defining diaspora "sharply," preferring "a loosely coherent, adaptive constellation of responses to dwelling-in-displacement" (1994, 310). Key here, again, is that Clifford locates the diasporic in "responses" to dwelling-in-displacement and not in the displaced people themselves. Drawing on a number of diaspora theorists,[9] I list the following as what I call *diasporic modes*, or positions and/or conditions in which diaspora can be invoked:

- Dispersal of a human population from a homeland across nation-state borders to multiple new locations
- A way of thinking about that movement, a state of group consciousness, present (performed) in expressive culture
- Exchange/circulation of expressive cultural production across the multiple sites of dispersal and (often) the homeland
- A political positioning, a discourse with real implications, particularly given that the notion of diaspora is generally invoked with reference to people who are marginalized (the powerful are those "in place")
- A scholarly theory and method—a paradigm for the study of human movement

In certain cases, all of these modes are present, but not all of them must be present for expressive culture associated with a dispersed population to exhibit, or be interpreted as having, "diasporic sensibilities." These "modes" can be found in and/or applied to any diaspora, whether "old" or "new."

Table 1.1 Contrasting scholarly representations of "old" and "new" African diasporas (drawing on Paul Tiyambe Zeleza 2009)

"Old"	"New"
Precolonial forced *group* Displacement (slavery)	Postcolonial voluntary *individual* Displacement (migrant labor) in the context of global capitalism
Slavery as unifying experience	Lack of comparable unifying experience
Relatively unified identity (African American)	Heterogeneous identities (American African? Kenyan American? Ivorian? West African? African?)
Place of origin unknown, imagined ("Africa" as homeland)	Known, specific place of origin
Individuals primarily rooted in nation	Individuals whose life experience fundamentally transnational

So, do Ivorian immigrants perform a New African Diaspora? Many would say yes. Many would go farther still and identify not just the expressive culture of these immigrants but the people themselves as its representatives. The term *New African Diaspora* began gaining currency in scholarly discourse in the 1990s to identify the dramatically increasing numbers of Africans migrating to the Global North.[10] As these numbers began growing almost exponentially from the 1990s through the early years of the twenty-first century, the volume of scholarly publications bearing the name *New African Diaspora* increased in parallel. Drawing from Paul Tiyambe Zeleza (2009), I contrast the scholarly representations of "old" versus "new" diasporas in table 1.1.

Note in the table the plural form of both old and new diaspora*s*. I choose the plural because I reject the idea of two singular diasporas (old versus new) and argue that both old and new are plural and historically dynamic.[11] However, recent diasporic movements *are* generally distinct from those of the slave era. My Ivorian consultants, despite the fact that they do not self-identify as such, match nearly identically the characterization of the New African Diaspora. This point becomes abundantly clear in the life story chapters of this book, so I only summarize it in the following paragraphs.

Postcolonial voluntary individual displacement (migrant labor) in the context of global capitalism. All four of my primary consultants—Vado Diomande, Samba Diallo, Sogbety Diomande, and Dr. Djo Bi Irie Simon—voluntarily moved from Côte d'Ivoire to the United States (via Europe in the case of Djo Bi). And all four are participants in the transnational labor market in that each came to the United States seeking economic opportunity (though Vado Diomande's goal, better health care, was ultimately more specific). *Global capitalism* is a phrase that describes the broader context of their movements: the far reach of US economic hegemony (and that of other countries in the Global North) has created one-way migratory pathways, legal and illegal, for Global South migrants to follow.

The four artists can be further characterized in economic terms as skilled laborers. Each has training and experience in the staging of Ivorian music and dance and in the Ivorian version of the transnational discourse of "ballet." However, whether they are "migrant" or "immigrant" laborers is an open question. Not a single one imagined that his move to the United States would be permanent, and since migrants tend to relocate for work and return, the phrase *migrant laborer* does connote something of their self-definition. Yet all four now seem to be ensconced in life in the United States to the extent that they do not see themselves returning "home," at least anytime before retirement if at all. Their sense that their move is permanent supports labeling them immigrants.

Finally, Ivorian immigrant performers tend to migrate alone, individually, in great contrast to the forced group relocations of the slave era. However, Peter Geschiere offers the caveat that, because of the heavy expectation of remittance that follows individual migrants abroad, "the general perception in affluent countries of the North of transcontinental immigrants as individual actors is highly misleading" (2013, 62).

Lack of unifying experience (comparable to slavery). It is not as if the four men have no unifying experience. They are all from the same West African country, all men, all trained in the Ivorian version of ballet and all immigrants who came to the United States in the 1990s. Nothing they have experienced, however, is on par with the life-transforming experience of slavery. Trauma such as slavery bonds survivors, providing them with a shared perspective so deep as to be incomparable to anything other than, perhaps, other horrific, human-generated traumas (such as concentration camps or group massacres).

Heterogeneous identities. Here I refer both to identities expressed by these four men in everyday life and to those expressed in a more explicitly performative mode—on stage, in promotional materials, and in the naming of performing ensembles. Effectively, I find no great difference between these two domains, both of which reflect broader trends in terms of recent African immigrants. As others have noted (Humphries 2009), compared with *African American*, there exists no unifying identity label among recent African immigrants in the United States. I have observed my four primary consultants, in daily speech and in performance, refer to themselves by the names of their ethnic groups (such as Mau or Guro) or as Ivorian, West African, or African. Occasionally, one of them identifies as an immigrant, usually using *Ivorian* as a modifier. Like most recent arrivals, they distinguish themselves from African Americans (whom they call, in French, *Américains noires*).

Some scholars have advocated for a broad, unifying label for all peoples of African descent in the United States; others have called for a slightly less broad label for all recent immigrants (e.g., American Africans). However, the reality is that communities of recent African immigrants are splintered in terms of their self-identification, and depending on the situation, might identify along ethnic, national (Ivorian or, rarely, Ivorian American), regional (West African), or continental lines (African).

Known, specific place of origin. Here I state a fact that is as obvious as it is profound. In contrast to descendants of slaves, nearly all recent immigrants know where they come from. The existential effect of that knowledge cannot be overstated. Furthermore, known origins, coupled with increased mobility and expansions of mass communication technologies and mass media, set the stage for the final major point distinguishing the lives of "new" diasporans.

Individuals whose life experience is fundamentally transnational. In this book, I use several terms (*transnational, diaspora, global, globalization, global capitalism, cosmopolitanism*) that, while distinct, are also potentially overlapping in scope and meaning. What do I mean by "transnational"? In answering this question, I draw from Steven Vertovec, who defines it as "multiple ties and interactions linking people or institutions across the borders of nationstates" (2001, 447). Vado, Samba, Sogbety, and Dr. Djo Bi—indeed, all Ivorian immigrants I have come to know—routinely operate in social fields that cross geographic, cultural, and political borders. Ivorian immigrants have regular, often daily contact with people in the homeland, on cell phones, through social media, and via Western Union money transfers. They keep up with daily Ivorian print and broadcast news on sites such as Abidjan.net. Some receive visits from Ivorian spirits in dreams. Those with the means travel back to visit, to bring money and gifts, or to make sacrifices to ancestors to secure permission to perform sacred masks abroad.[12] They have performed in touring groups crossing national boundaries and crossing continents; the most successful of them still do so from their new US base. Finally, of course, they live in one nation and struggle to make a living by representing, on stages and in schools, in classes and at camps, at festivals and in workshops, another nation, albeit in a form, ballet, that is itself transnational. That is, they perform a transnational form of nationalism transnationally. While I do not wish to suggest that earlier diasporans were/are provincial, most of them occupy space more centrally located in a single nation and very few know their specific point of origin on the continent.

My consultants' stories and shows suggest a concept of diaspora characterized less in terms of home and abroad and more in terms of transnational cultural movement—including that of people, ideas, artistic forms, and instruments

(Muller and Benjamin 2011; Gilroy 1993; Monson 2000; Okpewho and Nzegwu 2009). In their performances, I find the transnational, rather than some kind of singular authentic homeland, emphasized. In that sense, this study follows Ingrid Monson's call for research on music related to the African diaspora to focus on "examining the social and cultural processes through which contemporary Africans revise and reinvent notions of cultural legitimacy from generation to generation rather than on an original cultural baseline to be reclaimed" (Monson 2000, 12).[13]

* * *

Each of the characteristics associated with the "New African Diaspora" is evident in the life stories I recount in this book. Integrating those life stories with performance analysis, I highlight two issues that are underemphasized in the relevant literature: the arts and individual experience. Clearly my application of Zeleza's model, discussed previously, to the lives of the Ivorian immigrant performers in this book shows that the shoe fits. But, again, I have never heard a single one of them use the word *diaspora*, without my prompting. If diaspora is partly a state of consciousness, can a person be a member of a diaspora without knowing it? Recognizing that, as an academic researcher, my choice of words is an exercise of power, I choose not to represent my Ivorian consultants as diasporans so as to align this book's discursive framing with the ways in which these four men understand and define themselves.

Cosmopolitan?

In my Skype conversation with Lisa and Vado Diomande, we discussed other terms in scholarly literature that seem to apply to him and his friends but that, in my experience, they do not use to identify themselves. One such word is *cosmopolitan*. Once again, though I see Vado as very cosmopolitan, this was not a word he knew. I explained what I meant by the term by paraphrasing Tom Turino's formulation: "Objects, ideas, and cultural positions that are widely diffused throughout the world and yet are specific only to certain portions of the populations within given countries" (Turino 2000, 7). I said that, through media, mobility, mass communications, and financial means, "cosmopolitans" in African cities might feel that they have as much or more in common with people of similar social positions living in Paris, New York, or Seoul as they might with more provincial citizens in their own countries. Both Vado and Lisa seemed warm to the idea of categorizing Vado in such a way, but then Lisa offered this incisive, problematizing intervention:

> The difference between Vado, though, and a lot of performers who are cosmopolitan or transnational . . . is that he seems to be hyperaware of the role of

tradition. [To Vado]: Because you are still connected in really profound ways with *Toufinga* [his natal village].... So you are in my mind cosmopolitan. Unquestionably cosmopolitan. But you are also very traditional in certain ways. So how to describe you this way is very interesting. You are this transnational guy, you're cosmopolitan, you have traveled the world, you live in New York City, but you still make sacrifices.

Here I again find myself wanting not to label Vado with a term not of his choosing while at the same time wanting to connect his story and performances to a scholarly literature that needs to hear about them. In Vado, Samba, Sogbety, and Djo Bi, I see a kind of worldliness, a kind of cosmopolitanism, distinct from the conventional elite connotations of those terms. Steven Feld (2012) very effectively argues that heterogeneous conceptualizations of both diaspora and cosmopolitanism are essential for an understanding of the lives of jazz musician interlocutors in Accra. He claims that cosmopolitanism is no more guaranteed in the lives of the highly educated, privileged, wealthy, and powerful than it is certain to be lacking in the lives of people struggling to survive. And he asks us "to clear space to talk about cosmopolitanism from below, to reimagine cosmopolitanism from the standpoint of the seriously uneven intersections, and the seriously off-the-radar lives of people who, whatever is to be said about their global connections, nonetheless live quite remotely to the theorists and settings that usually dominate cosmopolitanism conversations in academia" (Feld 2012, 7).[14]

Drawing ideas from Pnina Werbner, Feld asserts that the worldly perspective, openness, tolerance, multicultural awareness, and sensitivity to diverse perspectives often associated with cosmopolitanism are not the sole province of wealthy elites. Werbner advocates a concept, originally introduced by Homi Bhabha (1996), called "vernacular cosmopolitanism" (quoted in Feld 2012, 230) that can gain purchase on diverse types of cosmopolitanism and so offer perspective on the ways of being cosmopolitan (Werbner 2006). As early as 1997, Feld said of James Clifford that he conceived the idea of "discrepant cosmopolitanism, a notion that came out of his concern to explore differences between privileged and nonprivileged travelers, and his loud insistence that it is shortsighted to imagine cosmopolitans as necessarily elite" (Clifford 1997, qoted in Feld 231).

Vado, Samba, Sogbety, and Djo Bi are not jet-setters. They lack high levels of Western-style, formal education, and they are far from wealthy. Yet they are world travelers. They have lived on multiple continents. They consume mass media. They receive visits from village spirits in dreams. They promote ideals of international peace and tolerance. Like Feld's Accra jazz musicians, these four ballet performers force us to problematize simple binaries that imagine the marginalized and powerless in diasporas and the hegemonic and powerful as cosmopolitans.[15]

Beyond questioning such limiting binaries, though, I ultimately choose the same epistemological position on cosmopolitanism that I do on diaspora: that is, I resist the temptation to *label* my four Ivorian consultants as "cosmopolitan" and instead see aspects of their lives as exhibiting cosmopolitan sensibilities. Again with a tip of my hat to Jason Nguyen, the term *cosmopolitan sensibilities*, rather than reducing complex human beings to a label, describes the *behaviors* of those complex human beings and analyzes them within a particular framework (personal communication). This, I find, enables me to comfortably invoke cosmopolitanism and challenge it to expand without feeling I am misrepresenting my consultants in terms they themselves do not use.

Scholar?

But what of Lisa Diomande's first provocative challenge, which questioned my implicit epistemological separation of "scholars" from whatever label one might use for the Ivorian immigrant performers in this study? Just as I have never heard Ivorian immigrants self-identify as members of a diaspora or as cosmopolitan, I have also never heard them call themselves or each other scholars. Is it apt, then, to describe some of their behaviors as displaying "scholarly sensibilities?"

Before answering that question, let me toy for a moment with the idea of *scholar* as label. Lisa's observation brings up the long debated issue of naming providers-of-information in ethnography. Most popular by far has been *informant*, a term I avoid because its French translation *informateur* connotes a spy or an undercover agent. One of my former teachers, folklorist Roger Janelli, when doing ethnographic research in a Korean corporation, chose *consultant* (see Janelli and Yim 1993), and I was immediately drawn to this option and have employed it in publications ever since. What is a consultant after all? A consultant has a certain degree of expertise on a subject, to the extent that the ethnographer *consults* this person about it. Sounds right to me. But consultant and scholar conceptually are far from mutually exclusive. The *Oxford English Dictionary* defines *scholar* as "a specialist in a particular branch of study, especially in the humanities." Excluding the last part, and, I would argue, the language "branch of study" (which to me epistemologically suggests a western academic frame), the idea of a specialist in a particular area of knowledge glosses quite well the role that Vado, Samba, Sogbety, and Djo Bi have played in this work. In other words, I consider them scholars and I consider them as a group to be a scholarly community. My hope is that this work of scholarship will appeal to multiple communities—in the academy, including those in ethnomusicology, folklore, anthropology, art history, sociology, African studies, international and global studies, immigration studies, diaspora studies, and even economics—and outside the academy, including the people about whom this book is written.

Once again, although it feels politically good to name them as such, Vado, Samba, Sogbety, and Dr. Djo Bi do not self-identify as scholars but as Ivorian artists—musicians and dancers—and as immigrants, among other things (in categories such as ethnicity and gender). However, I choose to look at certain of their behaviors as revealing scholarly sensibilities. All four of them have studied ballet intensively for years and the work they have engaged in—thorough, long-term, comparative, and subject to regular analysis, questioning, and experimental tests—is of a scholarly nature. Some of their scholarly activities, including learning and transmission, are oral while others are written. All four men to greater or lesser degrees tout the educational aspects of their work. Samba Diallo even labels his troupe Attoungblan an educational cultural art entertainment group. Djo Bi, prior to this project, participated in other research projects that were scholarly, especially one with Anne-Marie Bouttiaux that resulted in publications and a museum exhibit. Finally, as just suggested, I do not consider Vado, Samba, Sogbety, and Djo Bi merely objects or even subjects of research but participants in this project. In helping me understand and interpret their worlds, they have clearly exhibited scholarly sensibilities.

For convenience's sake, though, and because I think it is neutral, nonreductive, and most accurate (not denying or undercutting any other label), I persist in labeling as *consultant* the professional role the four Ivorian men play in this work, if only to avoid listing their names every time I invoke them as a group.

Individuals, Life Story, and Performance as Analytical Frames

Ethnography Focused on Individuals

This book builds on a long tradition in ethnographic disciplines, and enhances more recent literature on immigration and diaspora, by focusing on individuals. In social science research, scholars have recognized the paradox that culture—by definition communal, social, shared—can be learned only through research with individuals. This being the case, even studies that do not represent individual voices (as in "the Yoruba do X") are still fundamentally collections of individual perspectives. Over the past several decades, however, in part as a result of the reflexive turn in ethnography that emphasizes the representation of field experience with individual subjects, ethnographic publications have featured individuals more and more. The manner in and the extent to which individuals are represented ranges from direct quotes to whole sections or chapters to full-fledged book-length biographies.

In a number of disciplines, including ethnomusicology, the late 1970s was the moment when the representation of individual subject positions rose in prominence. In 1978, in an article in *Ethnomusicology*, Kenneth Gourlay critiqued the pretense of objectivity in ethnomusicological research, insisting that the research process be understood as "a dialogue between historically and socially positioned individuals" (Gourlay 1978, quoted in Ruskin and Rice 2012, 300). That same year, in a pioneering work Charlotte Frisbie and David McAllister shifted the authoritative focus from researcher to research subject by naming Navajo singer Frank Mitchell the author of his musical biography (Mitchell 1978, cited in Ruskin and Rice 2012, 300). The next year, Paul Berliner's *Soul of Mbira* based an analysis of a musical instrument tradition in part on large sections of biographical writing about named individual musicians (Berliner 1979).

Following this initial blossoming, an increasing (though overall still relatively small) number of books representing individuals were being written by ethnomusicologists. In 1988 Jeff Todd Titon's *Powerhouse for God* prominently featured life stories, which he emphasized were first and foremost stories affirming "the identity of the storyteller in the act of telling" (1988, 290). Tim Rice's *May It Fill Your Soul* used the biography of the Varimezov family as the basis for a book about twentieth-century Bulgarian folk music history (Rice 2004). Perhaps because it has become more commonplace, in the 2000s more books have been published in which theorizing the representation of individual voices is implicit. Some ethnographies make a profound statement by recognizing individuals not just as research subjects but as coauthors (e.g., Dutiro and Howard 2007; Muller and Benjamin 2011).

Of course, reflexivity became a growing concern not just in ethnomusicology but across ethnographic disciplines starting in the late 1970s. In anthropology, books about individuals also began emerging in the late 1970s/early 1980s, including two noteworthy examples spotlighting Africans. Vincent Crapanzano's *Tuhami: Portrait of a Moroccan* (1980) focused on one man, Tuhami, and especially Crapanzano's relationship with him, which the latter characterized as researcher and research *subject* rather than research *object*. *Tuhami* was followed closely by Marjorie Shostak's *Nisa: the Life and Words of a !Kung Woman* (1981), which centered on a woman narrating her life story.

The birth of reflexivity was not, however, the first emergence of anthropological texts about individuals. Folklorist Henry Glassie points to much earlier examples: Peter Nobakov's *Two Leggings* (1923) and a remarkably early example of a co-authored monograph, *Sun Chief* (Talayesva and Simmons 1942). Nor has interest in this issue waned in recent years. A case in point is the edited volume *Anthropology and the Individual: A Material Culture Perspective* (2009), in which editor Daniel Miller claims that "approaches created by anthropologists for the purpose of contending with society turn out to be singularly and unexpectedly appropriate for the study of the individual" (2010, 3).

Art history, according to Patrick McNaughton, lags behind in individual-centered research. Critiquing his discipline, McNaughton argues that "individuals ... have not yet received their share of attention" (2008, 3). This is unfortunate, he says, because "even though [individuals] come together in groups, their uniqueness—too often shortchanged or patronized in scholarship—is ultimately what forms society and gives rise to history" (ibid., 4). At least as much as other disciplines, African art history epistemologically organizes itself according to ethnicity and geographic area. This persists despite the efforts of several scholars who have represented individual perspectives in their work. In 1963, Eberhard Fischer published an innovative study of Dan sculpture through the life story lens (coincidentally) of four carvers. Because it was published only in German, this piece, far ahead of its time, arguably did not receive the attention it warranted. However, its release in English translation fifty years later (Fischer 2013) just as I was finishing this manuscript, reinforced my belief in the value of this approach. In the interim, art historian Barbara Johnson's *Four Dan Sculptors: Continuity and Change* charted an innovative course by considering the role of individuals in creating style. Despite these innovations and Warren D'Azevedo's *The Traditional Artist in African Societies* (1991), which is an often cited call for the study of individual African artists, the ethnicity-as-analytical-frame epistemological model remains common in the field.

Henry Glassie fully embraces the individual, as opposed to the group, as an analytical frame for the study of expressive culture. In his monograph on Yoruba immigrant painter Prince Twins Seven-Seven, he says:

> Prince is not an example of some force or process or condition. He is a man.... I am not an Africanist with a need to reconcile the conflicting authorities and make of Prince a representative African man–though he is a man of Africa who offers glimpses through a slim aperture of Nigerian history and Yoruba culture. Nor am I an art historian with the need to fit his works into some scheme, reducing them to examples of African art or Yoruba art or traditional art or heritage art or self-taught art or outsider art or folk art or fine art or modern art–though they are in part, all of these things.... I do not intend a historian's biography, testing his statements against ostensibly objective evidence for their veracity. A folklorist, and a photographer, I am after a subjective revelation. The truth I seek is the truth as Prince sees it. (2010, 6)

Glassie's approach results in a vivid portrayal of details of Prince's life and aesthetic practice. Despite arguing that by necessity "all understanding begins ... with individuals in their acts of creative will," Glassie acknowledges that "study will expand to groups, movements, communities, societies, all nations (ibid., 7). However, he resists such expansion, choosing instead to write about Prince the individual artist as exactly that: an individual artist.

* * *

My approach here builds on many previously mentioned ethnographies and others, including my own *Dan Ge Performance* (2003). I *am* an Africanist who thinks not only in terms of individual artists' lives and performance practices but also in terms of broad social formulations (such as diaspora, transnationality, nationality, ethnicity). My goal, in fact, is to productively weave together interconnections between these different but mutually informative levels of analysis so as to better understand each.

Broadly speaking, in my first book I learned from two categories of consultant: primary—a small number of people, including performers, knowledgeable elders, and others with whom I spent the most time; and secondary—people whom I got to know but not as well, people with whom I spent considerable time but did not engage directly in research, and those whom I met and interviewed just once. This book wove together these multiple perspectives, informed by the phenomenological notion of intersubjectivity, to create a portrayal of uses of mask and music performance in late 1990s western Côte d'Ivoire. In the present project, in contrast, primary consultants are even more centrally placed than in *Dan Ge Performance*, both during field research and here. That is to say, this book is arguably about four individuals. In eliciting life stories, I came to know Vado, Samba, Sogbety, and Djo Bi deeply, in relationships now ten years old and still growing. In many cases, my secondary consultants I also know reasonably well (especially Lisa Diomande, Harmony Harris, and Melanie Seaman but also many others, including Tra Bi Lizzie, Moha Dosso, Papa Diarra, and Blaise Zekalo); however, I chose to involve them less centrally in the research. Ultimately, in terms of the relationship between individuals and community—which is fundamental to all ethnography—this book is about four performers in the *contexts* of the broader community of Ivorian immigrant performers, the United States, and transnational cultural interactions.

In ethnomusicological studies of African music, several recent publications resonate with my approach. Kay Shelemay's article "Ethiopian Musical Invention in Diaspora" bases a study of diasporan community formation on three individual musicians "because to do so enables us to link individual musical activity to broader social processes as well as important institutional settings" (2006, 304). As I was writing this book, two works were published that, in terms of scope, approach, theoretical concerns, and subject matter, could be considered my work's slightly older siblings. Carol Muller and Sathima Bea Benjamin's *Musical Echoes* (2011) offers a coauthored call and response–structured, life story–based rethinking of notions of ethnography, race, and diaspora. Steven Feld, in *Jazz Cosmopolitanism in Accra* employs "the analytical power of narrative" (2012, 8) to address diaspora and cosmopolitanism through the life stories of three Ghanaian jazz musicians. With these works, I share an approach—the life story—that, while becoming a trend in ethnomusicology and related fields, has a long history in ethnographic writing.

Life Story

Life story has been an emphasis in ethnography at least back to Paul Radin, who "believed that history and culture are grounded in the lives of specific individuals. Life histories revealed history and culture as lived" (Peacock and Holland 1993, 367). Peacock and Holland noted the vexed history of life story, with scholars debating the extent to which it accurately reflects reality or is constructed. That is, is the self reflected in life story or is it generated by it? Like Peacock and Holland, I chart a middle ground: life story telling, though rooted in actual experience of the "real," is subjective, interpretive, contingent, and contextual (cf. Cohen et al., 2001).

Life story telling is something we rarely do. Historian Corrine A. Kratz asserts that anecdotes about particular incidents are common features in everyday conversation, but states:

> Accounts that span an entire life in some detail, however, are told less often, only in particular kinds of situations. The terms "life history" and "life story" usually refer to these fuller accounts. They are sometimes told in therapeutic or legal settings, after ritual investitures, at high school reunions, or during intimate moments that help establish close friendships, but those that become published accounts are most often elicited by researchers. (Kratz 2001, 127–128)

Life story telling, then, is not as "natural" or common a genre as it might seem to be. Interview settings—whether for journalistic or scholarly research purposes—are a common context for the emergence of this genre. This is not to suggest that it is a false genre; rather, it is rare and contingent on particular situations and contexts. Building on Kratz, I argue that life story is as much a scholarly genre as a form of personal narrative. As a form of ethnographic representation, not only can life story make scholarly writing "more accessible and engaging"—a laudable goal in and of itself—it can also foreground individual, too often "submerged voices" (Clark 2010, 11) of consultants as well as the relationships between ethnographer and research subjects on which all ethnography is based.

As a scholarly genre, life story represents a form whose creation inherently requires "a considerable degree of trust and commitment on both sides, which the critical reader needs to verify" (Clark 2010, 8). I have taken that trust very seriously because publishing versions of their life stories places Vado, Samba, Sogbety, and Djo Bi in positions of great vulnerability. This is one reason I have followed the lead of Elaine Lawless (1993) and many in her wake by sharing chapter drafts with my four primary consultants, who read, edited, and corrected them and talked with me about how I chose to represent them and their lives. In some passages, consultants asked me to remove sensitive material, and in every such instance I abided by their wishes, regardless of how important I felt the deleted content to be. What I present to the reader in these pages, then, are stories that have been reciprocally created and approved by the men whose lives they represent.

I thought carefully about my representation of these narratives and the extent of my presence in them—as interviewer, editor, and author. At some moments in these pages, my voice and presence are neither transparent nor observable, though I am inherently ever present in my role as mediator, silently selecting narrative excerpts and placing them in the context of a chapter in an academic monograph. At other moments, however, I follow Alessandro Portelli (1997), Gracia Clark (2010), and others who construct oral history or life story as a dialogue between researcher and subject. Often it simply felt right to represent myself as the interviewer engaged in conversation with the interviewee. This reflexive move is important at moments because it underscores the role I played as researcher in driving and guiding aspects of the stories with my questions and the research interests that informed them. The life stories in this book are not, in other words, neutral, objectifiable narratives divorced from the context of their telling. Nor are they nostalgic, stereotypical stories emanating from a proverbial elder with a child on his knee recounting his life's journey. What follows, rather, are stories resulting from a collaborative process in which an ethnomusicologist interviewed four immigrant artists (cf., Tang 2007, 68). As I always tell my students, ethnographers must emphasize how we know what we know and openly reveal that process in our published representations.

The vast majority of my interviews took place in French. This was a natural choice for several reasons. First, whether the formal French spoken by highly educated elites or the more fluid French of the streets,[16] this is the most common language used to communicate across ethnic lines in Côte d'Ivoire. Thus, it should come as no surprise that it is also the most common linguistic code for the multiethnic community of Ivorian immigrants in the United States. Even though most of my consultants are proficient in English, French is their default, especially when discussing their lives, their work, and things Ivorian, so it was a natural choice for that reason as well. There were moments when an interviewee—most commonly Vado Diomande—would shift into English in the middle of our conversations. However, to keep the focus on content and improve narrative flow, I chose not to represent the original language, including language changes, in this ethnography.

Not only do I not indicate when interviewees change languages, I also edited their language sometimes, especially when they spoke in English. Having been exposed, while studying folkloristics, to the representation of "real" speech as it is uttered, it is with some trepidation that I made this choice. I did so, however, because I wanted to represent my consultants accurately *and* in their best light. For no one was this more of an issue than Vado Diomande. I do not wish to romanticize him, but the fact is that Vado is a highly intelligent, articulate, and creative man. He represents himself well in French, but his English is rough enough that, removed from context and placed on a page, it does not accurately reflect the person he is. In making the choice to occasionally "fix" Vado's grammar, I ran the risk, articulated by Babiracki (2008, 2–3), of rendering the messy nature of his life story more coherent than it would be in unedited form. I am, however, willing to accept that risk, which is inherent in the responsibility I assume in my authorship of Vado's life in this context. I know what it feels like to sit in his presence, and I made representational choices in an effort to translate from the medium of the interview to the medium of written text something of his personality and character.[17] While interviews of the other three immigrants required less frequent and more minimal massaging, they too were subject to alteration in the interest of aligning my textual representations with my experiential memories.

The life stories in this book portray the immigration experience from unique, individual vantage points based on individual experience. In most cases, they have not been told elsewhere in print, and thus they have inherent value as records of individuals in this mobile, fluid era of globalization who are making new lives for themselves as transnational immigrants. Through their unique, individual subject positions, then, the stories complement social scientific writing and mass media portrayals of African immigrant experience. In a few instances, the stories herein offer different perspectives on information that is part of the written public record. For example, Vado's bout with anthrax (in chapter 3) was a national news story—its representation in that form is widely available and systematically distributed. In this case, the individual life story does not complement but rather interrupts the public record, as Vado disagrees vehemently with some of the ways in which he and his illness were explained and characterized in the press (Shuman 2011).

Another consideration is the highly selective nature of life story, which emphasizes some things and deemphasizes others. Because I had shared my research interests and goals with my consultants in advance of interviews, regardless of what I asked, the artists would naturally talk about their performance histories and immigration narratives. Because these two topics are the focus, each story also has particular foci. This is but one of a number of ways I influenced them. Additionally, even though in nearly every instance I tried my best to avoid asking leading questions, I began each interview interested in certain topics and issues that, through my questioning, influenced direction and content. Of course, I then selected parts of the stories to present here, further adding my own voice and perspective to the those of the Ivorians. All in all, the narratives are contingent on many factors that influenced their telling and content.

Furthermore, the narratives occasionally exhibit a nonlinear, kaleidoscopic flow. The opening of chapter 4, about Vado Diomande's national ballet audition, for example, cycles back to a narrative of dancing for doctors when he was a child and then returns to the audition. Such flow was common in the formal and informal conversations in which my consultants' life stories emerged. The grand arc of our conversations was roughly chronological, but at a fine-grained level they were anything but. Our chats flowed organically just as good conversations usually do. We followed tangents, responded to circumstances in our immediate environments, analyzed performances, got interrupted, discussed current events or that day's activities. In constructing this book, I retained some of that non-linear narrative flow. One could reasonably argue that life stories are often not strictly chronological regardless of the teller, but an equally strong case can be made for the argument that West Africans in particular think of history less in chronological terms than in terms of social relations (Jackson 1982; Stone 1988).

Performance

I chose to focus this book on Ivorian immigrant performance for two main reasons. First, performance is central to my consultants' lives and stories. They define themselves as performers—musicians and dancers—and their decisions to immigrate were completely and inextricably intertwined with performance. In other words, to tell their stories as immigrants is to tell their stories as performers and vice versa. Second, as a specially framed site of "heightened reflexivity," (Goodman 2005, 167), performance itself serves as an effective arena in which to seek understanding of participants' lives.

My approach to performance in this book is informed by a number theoretical models for analyzing the performance process.[18] Most profoundly influential has been Richard Bauman's body of work articulating a model of performance theory advanced in his landmark *Verbal Art as Performance* (1977), and further developed in subsequent works that elaborate on his initial insights about performance, genre, and intertextuality (see for example Bauman 1986, 2004; Bauman and Briggs 1990). When deciding how to write the performance chapters, however, I chose not to explicitly foreground this theory and its language. Instead, I foregrounded a narrative approach and, to the extent possible, the accessible language of my consultants—in their performances and promotional materials and in dialogue with me in feedback interviews and other contexts. I endeavored to embrace their scholarly sensibilities in my writing, and I hope they will recognize not only themselves but their own analyses in these pages.

Having said that, I must also say that I make use of academic terminology, especially when writing about performance, that must be explained. Careful readers will note that I alternately refer to ballet as genre and discourse. I do so intentionally because I believe that ballet is both a form—a genre—and a kind of performative language—a discourse—that can be used both within and outside of that form. To clarify, following Bauman I use the word *genre* to refer to an order of style, "a constellation of systematically related, co-occurrent formal features and structures that serves as a conventionalized orienting framework for the production and reception of discourse" (Bauman 2004, 3). Adapting ideas from Foucault, Bourdieu, Butler, and others, I define discourse as "normalized ideas and beliefs that are intersubjectively constructed over time through communicative utterances that cross-reference or cite previous utterances." I interpret my consultants' performed references of ballet (in conversation and on stage) as sometimes referring strictly to its formal elements—its genre-ness, and other times to its discursive-ness—its paradoxical blends of the national, transnational and personal, reification and integration of ethnicity, and cooperation and competition. Not unusually, I sense both the genre and the discourse in ballet references and utterances.

In certain respects, immigration favors performers such as my four consultants, for whom ballet serves as valuable preparation for participation in a transnational labor market. Again, ballet is in part a multifaceted skill set that performers can readily adapt to professional opportunities in the United States. Fluency in the language of the Ivorian state ensemble or ballet includes mastery of a certain core number of the most popular dances (including basic rhythms/dance steps, solo "breaks," and "cuts"), familiarity with the formal transformations associated with staging rural traditions, skill in interweaving traditions from disparate sources, knowledge of at least some Guinean rhythms (at the very least *kuku*), and the ability to transpose rhythms from their original instrumentation for an ensemble of *jembes* and *dunduns*.

On a very practical level, my consultants benefited from touring with the Ivorian National Ballet and/or other ballet-style ensembles because it allowed them to experience life abroad and become gradually acclimated to sociocultural environments of the Global North and to cosmopolitan lifestyles. Most concretely, touring provided my consultants with their tickets to America and the chance to draw on their creativity in finding ways to remain.

For Ivorian immigrant performers, performance is not only an economic resource but also the primary venue for reinforcement and maintenance of community. Dispersed across the eastern United States, from New York to St. Louis, from Indianapolis to Orlando, the community of Ivorian immigrant performers generally reunites when one of them secures a lucrative performance contract and can afford to invite his friends to join him for the show. While also relying heavily on cell phones and social media to stay in touch, in physical terms the community literally (re)constitutes itself because of, and via, performance. In this sense, it exemplifies Kay Kaufman Shelemay's model of a "musical community" in that it is "constructed through and sustained by musical processes and/or performances" but need not "be anchored in a single place" (Shelemay 2011, 364–365). Shelemay notes that such a community can be "socially and/or symbolically constituted" in real-time or virtual settings and in the imagination (ibid.). Face-to-face, mediated, and imaginary, Ivorian immigrant performers' sense of community is multiple: local, national, and transnational. Like others in the era of the New African Diaspora, Ivorian immigrants are severed neither from their histories nor from their homeland. Rather, they are in daily communication with Ivorians all over the world, including those (if there are any) in their local communities, around the United States, in Europe, and remaining in Africa. Those with sufficient means even go back periodically to visit home and family.

Just as the state ensemble looks inward to build community (i.e., the nation) while simultaneously being charged with representing that community to the world, the Ivorian immigrant community uses music and dance to reconnect while also representing themselves to their society-at-large. In diasporic settings, performers are often the most visible and audible community representatives to the multicultural society around them; African immigrant performers can function as the face of the New Diaspora, symbolically representing "Africa," "West Africa," and/or "Ivory Coast." Given the polysemic nature of performance, ethnicity, nation, region, continent, the transnational, the global—all can be expressed simultaneously.[19] Audiences, for their part, can read various meanings in the performances, which can be connective or contentious or even both at the same time. My consultants' shows and stories shine a spotlight on such interactions.

Yet even if performers have some advantages in emigration and immigration, they still struggle. In nearly every case, my four consultants' classes, workshops, and school shows pay little, and their bigger, higher-profile shows (such as Vado's *Kekene* or Samba's *Ayoka*) often fail to break even. They must deal with a complex and frightening immigration legalization process and struggle to make ends meet (which for African immigrants is a matter not just of feeding oneself and paying the bills but also of supporting family members back home, who often have idealized notions of life in the United States that result in unrealistic expectations). And they must compete for often low-paying work in the face of American racism in its many guises. In immigrant America, sometimes romanticized as a land of tolerant, multicultural unity and great economic opportunity, life can feel like a fractured, lonely existence of misunderstandings and disconnection, of separation from family and friends and familiarity (Coe 2013). Vado, Samba, Sogbety, and Djo Bi all remain optimists, full of gratitude for their lives, and believers in the value of the work they do, but that is not because they have it easy; rather, it is because of their strength of character and their seemingly superhuman ability to endure hardship and pain.

Methods

Social relations are key to ethnography; indeed, ethnography ultimately is founded on specially framed human interactions. My years of area studies training, including one year living in the country from which my consultants emigrated, created a basis of shared knowledge—of Ivorian history, politics, religion, geography, culture, art, music, current events, indeed, *life*—that makes possible the relationship I have with my consultants. This previous experience was essential for me to write this book.

In keeping with a recent trend in ethnography, research for this project was multisited, allowing me to better follow the mobile, dispersed Ivorian population and the circulation of cultural meanings (Marcus 1995). I have been using participant-observation methods since 2006, attending dance and drum classes, workshops, and performances in Indiana, Ohio, New York, and Georgia. Many events I have documented in the form of video and audio recordings and photographs. Sometimes I have participated, as a student in dance classes and as a musician in performances and recording sessions. I have served as a booking agent, mediating between event organizers and Ivorian performers. I have conducted dozens of hours of interviews, including life stories and feedback interviews, in which I watch field videos with event participants to incorporate their interpretations into my analysis (V. Stone and R. Stone 1981; A. Stone and R. Stone 2013). I have also collected and analyzed promotional materials and historic videos from these performers' pasts, including materials dating prior to their emigration from Côte d'Ivoire, which provide a different historical angle. Finally, I have spent time with my four principal consultants—socializing, moving with them through their daily lives, driving with them to dance and music events, sharing meals. I have learned as much about my consultants' life stories in informal settings as I have in formal interviews (White et al. 2001). As of this writing, I continue to interact with my consultants, face to face and via cell phone, e-mail, Facebook, and Skype. Using mass communications is consistent with the communicative patterns of members of the dispersed immigrant community, who make extensive use of such networks to maintain connections (cf. Wood 2008). As I write, then, I remain in "the field," which for a project such as this is a figurative place where I expect I will "remain" long after this book is published (Cooley 2008).

Music and dance performance are multifaceted and polysemic, and can be used to communicate different messages through different channels simultaneously. Of these channels, my primary research focus is sound, not only because of my skills as an ethnomusicologist but also because in analyzing the sounds of Ivorian immigrant performances I find meaning that helps me better understand immigrants' lives. I do attend to other channels of communication, if less directly. All of the performances in this book involve dance as well as music; many also involve masks. One cannot study such music in Africa without attending to dance, which is conceptually linked to music. In my earlier research, for example, a single phrase described both the sound of the solo played by the master drummer and the movement of the dancing mask's feet (*baa gen* or "foot of the drum"; Reed 2003).

This book deals with the interweavings of many performance traditions with terminologies in multiple languages, but they are discussed in interethnic contexts—from Abidjan to America—by performers speaking French. When discussing, for example, *zauli*, consultants sometimes use the word *danse* and sometimes *rythme*, in certain contexts referring more specifically to movement or to sound, respectively, but often referring holistically to both. In such moments, I use the compound "rhythm/dance" to represent the inherent link between music and dance (cf. Wolf 2013). More generally, this book responds to the call from certain ethnomusicologists and dance scholars to attend more carefully to the interdependence of music and dance in Africa, even if my emphasis is the sonic side of the equation (Henderson 2009). Likewise, because art historians focus on the visual dimensions of mask performance in Africa, for the most part I leave the crucial visual element to their expertise. Yet another expressive channel—spoken and sung text—I have found to be less important in this study than in my previous work. In what my consultants (and I) call ballet performance, which is expected to feature traditions from all over Côte d'Ivoire, the performers themselves sometimes do not know the language or the meaning of the words they sing. The importance of text in immigrant performance sometimes lies in its sonic quality and what it indexes—which can be read as markers of various things, including a foreign sound, a kind of otherness, or an "authentic" Ivorian or African language.

Chapter Descriptions

This book is organized in two parts. The first part, "Program Notes," like the metaphor I have chosen for its title, provides background information that sets the stage for the heart of the book—the chapters about staged shows and stories. It consists of this introductory chapter, and chapter 2, "'Ballet' as Nexus of Discourses," where I investigate African ballet, both historically and in terms of its various parts. Charting the history of transnational African ballet, I focus on its origins, its spread across Africa and other continents, on various discourses that have been perpetuated through and in response to ballet as it has spread transnationally, and on the development of the Ivorian national version of ballet in 1974. Using material from my ethnographic work with Ivorian immigrants, I then focus on the embodiment of Ivorian ballet in the lives of immigrant performers and performance, detailing its specific formal elements (instrumentation, repertoire, and aesthetic practice in staged performance). Finally I discuss one of the ironies at the center of ballet social practice: cooperation and competition. Though cooperation lies at the very heart of the ideology of the national ensemble and as such is a principle central to the very idea of ballet, competition is also pervasive in everything from the formation of ballet troupes to ballet performances on stage to ballet veterans' struggles to find work in North America.

Part II, "Stages and Stories," is the core of the book. In it each performer has his own "act" consisting of two chapters—a relatively brief one based on a performance event and a more extensive one based on that individual's life story. Each life story chapter includes abundant excerpts from interview transcripts to highlight my consultants' voices. The performance chapters each feature a performance I attended, and the narratives and analysis are built from my field notes; video, audio, and photographic documentation; and feedback interviews with participants (especially but not exclusively the featured performer). Threaded throughout the stories and performances is ballet. The stories offer firsthand accounts of initial exposure to music and dance, introduction and eventual training in ballet, and ballet's role in creating opportunities for Ivorian performers to navigate the transnational networks of the immigrant performance labor market. In each act, on stage and in story, these four performers are shown to live transnational lives, at turns conforming with and resisting prevailing discourses of Africa and expectations for how Africa should be represented on stage.

Act I: Vado Diomande begins with chapter 3: "*Kekene*: The Performance of Oneness in NYC." A show organized and structured by Vado himself, *Kekene* ("oneness" in the Mauka language) is an annual performance series designed to showcase his Kotchegna Dance Company in collaboration with other Ivorian immigrants he calls the Ivory Coast All Stars. As the title suggests, Kekene is a forum for Vado to propogate a discourse of unity, which he accomplishes by extending ballet's integration of forms of difference to include not just ethnicity but also various nationalities and races. Vado profits from the polysemous potential of performance, simultaneously performing oneness and "traditional Ivory Coast dance." But *Kekene* also celebrates something more personal: Vado's return to health following a bout with anthrax that nearly killed him in 2006. A dance magazine review of Kekene exemplifies some of the resistance Vado receives from American audiences to his "multicultural" performance of African dance and the friction that results.

Vado's life story (chapter 4), among other things, explains both how he developed his interest in performing discourses of unity and his focus on his health. As a founding member of the Ballet National de Côte d'Ivoire, Vado developed a performative philosophy and approach that he has continued to adapt as a choreographer and director of Kotchegna. Competition-inspired sorcery attacks and healing and/or protective countermeasures have punctuated Vado's life ever since he tasted fame as a late teen representing his nation on stage. While skill developed through training and experience bought him his ticket to the United States, the search for better health care motivated him to stay. Yet on the phone, on Facebook, through trips home to offer sacrifices, and via spirit visits in dreams, Vado maintains a fundamentally transnational existence in daily life and on stage.

In act II, the spotlight shifts to Samba Diallo. Like Vado, Samba produces an annual show, *Ayoka* and chapter 5 narrates a portion of its 2010 performance in suburban Atlanta. Performed by Samba's dance troupe, Attoungblan (the Baule name for Akan "talking drums"), and other Ivorian immigrants, West Africans from other countries, and Americans, Ayoka ("thank you" in Bete) mixes languages, rhythms, and masks of various origins, sometimes in a single piece. Even more explicitly than Vado, Samba articulates a discourse of unity in words ("Culture brings everybody together") and music/dance (conforming to ballet norms in instrumentation, style, and repertoire). In so doing, he reinforces (and in publicity materials literally promotes) discourses of the global village, in which music and dance do not divide but unite. Yet nationalist discourse is also prevalent in Ayoka, showing performance to be a space in which seemingly incompatible notions can be expressed.

Threaded through Samba Diallo's life story (chapter 6) is the theme of exceptionalism. Born and raised near Abidjan, Samba might be described as "postethnic" in that he identifies with neither parent's ethnic heritage. His early experiences of difference occurred in the neighborhood where he grew up surrounded by people of many ethnicities who played music and danced together, interweaving traditions in the style of ballet, which was already influencing performance practices well beyond the stage. After stints with a popular competitive dance ensemble and the national ballet, Samba was invited to participate in the Memphis in May festival in 1994. He chose to stay, eventually making his way to the Atlanta area (without passing through New York as the other three performers did). Joining a dance studio in a largely white suburb, where he was adopted by a white family (through which he obtained legal status; the other three did so through marriage), Samba has danced in performances ranging from ballet-style Ivorian performance to the controversial musical *Song of the South*.

Samba's decision to immigrate to the United States has led not just to greater opportunities to transform his ballet training into an economic resource, transcend difference, and pursue visions of unity; it has also led to a life of loneliness, suffering, struggle—including financial struggle—and plenty of cultural *mis*understanding or friction. Ever the optimist, however, Samba dances on, embracing his roles as an educator, fitness instructor, and third-shift factory worker, all the while dreaming up future plans to establish a school that will teach tolerance through culture and dance.

Act III, which features Sogbety Diomande, begins with chapter 7, in which I narrate the performance of Sogbety's West African Drum and Dance Ensemble at the 2008 Lotus Festival in Bloomington, Indiana. Like "world music" recording artists, Sogbety adapts his performance in such a way as to familiarize the "exotic" (Taylor 1997). Identity being situational and contextual, Sogbety strategically tailors his self-representation to the American market, choosing an English-language name for his troupe and "West African" rather than "Ivorian" as a familiar geographical handle. Adapting the transnational concept of "ballet' and his Uncle Vado's discourse of universalism, Sogbety's performance fluidly blends ethnicities, nations, genres, and aesthetics, but not races, conforming with expectations for the representation of "Africa" on stage.

Chapter 8 narrates Sogbety's life story. He tells of village daydreams of a life abroad, teen years in multiethnic, cosmopolitan Abidjan, where he learned ballet in Kotchegna, at home and on the street. He portrays himself as an artist who finds the interweaving of difference second nature. Just seventeen when he moved to the United States, Sogbety spent nine years in New York, after which he moved to the small city of Mansfield, Ohio, where, as the only African performer during the years of this research project, he has worked more than any Ivorian artist I know. Sacrificing community for professional success, Sogbety has followed a path similar to that of earlier generations of immigrants who headed West in search of freedom, opportunity, and reduced competition.

The final act belongs to Dr. Djo Bi Irie Simon and begins with chapter 9, "'Open Village,'" the name Djo Bi gave his 2008 wedding, which took place in a cornfield in west-central Indiana. The informal performances before and after the formal wedding performance are intriguing for what they reveal about immigrant life and ballet discourse offstage, that is, when performers' intentions are to represent something not to an audience but to themselves and their close family and friends. The ritual within a ritual of the wedding ceremony—the moment of the formal performance framed as "wedding"—extended ballet interweaving beyond convention to include everything from iconic symbols of "traditional Africa" such as *kente* cloth to a reggae-influenced pop tune celebrating immigrant life in America. The open village demonstrates that ballet discourse, which enabled Ivorian performers to become migrant laborers, is sufficiently fluid and dynamic to allow immigrants to embody and express complex, sometimes contradictory meanings.

Chapter 10 chronicles Djo Bi's life story. Unlike his colleagues', Djo Bi's path toward international stages started in church, where he began drumming in interethnic ensembles as a child. This led to secular but private ballet groups in Abidjan, eventually that of famous dancer/choreographer Rose-Marie Giraud. A true transnational migrant, Djo Bi lived in Belgium, France, and England, playing both traditional and popular music, before settling in New York in 1997. Like

Sogbety, Djo Bi eventually moved to the Midwest, spending five years in Bloomington, Indiana, before relocating to his wife's hometown in a farming area of west-central Indiana in late 2012. While he makes nearly all his income teaching and/or performing ballet repertoire, Djo Bi's preference is writing and arranging his own compositions, based on ballet rhythms, that he performs in rock bands and other ensembles.

Chapter 11, "Thoughts on the Way Out," revisits some of the central questions raised in the introduction. Do the four artists engage in practices that can be interpreted as exhibiting diasporic, cosmopolitan, or scholarly sensibilities? What purchase do we gain by thinking about their lives and performances as exhibiting such sensibilities? Furthermore, what do these four performers' stories and shows add to the literature on migration and the New African Diaspora? Does approaching these issues via performance, with its heightened reflexivity, polysemous potential, adaptability, and transportability, paired with the subjectivities of rich, detailed immigrants' stories, shed any new light on such issues?

* * *

Abidjan USA is accessible in two, interlinked locations: the pages of this book and the Ethnomusicology Multimedia (EM) website at http://www.ethnomultimedia.org (accessed April 14, 2016), where annotated video, audio, and still images supplement the text. Connection between the two occurs through persistent URLs, or PURLs: hot links found in passages of this book where specific performance practices are discussed and analyzed.

2 "Ballet" as Nexus of Discourses

> Unity behind apparent multiplicity. *That is the music.*
> —Ernesto Cardenal[1]

ONE AFTERNOON IN 2008, Dr. Djo Bi and I were watching a video of his wedding. We came to a passage in which the Djo Bi on the screen began playing the *gbegbe* rhythm on his *jembe*, then smiled widely as the other drummers enthusiastically joined in with appropriate accompanying patterns and the dancers' bodies began moving. Turning to the Djo Bi with me in the room, I commented, "Clearly you are happy playing that rhythm!"

DJO BI (DB): Ah, yes! Everyone knows it!

DANIEL REED (DR): Everyone knows it regardless of whether you are Guro or Bete or some other ethnic group?

DB: Yes. Because everybody who was there, you know, we call it "ballet." We call it ballet because when you arrive in Abidjan, to prepare yourself to travel to Europe or to go to the United States, to go all over, you have to know other people's rhythms. You have to know all the rhythms. If, for example, I am Guro, a drummer from a non-Guro village can't drum that [my rhythm]. It's when we all come together, each one learns from the other.

DR: And so for you, being Guro, you learned that rhythm in the village?

DB: Yes.

DR: It's a rhythm of your neighbors, the Bete?

DB: Voilà.

DR: But for the others, the Senufo and other groups, where exactly do they learn this?

DB: They learn it in the ballet. In Abidjan.

How did it come to be that in 2008 a group of Ivorian immigrants in a west central Indiana cornfield could join in performing a rhythm based on shared experience of something they call "ballet?" In this chapter, I address this question using written and oral histories, ethnographic interviews, and archival sources. Drawing on research by others, I begin by briefly tracking the history of African ballet to provide historical context for the development of its Ivorian version and for the specific life stories and performances that form this book. I also take apart the polysemous discourse of ballet, including its seemingly incompatible blends of the national, transnational and personal, and its reification and integration of ethnicity and cooperation and competition. I furthermore discuss the various components of the embodiment of that discourse—that is, the elements of ballet that immigrant performers like Vado, Samba, Sogbety, and Dr. Djo Bi have mastered, including a canonized repertoire of prearranged pieces with set drum rhythms and dance steps, sometimes condensed and interwoven into choreographed dance dramas; standardized rhythmic changes, including cues, signals, and "breaks"; standardized instrumentation; and a disposition toward combining and interweaving traditions and peoples from diverse sources into a coherent whole. When Djo Bi said, "We call it ballet," he was referring to a shared experience, discourse, and practice that Ivorian immigrants have transformed from a type of training representing the Ivorian nation into a skill set ready-made for the transnational African performance marketplace.

However, as Castaldi (2006) notes of Senegal and as Schauert (2015) notes of Ghana, neither ballet versions of dances/rhythms nor ballet performers can be restricted to the national performance stage. Ballet as a genre, and its various embodiments in rhythms, breaks, choreographed pieces, narrative dances, and instrumentations, is itself as mobile as the people who perform it.

Training for the national stage to prepare performers for a migrant labor market abroad is a transnational phenomenon not limited to Côte d'Ivoire or even West Africa for that matter. Because there is a shared history in the creation of West African and, especially, francophone West African varieties of ballet, a comparative perspective that analyzes Ivorian ballet within its regional context is revealing. Castaldi writes that the grueling training for the national ballet of Senegal enabled performers to accumulate "precious cultural capital" (2008, 173) that they could later employ to make a living abroad. Given how little they are paid for their work in the Senegalese ballet—at the time of Castaldi's research, a maximum of $64 a month—dancers come to "consider their participation . . . as a long-term immigration strategy" (196) rather than a permanent position in-country. Schauert writes that in Ghana's two national ensembles, the Ghana Dance Ensemble and the National Dance Company, the idea that performers view tours as opportunities to "seek . . . greener pastures" abroad is well known to the point that rules and strictures are in place as disincentives (2015, 146–148).[2]

Even within West African countries, ballet and its performers are mobile and fluid and not controllable by the state. Despite the rules prohibiting them from doing so, many members of Ghana's state ensembles earn income with private groups. Castaldi notes that many ballets exist in Dakar and dancers compete for positions in the few groups that pay a decent wage (2006, 150). Likewise, in hotels and on private concert stages in Abidjan and smaller cities in tourist regions of Côte d'Ivoire, such as Korhogo and Man, groups perform Ivorian ballet traditions. As Sogbety once told me, "[The word] 'ballet' we use not just for the national ballet but for little groups.... When they play weddings, funerals, if they do the traditional stuff, with no *dunduns*, it's not ballet. But when you see a ballet group, then you see *dunduns*." Often these groups include at least some veterans of the national ensemble, which accords the groups authority and reputation. But one need not have actually spent time in the national ballet to learn aspects of its approach and repertoire. Djo Bi, for example, learned and eventually mastered Ivorian ballet traditions first by watching the Ballet National de Côte d'Ivoire (BNCI) and then by spending years performing with various private ballets based in Abidjan; his extensive training occurred completely outside the national ballet. Via media and mobility, this knowledge spreads. Ballet is mobile and can hardly be controlled or contained.

Because of global financial inequities, West African national ensembles routinely lose dancers during tours of wealthy nations in the Global North. Some performers obtain their skills through ballet training and are fortunate enough to land legal employment through which they initially establish themselves in Europe or North America. In such cases, it is common for them to remain long after their initial visas have expired while they seek out ways to remain legally in their adopted country for the long term. Vado and Samba are classic examples of the former; Djo Bi and Sogbety, of the latter. In either instance, ballet serves as a gateway for West African dancers and musicians to participate in a global capitalist market.

Anthropologist Rainer Polak, in his work on the transnational spread of the *jembe*, writes, "Capitalism generates a permanent demand for new cultural forms that are to be commercialized.... In most cases contacts between the world market and local culture are mediated through certain institutions or agencies.... One example is the nation state." (2006, 168). Like Debra Klein (2006), I concern myself with agency in this mediation by focusing on specific individuals as representatives of what Polak calls "local culture." In contrast to Klein's Yoruba *bata* drummers, who engaged in long-term, direct collaborations with individuals in their efforts to reach lucrative world markets, the Ivorian immigrants in this book profited from *state* mediation at the *beginning* of their pursuit of opportunities abroad. Ironically, in providing these performers with training to represent the nation, West African states have given them a skill set that serves as their ticket to a *trans*national capitalist market. As Polak notes, the market for African *jembe* players in Europe and America is supplied by former national ballet drummers, which suggests an "interesting relationship between nationalization and globalization" (169). In the context of West African government institutions, music and dance forms have been selected and repurposed for the stage to allow individuals to sell their performance skills in the international market for African music and dance.

The Transnational Genre of the (Nation-) State Ensemble

The literature on music, dance, and state ensembles is filled with examples of performance used to develop and express a unified national identity based on the interweaving of difference (Gilman 2009, 32ff; Turino 2000, 179; Castaldi 2006; Askew 2002; Schauert 2011, 2015; Flaig 2011). State ensemble creation is typically based on revaluing local, rural, often "indigenous," and/or "traditional" cultural practices that previously had been marginalized if not made objects of disdain (Gilman 2009, 36). Typically it is a country's urban elites who mine practices from rural community contexts, which they recontextualize, blending them with the formalized performative structures and professionalism of the concert stage (Buchanan 2006, 82).

State ensembles are known for their spectacle-like performances, including fancy light shows, athletic choreography, and strikingly colorful costumes. These performances draw on and create "visual and musical iconicities" that are "especially effective in rallying entire populations" (Herzfeld 1997, 27). Ethnomusicologists Sue Tuohy (2001) and Thomas Turino (2000) both point to the emotive affect of dance and music as key reasons for their use in nationalist projects (cf. Shay 2002, 3ff). Tuohy observes that music performance can be an "active means by which to experience the nation, by which to feel and act national" (108).

The transformation at the heart of the state ensemble has been labeled by some scholars "folklorization," which anthropologists Greg Urban and Joel Sherzer (drawing on Turino) define as "the relocation of native customs (typically music and dance, but other art forms as well) from their original contexts to new urban contexts, usually under the direct sponsorship of the state" (1991, 10). While this is useful, I take issue with the very concept of an "original context," which implies a time of purity and stasis before things begin to change. Rather, with John McDowell (2010), I argue that folklorization is a process in which expressive cultural practice is moved from historically situated, contingent community contexts into other contexts such as state ensemble stages, where they are manipulated and changed according to new, specific agendas.

Performing nationalism on stage necessarily essentializes not only the nation (Shay 2002, 1) but also forms of difference, such as ethnicity or class, that are united by the unifying nationalist discourse. Anthropologist Kelly Askew writes that in Tanzania so-called traditional dances "are valued for essentializing both 'tradition' and the ethnic groups that perform them. At the same time, however, they are subjected to modification to accommodate nationalist goals and objectives" (2002, 14). In West African ballet, ethnicity tends to be the most significant difference that must be massaged into a unified representation of the state. Its very selection as a focus and subject of the nationalist unification project ironically reifies its importance even as the project endeavors to relieve it of that importance. Simply put, states promote a postethnic discourse using representations that are ethnically marked and defined.

In the modification required to transform difference into unity, a tension surfaces that anthropologists Greg Urban and Joel Scherzer (1991) see as between "assimilation and differentiation." That is, to unify there must be difference that is in need of unification. Ethnomusicologist Peter Wade, writing about nationalism in Colombia, refers to the homogenizing process through which attempts to create coherence and meaning in diversity inherently acknowledge the presence of a nation's diversity (2000, 3–16). Herein lies another irony—nationalist expressions of unifying diversity inevitably include and elevate certain expressions of difference and, by extension, exclude and erase others. For Askew "there must be some degree of mutual engagement for nationalism to flourish, but this very element of mutuality, of sharedness, of common participation, admits the possibility of dissension from those excluded from state activities" (2002, 12). Wade brings this last point into sharp focus by acknowledging that the nationalist project is one of active *reconstruction*, not one in which diversity is merely denied, suppressed, or channeled (1998, 6). Castaldi believes that West African ballet has tended to favor Mande dance traditions, specifically those based on *jembe* drumming, to the extent that she invents the term *Mandification* (2006, 154) to refer to the hegemonic dominance of the traditions of descendants of the Mali Empire in ballets of the region, including Senegal. In Senegal, however, a country whose population includes significant numbers of Mande but ultimately is dominated by the Wolof, the ballet is also subject to *Wolofization* (2006, 13), including prominent ensembles of *sabar* drums. Reasons for the selection and highlighting of certain ethnic traditions and the rejection or silencing of others vary from country to country, but the processes remain consistent.

Yet another irony of West African ballet is its expressions of group identity through which individual stars are born. In Ivorian ballet, as in others, specific individuals such as Vado were designated "soloists," becoming well known in their own right, and effectively personal representatives of the state. Not surprisingly, individual stars are strong candidates for eventual defection abroad. The polysemic nature of performance thus can accommodate transnational, national, ethnic, regional, and individual identity expression simultaneously.

A Brief History of West African Ballet

A number of scholars have traced the history of West African ballet, showing its development to be a fundamentally transnational and international process

(Charry 2000; Polak 2006; Cohen 2008; Miller 1990; Flaig 2010; Castaldi 2006). In the late 1940s, Guinean Fodeba Keita, in Paris to pursue a law degree, formed an ensemble that became the first Les Ballets Africains, made up of his African student friends from the exclusive Ecole Normale William Ponty outside of Dakar, Senegal.[3] A French colonial teacher's college, Ecole Ponty was the choice for elites from across French colonial Africa. Among its graduates were men who later became prominent artists, writers, and politicians and would lead the movement for independence from France. Several—Modiba Keita of Mali, Félix Houphouët-Boigny of Côte d'Ivoire, and Daniel Ouezzin Coulibaly of Burkina Faso—would become the first presidents of newly independent African states (Cutter 1985, 121–125; Gardinier 1985, 334–335). Ecole Ponty was thus a hotbed of intellectual and artistic activity in which the future of Africa was debated, imagined, and realized. The seeds of an African ballet were planted in this context, seeds that would germinate and flower in the colonial metropole of Paris, where Keita and fellow Ponty graduates created "a new form of West African dance theater" (Flaig 2010, 58; Charry 2000).

Given the strong nationalist emphasis of its eventual manifestation as a state ensemble, Keita's ballet, initially called Les Ballets de Fodeba Keita, was surprisingly *inter*national in its performers, who hailed not just from the territory that would in 1958 become the Republic of Guinea but from across French West Africa. No less surprising, given the exclusive emphasis in the eventual state ensemble on rural, village settings on stage, was the instrumentation of Keita's group, which blended Mande instruments such as the *kora*, *bala*, and *jembe* with guitars and other Western instruments. "Keita's ballets amalgamated various elements from the outset: indigenous, traditional forms, pan-Africanist *Ponty* theater, and the values of European show business" (Cohen 2008, 24). Keita himself described the ballet as "modern folklore, that is, traditional Mande music and dance adapted to Western means of presentation" (Miller 1990, 53, quoted in Flaig 2010, 15). Keita, in 1957, made no pretense of representing any kind of ossified authentic Africa:

> We heard so many times the word "authenticity" employed haphazardly in relation to folkloric spectacles! Really, authentic in relation to what? To an idea more or less false that one holds of the sensational primitivism of Africa? No! . . . For us, authenticity is synonymous with reality . . . with living expression. . . . That is why the folklore of modern Africa is as authentic as the folklore of ancient Africa, both being the real expression of life in our country at two different moments of its history. The contemporary tendency of a folkloric company like ours must be to inform the whole world of the cultural values of those two Africas: the traditional and precolonial Africa of our ancestors, and today's Africa, which little by little is imprinted by western civilization. In fact, it would be even more absurd to fix our folklore only to the past of our country, since no folklore in this world is not partly hybrid. (quoted in Castaldi 2006, 63)

Keita's contention that all folklore is hybrid and historically contingent, and that both "modern" and "ancient" Africa should be represented on stage, informed his decision to create a ballet featuring everything from guitars to grass skirts.[4] That African ballet was initially so sophisticated renders all the more surreal Memphis in May's Ivorian ballet performance as a representation of a primitive past more than forty years later.[5]

Keita's ensemble debuted in Paris in 1952, then spent the next several years touring Europe, Africa, and the Americas. So successful was this venture that, on Guinea gaining independence from France in 1958, Guinean President Sekou Touré invited Keita to take part in his nation-building enterprise. Touré was determined to forge a new, anticolonial (that is, anti-French) path in every domain from economics to dance.[6] For this reason, he appointed Keita Minister of the Interior (Charry 2000, 252) and Keita's ballet became redefined as anticolonial and nationalist. Touré, motivated by his desire to revive pride and value in things African, sought to represent to the world an image of his new nation and the continent itself as one of great cultural and artistic achievement. "The National Ballet," he wrote, "should present Africa, make her known and esteemed" (1963, 261; n.d., 87).

Charry writes that "ballet as a genre must be understood within the context of the *orchestre, ensemble* and *ballet* as part of revolutionary cultural policy" (2000, 252). *Ensembles* perform exclusively local, ethnically marked traditions using indigenous instruments; *orchestres* play traditional music and new compositions inspired by local traditions but with "Western" instrumentation often featuring drum kit, guitars, bass, and horns (Flaig 2010, 58; Charry 2000, 251–253). Completing the triumvirate is ballet, which Charry defines succinctly: "Although rooted in village traditions, regional and national ballets combine diverse local styles, which would rarely mix in a village context, with European ideas of group choreography and stage presentation" (194). Underscoring the ideology behind the name of this new genre, Castaldi argues that "the concept of African Ballet serves as a challenge to European racist assumptions, suggesting that African dances are classical forms that offer their own aesthetic, equal in sophistication and beauty to the ballet tradition" (2006, 9). And yet the choreography, sets, and staging of Les Ballets Africains (LBA) represented exclusively "the trope of the African village as the marker of a tribal African world" (Charry 2000, 30).

So it was that the idea of African ballet began to travel across Europe, North America, and beyond, manifesting on concert stages featuring LBA. West African nations began forming national ensembles in the wake of Guinea's success, the other former francophone nations among them following suit by naming their troupes "ballets." An early exception was the Ghana Dance Ensemble (GDE), which had an ideology similar to that of Guinea's national performance troupes but was distinct in certain key ways. Sponsored by President Kwame Nkruma, the GDE was developed by ethnomusicologist Kwabena Nketia and others at the Institute of African Studies of the University of Ghana at Legon. Promoting an ideaology of "unity in diversity" (Schauert 2015, 75), the GDE sought both to instill a sense of nationalist identity among citizens of the new nation of Ghana and to educate audiences around the world about Ghana's cultural traditions.[7] The educational dimension of the GDE's mission resulted in the Ghanaian national ensemble model spreading as much in European and US institutions of higher learning as on concert stages (Flaig 2010, 66; see also Locke 2004; Dor 2014).[8]

The LBA model, while initially far less influential in university contexts, had a profound impact throughout Europe and North America because of the consistency and popularity of those early tours. The instrumentation of Keita's early ensembles blended "European" and African instruments, but, following the redefinition of LBA as a national ensemble, it began to evolve in a more exclusively West African and in particular Mande direction. As the LBA model continued to evolve, the *jembe*, originally from the region near the contemporary border between northern Guinea and southern Mali, became increasingly prominent, along with the *dundun*, which is usually two or three drums of the *dundun* type (the medium-sized *sangba*, the small *kenkeni*, and the large *dundun*). While the LBA from its inception featured amalgamations of instruments from various traditions, the ballet stage increasingly became the scene of large groups of *jembe* players with many accompanying parts. Flaig asserts that the *jembe* was deliberately foregrounded by the socialist Touré because it was "a common person's tradition," allowing the new president to use the LBA to minimize ethnic difference and local, ethnic-based power as represented by the "professional" *jeli* (griot) caste (2010, 8–9). The ballet transformed meanings associated with *jembe* playing, which became increasingly seen as an urban profession, even an art form (112).

Whether the large *jembe* ensemble originated on the ballet stage or with African teachers of large drumming classes is not known (Charry 2000, 195), but by the 1980s a concert drumming tradition, removed from its dance origins, had developed. The increasing dominance of the *jembe* on concert stages and as an icon of Africa was encouraged by ballet performance and by LBA drummers who had settled in New York and began teaching it in the 1960s.

Beyond popularizing the *jembe* and *dundun*, the LBA also set in motion other performative patterns that became normalized in stagings of ballet. Charry notes that ballet practice altered village performance traditions in several key ways. For example, Keita's "amalgamation" of various traditions in new forms has persisted. Charry writes, "Not only are dances from different regional traditions combined, but so are their associated musical instruments, an equally rare village event." (2000, 30). This amalgamation has created choreographed, danced narratives "combining different dance styles sequentially in long suites that take on a life of their own, telling a story with a specific sequence of dances, rhythms,

Figure 2.1 Dr. Djo Bi playing the *jembe* at his June 2008 wedding in St. Bernice, Indiana. Photograph by Christy True.

and costumes" (211). As choreographers in each country build up a repertoire of danced narratives, this repertoire becomes "the reification of national canons or repertories of dances" (ibid.), in which performers in national companies become trained. Those who later cross paths in immigrant settings—such as Djo Bi's wedding (as seen in figure 2.1)—can draw on shared knowledge—of forms, aesthetics, instrumentation, performative tendencies—quickly falling in together in a celebration of shared culture even if they had never previously met.

LBA and the Spread of the *Jembe* in the United States

Shortly after adopting LBA as a state ensemble, Sekou Touré founded Ensemble Djoliba and Ballet de l'Armée. From the late 1950s into the 1960s, as the three groups regularly toured Europe and North America, "Guinean cultural diplomacy operated quite actively through globally touring staged productions" (Cohen 2008, 4). LBA was not just the first but also by far the most popular and influential group. Its influence took a new form when one of its lead drummers, Papa Ladji Camara, relocated to New York in the early 1960s to perform and teach (Charry 2000, 193). As LBA had done on the concert stage, Camara established a tradition of *jembe* and *dundun* drumming in North America that would proliferate dramatically in the decades to come.

The most serious interest in *jembe* drumming and dance traditions in North America initially developed in African American communities in New York. This was the period of the African Independence, Civil Rights, and Black Power movements, and many African Americans saw in the Guinean ballet tours and in Guinean drum and dance classes opportunities to use the performing arts to reclaim their African heritage and identity (Watson 2008, 537–538; cited in Cohen 2008, 17). The *jembe* thus became "politically potent" as a medium connecting "the emancipation of Guinea (followed by the rest of francophone West Africa) from French colonial rule and the emergence of Black Nationalism in America" (Flaig 2010, 239).[9]

Roughly concurrent with the early LBA tours and Camara's immigration to New York, another trend joined the growing popularity of African drumming and its signification as a point of pride for African Americans, this one generated by Nigerian immigrant Michael Babatunde Olatunji. Charry observes about Olatunji's ground-breaking debut album:

> *Drums of Passion* was recorded several months before, and released a few months after, the February 1960 sit-ins in Greensboro, North Carolina, which would transform the growing civil rights struggle into a national movement overnight. Both events—one cultural (the release of *Drums of Passion*) and the [other] social (the rapid spread of the sit-ins) permanently changed the consciousness of many Americans and helped jump-start one of the most dynamic and volatile decades in American history. (2005, 1–2)

According to Olatunji, in his 2005 autobiography:

> *Drums of Passion* played a significant role in all the social change taking place around that time. It was the first percussion album to be recognized as an African contribution to the music of African Americans. It also came right at the beginning of the Civil Rights Movement. This meant that we were recognized as pioneers in the "Black is Beautiful" Movement. The whole idea of "black power" came along at this time too. And so did the wearing of the *dashiki* and natural hair. We found ourselves right in the middle of this, going from one rally to another, sponsored by different organizations fighting for freedom: from the NAACP to CORE to SNCC to the Black Muslims. (157)

In 1967, Olatunji opened the Olatunji Center for African Culture in Harlem, where he taught drum and dance classes. By the early 1970s, both Olatunji's school and one founded by Camara in the Bronx were facilitating and nurturing interest in African drumming. "It should be noted, however, that for a long time neither Olatunji nor Camara enjoyed widespread support outside the small community of culturally aware African Americans actively pursuing this part of their heritage" (Charry 2005, 12). Nonetheless, the two trained a generation of African American hand drummers who, as they deepened their study of African music, increasingly focused on the *jembe* (and to a lesser extent on *sabar* and other Senegambian drumming styles). *Jembe* traditions continued to spread through New York and beyond because of their prominence in Africa-focused dance companies. In 1977 the founder of one such company, Chuck Davis, inaugurated an annual African music and dance festival called DanceAfrica that has persisted well into the twentieth-first century. *Jembe*-related traditions thus continued to dominate representations of Africa on stage in New York and beyond as dance companies, inspired by Davis and others, began to be formed in smaller cities and universities around the United States.

In the meantime, American interest in African music continued to grow steadily, although it remained relatively isolated in universities or particular urban settings. Ghanaian ethnomusicologist Kwabena Nketia initiated a trend of teaching Ghanaian drumming and dance at American universities (often with Ghanaian musicians as instructors), and drumming and dance communities took root in various other cities, including Philadelphia and Washington, DC (cf. Charry 2005, 13). But the *jembe*, already a familiar feature in concert stage representations of Africa, would catapult toward its eventual iconic status as a result of two unrelated events in the 1980s.

First, the death of Sekou Touré in 1984 and the subsequent destabilization of the Guinean government, including its performance troupes, left prominent Guinean musicians without work and "in search of new forms of patronage" (Charry 2000, 193). Perhaps most noteworthy among these musicians was Mamady Keita, who relocated to Brussels and became a kind of world music phenomenon and arguably the most famous and widely recognized drummer in the history of the *jembe*'s transnational spread. Flaig also points to Famoudou Konaté, who, like Keita, began a successful solo career during the post-Touré era through concerts, workshops, and recordings. Flaig goes so far as to assert that the "globalization of the [*jembe*] occurred in two stages, first, with Guinea's national ballet companies and then through the concerts and workshops given by Konaté and Keïta as they embarked on solo careers outside of the ballet" (2010, xiii). The increasing prominence of the *jembe* as a performance focus has led, since the 1980s, to the establishment of "a concert drumming tradition removed from its dance origins" (Charry 2000, 9).

Separation of the *jembe* from the dance developed further in the wake of a second significant event: when Grateful Dead drummer Mickey Hart, who had first met Olatunji when Olatunji appeared at Hart's Long Island school in 1964, invited Drums of Passion to open for the Grateful Dead at their 1985 New Year's Eve show in New York. According to Flaig, "The 1980s was the beginning of the 'Dead Heads,' a community of fans who followed the band from one show to the next across the nation. The performance of Olatunji and *Drums of Passion* inspired the beginning of the 'Dead Head' drum circle, which took place in the parking lot hours before the start of each Grateful Dead concert" (2010, 250).

Olatunji is from Nigeria, far from the original homeland of the *jembe* along the Mali-Guinea border, and yet, probably because of his deep involvement in African American drumming communities in and around New York City, "by the 1980s, [he] had four [*jembe*] players and two [*dundun*] players featured in the ensemble" (Flaig 2010, 251). Dead Head drum circles followed, and *jembe* drum circles began spreading across North America among Dead Heads and other primarily white middle-class liberals. Then the spread of *jembe* came full circle when Dead Heads and others who had been introduced to it by them began showing up as students at *jembe* workshops led by Keita, Konate, and other former ballet drummers (ibid.). Though many drum circles were based on the idea of free improvisation, some people initially exposed to the *jembe* in such contexts began attending workshops lead by Mande drummers teaching *jembe* and *dundun* patterns from West Africa.

Thus began what Polak calls the *jembe*'s "unparalleled boom in Europe and North America" (2006, 161–162), with increasing numbers of concerts, CDs, instructional books, classes for and playing by amateur drummers, and exponential increases in the *jembe* export market. Charry (2000) describes the "unprecedented upturn" of the *jembe* in the 1980s thus:

> Former members of national ballet troupes of Guinea, Mali, and Senegal routinely settle abroad to teach and perform, *jembe* students flock to drum classes and camps, and major drum manufacturers have found a market for industrially produced synthetic *jembe* like instruments. (193)

As a result, by the 1990s the *jembe* had attained a level of "world exposure . . . unprecedented for any African drumming tradition. . . . The stage presentation of *Mandenka* [Mande] drumming and dancing has a history that is now over half a century old" (Charry 2000, 241) Even though these traditions are in fact new, "the general recognition of Africa as a wellspring of a deeply entrenched culture of drumming and dancing still operates" (ibid.).

The Transnational West African Ballet

Jembefication (my admittedly playful response to Castaldi's term *Mandeification*) is but one of many qualities that the Ivorian version of West African ballet has in common with LBA and ballets from other former French colonies in the region, such as Senegal and Mali. Polak (2006), writing specifically about changes in *jembe* "celebration" music as performed in villages and communities in Mali, succinctly describes some of the qualities that generally distinguish ballet from community performance traditions in West Africa. First, ballet performers learn that staging requires fundamental changes to performance kinesthetics and proxemics. In typical community contexts, lead musicians are at the center of a human circle that creates a performance space integrating almost everyone present, defying easy distinctions between performers and audience members. This spatial organization is consistent with the West African participatory performance model (Turino 2006), in which everyone present contributes, even if only by clapping, singing a response in call-response songs, or dancing or moving to the beat. On the ballet stage, circles open up into lines[10] and the audience becomes physically separated from performers, with the result that "the role distinction between audience and performers is far more rigid" (Polak 2006, 164).

Second, ballet "repertoire is condensed, arranged into pieces, made uniform and pre-established. It artistically blends elements of different sources into a new aesthetic whole" (ibid.). Such musical and choreographic rearrangement necessitates more rehearsal than is typical in community contexts, where rehearsal is rare outside the actual performance context (ibid.). Elements that are added and/or transformed include

- Signal phrases marking the beginnings and endings of pieces
- Prearranged rhythmic changes
- Enlarged ensembles
- A canonized repertoire

Polak observes that the ballet version of *jembe* drumming—with its attendant changes in spatial organization, repertoire, and performance—is what has spread transnationally, not the community celebration version:

> The *djembe* playing in recording studios, concert stages, drum and dance workshops, and schools, does not simply consist of "traditional" repertoires and styles of local African celebration music. The arrangement techniques and transformations developed in the ballet context form a constituent part of the mediation process of *djembe* music in the West. (2006, 166)

This is precisely the case in the Ivorian immigrant community, nearly all of whose music and dance feature ballet material whether in grand-scale performances or in workshops, school assemblies, or dance classes. The national ensemble experience thus serves as a kind of mediator between Ivorian community contexts and immigrant performance experience.

Substantiating her understanding of the ballet transformation of local performance, Flaig (2010) quotes Fodeba Keita's (1958) explanation of the process:

> On the stage new conditions have to be created by means of different devices in order, on the one hand, to retain the freshness and reality of the dance and, on the other, to destroy the monotony which is quick to arise due to the non-active participation of the audience. That is the reason why we must take our

dances only at their culminating point, shorten them and cut out a thousand details which are not important except in the public place of the village. For instance the "Dance of Possession" easily takes most of the night in the Sudan whereas, on the stage, five or six minutes are quite sufficient in order not to tire a foreign audience. (74)

Castaldi writes that even the dress for Senegalese ballet performance is adapted—inspired by village clothing but not the same. The tendency for all performers to be in smart, matching costumes is yet another example of what Castaldi terms the "cultural translation" required to meet the audience on its own terms (2006, 74).

The Ivorian National Version of the Transnational Ballet

When I was first becoming familiar with Ivorian performers living in the United States, I knew little about their pasts and not much at all about African ballet and its importance in their lives. Shortly after meeting Sogbety Diomande, I arranged for him and his cousin Moha Dosso to perform Gue Pelou, the Mau *nya yan* (stilt mask), as a late addition to the 2006 Lotus Festival in Bloomington, Indiana. When Sogbety and I were negotiating the terms of this performance and it became clear that the festival could only afford two mask spirit performers, the question became what to do about a drum ensemble. Knowing my familiarity with West African music, Sogbety asked me to put together a group of drummers for the event. I swallowed hard but accepted the responsibility. To be on the safe side and to confirm what I was sure would be the case, I asked, "You want *baa* drums, correct?" Here I was referring to the drums (see figure 2.2) I had always seen played in Mau and Dan communities in Côte d'Ivoire, which I had been taught were essential for the spirits called *yinan* to be drawn into the performance space to enable the masked spirit himself to appear and be empowered to perform. I was completely caught off guard by Sogbety's response: "No, *jembe* and *dundun*." Once I recovered from my shock, I easily put together a group of students and local residents with *jembe* and *dundun* experience. At Sogbety's request, we played variations of *kuku*—a Guinean rhythm from a region and ethnic group totally outside the Mau mask spirit performance tradition but arguably the most popular in the *jembe* repertoire in the United States (PURLs 2.1, 2.2, 2.3, 2.4, 2.5, and 2.6).

The transnational spread of the *jembe* began decades before Côte d'Ivoire had even begun planning for its own national ballet. The Guinean ballet predated and informed the Ivorian ballet from the moment of its inception, and Ivorians gradually began "jembefying" many dances in their standard ballet repertoire. In the United States, they continued encountering the dominant popularity of the *jembe*, which affected very substantially and specifically their establishing themselves as performers and teachers of African music and dance. Many jobs

Figure 2.2 Vado Diomande playing the *baade* during a sound check for the September 2008 Lotus Festival in Bloomington, Indiana. Photograph by author.

that Vado found when he first arrived in New York were with Guineans, including repairing *jembe*s and playing them for Guinean dance classes. Like his uncle Vado, some of Sogbety's first jobs involved the *jembe*, that drum he had only learned to play in Abidjan. One of the standard rhythms in the Ivorian immigrant dance repertoire is the well-known *kuku*, and the instrumentation of Ivorian immigrant performance is often, if not almost, exclusively, multiple *jembe*s and one or two *dunduns*.

Jembefication is, however, just one facet of the complex phenomenon of Ivorian ballet. Ivorian ballet discourse began in 1969, when Côte d'Ivoire sent a private, nongovernment music and dance group led by Moussa Kourouma to perform at the historic first Pan-African Festival in Algiers. Reaction to the group's performance was so positive that Ivorian President Félix Houphouët-Boigny, now determined to create a national music and dance group, charged his Director of the Ministry of Cultural Affairs, Jules Hié Nea, with creating the Ballet National de Côte d'Ivoire (BNCI). Nea hired former LBA dancer Mamadou Condé to serve as first director, thereby establishing a direct line of influence between the internationally successful Guinean troupe and Côte d'Ivoire's nascent model of representing Africa and the Ivorian nation on stage.

That similarities abound between the two national ballets is surely no accident. An internal policy document in the BNCI's archives states that the BNCI was formed "with the noble mission of promoting the image of the country's prestige through dance" (BNCI). This statement, which echoes Sekou Touré's stated purpose for the founding of Guinea's LBA, would be used to promote the BNCI and its successor, formed in 1994, the Compagnie Nationale de Danse de Côte d'Ivoire, for decades to come. Promotional brochures for the Compagnie Nationale published as late as 2006 continued to state its mission as "the promotion of the image of prestige of the country through dance." Intriguingly, an additional purpose was this:

> Through their art, the dancers of the National Dance Company of Côte d'Ivoire participate in the return of peace to their country. And their message of peace is contained in different choreographies presented to the public. In a varied repertoire the National Dance Company preaches for peace and reconciliation in Azoumadre and Seri Yama. These creations, in which certain dancers are dressed as priests, marabouts, and traditional fetishers, present different religions evolving in harmony and in the respect of mutual differences ... The philosophy that underpins this choreography is the magnification of peace and tolerance between people of Côte d'Ivoire after the breakout of war in 2002. (CNAC 2006)

While the mission of the Ivorian national ballet seemed to be, like that of Guinea's, to project an image of cultural prestige to the world, implicit was also the uniting of peoples of diverse regional, linguistic, ethnic, and religious backgrounds into a national vision. However, it seems that the idea of national unity in difference became explicit only after the period of instability and civil war that plagued the country for most of the first decade of the 2000s.[11]

Condé led a series of tours around the country, selecting about a hundred artists from the various regions and gathering them in Bouaké for final auditions. In the end, the company consisted of about twenty female and thirty male dancers and musicians, the director, a general manager, and a stage manager. The company purchased a bus for local tours and constructed a building in the Abidjan suburb of Yopougon for lodging and training performers. Selected for their "artistic technique, physical and vocal qualities," the performers brought to the BNCI a repertoire of dances that were "the most significant and original of their [respective] regions" (Ministère de la Culture et de la Francophonie, n.d.). Côte d'Ivoire is particularly well known for its masks, with roughly forty of its sixty ethnic groups having some masking tradition. Naturally, the national ballet selected masks that represented these groups. Listed in the ballet repertoire were thirty-six dances, of which at least half a dozen featured masks. Also included were the following examples that I have seen performed by Ivorian immigrants in the United States over the past decade (BNCI):

Dance	Description
Abodan	Agni women's rejoicing dance
Adjoss	Baule rejoicing dance
Gbegbe	Bete funeral dance
Tématé	Wè/Dan girls' circumcision/initiation dance
N'goron	Senufo young girls' dance
Goli	Wan rejoicing mask
Zauli	Guro rejoicing mask
Flali	Guro rejoicing mask
Gla	Wè rejoicing mask
Echassier	Dan/Mau rejoicing mask (*nya yan* in Mau; *ge gbleen* in Dan)

Of the most common Ivorian dances performed by the immigrant community during my research for this book, only the Senufo panther mask Bolohi is missing from this partial list. Also missing is *kuku*, though this is less surprising because this rhythm is of Guinean origin.[12] The Ivorian ballet drew much influence from Guinea, including its mission, instrumentation, and various aspects of performance, but I have no evidence that it performed actual dances/rhythms from across the Guinean border. That *kuku* was a cornerstone of the Ivorian immigrant repertoire in the 2000s was most likely because of the influence of LBA and Papa Ladji in the United States.

Ivorian Ballet Embodied

What is it, then, that the Ivorians at Djo Bi's wedding had learned? What is Ivorian ballet discourse, and how is it embodied in performance? Some of its elements are specific to the Ivorian national version of the transnational genre, while others are more generally in the West African tradition of ballet whose roots are in the LBA. Moving the frame back, elements in Ivorian ballet are inextricably bound up in the very idea of a national ensemble and are likely present in any national performance troupe.

Instrumentation (Jembefication)

So struck was I by the pervasive use of the *jembe* in Ivorian immigrant performance that instrumentation became one of my first questions when I sat down with Sogbety for our first formal interview. To be clear, the *jembe* is a common instrument in Côte d'Ivoire. It has been widespread throughout the Mande heartland region, which includes the country's northern savanna, certainly since well before the colonial period. Colonial "pacification"—the euphemism for diminishing tensions between various ethnic groups as a result of the territorial takeover by the French (and the sudden presence of a more powerful shared enemy)—was one of the factors that increased north–south traffic in trade and led northern traders (*Jula*) to move in greater numbers to colonial outposts in the south (Reed 2003, 38–39). These traders brought their instruments and, as trading outposts grew, more northern Mandes moved south, bringing their instruments, including the *jembe*, with them. By the late twentieth century, cities such as Abidjan and Bouaké were home to large numbers of *jembe* drummers. Even smaller cities such as Man or Daloa had significant populations of northerners and their *jembe*s. Throughout the country and especially in rural regions, however, the *jembe* is often nicknamed "the city drum" in French, distinguishing it from the dozens of drums favored by other Ivorian ethnic groups. In my time in Côte d'Ivoire, I rarely saw a *jembe* in villages, and when I did it was in the hands of young people.[13]

I asked Sogbety, who hails from the small village of Toufinga in northwestern Côte d'Ivoire, if he could remember the first time he saw a *jembe*. He said that the first time was in Toufinga, but it was being played by someone who had moved away from the village and then come back to visit. "It was in Abidjan that I myself began [to play]." I told him that I had seen the *jembe* used in the United States for many dances/rhythms from all over Côte d'Ivoire, including those of the Dan, Guro, and other ethnic groups who typically play other drums. Sogbety's response was informative:

> You know the reason is that we are not all living in the same place here.... Everyone is spread out in different places. In Africa, we are still very much together. If it's a Mau, there are many Mau around. If it's a Dan, there are many around who can play. If it's Guro, there are many Guro who can play. But when we come here, there are how many Guro here? There is Tra Bi, Djo Bi, and Bi Bo Ti and Titos.[14] Those are the Guro who are here. Of those four, it's only Tra Bi and Djo Bi who know how to drum the Guro rhythms. Bi Bo Ti and Titos know how to dance. If they want to dance, for example, *zauli* like they do in the village, they will need at least ten people—they'll need five people who can play different [instruments]. But how are they going to do that here?
>
> Here, the Guineans who arrived ... before we did, they introduced the *jembe* and the *dundun*, so everything is based on that now. No matter where you go, the Guineans have already been there, and everyone knows *dundun*, *jembe*. Instruments like this [plays my Dan/Mau *ɓaaɗe* drum], they don't know here. It's only now that people are starting to send them here. And there are other instruments than the *jembe*.... I can't play [the *ɓaaɗe*] here because there is no one who can accompany me, there is no one who can drum in the way that I feel. Voilà. So what remains is just the *jembe* and *dundun*. The mask comes, [and] we play *kuku*, everyone goes *kuku*, we play the loud drum, and that's it. But back home it's not *kuku*. It's different music.

Among my four primary consultants, there was no consensus on precisely when Ivorian ballet drummers began transposing Ivorian dances for *jembe*. Sogbety insists that this transition occurred in the United States, but Djo Bi says that the *jembe* began to be incorporated into ballet contexts in Abidjan. Vado agrees, pointing not to the national ballet, however, which initially was determined to approximate the instrumentation used in village contexts, but rather to his own Ensemble Kotchegna and comparable private ballets. On one point, however, everyone agrees: *jembe/dundun* arrangements of Ivorian dances/rhythms are a central aspect of ballet that has become increasingly dominant in the United States, where it is now a fixture in North American audiences' imaginaries and expectations for Africa on stage. The Guineans came first and set the stage with a *jembe*.

The *jembe*'s popularity has affected many Ivorians' choices regarding their music in the United States. Sogbety talks of playing *kuku* in mask performances which he contrasts with the rhythms played "back home." The *jembe* for Sogbety is a kind of mediation, a connecting point between his experiences prior to immigration and his North American experiences and Americans' expectations regarding African music. In Sogbety's life, the *jembe* renders the unfamiliar more familiar; that is, it has become well known in the United States to the point that, like world music, it can be seen, according to Timothy Taylor (2006), as a means of familiarizing otherwise exotic African music, especially for young audiences. "When you arrive at a school," Sogbety explained, "If they see a drum like this [points to my Dan *baade*], they'll say, 'What is this?' But if you arrive with the *jembe*, they know what it is; they say, 'That's from Africa.' If you play [the *baade*], they say, 'That, that's really different [quizzically].'" Just as Grammy awards for world music tend to go to collaborative ventures between European or North American stars and musicians from elsewhere, and/or to highly "Westernized" music of the Other, Sogbety finds it eases and increases his work to have a means, in the *jembe*, of increasing the accessibility of his performances and workshops to North American audiences.

The practical aspect of jembefication makes a considerable difference in the choices of ballet performers as well. Once I asked Djo Bi when the transformation to the *jembe* began. "In the ballet!"

> I am Guro, you understand? I am Guro, and I come there and there is no Guro drum. . . . And the others there don't know [Guro music]. And you have to do *zauli*. But they are the master drummers of their ethnic groups. So you touch a little bit of everything. It's like you—today you know how to read and write. If someone gives you a book in French, and you copy it, you're not going to write in the way a French person would write. You're going to copy it in your own manner. In the way people write here. . . . So here it's the ballet, it's the public, it's the huge public. You need something spectacular. So we take three *dunduns*, and the *jembe* rhythms.

Ivorian ballet performances in the United States nearly always consist of rhythms transposed from instrumentation marked as "traditional" and "ethnic" (such as *bɔlɔnye* single-stringed harps and calabash rattles for the Senufo dance *bolohi*, or the *baade*, *zikri*, and associated accompanying drums for the Wè/Dan *tématé*) to the ballet standard of multiple *jembes* and *dundun*. According to the oral histories I have collected and videos from as far back as the late 1970s, the BNCI originally employed a range of instruments, likely for performances in villages and/or other community contexts from which a genre originated (though often using more instruments than would be used in those contexts). However, as Vado explained, this resulted in great expense and difficulty when the BNCI toured, so at a certain point it began transposing rhythms for ensembles of *jembes* and *dunduns*. By the time Vado was running his own group, transposition to *jembe/dundun* had become the norm for practical reasons.

While the *jembe* and *dundun* dominate in Ivorian immigrant performances, other instruments are occasionally used. For example, Sogbety and/or Vado will play a piece or two during a set on the *baade*—the multiple-head drum associated with the Mau and Dan people in the mountainous west of Côte d'Ivoire. Rarely, however, is the *baade* used during performances of the Mau stilt mask Gue Pelou, whose music is almost always among the many transposed for *jembe* and *dundun*. Rather, *baade* pieces are usually interludes between big, full ensemble dance pieces, played either solo or with light accompaniment. Performances occasionally include the musical bow (*arc musical*) expertly played by Florida resident Zagbo Martin, who like Vado is a veteran of the BNCI dating back to the 1970s. Some performances also feature wooden xylophones, the most common being the pentatonic Senufo *jegele* played by virtuoso Seguenon Kone while he acrobatically spins and dances. Occasionally the Ivorians are joined by a Guinean Maninka *jeli* (griot) named Kierno Diabate, who plays a heptatonic *jelibala*, usually layering rapid melodic runs over standard *jembe* and *dundun* polyrhythms, which adds a distinctly different element of the *jeli* tradition to Ivorian dances such as *zauli* and *bolohi*. When the Guinean Diabate joins the group, performing Ivorian nationalism is somewhat problematized, even though the Maninka *jeli* tradition he represents is also found in northwestern Côte d'Ivoire. In ethnic terms, however, and in terms of performance genres, the addition of *jelibala* melodies to rhythms/dances from across Côte d'Ivoire further deepens the already profound interweaving of ethnicity in these performances.

Canonization of the Repertoire

Just as the instrumentation for Ivorian ballet performance in the United States has become standardized, so has the repertoire become common to the point that there is unquestionably a canon. The dances/rhythms that constitute this canon have been performed so regularly in the national ballet that they have become imbued with a nationalist meaning in addition to their ongoing association with ethnicity. In the United States Ivorian immigrant performers can select from a whole set of such dances/rhythms that have been transposed for *jembe/dundun* and can now be considered standards. While noncanonized Ivorian rhythms/ dances occasionally show up on set lists, my consultants nearly always perform *gbegbe, zauli, bolohi,* and *baanya*. Of these, only the Bete *gbegbe* is not a mask dance. *Zauli* is the name both for a Guro mask dance celebrating the legend of a beautiful young girl (Fischer 2008, 294)[15] and for its rhythmic accompaniment; *bolohi* is a Senufo panther mask and its rhythm; and *baanya* is the general term for the rhythms played in immigrant performances of the Mau stilt mask Gue Pelou, a spirit from the forest. Specifically, the two most common rhythms played for Gue Pelou are *tindin* and *zikinin*.[16] The canon also includes *soli wule*, a rhythm for a Guinean mask of the same name, and *kuku*. Dances/rhythms sometimes appearing in the Ivorian immigrant set list are *témaké* (Dan/Wè), *adjoss* (Baule), *zanloba* and *zambele/flaly* (Guro), *tibloklalo* (Dida), *n'goron* (Senufo), and *abodan* (Agni). Occasionally Ivorians add other core *jembe* rhythms from the Maninka area around the Mali-Guinea border, such as *dundunba*.

Gbegbe, which Djo Bi introduced at his wedding, is arguably the most popular rhythm in the Ivorian immigrant community (see table 2.1). It is typically attributed to the Bete people, though Djo Bi says that it is also played at funerals by his Guro ethnic group, who call it *ury*. *Gbegbe* has become so common and popular that I have heard both Sogbety and Samba jokingly refer to it as the "Ivorian national rhythm." The fervor and enthusiasm with which Ivorians play it makes it stand out from the rest of the repertoire. Because its rapid tempo featuring fast-paced repeating patterns makes it a suitable showcase for virtuosic drum and dance solos, it is frequently performed toward the end of a set.

Gbegbe is also popular in informal, nonperforming contexts such as parties the night before or after a staged performance, or when everyone has gathered after having not seen one another for a while (see PURL 9.13). Having observed this again and again, I once said to Sogbety, "*Gbegbe* is like the national popular dance of Côte d'Ivoire!" He agreed: "Yes, everyone knows it. When Ivorians want to relax, *gbegbe* has to be there. It's always either at the end of a show, or it can be at the beginning. In Africa . . . they have a *gbegbe* group. They just do this dance [exclusively]. If they have a funeral, they call this group and they start and there's no stop."[17]

At least as common as *gbegbe* is the ever popular *kuku*, which, though it originated in a West African region now part of Guinea, is often selected by Ivorians in dance classes and/or performances because of its familiarity in North American *jembe* circles. While I have (only rarely) seen performances without *kuku*, I have seen performances in which it makes up half or more of the music. There are several variations of the basic *dundun* and *jembe* patterns for this rhythm. Table 2.2 is a transcription of only the most common *dundun* pattern and two of the most common *jembe* patterns in *kuku* that I experienced during my research:

Table 2.1 Rhythm gbegbe

Drum	1	2	3	4	5	6	7	8	9	10	11	12	13	14	15	16	17	18	19	20	21	22	23	24
Dundun H	•		•	•		•		•		•	•		•		•	•		•		•		•	•	
Dundun L																								
Jembe	B	T	T	B			B	T	T	B			B	T	T	B			B	T	T	B		

Note: Shown are only the most common *dundun* and *jembe* patterns, typically played on a two-drum *dundun* with one drum higher in pitch (H); the other, lower in pitch (L). The *jembe* strike is indicated as B = bass or T = tone.

Table 2.2 Rhythm *kuku*, one cycle only

Drum	1	2	3	4	5	6	7	8	9	10	11	12	13	14	15	16
Dundun H	•															
Dundun M				•			•									
Dundun L									•							
Jembe 1	tun		pe	de			pa		tun		pe	de			pa	
Jembe 2	B				B				T		T		T	T		

Note: Included are the most common *dundun* pattern and two of the most common *jembe* patterns. For the three *dundun* drums, H, M, and L indicate relative pitches (high, medium, low); for *jembe* pattern 1, "pa" = slap, "tun" = bass, "pe," and "de" = tone. *Jembe* pattern 2 indicates the type of strike: B = bass; T = tone.

In addition to multiple variations of *kuku*, Ivorians at times also insert its patterns into other rhythms/dances. According to Sogbety, drummers may not know or cannot remember a pattern for the rhythm/dance being played and so play a *kuku* pattern. In other cases, however, *kuku* patterns are substituted more formally. Particularly interesting to me, given my study of mask spirit performance, are the times when drummers insert *kuku* patterns into *tindin*, one of the common rhythms used for Gue Pelou. Before representing a version of *tindin* with a *kuku* pattern added, let me first show, in table 2.3, a version played in Mau communities in Côte d'Ivoire (on Mau drums called *zikinin* and *ɓaanya* or *ɓaadè* with the *yado*, a gourd rattle).

Table 2.4 represents drumming patterns from a Gue Pelou performance at Djo Bi's wedding that demonstrate the transposition of both the *zikinin* pattern (*tindin*) and the *ɓaanya* or *ɓaadè* pattern (*kpi ki li kpi gblin*) from the Mau version of *tindin* onto *dundun*, played simultaneously by one person on three differently pitched *dundun* drums. Also shown is a *shekere*, or a net-strung calabash rattle, playing a *yado* pattern from the Mau version of *tindin*.

At a second Gue Pelou performance at the same wedding, drummers added *kuku* patterns. For example, Table 2.5 shows the *kuku* pattern "pa tun pe de" being played on *jembe* along with the *tindin* patterns on *dundun*, here played by two drummers, one playing just "*kpi ki li kpi gblin*" and a second simultaneously playing both "*kpi ki li kpi gblin*" and "*tindin*."

This insertion of "pa tun pe de" into *tindin* is what Sogbety calls a "mixture" of *tindin* and *kuku*, a kind of an accommodation that makes it easier to perform Gue Pelou regardless of the drummers' experience with Mau mask rhythms. Sogbety accepts such mixtures and is grateful for the flexibility that allows Gue Pelou to be performed more frequently than it would be if Mau immigrants were more rigid about rhythmic specificity. That said, he expresses pride in his knowledge of how rhythms/dances are performed in western Côte d'Ivoire, his home region. As we watched a video of his group performing the young girls' dance rhythm from the Wè/Dan region called *témaé*, Sogbety sighed and said:

> Not everybody knows how to play the real *témaé*. These guys, many of them learned it in the ballet. They just know how to play it on the *dundun*. Even though all those guys come from Côte d'Ivoire, nobody knows how to play the real *témaé* on this type of drum [points to his *ɓaadè*]. Everybody learns in the ballet the *dundun*/ballet kind of way.

In his use of *real* to describe the "preballet" instrumentation associated with the rural village and ethnic group considered to be its origin, Sogbety strongly suggests a valuing of that "original" version. Ballet performers who grew up in such contexts can claim a special authority, a higher level of competence (Bauman 1977), that in the case of *témaé* is accorded to Vado and/or Sogbety because of the proximity of their home village of Toufinga to the Dan region.

Table 2.3 Rhythm *tindin*, as typically played in Mau communities in Côte d'Ivoire

Zikinin	tin		din		tin		tin		din		tin		tin		din
baade		x	kpi	ki	li	kpi	gblin	kpa*	kpi	li	kpi	gblin	kpa*	kpi	ki
Yado			x	x	x	x	x	x	x	x	x	x	x	x	x

Note: Included are the most common *dundun* pattern and two of the most common *jembe* patterns. For the three *dundun* drums, H, M, and L indicate relative pitches (high, medium, low); for *jembe* pattern 1, "pa" = slap, "tun" = bass, "pe" and "de" = tone. *Jembe* pattern 2 indicates the type of strike: B = bass; T = tone.

Table 2.4 Rhythm *tindin*, showing only *dundun* and *shekere* patterns as performed during Gue Pelou's second appearance at Djo Bi's wedding

Dundun left	tin		din				tin		din				tin		din	
Dundun center		tin					tin	tin					tin	tin		
Dundun right	Kpi	gblin	kpi	ki	li		kpi	gblin	kpi	ki	li		kpi	gblin	kpi	ki
Shekere	X	X	X				X	X	X				X	X	X	x

Note: Performers were also improvising on *jembes*.

Table 2.5 Rhythm *tindin*, showing *dundun* and *shekere* patterns and *kuku* pattern "pa tun pede" on *jembe*

Dundun 1 left	tin		din				din				din	
Dundun 1 center		tin			tin	tin			tin	tin		
Dundun 1 right				ki				ki	kpi	gblin		ki
Dundun 2 left	kpi	gblin*	kpi		kpi		kpi		kpi		kpi	
Dundun 2 center		gblin*		li		gblin*	kpi	li		gblin*		
Dundun 2 right						gblin*				gblin*		
Shekere	X	X	X	x	X	X	X	x	X	X	X	x
Jembe	pa	tun	de	pe	pa	tun	de	pe	pa	tun	de	pe

In addition to the individual, ethnically marked dances/rhythms mentioned thus far, some Ivorian ballet performers count choreographed dramas in their repertoire. As creations of choreographers in the Ivorian national ballets and/or in private groups, these pieces interweave condensed versions of dances/rhythms from around Côte d'Ivoire with sets and costumes. They can be thirty minutes or much longer and frequently end with a celebratory dance party consisting of many ethnically marked dances/rhythms performed in rapid succession. Vado Diomande is well known for such creations, and his particular version of Ivorian ballet, best represented in his annual Kotchegna Dance Company showcase that he calls *Kekene* (oneness), always features one as at least the first act. His dramas are typical of the genre in that they tend to be based on moral themes. For example, "The History of Mahou Masks" narrates the cosmological myth of Mau masks, a story about the importance of sharing what is of highest value with everyone in a community; "The Vampire" addresses the spread of HIV-AIDS.

Occasionally some of Vado's fellow immigrants feature choreographed dramas in their shows. For instance, two of Sogbety's performances that I attended during my research (at his festival in Mansfield, Ohio, in 2007 and at one of his showcases at the 2008 Lotus Festival in Bloomington, Indiana) were built around "The Marriage," a choreographed drama about a woman who is courted by, and eventually accepts, a male dancer in the form of a *zauli* mask. More typically, however, Sogbety chooses not to perform choreographed dramas, considering them somewhat old-fashioned and unintelligible to North American audiences, who are more interested in simply watching virtuosic drumming and dance. He prefers to write individual pieces for his American performances, which is also generally Samba's approach.

Even when simply performing a set of individual dances/rhythms, Ivorians have established standardized sequences for them, especially masks. Gue Pelou is a case in point. Nearly every staged Gue Pelou performance that I experienced in the United States between 2006 and 2015 followed this structure:

> I. Rhythm *tindin* (or *kuku*), at times also a call-response song sung in Dan, while Gue Pelou dances and does acrobatic moves such as twirling around on one leg and falling into splits.
>
> II. Gue Pelou gestures for the musicians to stop and then, in his characteristically high falsetto, offers benedictions in the Dan language to the crowd, the "fathers of the mask spirit," the drummers, and all who have come to see the mask spirit.
>
> III. Gue Pelou initiates the Dan song "Ee! Ge ya yi kan bo" (The mask spirit has crossed the river) sung to the *zikinin* rhythm (or *kuku*). The mask dances and wows the crowd with more daredevil acrobatics before walking off the stage to find the sacred space reserved for its dressing and undressing.

Other mask dances, such as *bolohi*, are similarly standardized, though the structure for Gue Pelou is the most predictable. As this example shows, the shared knowledge that Ivorians draw on to perform in the United States is deeper than just a set of rhythms that form a repertoire. Ballet discourse is also about *how* one performs that repertoire. Cues of various kinds are a critical part of that knowledge.

Signals

For each dance/rhythm in the Ivorian ballet repertoire, the basic rhythmic patterns and dance steps represent only the beginning of what drummers and dancers must know. They also must know the standard signals that coordinate sound and movement, including cues for starting, stopping, and making transitions within rhythms, and the extended, rhythmically coordinated interludes.

The most common signal is one that has traveled with the *jembe* and associated ballet discourse across Africa and around the world, becoming standardized in many ballet-related and/or ballet-inspired settings, from performances by national ensembles in Ghana to drum circles in California. Often referred to in French as *appel* (call), this signal has two common variations (and an endless number of more nuanced variations of variations). The first is usually played by drummers to mark the beginning of a dance. In the transcriptions that follow, x represents a tone strike on the *jembe*; • represents an equivalent rest.

x/•/x/x/•/x/•/x/x/•/x/x/x

Then a slight alteration to this call, an additional slap (S) following three beats of rest, signals a coordinated stopping point for all performers:

x/•/x/x/•/x/•/x/x/•/x/x/x/•/•/•/S

A signal that marks transitions during a dance/rhythm, such as beginnings and endings of choreographed drum/dance interludes and solos, is called a break (in French and English) or occasionally a *changement* (change). The pattern transcribed previously, which serves as the standard "call" for a dance/rhythm to begin, is also employed in many different dance/rhythms as a break, though there are many breaks that are specific to certain ones. Yet another specific form of rhythmic coordination between drummers and dancers is the flourish that marks the end of a break, called a *coup* in French (cut) or a *bloc* (block, as in a block of stone). The block or cut is crucial, for the drummer and dancer must end in a precise rhythmically coordinated way to elicit the kind of applause and shouts of approval desired.

Ballet drummers and dancers whom members of their community consider the best at a particular dance are evaluated in part on their mastery of a significant number of breaks. Some breaks are so complex that Djo Bi gives them another name altogether, "compositions." As we watched the video of his wedding, Djo Bi described a composition that Ivorians sometimes incorporate into *gbegbe*. Dancers alternated solos in the center of the space while Tra Bi Lizzie soloed on his *jembe* and the rest of the drummers played the *gbegbe*'s rapid, layered ostinato patterns. Suddenly everyone stopped. Instantaneously, the drummers began a long and complicated series of phrases played in unison.

> That's a part of *gbegbe* that we all know. It's a break that marks the end of a solo. [It was] composed back in Côte d'Ivoire and is well known. We all know it then, where you're going to finish. . . . If you are a drummer, you know how to finish. What they did there, they all learned that in Côte d'Ivoire.

As the *gbegbe* break on the video came to a dramatic finish, Djo Bi smiled and said, "That's what we call the mathematics of African dance." I asked what he meant. "When everyone plays the same thing as opposed to repeating parts with a soloist. . . . What I mean is that those who do this playing altogether are mathematicians. They know the dimensions of things. They know how to finish all together. It's clear. Everything is equal."

But how do all of the performers know when to transition from *gbegbe* to the break or to a composition? As we continued watching the video, Djo Bi taught me a cue that the lead drummer plays to signal the beginning of a particular mathematical composition. At this passage, the performers were drumming and dancing another of the most popular pieces in the ballet repertoire, *zauli*. Djo Bi, being Guro (and furthermore the groom and host), was on solo *jembe* at the moment during the formal wedding celebration when *zauli* was played. As we watched, the Djo Bi in the room with me became irritated with the performers on the screen. "Tan tan krididi!" he cried out. "Oh!" he sighed. "Here they make a mistake. I try to do some mathematics—everyone should be together. But those others, they just came to dance [in any old manner]. Right now what I'm doing *all* the drummers should be doing *together*. That's the problem!" He repeated, "Tan tan krididi! That's the part they don't know!" The video continued showing Djo Bi trying again and again to cue the *zauli* composition. He sighed, moaned, and eventually *shouted* at the screen: "*TAN TAN KRIDIDI!*" Finally Tra Bi Lizzie caught on and joined Djo Bi for the break as the others continued their ostinato parts. "It's only Tra Bi who can play for me!" Djo Bi exclaimed.

In an interview years later, Djo Bi confirmed what I had learned from him and others about breaks:

> Everyone must know all the breaks. When you know how to dance something you have to know how it's going to start and how it's going to end. That's why you are in the ballet. So we know the breaks. We know *all* the breaks . . . so you

learn the rhythms, the dance and the breaks. Voilà, you learn all that. If you say you know *zauli*, it's all that that you know. When you say I know *zauli*, one knows what that means. So when the dancer does something . . . you know what's coming afterwards.

I asked if the breaks themselves have names as the rhythms/dances do. "No," replied Djo Bi. "When you say *zauli*, when you say *tématé*, [you mean] all that. There is no name for the breaks themselves. When you say *tématé*, it's *tématé*. It's a package. It goes together. . . . When you say you know *zauli* or *n'goron*, it's a package."

Many breaks regularly performed in a given rhythm/dance originated not in rural villages but in ballet. As Polak (2006) notes, ballet versions of dance/rhythms tend to be performed in a condensed and cleaner manner, with preset beginnings and endings cued by signals for fancy and impressive breaks. Flaig (2010) observes this same process in Guinean ballets, where so many changes were made to village or community performances that the LBA drummers, performing abroad in Europe or North America, might well have found the music they played "often as foreign an experience . . . as it was for the audience" (74):

> The condensed version of rhythms, songs, and dances, from various parts of Guinea, used for divergent sets of occasions, often hundreds of kilometers apart, patched together with a series of signals and solos are what, for the drummer, defines the difference between the ballet and village traditions. The two most challenging aspects of adapting to the ballet consisted of learning all of the newly composed parts made up of signals, breaks, and pre-composed solo passages that connect one rhythm to the next, as well as learning solo patterns which corresponded directly to the movement of the dancers. (74–75)

Built into each dance and rhythm in the ballet repertoire are many possibilities for precise drumming and dancing. That is, there are beginners' versions of dances and rhythms, and there are far more nuanced, subtle, complex versions. As a regular participant in Djo Bi and Harmony Harris's dance classes and as an occasional visitor to classes led by Samba, Vado, and Sogbety, I noticed that, when first introducing a series of dance steps to a class, teachers would simplify the movements to make them more obvious and accessible for less skilled students. As we learned complete choreographed routines, which might consist of ten, fifteen, or more dance steps strung together, and as the class began transitioning from "learning" to "performing," the teachers would introduce far more complex and subtle versions of the dance. I can do little more than describe the dances with words. The corollary for drumming patterns is also true. I recall learning Dan *getan* drum rhythms in Côte d'Ivoire in the 1990s. I spent hours on basic ostinato patterns for each drum in each rhythm. When I attended a *ge* performance, I sometimes did not even recognize in the complex polyrhythms the individual patterns I had so doggedly practiced. Over time my ears became more attuned, allowing me to recognize that truly fine drummers can improvise not just in solos but even in the repeating, accompanying patterns, adding subtle variations that extend, modify, and nuance the basic patterns without losing their essential integrity (Reed 2003, 141–143).

Competition and Cooperation

A principle of cooperation is at the heart of the very idea of ballet. Even on a basic level—the social organization of much of the music featured in these staged settings—the emphasis is on the rhythmic coordination of individual, interlocking parts through fundamentally cooperative interaction. Movement and sound are coordinated through tight cooperation of drummers and dancers. Then, of course, when performers from many different ethnicities come together to form an ensemble, they engage in a cooperative social effort that transcends ethnic and often regional, religious, and other kinds of difference. Specifically, choreographed dramas, and for that matter any ballet performances, blend traditions from various sources into a unified whole. The concept of ballet, the form, and the social processes required to produce it, are all cooperative at their core.

The cooperative spirit and practice in ballet has its genesis in postcolonial nation building. Through ballet, people thrown together by a political project, colonialism, unite to represent to the world an idealized portrayal of a nation that transcends difference. As Djo Bi saw it, the ballet, like big cities such as Abidjan, created a space for people of very different backgrounds to come together, to work together, and to become better, more understanding neighbors:

> Look, when we are there, Seguenon, he comes from the north. If it was not [for] the ballet, he could never be my friend. He wouldn't understand me at all. And I wouldn't understand him. We are not the same. Someone like Vado—I wouldn't know him at all! I have never been to Touba [the main city in the Mau region]. I've never gone there. But in the ballet, everyone finds each other there. It's like when you go to Abidjan, you go to work; or even your neighbor, he's a Guéré, he's a whatever, he's a Baule. So it's *life* that makes the ballet also.

And yet another of the ironies of ballet is the pervasiveness of competition. Prior to my research for this project, I quite honestly was not expecting and certainly was not looking for competition as a theme in the lives of my four consultants and/or their larger communities. However, in the life stories and performances of Ivorian immigrants, competition came up again and again.[18] Indeed, from the very creation of the BNCI, access to the stage was determined by competition. And once in the ballet, performers competed for the most lucrative shows and international tours. In auditions and on stage, drummers competed against drummers, dancers against dancers, and drummers and dancers against each other for social standing, with each expression of brilliant skill inspiring others to do better. Once in the United States, Ivorians and Guineans competed for jobs, students, and resources. Individuals from across the African Diaspora competed for reputations as the finest dancers and drummers.

Competition is still so fierce that performers resort to mystical attacks on one another. Different constituencies compete for "Africa" as a discourse and representational resource to support conflicting agendas. Ivorians keep moving to find less competitive places to live and pursue their work. The understanding and framing of ballet performance as a skill set that provides access to an international labor market is by nature founded on engagement with global capitalist ideas and processes with competition at its center.

Competition in Performance

Ballet involves a considerable amount of intra-ensemble competition that is built into the drumming and dancing on which it is based. Certainly part of this aesthetic is drummers and dancers playfully challenging each other, taking turns in the lead and initiating breaks, each trying to perform sequences that are more spectacular than the any other's. Even more fundamentally, drummers and dancers have an *interdependent* relationship in which each relies on the other to succeed and do his or her best. Tensions between drummers and dancers can easily invade their rhythmic communication, which can exacerbate feelings of jealousy and competition. Sogbety explained:

> There is a lot of jealousy there, and why is there so much jealousy? In music, there is nobody who is number one.... Everyone is number one.... Everyone has their own manner of playing music. It's the same thing for dancers. They believe they are great at dancing. The drummers say they are great at drumming.... The two have to like each other [for the performance to be good].
>
> Say I want to drum for Clarice [Toa, an Ivorian dancer who lives in Indianapolis]. She dances so well! But if there is a problem—we're not getting along and then we arrive on stage and we have to play, I cannot—I know how to play for her; I know what sound to play for her so that she really *dances*, but I won't play that sound. We don't speak with each other. But if someone else comes, I play that sound LLLLLAAAA!

Sogbety also spoke of competitive tensions that can surface between drummers. The concert *jembe* tradition and the growing fame and social status of *jembe* drummers have certainly heightened rivalry. According to Sogbety, "Between drummers, you also have these problems. There are some who want to play fast but not musically. And there are some who play nice sounds so people listen to what they play . . . and people get jealous and want to be known as the best." He then took our discussion in a philosophical direction:

> To be jealous of someone is another form of work. It's hard already—the world is already hard. If you put this into it, you wear yourself out more. You've got to forget that stuff and search for a good way to live. Jealousy—those who do that don't understand life. Jealousy doesn't get you anywhere, it destroys you. I am not the best. I know what I do. But I am not the best drummer. I am not the best dancer of the tall mask. But I do what I can do.

Notwithstanding the character Sogbety shows in resisting it, competition is, and always has been, an undeniable feature of the discourse and embodiment of ballet. At its core, ballet positions Ivorian immigrants to compete—with each other and with immigrants from other countries—to find footing on lucrative stages from Abidjan to America.

Competition between Guineans and Ivorians in the Immigrant Marketplace

The spread of African ballet in the United States naturally involves competing ballet discourses. Given the early arrival of Guinea's LBA and Papa Ladji Camara's Mande-based *jembe/dundun* version of ballet as at least one normative discourse, it stands to reason that Ivorians arriving much later would encounter a landscape in which their ballet's relative likeness to the Guinean model would be an advantage and its difference would be a liability. Of course, musicians and dancers from other African nations were also here when Vado, Samba, and others arrived in 1994. However, given that their home countries are neighbors and given the intertwined histories of their ballets and, again, the precedent-establishing LBA, I was not surprised to find Ivorians rubbing shoulders with Guineans more frequently than with Africans from any other nation.

Many of the jobs that Vado found when he first arrived in New York were with Guineans, including *jembe* repair and *jembe* playing for Guinean dance classes. Some of Sogbety's first jobs also involved the *jembe*, that drum he had only learned to play in Abidjan. Meanwhile, Guineans sometimes play with Ivorians in Ivorian music and dance. Such was the case at Sogbety's annual festivals I attended in Mansfield in 2006, 2007, and 2008. Nearly all of the drum (read *jembe*) and dance teachers had come from New York, and about half of them were from Guinea. One Guinean, dancer Hamidou Koivogui, appears frequently in performances of Ivorian dance; another, *jelibala* player Kierno Diabate, occasionally does as well.

One day I asked Sogbety what his experience of Guinean-Ivorian relations had been during his years in New York. "There [was] no relationship" was his surprising reply.

> We know each other, but we don't play the same music. No, there is no relationship. Each one plays what he knows how to play. . . . All over the world, and here in the United States, everyone knows Guinea, Guinean music. So it's no longer important for everyone to play. People are tired of it. It's that the same thing continues.

They know each other, they play together, but there is no relationship? So accustomed was I to Sogbety's charitable views on nearly everyone and everything that I was taken aback by this implication of nationalist competition. I listened carefully as he continued:

> There are many Americans here that, when they play Guinean music, they are very good at it. So the Guineans show [teach music] to [other] Guineans, and then black Americans, and often there is competition between them because the black Americans often can play better than the Guineans.

Again, the majority of Ivorian immigrant performers arrived after the 1960s–1970s heyday of Guinean–African American cultural collaboration. I sometimes noticed in them a subtle and often not so subtle jealousy and competitiveness toward their Guinean counterparts. Still, at many events—Sogbety's festivals in Ohio, Samba's in the Atlanta area, and others—I encountered African Americans, Guineans, and Ivorians performing together. At a fundamental level, there is a shared "ballet" discourse uniting them that is evident in a general understanding of the ways dance and drum soloists interact, the flow of a West African ballet performance, and specific rhythms and dance routines (e.g., *kuku*). This is the generally shared knowledge that allows performers who have never met to work together. But just as often I noted that many African Americans who have mastered the Guinean drum and dance repertoire are far less familiar—and often completely unfamiliar—with Ivorian traditions. There are economic implications arising from this disparity, and Ivorians sometimes seem to resent Guineans for them.

Sometimes, however, reaction to Guinean dominance of not just the African American but also the entire North American market is just the opposite—a claim of Ivorian distinctiveness as a point of pride and a potentially lucrative future in which those tired of "the same old Guinean stuff" will be drawn to the next new thing: music and dance from Côte d'Ivoire. According to Sogbety:

> We [Ivorians], our music, we are rich with our music. Not everyone knows it, [but] it's coming now, and even if you know it, we play . . . [music of] each ethnic group. Even the Guineans are learning our music so that they have something new. . . . It's like that in New York. But there's not competition, like "You, you're Guinean . . ." Well, there *is* that, but there is [also] the language of the drum—they *want* to learn what we do. And in Côte d'Ivoire, we have everyone there; there are Guineans. When you play [music in Côte

d'Ivoire], you might have a Guinean there with you. But in Guinea, there are not very many Ivorians.

I had not thought of that difference before. The post-independence economic disparity between the two countries, and Houphouët-Boigny's policy of meeting labor needs by encouraging people from neighboring countries to migrate to Côte d'Ivoire, had resulted in many more Guineans living in Côte d'Ivoire than Ivorians living in Guinea. In fact, following the death of Guinean president Sekou Touré, even the famous Mamady Keita spent two years in the Abidjan area in a private ballet called Ensemble Koteba (Flaig 2011, 22).

According to Sogbety, beyond general economic policy differences, there were specific differences in the national mentalities of the West African neighbors, differences nurtured by their respective first presidents and their contrasting political philosophies:

> After Independence, Houphouët ... wanted everyone to be content [to be in Côte d'Ivoire]. He said, "Let's stay here and keep to ourselves. Yes. We are going to take care of ourselves." ... So Ivorians are like that. ... Sekou Touré showed [Guinean culture] to all the other countries. Sekou Touré said, "Let's go to other countries, and show them." ... That's why Guinean *jembe* is so well-known in other countries compared to Côte d'Ivoire. [Whereas] Houphouët said, "Stay here, we'll make peace. Come here [gesturing as if encouraging others to migrate into the country]."

The difference of almost twenty years between the founding of LBA and the founding of BNCI is arguably evidence of the contrast between the nationalist discourses and related policies of Guinea and Côte d'Ivoire in the early postcolonial period. Houphouët-Boigny was ardently pro-Western and virulently anticommunist, which put him at great odds with Touré. The Ivorian leader routinely emphasized his young nation's modernity and its readiness to participate in global capitalism, and so naturally he did not initially follow Touré's socialist, revolutionary, anti-French state support for indigenous cultural expression. Houphouët-Boigny's political philosophy nurtured the development of a pro-Western mentality in Ivorian elites—an embrace of the fashion, language, and culture of the West in contrast to village lifeways and attitudes. Even today, among Ivorian immigrants in Atlanta, Samba Diallo encounters opposition to what some see as "backward" cultural expressions like drumming, dancing in grass skirts, mask performance, and other symbolic links to a stereotypical primitive imaginary of Africa. What Touré embraced Houphouët-Boigny initially downplayed, eventually contributing to a competitive advantage for Guineans in the immigrant performance marketplace.

Ballet and Immigrant Life

Throughout the following four acts and their accompanying chapters, ballet discourse becomes embodied in its staged forms and in its formative influence on my consultants' life stories. Performers as agents enact ballet selectively and variously depending on their needs, communicative goals, and creativity. They transform it into expressions of unity, educational initiatives, and fitness programs. They collaborate with other African descendants, rock musicians, museum curators, world music festival promoters, elementary music teachers, and ethnomusicologists. They meet and challenge the expectations of American audiences. They try for but nearly always fall short of the financial expectations of their family members back home. They struggle, and they celebrate. Drawing on ballet, which has made possible their lives as transnational immigrants, they keep dancing and they keep drumming.

PART II

STAGES AND STORIES

ACT I
Vado Diomande

3 *Kekene*

The Performance of Oneness in NYC

FLASHBACK: NEW YORK CITY, February 22, 2009. Ivorian immigrant Vado Diomande's Kotchegna Dance Company began its third annual performance of *Kekene* (Oneness). An original member of the Ballet National de Côte d'Ivoire (BNCI), Vado had long ago adopted that ensemble's practice of representing unity through diversity. He had transformed ballet from a representation of national unity through ethnic diversity into a discourse of global unity through national, ethnic, and racial diversity and, simultaneously, into an "authentic" representation of traditional Ivorian dance. As the ensemble took the stage, the audience heard the first SLAP resounding from a *jembe*, that sonic and visual icon of Africa. The drummers—Ivorians, a Jamaican, a Trinidadian, and a Spaniard—sat before a tapestry featuring three colorful twenty-foot high masks. Dancers streamed in from stage left: Ivorians, African Americans, European Americans, a Japanese American. The audience, consisting of whites, blacks, Asians, and others, applauded enthusiastically in anticipation of what was billed as "Traditional Ivory Coast Dance." Weeks later, however, a reviewer for the dance magazine *Attitude* blasted the show: "When other cultures perform one's traditional folklore . . . it results in the authenticity of the tradition being compromised because . . . they do not look like the indigenous people that they are trying to represent" (Waltrous 2009, 34).

Recall the conflicting discourses at Memphis in May. There, in 1994, Vado had been unaware of the social evolutionary narrative and thus unaware of the resulting friction. At *Kekene III* in 2009, however, he was fully conscious of the friction, even before *Attitude*'s review was published. Backstage, audience members told him that they had watched the African American reviewer gather her things and storm out long before the end of the show. Her subsequent review suggested the reason for her early exit: she wanted to claim Vado's representation of African dance as part of her culture. Her seemingly Afrocentric discourse and Vado's universalist discourse had collided, causing an unresolvable friction. In conversation with me, Vado said that authenticity—an essential aspect of his performances—runs deeper than the color of one's skin.

* * *

From 2006 to 2014, the period during which I conducted research for this book, Vado held fast to his universalist beliefs and their representation in the blending of all manner of difference into performed discourses of unity. Such was certainly the case at the following year's show, although Vado's 2010 performance of oneness added yet another discursive dimension. *Kekene IV* was about to begin, with Haitian immigrant Girlane Zetrea (known as TC), a longtime member of Kotchegna, making the introduction. Under the glare of a spotlight, she began (PURL 3.1):

> Kotchegna and Ivorian dancers have been celebrating our annual recognition of Vado's great health from the time that he contracted anthrax four years ago. And from that moment on, we've taken every opportunity to show the power and strength of our unity, of our unity and our love that was vested into his health, that helped bring everything to fruition, so that everything that occurs here today that you will see on this stage. Now, you know this is *Kekene IV*, we are up to year four. . . . in the end, we will see who the mask really belongs to, and who really should hold the history, the culture, and the celebration of the Ivory Coast.

TC's introduction defined the annual *Kekene* series as a celebration of Vado's return to health from his nearly fatal bout of anthrax four years earlier. With health as the purpose and the overall frame of the event, TC then articulated some of the discourse of "oneness." In an almost prayer-like passage, she interwove discourses of health and unity, noting that Vado's recovery inspired the group to "show the power and strength of our unity, of our unity and our love." Ballet discourse, refashioned for a New York stage, inspired by a miracle recovery.

Just as he had done in Côte d'Ivoire, Vado used Kotchegna in the United States to promote unity, now by showcasing his natal and adopted countries' diversity. The fourth annual *Kekene*, which took place at the Jacqueline Kennedy Onassis High School auditorium near Times Square in 2010, consisted of two acts: the first a choreographed drama (spectacle *chorèographique*), "The History of Mahou[1] Masks"; and the second, a set of ethnically marked Ivorian dances.

"The History of Mahou Masks," created by Vado, recounts a mythic battle fought between Mau men and women over control of mask spirits, which originally were the province of women. The men attempt to wrest control, accusing the women of selfishly guarding the power of the masks for themselves. They start the battle, ostensibly so that the masks can be shared by all in the village and, not surprisingly, they win. This narrative was familiar to me, as I had heard it told orally in Dan country in the 1990s and even earlier had read it in a 1971 book about Dan masks in Liberia (Tabmen 1971). I even heard this theme recounted by other immigrants: Dr. Djo Bi, for instance, said that the Guro tell this same story when recounting the origin of their mask traditions. Guro and Dan are both southern Mande groups, and the Mau are the southernmost northern Mande population, so this story likely betrays their shared history. It is clearly ripe for analysis from the perspective of gender, especially given western Côte d'Ivoire's patriarchal power structures.

Of interest here, though, is the narrative's emphasis on unity (albeit from a male power point of view), which again reflects the ideology of the BNCI. In ballet, transnationalism and unity intertwine with nationalism in a complex, seemingly contradictory discourse that was manifested in various ways in *Kekene IV*: in the demographic makeup of the ensemble, in its interweaving of dance and musical elements from various ethnic traditions, in its instrumentation, and in its images.

Verbal Discourse

What's in a Name?

Vado selected the name Kotchegna (messenger in Mauka) to emphasize one of his central motivations: to spread a message of unity through music and dance performance. Although to secure work in the United States he sometimes must compromise his approach or ideals of representing both tradition and unity, once a year he books a theater for his annual Kotchegna showcase, where he assumes complete control and his ideals are fully realized, reflected in his message of *kekene*, or oneness:

> Come from everywhere [to my shows, where], we all become one.
> You might come from anywhere, but we are the same thing.
> We have to do it together.

Kekene is about more than oneness and unity, however. When I asked why he had chosen the name, Vado replied:

> I chose it because, since Ivorians have been here, people haven't known us. So I want people to know us. So everybody, if everybody comes together, people will know us. So all Ivorian dancers, come be together. With my students from here. I need everybody to come become one person.

In addition to the message of unity, universalism, and oneness, then, Vado chose the name to promote a sense of national Ivorian identity. The nationalism instilled in him by the BNCI remains a concern in New York, where, compared with other African nationals, most notably Guineans, Ivorians feel that they do not have a seat at the table. In any case, the polysemic nature of performance allows for seemingly incompatible discourses, such as global unity and nationalism, to be expressed simultaneously.

Vado defines his Kotchegna troupe in nationalist terms, and its expressive forms of Ivorian traditional dance have over time become imbued with nationalist meaning—symbolic representations of the Ivorian nation on stage. A dance/rhythm with nationalist meaning does not erase other meanings Ivorians or others might associate with it, however. Perhaps the most famous Ivorian mask, Zauli, is considered by Ivorians to be of Guro ethnic origin. It was incorporated into the BNCI repertoire and ultimately became the favorite mask of President Félix Houphouët-Boigny (Reed 2003, 61; Bouttiaux 2013, 129). Ivorians still identify it as ethnically Guro, but also associate it with Ivorian nationalism and the country's first president, who ruled from independence in 1960 until his death in 1993. When dancing Zauli, then, Kotchegna performs a mask dance that has strong associations with (1) one of Côte d'Ivoire's sixty ethnic groups, (2) the nation, (3) the nation's first president, and (4) "oneness" or unity. Nations are complex, ultimately ambiguous entities brought into sharp focus in the heightened reflexivity of the performance stage.

Promotional Discourse

The tension in Kotchegna's discourse between universalist and nationalist ideologies shows in various expressive forms, including the group's promotional materials, which highlight the complexity of Vado's vision: "We are Kotchegna Dance Company! We are a multicultural, racially diverse dance company specializing in the traditional dances of the Ivory Coast under the direction of Vado Diomande." Drawing on his experience with the BNCI, Vado's vision is founded on a strong sense of nationalism. The colors of the Ivorian flag, for example, are ubiquitous in posters and postcards (see figure 3.1). Vado explicitly expands his nationalism discourse into a transnational if not global discourse, which at points he embodies as an individual. Consider the following from Kotchegna's promotional package: "As a multicultural, ethnically diverse company of dancers and musicians, Kotchegna Dance Company mirrors the richness of Ivory Coast culture."

The shift in discourse might be read as follows:

nation = dance company
rich = diversity

In other words, nation is to dance company as rich as to diversity.

Expressions of Ivorian nationalism permeate the group's promotional materials, and this, not surprisingly, is picked up by reviewers. A 2002 review in *The Morning Call* in Bethlehem, Pennsylvania, featured the headline "Mask dance tells story of Ivory Coast music and folklore" (Craft 2002). At turns, the Kotchegna Dance Company and Vado himself are discursively portrayed as representing the

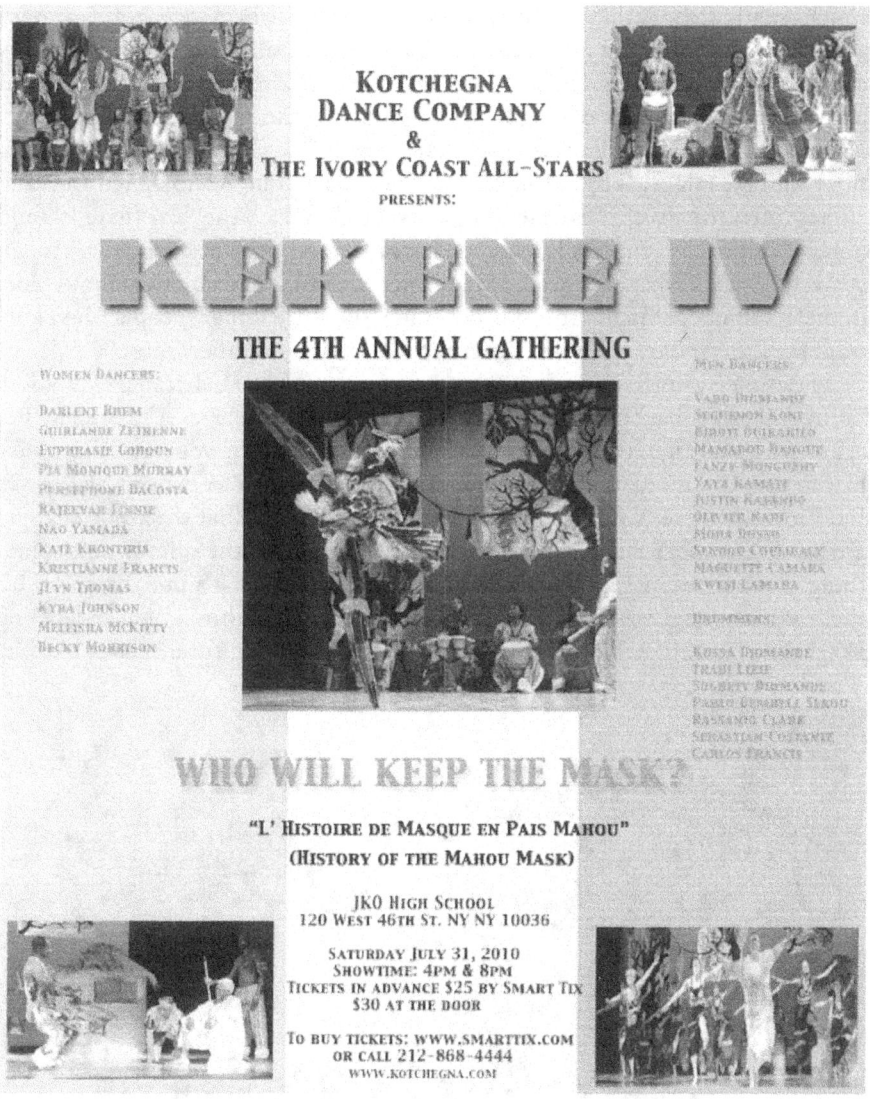

Figure 3.1 *Kekene IV* poster, July 2010.

Ivorian nation, having effectively appropriated that role from the BNCI on American stages. This is a fascinating transformation of the representation of nation, particularly when it becomes embodied in an individual immigrant.

Racially diverse, ethnically diverse. A number of similar descriptors are used to promote the ensemble, but none is as common as *multicultural*. In fact,

Kotchegna is frequently *defined* as a multicultural performance troupe. I once asked Vado why. He told me, "Because I came here to share my culture with any color. So any color that wants to do it—welcome! ... I am here, among white people and among all kinds of people—they choose to dance with me. That's why." His wife and manager Lisa (see figure 3.2) added, "That reflects the population of this country." I then asked, "How has that worked for you?" Vado sighed and said, "It has often not worked. Because often, in the shows ... they say there [should not be] whites here [on stage]. So often I have to bring only black people.... When you send a press kit somewhere ... they often say, 'No, there are too many colors in there, I'm not going to hire you.' But [then] there are [other] people who really want the group who say, I want the group but I don't want the whites."[2]

Friction—a form of connection. Representations of Africa. Expectation. "Why might people be looking for a group that only has blacks?" I asked. "Because it is traditional—the blacks," Vado replied. "When you say Africa—it's blacks who are there. So, if it's African dance, you have to present blacks ... [but] for me, there is nothing that has changed. It's not that the color changes anything. But that's me. It's [people who hire us] who say the color means something. For me, what I came here with is what I present. It's not the color. It's the tradition—and we are on that path." Vado saw no contradiction in labeling Kotchegna "traditional" while performing with a "multicultural" ensemble. The

Figure 3.2 Lisa and Vado Diomande at home in New York City in 2008. Photograph by author.

American market, however, and some other Ivorian immigrant performers have difficulty reconciling the two.

As in the 2009 *Kekene*, this disjuncture surfaces constantly in the work of Lisa Diomande, who in discussing her experiences booking Kotchegna, told me, "We allow people to dictate [race]. Because it's a marketplace, we allow people to dictate color terms if they need to. Yeah, we just go along with it. . . . We do let them know that this is a multiethnic dance company, and our philosophy is that dance is for everyone.[3] Vado has a multiethnic dance company because he believes that everybody can dance African dance. So that's what he draws from. . . . He's much more inclusive than exclusive." But just as with the Ivorian ballet, Vado's inclusive approach is one part ideological and one part practical. Many Kotchegna performers come directly from his drum and dance classes, in which he teaches the same dances and rhythms that Kotchegna performs. He chooses dancers for shows based on ability, not race.

All dimensions of the complex discourse of Kotchegna appear in its advertising, which does not hide but rather celebrates the company's diversity, albeit selectively. Its website, business card, and poster emphasize "traditional Ivorian dance." Telling, however, is a video clip from the promotional DVD which shows one of those performances in which only Africans or African descendants perform. Sensitive to the controversial nature of this choice, the company conforms to expectations in this most crucial part of its promo package. Vado sometimes strategically dances around this problem in his initial presentation of his work, and only in later negotiations reveals his troupe's multiracial composition and the philosophy behind it.

Program Notes

Vado Diomande & Kotchegna Dance Co.

There are as many ways of dancing as there are dance forms. Formal forms, like ballet, are highly technical and specific; others, like hip hop, are communal, and can [be] danced by anyone, in any style desired. What defines each form comes from the movements and music. Dance lovers of all forms share in the joy of the music and movement. Communal dancing in particular has an additional joy of sharing in the individual expression of the dancer. West African dance as the epitome of communal dancing, has a power that is undeniable, and its influence is felt in modern and youthful expressions throughout the world.

Vado Diomande is passionately committed to the sharing of this powerful form of communal expression from the Ivory Coast. With Kotchegna Dance Company as the "Messenger," these dances are kept alive as an expression of communal living that is quickly disappearing. Vado and KDC are committed to giving these village dances to the world, so that all can enjoy and dance this expression of universal community. These dances are a wonderful antidote to our complex, modern lives. We are enriched by the power and joy in this traditional form of expression. As we keep alive the purity of the steps through our multicultural world, we breathe life into a valuable form of inspiration. We are inspired to watch, dance and share in this universal village life.

Discourses of unity and multiculturalism, along with a universalist, "global village" rhetoric, also inform the program notes (see above) handed out to the audience at annual *Kekene* shows. For example, the notes for *Kekene IV* describe the performance as "an expression of communal living" shared "so that all can enjoy and dance this expression of universal community." Referencing "our multicultural world," they invite all to "dance and share in this universal village life." Furthermore, "West African dance is the epitome of communal dancing . . . [with] a power that is undeniable." This undeniable power feeds directly into common discourses of Africa and African music, evoking a primal sensuality if not sexuality that is relentlessly seductive. It is present in staged representations of Africa in the form of muscular dancers and their strong movements; loud, powerful sounds of *jembes* and *dunduns*; danced narratives about the powers of sorcerers or mask spirits. The program notes are filled with the discourse commonly used to promote African music performance in the United States. They read as an invitation to all members of the global village to dance and share these traditions.

Discourse on Stage

Vado's discourse of unity is manifest not just in words but in many facets of his performance: the demographic makeup of the ensemble; the repertoire, including dance and musical elements from various ethnic traditions; the instrumentation; drum and dance "breaks"; the images, and more—ballet as a discourse of unity through diversity, of difference interwoven toward an ideological goal.

Images

The backdrop for "The History of Mahou Masks" was a colorful tapestry designed by Vado's wife Lisa, featuring three twenty-foot-tall masks representing three ethnic groups well known for their masks—Baule, Guro, and Senufo. In conversation with Vado, I noted that this backdrop seems to reflect the philosophy of the dances: a Mau legend told not just through Mau movement, sound, and image but through the expressive culture of various Ivorian ethnic groups. I began to say, "So it's an expression—" but Vado interrupted, completing my thought: "Ivorian," reflecting the phrase Vado uses to describe Kotchegna: "Traditional Ivorian Dance." While on one hand Vado identifies his work as universal, on the other hand a nationalist spirit persists, which appears in other visual forms as well. Just as they grace all Kotchegna promotional materials, the colors of the Ivorian flag appeared throughout the performance, most prominently in the drummers' matching outfits as well as in the last of several outfits worn by the dancers. Through much of the performance, the dancers wore costumes of green, gold, and red—the colors of the Ethiopian flag that became Pan-African symbols through their association with Rastafarian religion and reggae. Costuming alone, then, suggested a mixture of Ivorian nationalism mixed with a Pan-African or perhaps African diasporic sensibility. The polysemic nature of performance makes possible such rich, multilayered expressions that might seem contradictory in another venue but are compatible on stage.

Performers

The diversity portrayed in *Kekene III* in 2009 was also present in *Kekene IV* in 2010. There was a core of performers from Côte d'Ivoire, with the rest of the company European Americans, African Americans, an Asian American, a European, and Caribbeans. Table 3.1 is a demographic representation of the *Kekene IV* performers, including Kotchegna members along with several Ivorian immigrants from around the eastern United States whom Vado labels the Ivory Coast All Stars.

As the table shows, in *Kekene IV* fewer than half of the performers were from Côte d'Ivoire. Nearly a third were from the United States, most of them African American though two were white. Rounding out the group were four Caribbean immigrants and a woman originally from Japan. Demographically the group represented two types of interweaving. Considering the Ivorians alone, we see the diversity represented in the BNCI married to an international diversity. I stop short of calling it a global because of the uneven representation, but Vado clearly intended to represent a global village of sorts. Consistent with its verbal discourse, Kotchegna on stage simultaneously represents nationalism and universality or globalization. Difference interweaves with difference. Once again, this is not a sacrifice in Vado's mind but an intentional choice.

I once commented to Vado that I found his philosophical approach interesting. "So it's clear that you [intentionally] chose people for the show who were not necessarily Ivorian." "Yes!" he replied. "No matter what you are . . . you can come from anywhere but we are the same thing." Are the performers viewed as different but equal? Clearly not, depending on whose view is considered. Performers enact ideological discourses on stage, which viewers read from the perspective of their own ideological discourses; at times the two clash. The *Attitude* reviewer mentioned earlier was troubled by the nonblack faces and bodies representing Africa in 2009. Her concern seemed based on race—only African descendants should perform African dance—given that she did not express concern about African Americans or Caribbeans representing Côte d'Ivoire.

I was unsuccessful in contacting this reviewer, so I can only speculate as to her interpretation of Vado's performance of oneness, which suggests an African diasporic sensibility. But Vado, while favoring Africans and African diasporans

Table 3.1 *Kekene* IV performers

Artists	Country of origin	Ethnicity or race or nationality
Drummers/musicians (all male)		
Bassanio Clark	Jamaica	Jamaican
Sebastian Costante	Spain	Spanish
Pablo Dembele	Côte d'Ivoire	Maninka
Sogbety Diomande	Côte d'Ivoire	Mau
Carlos Francis	St. Lucia	St. Lucian
Justin Kafando	Côte d'Ivoire	More (Burkinabé)
Seguenon Kone	Côte d'Ivoire	Senufo
Tra Bi Lizie	Côte d'Ivoire	Guro
Dancers/actors (all female except *)		
Kwesi Camara*	USA	African American
Mamadou Dahoue*	Côte d'Ivoire	Koyaka
Vado Diomande*	Côte d'Ivoire	Mau
Yahya Kamaté*	Côte d'Ivoire	Maninka
Persephone DaCosta	Guyana	African Guyanese
Rajeeyah Finnie	USA	African American
KristiAnn Francis	USA	European American
Euphrasie Gohoun	Côte d'Ivoire	Bete
Kate Krontiris	USA	European American
Pia Murray	USA	African American
Becky Morrison	USA	European American
Darlene Rhem	USA	African American
Nao Yamada	Japan	Japanese American
Guirlande Zetrenne	Haiti	Haitian

Note: "Ethnicity or race or nationality" is obviously problematic and begs explanation. Essentially I tried to use whatever primary label these people would use, beyond their country of origin, in identifying themselves. Ivorians would default to one of the sixty ethnicities in their home country. US-born citizens are either African American or European American (or "white"). Caribbean Islanders vary. Because roughly 95 percent of Haitians and 92 percent of Jamaicans are of African descent, they tend not to specify beyond nationality. African Guyanese, on the other hand, are distinguished from Indian Guyanese and thus are specifically labeled.

as drummers, emphasized *kekene*—a message of universal unity. He connected this review to similar reactions to his choice to perform with people not of African heritage—and especially *whites* of European heritage—in his Ivorian music and dance. Vado's discourse of oneness resonates with Martin Luther King, Jr., and the Civil Rights Movement's goal of racial integration. In contrast, many

African Americans, particularly in New York, who embraced the *jembe* and West African dance in the 1960s, were connected to the Black Arts Movement and its separationist agenda (Flaig 2010, 236; Sell 2001). Theater scholar Larry Neal, who participated in the movement, describes it:

> [It was] the aesthetic and spiritual sister of the Black Power concept. As such, it envisions an art that speaks directly to the needs and aspirations of Black America. In order to perform this task, the Black Arts Movement proposes a radical reordering of the western cultural aesthetic. It proposes a separate symbolism, mythology, critique, and iconology (National Humanities Center, 2007)

The Black Arts Movement, though different from Sekou Touré's anticolonial African nationalism (Cohen 2008, 19), resonated with Touré's appropriation of the European ballet. As an elite art form, ballet exemplified the Enlightenment-era imaginary that placed Europeans at the pinnacle of human social evolution. When peoples of African descent mounted concert stages and defined their art as ballet, they indeed em*bodied* a deeply moving political discourse against white supremacy and for the valuing not just of African arts but of the black body as well.

According to dance scholar Eleni Bizas, the tension between Afrocentric and universalist discourses has been mapped onto New York City dance class geography. She writes, "Uptown classes are primarily taught and attended by African-Americans. Downtown classes are taught by West African migrants and attended by an ethnically mixed group of students" (2014, 12–13). Bizas characterizes the latter as fee charging but inclusive; the former, as often free and in school gyms, YMCAs, or community centers, which are generally sites for African American heritage reconstruction. One student told Bizas that the mixed population of downtown classes kept uptown residents away (47). Echoing Vado, a Senegalese dance instructor who chooses to teach downtown told Bizas that African dance "is not about black or white, it's for everybody" (62). During the time I was researching this book, Vado's two regular teaching gigs were not in Harlem but rather in midtown, at the Alvin Ailey Dance Theater, and downtown, at Djoniba Dance and Drum Centre.

African American dance scholar Katrina Hazzard-Gordon says that "dance can serve as a 'litmus test for cultural identity'" (1985, 431) in which posture, gesture, and movement may be read as reifying African American cultural values based on dance's African roots. As such, they "help define one as a black person, but especially as a black person who has not been removed from one's people and cultural roots" (ibid., 434, quoted in Bizas 2014, 51–52). From this perspective, one can certainly appreciate the shock that African Americans might feel when faced with white bodies on stage representing African ballet. Think of the history. Europeans and Americans took everything Africa had—land, resources, sovereignty, people—for their own benefit. European and American slave traders conceived the black body itself as nothing more than a resource to control and use for their own profit. In the process they redefined things African as primitive and unworthy compared with Europe's "enlightened" achievements in all realms, from government to religion to industry to science, and, of course, to the arts. Africans struggled to "decolonize the mind" (the name of Ngugi wa Thiongo's 1981 book) as they threw off the shackles of colonial rule and created independent states. Independence-era Africans and then African Americans appropriated the concept of ballet, and now whites are taking that, *too*?

True enough. Not only do whites sometimes perform Africa on stage; a number of white *jembe* players teach African music, arguably displacing market share from African immigrant musicians. Indeed, as a white ethnomusicologist whose career has been built largely on the study of African music, I cannot deny my own complicity. On one hand, I want to defend Vado from an attack on grounds other than what he intends; on the other, I am sympathetic to the *Attitude* reviewer's discourse, which is founded on a reasonable and defensible position. Yet her discourse clashes with Vado's, which is equally valid. Both make sense within their own logics and underscore anthropologist Marvin Sterling's assertion of the "value of ethnographically situating global performativities of race, nation and culture in time and place" (2010, 255).

This clash of discourses is far from isolated. Joshua Cohen shows that, notwithstanding the great enthusiasm with which African Americans received early Les Ballets Africains (LBA) performances, the meanings of those performances were sometimes lost in translation: "Critical excavation of the Ballets' U.S. reception may also benefit from Brent Hayes Edwards' [2003] insight that processes of cultural and linguistic translation—with their attendant misinterpretations and disjunctures—have been integral to 20th-century diasporan exchanges" (Cohen 2008, 18).

Most of Vado's performances do not engender such controversy. I have to wonder how often booking agents and/or audiences take note of or even care where the dark-skinned people in a Kotchegna show come from, as long as they are black. In Kotchegna African descendant performers from the Americas are able to "pass" as African. And here I am aware of the profound irony of the term *pass*. In fact, one might describe Caribbean and African American performers blending in with and being taken as Africans as *reverse passing*. Far from distancing themselves from their African ancestry to fit into the white world, these artists embrace their racial and cultural roots as Africans and might be understood to be *more* African, not less.

Again, in booking shows the negotiating point is not "African or non-African" but "black or other (white or Asian)." Similarly, the *Attitude* reviewer seems to accept all Kotchegna performers of African ancestry, but is critical of those who she claims do not embody the "essence" of the dance, "because [they are] incapable of ever fully understanding that which [they are] not" (Waltrous 2009, 35). Critical of the racial integration, she expresses no concern over the many other integrations of difference in Vado's vision of unity. In several respects less obvious to Americans, most of whom know little about the distinctions between Ivorian ethnicities and their music and dance genres, the ensemble mixes and blends its aesthetic materials. The performers sing Mau songs over Senufo rhythms and dances, blend Senufo xylophones with Mau drums, and, most commonly and throughout the show, perform rhythms from many Ivorian groups on the Mande *jembe*.

Instrumentation

The instrumentation of nearly the entire *Kekene* and every Ivorian immigrant performance, dance class, or workshop I have attended over the past nine years, consists of *jembes* and accompanying *dunduns*, which, while inconsistent with the traditions of Ivorian villages, is totally consistent with American performances of Ivorian ballet. Vado notes that the hegemony of the Mande *jembe*—what I call *jembefication*—began to dominate and transform the ballet not in Côte d'Ivoire but on American stages. Patty Tang (2012) notes the prevalence of the griot in staged representations of Africa in the United States, but audiences here have also come to expect "West Africa" to be represented by loud, densely polyrhythmic *jembe* and *dundun* ensembles and ecstatic, high-energy dance with big, sweeping, movements suitable for the stage. Again, history offers an explanation.

The early LBA tours, the immigration and influential teaching of LBA master drummer Papa Ladji Camara in New York beginning in the 1960s, the adoption of the *jembe* by African Americans in connecting to their African heritage beginning in the 1970s, the drum circle culture that began sweeping the nation in the 1980s (Charry 2000; Flaig 2010; Polak 2006, 2012)—all of these resulted in fixing the *jembe* in many Americans' minds as a quintessential symbol of Africa. Although almost none of the traditions performed by Vado and friends would be performed on *jembe* in community contexts in Côte d'Ivoire, on North American stages this drum represents yet another aesthetic and cultural interweaving consistent with Vado's discourse of unity and his desire to meet expectations and get jobs.

Genre/Structure

Kekene's structure follows the pattern established by the BNCI, which itself was influenced by the transnational genre of the national ensemble. Particularly influential for the Ivorian ballet was the LBA. Indeed, an LBA veteran, Mamadou

Condé, was brought to Côte d'Ivoire from Guinea to become the first director of the BNCI in 1974. At its inception, then, Côte d'Ivoire's performance of nationalism was directly influenced and shaped by its neighbors' version of the same.

The *Kekene*'s performative pattern is a choreographed drama that combines music and dance traditions from Côte d'Ivoire into a grand narrative that unfolds not through the spoken word but through dance and drumming. It typically ends on a happy note, with a celebratory showcasing of ethnically marked performance traditions from all over the country. As a founding member of the Ivorian national ballet, Vado Diomandé came to master this genre, and for years now he has been creating his own choreographed pieces, such as "The History of Mahou Masks."

Performing Oneness

One way in which Vado promotes oneness is through "The History of Mahou Masks," a Mau myth in which he integrates resources from many Ivorian ethnic groups.

> If an Ivorian is there, I can't do the whole thing in Mau. . . . We have lots of different ethnic groups in Côte d'Ivoire. If you go see the dance, each person will want to have something that comes from his area. That's why I mixed them all. So each person can have something that they connect with a little, and then we all feel that we are together.

The blending of ethnic elements is strategic for Vado as a way to promote unity. The 2010 *Kekene* is rife with examples. At one point in the choreographed drama, Vado sings a song in Mau accompanied by the well-known Senufo *n'goron* rhythm (originally played on xylophone). According to Vado, "I put this song with the rhythm because it goes well with it. . . . When the drummers hear that song they know to start playing *n'goron*." In so doing, he creates new traditions: "A lot of people here think this is the song for *n'goron*." Vado's innovations have become ballet standards in the United States.

At another point in the drama, a young African American woman, Pia Murray, initiates a call-response song in the Mau language (PURL 3.2):

Ma bo ba ee ma kieni
My mother and grandmother

Tama diani ne we
You must go to a good place

The song is sung in Mau, but the rhythm, *Maninkadon*, is Maninka. The Maninka people, whose homeland is northwest Côte d'Ivoire, southwest Mali, and northern Guinea, are a "core" northern Mande linguistic and cultural group. The Mau are related to the Maninka, but are a distinct ethnic group with a distinct language. Of course, the instrumentation is the standard *jembe* and *dundun*.

Kotchegna's performers broaden and deepen the interethnic, transnational, and diasporic nature of the ballet. Although some are Africans, African descendants from various parts of the diaspora form a majority of both drummers and dancers. Of the seven drummers, four are Ivorian immigrants (a Maninka, a Bete, a Guro, and a Mau). They are joined by a Jamaican, a St. Lucian, and a Spaniard. The dancers are an even more diverse lot. Only one, Euphrasie Gohoun, is Ivorian (Bete). She is joined by two African Americans, three European Americans, and four recent immigrants—two from Haiti and one each from Trinidad and Japan.

Leading the dance is the Mau mask spirit Gue Pelou. After he disappears behind the curtain, master drummer Pablo Dembele plays a pattern that cues the other drummers that he is ready to end the piece. All of a sudden, the drummers stop their individual repeating patterns and begin a unison "break." Understood as a process, a break is effectively a call and response—a call from the leader that functions as a cue and a response from the accompanying drummers in the form of a break. Such clearly defined endings are not often heard in Côte d'Ivoire when drummers play in nonstaged, community contexts; looser endings may be the norm because of the cyclical nature of this music, which has no fixed beginning or end. Drummers come in when they are ready, play the patterns in the right relationship to each other, and then, in response to a master drummer's cue, stop playing, not necessarily simultaneously but less formally. On stage, however, endings, and breaks in general, are more orchestrated and precise. "Ballet" includes not just mastery of a repertoire of dances and rhythms played on particular instruments; it also includes a repertoire of breaks and the knowledge of how they are employed.

"The History of Mahou Masks" ends with a song by Gue Pelou in the Dan language after he delivers a benediction to his fellow performers and the audience (PURL 3.3):

> ma lo ma ge ka Daloa
> I take my *ge* to Daloa
> The drummers and dancers respond:
>
> Daloa—o
> Daloa [name of city]—oh!

Textually this song is very typical of *getan*, the genre defined by Dan *ge* practitioners as the sonic manifestation of a *ge* spirit. It economically describes a person traveling with a *ge* to the city of Daloa in west central Côte d'Ivoire. Travel for the sake of performance is routine for *ge* spirits, which, like contemporary

Ivorians, are highly mobile beings. Thus, travel is a common theme in the *getan* repertoire.

Ge stilt mask spirits originated among the Dan people, the Mau's neighbors to the south, and were incorporated into Mau belief and practice. Evidence of this can be found in different performance elements, such as the Dan language in which the mask speaks and sings and the proper name of the spirit, the Dan *Gue* or *Ge*. This historical exchange demonstrates that interethnic interaction—so profoundly present in the ballet tradition—is a long-standing Ivorian practice historically, and though not invented on the ballet stage, it has been much more fully developed there. In ballet discourse, instrumentation, music and dance repertoires, and even sets and costumes form a body of raw materials from which ensemble directors like Vado select elements to blend into representations supporting broad ideological missions such as Vado's discourse of oneness.

4 "If You Aren't Careful, You Don't Know Where You Will End Up!"

Vado Diomande and Transcendence

DANIEL REED (DR): Why do you dance?

VADO DIOMANDE (VD): I don't know, but I love dance. I was born immersed in it. It was central to my father's life, and I myself, I loved it. . . . And when I was in the village I did not know that I would end up in the National Ballet, but I loved it. . . . So I dance. I love dance and it has become my work. When I feel sick, if I dance it goes away. I'm no longer sick if I dance.

I have spent many hours with Vado Diomande (see figure 4.1) in his Harlem apartment discussing his life. Nearly all of my formal interviews with him have taken place there, where I asked questions, cued up videotapes, and took notes while he (usually) repaired and set up *jembes*, multitasking as he politely answered my questions and told his story.

> 11-24-08, Harlem, NY. The morning of my third day staying with Lisa and Vado Diomande in Harlem. Their apartment is quite spacious—perhaps 400 square feet—on the ground floor of a 15-story apartment building [on] Lennox, which is also Malcolm X Avenue . . . off 142nd St. between Lennox and 5th Ave. Their apartment is very nicely furnished, with an obvious care for the visual, even though nearly everything they have has been given to them in the post-anthrax period, which is when they moved in here (2006). It's an intriguing combination of Africana—CDs, wall hangings, photos, and many drums—with a new-age sensibility—books by Deepak Chopra, healing texts, Enya-style music, etc. This [mixture] reflects their union, and also Lisa [who is] typical of one sort of contemporary North American African music aficionado—drawn to healing, to otherness, to art. . . .
>
> Vado is as I have always experienced him—quiet, somewhat shy, but very self-assured and confident, and, as Lisa says, very at home in his body. He prays just twice a day; as he told me, he's too busy to pray every time. Once in the morning and, before bed, he does "all the others." Just hearing his prayers emanating from the bedroom gives this place a certain character of Africa in a somewhat un-African place. . . .
>
> Yesterday was, in a day, quite something to behold in terms of Vado's work. He woke up and worked for several hours re-heading *jembes* for Aristide. Then

Figure 4.1 Vado Diomande. Photograph by author.

after lunch we drove to midtown to the Alvin Ailey American Dance Theater, where he taught a dance class. Then off to downtown to Djoniba—where he taught a drum class. He is clearly a multi-tasker, not unlike many American musicians I know who cannot make a living through performance alone and instead have to teach. He is very resourceful, though, in his ability not just to perform but teach dance, drumming, and make instruments. (field notes, 23–25)

Such was the context in which Vado told me his life story,[1] and as always with life story, Vado's was selective, focused primarily on his performance history and immigration experience. This was expected given the nature of my research project. But, another theme unexpectedly emerged from our conversations to become the most important, indeed the central, theme of Vado's narrative: health and health care. This is highly relevant for two reasons. First, illness, especially in the world of mask performance, is frequently attributed to sorcery inspired by jealousy and competition. Understanding Vado's performance history, then, requires engaging with a West African health care paradigm in which many illnesses are caused by social interaction on human and nonhuman planes. Second, the primary reason Vado decided to risk immigrating to the United States was better treatment for a life-threatening illness that had not responded to multiple surgeries in Abidjan. Economic issues were another engine driving major decisions in Vado's life, influencing aesthetic and religious practice, the decision to bring more family members to the United States, and the overall direction of his life and career. This particular version of Vado's life story, then, illustrates the interconnections between music and dance performance, health, money, and immigration. As Vado says, through dance he has chased illness away; in this life story, he dances his way across the Atlantic, migrating toward healing.

Discovered

One day, when Vado Diomande was just seventeen years old, he returned to his village of Toufinga in northwestern Côte d'Ivoire after a hard day of farming. There he found scouts from the Ballet National de Côte d'Ivoire (BNCI) preparing to audition villagers. Vado's father, well aware of his son's dance skills and sensing an opportunity, was already meeting with the visitors when Vado appeared. Vado later learned that his father had prepared traditional medicine to help his son's audition. Though clearly a favorite, Vado would need extra spiritual power and protection from malevolent attacks by those who wanted other competitors to win. This would be neither the first nor the last time Vado would require such protection; this type of attack has followed him throughout his career. In fact, it would be hard to imagine any version of Vado Diomande's life story that did not feature health problems, so prominent have they been. It was Vado's great skill as a performer that led to attacks on his health, and ultimately it was a desperate desire for better treatment that led him to make the difficult choice to leave his home country.

In the auditions that day Toufinga villagers recognized the seventeen-year-old Vado as a likely finalist because he had long been known for his superlative skills in dance. Stories abounded about Vado's dancing, which he seemed to do naturally from the time he could walk. For instance, when Vado was very small, a doctor visited Toufinga to give vaccinations. "I danced for him," Vado told me. "I was really little," he said, gesturing with his arm to indicate a height of less than three feet. "And afterwards, the villagers said, 'that guy, he's going to become something.'"

That Vado was singled out as a dance prodigy in his village is not surprising considering his family background. The Diomande are a "mask family," meaning that they have a long-standing tradition as guardians and performers of sacred masks.[2] These masks, called *nya* in Mauka—the language of Vado's ethnic group, the Mau—are spiritual beings, only some of whom manifest among humans in performance.

DR: What is the Mask?

VD: It's a spirit.[3] From what my father told me, it's between me and dead people. . . . If you are not initiated, you don't see it. The mask that you see outside is the dress. The real mask is somewhere around (gestures). You don't see it. Nobody sees it. So it's a spirit.

DR: So that spirit comes from the forest or . . .

VD: Yes it comes from the sacred forest [laughter].

As his laughter abated, Vado remained smiling and I wondered what was behind his grin. I then reminded him that, as we had discussed at the outset of our work together, if we were approaching the domain of secrets, he simply had to stop me if I went too far. He was not concerned but relaxed, and we proceeded. In my field notes later that evening, I registered that my interviews with Vado were becoming more comfortable the more time we spent together.

Vado was highly skilled in many forms of Mau dance, but it was his ability to dance Gue Pelou—the stilt mask spirit for which the family was known in the region—that most interested the BNCI team. Western Côte d'Ivoire, including the Mau region, is known for its masks (Reed 2003), and among the most spectacular and popular were those that dance on stilts. The BNCI founders likely were looking for stilt mask spirit performers, who were to be found in either the Mau region or the Dan region just to the south of the Mau. While living in western Côte d'Ivoire in the 1990s, I observed that no noteworthy event felt right without a mask dance; likewise, the BNCI could not represent the Ivorian nation without including these iconic symbols of the western region.

Vado says that the stilt mask spirit genre (*ge gbleen* in Dan; *nya yan* in Mauka) originated in Dan country and was borrowed by the Mau, who incorporated it into their belief system and performance traditions.[4] This history accounts for Vado's mask's name (Gue Pelou), which makes use of the Dan *gue* or *ge* for mask spirit. Gue Pelou speaks and sings exclusively in the Dan language. In performing the tradition, Vado engages in an interethnic move as a Mau singing and speaking in Dan while performing a Dan mask spirit. This shows that the performative interethnicity so fundamental to African ballet—whether in the form of individuals performing dances from an ethnic group not their own or in the interweaving of multiple ethnic traditions—did not begin with the staging of Ivorian dance. Mau performances of the stilt mask spirit problematize the absolute distinction between "ethnic" and "interethnic" because these performances, paradoxically, are both. Vado's current representational practice, with interethnicity and even internationality at its core, can thus be traced to his earliest Gue Pelou performances in his natal village (see Kopytoff 1987).

While Vado came from a so-called mask family, this alone did not guarantee his becoming a highly skilled practitioner. Generally in mask families, one man becomes the primary "proprietor" of the mask. Vado's father was the one in his generation who had what Vado alternately termed "the gift" and "the power." As among the Dan (Reed 2003, chap. 8), when a baby is born in a mask family, family members determine if he possesses the power (*fan* in Mauka). In fact it was even before Vado's birth that his father identified him as the next proprietor of the mask spirit: "I had lots of big brothers, but the mask doesn't come to everyone. They all danced, but it wasn't the same thing. The power only comes to one person." Because this was the first time he had identified this inheritance as the power, I asked him about it. "I don't know where the power comes from, but it comes to you. . . . It's a gift—my dad had it too." He told me that the power affects how you dance and sing. "Everyone can [dance and sing] well, but when they see me do it, they say, 'That's different!'"

This difference that Toufinga residents observed in Vado's dancing many people in western Côte d'Ivoire would interpret as the presence of spirits (*yinan* in Dan; *ginan* in Mauka). Vado acknowledged this: "The *ginan* make the dance powerful. When the good *ginan* come, the dance has a lot of power. Good energy." *Ginan* also accompany and empower mask spirits (*ge* in Dan; *nya* in Mau) when they perform among humans. Intermediaries between people and God, they appear most commonly as dancing figures. Vado confirmed what my Dan teachers taught me: a performing mask spirit personifies social ideals by being the best at whatever it does. Among Dan people, for example, no human can resolve sorcery conflicts as effectively as the *ge* (*zu ge*; see Reed 2003, chap. 8) charged with this task, and no human dancer can dance better than a dance *ge* (*tanke ge*; ibid., chap. 7). Not surprisingly, then, Vado said that Mau masks also personify ideals by being the best at what they do, comparing them to the BNCI's auditions: "It works just like this in the ballet. That is, you have to be the best at whatever it is that you do to be in it. . . . and even in the village before you are selected for the ballet you had to be the best."

Vado explained that the BNCI's initial visit to his village was but the first round in an audition process carried out in regions all over the country. Winners in the first round then competed in a second round in Touba—the capital of Mau country—where seventeen mask dance hopefuls tried out.

From that pool, just two mask dancers, one of whom was Vado, went on to the final round held in the regional capital city, Man. "They told us that they would take only these two masks to go to Man to do it again," Vado recounted. "That day my father was there. Yeah, my father went with us. Everybody from my village came." Vado recalled that among those villagers were healers/clairvoyants/religious specialists called *zo*.[5] "Every strong *zo* came. You know *zo*? They are the ones who can see everything." And why were the *zo* there? "We had to win. . . . Everybody wanted to win." Once again, competition emerges as a central theme, with indigenous religious resources strategically employed in the battle for victory. In the end, Vado and his mask spirit Gue Pelou were selected, heralding a new era in his life in which dance would transform from an avocation into profession and he would become a performer, tour the world, and, in the process, train and develop skills to prepare him for life and work as an immigrant in the United States (see figure 4.2).

Figure 4.2 Gue Pelou with drummer Papa Diarra at Djo Bi's June 2008 wedding in St. Bernice, Indiana. Photograph by Christy True.

Permission, Sacrifice, and "Voudou"

But Vado's success has come at a cost: "So they picked us. Then other villages in Touba, they don't like us now. They don't like me now. So we have competition everywhere. That's why any time I go to the village or anywhere [in Côte d'Ivoire], they shoot the voudou at me.... That's the problem for me now, everywhere I go." Competition, jealousy, and what Vado called "voudou" intertwine and endure as major issues in his life. As Ruth Stone (1988) and others have documented, West Africans may require those of great talent to adhere to strict social responsibilities. If you believe that a talented person is flaunting his skills, not adequately sharing the fruits of his labor, then you might resort to sorcery against him, using spiritual power for socially destructive ends. Ever since that fateful day in 1974, when Vado was selected for the BNCI, he has had to remain constantly vigilant and use powerful traditional medicines to protect himself and keep dancing.

The extent to which Ivorian performers will go to ensure success in competition is impressive. One day I said, "I have the impression that competition is really important, not only in masks but also among performers in general." "Yes," he replied, laughing. "It's like when you play soccer, when you play soccer, you want to win.... If you have a group, someone must be first."

> VD: There are people who don't like [competition]. But those who play, and those who dance, in order to be really good, you have to have a heart that says, "I'm going to be better than all the others." If not, you're not going to become a good dancer or drummer. You have to say to yourself, "I must surpass him. And then you become more powerful."
>
> DR: So it's a means of motivation?
>
> VD: *Voilà.*

Along with this passion to be the best, Vado recognized a countervailing culturally equalizing force:

> But if they do something and you do it better than them, [that's when the problems start]. If you're going to do something, you should not exceed [what others have done]. You must not be better than them. You must not do too much.... What you know, you do only a little bit and you leave the rest. You do it in a manner that you don't do more than the person who was before you. If you do more than him, then he will do to you what he knows. And it makes them happy to know more than you in the domain of masks.

Thus, he feels trapped between two opposing forces: a desire to succeed and ultimately make a living from his performing, and a social sanction against going too far or risk brutal attacks.

Even in the United States, Vado has had to watch his back, but when in Côte d'Ivoire to offer sacrifices[6] for permission to continue performing Gue Pelou outside the village, he feels particularly vulnerable: "You have to have a thing every time to clean your body. Medicine—*strong* medicine—you need it!" Vado's "medicine" comes from practices that, although veiled in secrecy, certainly involve some combination of herbology and mystical belief. Their use as spiritual protection is widespread in West Africa, and immigrants have imported them into the United States.[7] In Vado's case, however, because the required herbs must be procured from Africa, he often cannot prepare his defenses prior to his visits back home.

Describing his vulnerability when he travels back to Côte d'Ivoire, Vado invoked the metaphor of a papaya tree:

VD: When I go, my body is like a–you know papaya?

DR: Yes.

VD: You know the papaya tree?

DR: Yes.

VD: It's not a strong one. What is it like?

DR: I don't know.

VD: It's weak. When we get there, they think we are weak now. When you hit a papaya tree like that [gestures a karate chop], it will fall. If you don't have medicine in your body, then you are like a papaya tree. When they try a small thing, you will . . . [Laughs and gives me look suggesting there's no hope].

DR: Po po po [a nonlexical Ivorian expression suggesting "Oh, how terrible" . . .]

VD: That's why people try, because they think I don't have anything in my body anymore because I'm in America.

DR: As soon as you arrive in Abidjan, do you have to look for some medicine?

VD: Yes. Before I get there, I have to know where to go to get medicine before people see me!

LISA DIOMANDE: It's fascinating, huh?

VD: It's difficult!

DR: Fascinating, but dangerous!

A 2003 trip to Côte d'Ivoire for a show in Yopougon [a neighborhood in Abidjan] had dire consequences for Vado, which he described to me:

VD: My home is in Yopougon. So that time I arrived. We had to do a celebration for the mask because I had come from [New York] to [Abidjan] and I had to offer a sacrifice to the mask there. That same day, the Mau in Yopougon had their own celebration under way, the *sanwi* [a Mau women's social dance in which they all wear a special cloth chosen for the occasion].... Now that day, many people came from all over to see the mask show. But the *sanwi* performers ... wanted people to come too. So, [there was] competition between my people and theirs. The first week I was there, we did a show, but not a very powerful show. Now after that, the next week, I was doing my sacrifice. Now people, a lot of people, came to my show, and not to the other show.

Thanks to the large crowd, Vado's mask performance brought in 50,000 CFA (around $100)—a healthy offering to his family's mask spirit–which made the *sanwi* group jealous and angry.

The [other] group doing their thing, they're angry.... People from that group arranged for bad people to come to me. That's why they attacked me—you see, like my leg and everything. That was a bad day. That Sunday—my sacrifice day.

This leg injury was just as mysterious as it was debilitating. The problem first appeared just after this show, in his elbow.

I got a small swollen vein here [points to his elbow]. Every time I sat down like this [places elbow on knee], then it would swell here [gestures to show swelling of leg]. Eee! It was bad. The *sanwi*—oh. It was a lot of problem for me. So I had to perform in Holland the next week. After that, the following week, it was a lot of problem for me. Lisa went to see me in Holland ... at the hospital ... Before I got to Holland, it was bad.

Dutch doctors diagnosed the problem as a rare form of flesh-eating bacteria, which is highly contagious.

Mask performance can be a site of especially heated competition leading to jealousy and attacks. In Mau communities, the power of a mask is highly coveted and potentially dangerous to its proprietors. Vado has profited from the power, but he has also suffered its presence in his life:

Because of this [possession of the power], you cannot go anywhere. Whenever you go anywhere there is a lot of voudou[8] going on. Anyone who has good medicine, they try to get you. If it's not good it cannot do anything. If you fall or do something different [wrong], then they know their voudou is good.... the Mau have done voudou against me all the time. When you finish [performing], you have pain here and here [points to his legs].

A number of very serious health problems in the years following his selection for the BNCI were due to spiritual attacks, according to Vado. Just as he has continued offering sacrifices in his new immigrant community, so has the spiritual warfare persisted, following Vado and Gue Pelou to multicultural New York. One day I asked Vado about this:

DR: Today, since the mask is here in the US, far from Mau country, is it still the case that people attack the mask?

VD: It's the same thing that you find in Africa. It comes from everywhere. All ethnic groups, they are here. All things, are here. . . . People do the same things they do in Africa here.

DR: The Ivorians who are here?

VD: The Ivorians or people that come from anywhere. The Haitians, Malians, Guineans—everybody is doing the same thing here—competition, every time. In New York, there is more. Yeah. To get good here in New York? Very difficult. There's a lot of voudou here. They're doing voudou to everybody.

In describing his battles with spiritual attacks in the United States, Vado articulates an international, transnational, even an African diasporic sensibility. Immigrants from the continent and the Caribbean, some drawing on common cultural backgrounds rooted in African religious practice and belief, use powerful resources to gain advantage in the competition for scarce resources in immigrant America. To remain safe from such attacks, Vado is supposed to return each year to Toufinga to offer his sacrifice, but this has not always been possible. For many years after his arrival in the United States, for example, he could not leave the country because he had no papers.

I find it telling that Vado labels the attacks against him *voudou*. Of Fon origin (a language in contemporary Benin), although better known in the United States via the West African–derived religion practiced by descendants of slaves in Haiti, *voudou* is applied in Vado's discourse metaphorically—indeed, you might say metonymically—to refer to the negative use of spiritual power in the transnational, African diasporic community in New York.

Vado has endured sorcery attacks for decades, beginning the moment he was selected for the national ballet. These attacks have been motivated not just by jealousy but also by opposition to a sacred mask being taken from the village to perform on the national concert stage and beyond. Once Gue Pelou was selected to join the BNCI, much debate ensued among Toufinga residents as to whether to approve of the mask spirit's departure. Vado recalls:

People did not want the mask to leave there. . . . they approved for the mask to go away for just one year. Now . . . doing the choreography to create the Ballet National, it was a lot of work and it took us three years to finish. Three years. It took three years to put everything together.

Although it was controversial, the elders and overseers of the family's sacred house did grant their approval for the mask to join the national ballet, initially for one year. This approval came only after Vado's father offered a substantial sacrifice to the ancestors via the overseers of the family's sacred house. Approvals for subsequent years have had to be annually renegotiated. with Vado required to make annual pilgrimages to Toufinga to offer sacrifices. Only by respecting the authority of his fellow "fathers of the mask,"[9] can Vado assume the authority to take Gue Pelou along on his travels.

Vado is also expected to make annual pilgrimages to Toufinga for sacrifices to the "great mask"—the most powerful mask in the Diomande's sacred house and the source of Gue Pelou's power. For many years, honoring this commitment required an annual journey of about 500 kilometers each way from Abidjan to Toufinga. These pilgrimages continue, with Vado struggling to find the time and money for them.

Vado explained the sacrifices, beginning with those required initially to remove the mask from the village:

VD: They made me pay many chickens! You had to pay! If you don't, your power, can't dance—it's finished! You have to have power if you want to do something great. So I had to pay something like six chickens the day before I came to Abidjan with the mask.

DR: Is it still necessary for you to ask permission to continue to manifest the mask here? From time to time is it necessary to make sacrifices?

VD: Each time I make sacrifices. I do that here, yes. . . . When they call me, before going somewhere, I give some kola. Sometimes I give a chicken. That's what we do. The mask must be adored. If he needs something, I dream it. I have to follow that. If I don't, the power cannot go.

Sacrifices are also made in the United States each time a performance is requested.

Vado sometimes learns what a particular sacrifice to the mask must consist of via his dreams. I was intrigued by the idea of the dream as a medium for communication with *ginan*:

DR: Do you dream like that often?

VD: Yes. If there is something going to be wrong, I dream. Or something good coming, I dream it.

DR: Can you give an example of a dream that you received?

VD: You see the mask in your dream. . . . Sometimes he doesn't explain himself, and it's you now who must interpret what he wants. . . . You see something afterwards, something like some food, like a chicken.

Food or animals encountered in dreams might be understood as sacrificial offerings the mask is asking for. They constitute a central part of the idea of sacrifice. There are also esoteric, secret elements of sacrifice that I choose not to expose here, but I can say that a major emphasis is effectively the underwriting of the cost of a big party in the form of food, kola nut, and/or monetary offerings. According to Vado,

> Every year when we were in the National Ballet, every year we had to go to the village with the mask. We brought the mask home, we celebrated, [had a] good dance. Every village near Toufinga, everybody [would] come. And we killed a cow, everybody came to eat, two days dancing, just dance, lots of masks.[10]

Vado continues to be involved in the bundle of cultural practices integrating permission, sacrifice, problem solving, competition, and jealousy. Ever since his marriage to Lisa made it possible for him to obtain a green card and legal status, the pressure from Toufinga for annual sacrifices has increased. Anything going wrong in Vado's life or in the lives of Toufinga residents might be interpreted as related to Vado's taking his mask spirit away from the village. In January 2010, for example, Vado was forced to make a trip to his village to participate in a family-wide sacrifice ritual decreed by people who, Vado says, "see things; people who see the future." Led by a "big brother who is ninety-something," it was called to address the general misfortune that had befallen the family, following family members wherever they went, from the village to Abidjan to Europe and the United States—truly a transnational, diasporic malaise. Vado described the state of affairs:

VD: Everything for me had been going badly. Also for my brother in Norway. It [had been] going well and we were able to send [family in Toufinga] money. Any problem we had, we could fix it. But right now . . . In the village, they are planting things, and they don't work either. Everything is getting bad–bad!
    So they [village elders/clairvoyants] called for a big sacrifice, for all of my family. Any descendent of my father—we were all supposed to be in the village, to talk about it. And they say when I came to the city, it was with the mask, right? I brought the mask to go into Kotchegna. Then Kotchegna came here [to America]. The young people in Abidjan—this mask that I have here they have there also . . . are taking the mask anywhere, including places it should not go. So they are making everything bad. Some were saying that everything is bad because of Vado's mask. But I was not there [in Côte d'Ivoire]. So when I went back I gathered all those masks in Abidjan and took them to the village.

Given the severity of the problem, the sacrifice demanded was substantial, according to Vado: "That time I had [to sacrifice] two cows, one goat, one lamb and lots of chickens."

Vado's life in the 2010s in New York City continues to involve social processes that he first encountered when the mask spirit was invited to join the BNCI nearly forty years ago. Once again, an aspect of the ballet experience—here the need for a social and spiritual give and take for permission to take a performance across borders—proved to be a kind of training, preparing future immigrants like Vado for life as artists in the United States.

Formative Years in the National Ballet

Returning to Vado's audition story, once the initial sacrifice was made and the controversy settled, he left to join the ballet, becoming one of its founding members. Vado recalls there being forty-six performers in the original BNCI, though not all played the same role. Many dancers made up the chorus; a select few, including Vado, were soloists. As Vado's skills continued to develop, he became lead choreographer—the third most important position in the BNCI's hierarchy, beneath only the director, Mamadou Condé, and the assistant director, Dagbo Faustin. Vado hinted to me that his inability to read and write prevented him from rising even higher in the ranks. And yet: "The Director didn't dance. For learning dance I am good but I don't know how to write.... We were three people. When they wanted to write something, [the assistant director] did that. I taught the dance." Focusing on dance instruction and choreography would prove greatly beneficial to Vado down the road, though, as it enabled him to develop skills that he put to use forming his own troupe, Ensemble Kotchegna, in Abidjan and later in New York, where he rechristened it Kotchegna Dance Company. Again, the ballet emerges as the most important experience for Vado in terms of preparing him for his life as an American immigrant.

Dancing Dreams

People around Vado interpreted his great skill as a choreographer just exactly as they had interpreted his great skill at dance: that he had "the gift," that the spirits (*ginan*) were guiding him. Here again dreams emerge as an important channel for communication with spirits. Art historians have documented the dreams of Dan mask carvers as sites where spirits reveal the face (or mask) they desire for their visual manifestation (Johnson 1986). Vado and I discussed his choreography-inspiring dreams:

VD: When you sleep, someone comes to show you the steps.... It's like research that we do often [laughter].

DR: Dreams are like research?

VD: Yes. It's like that. When you think about something, someone comes to show you. Someone comes to show you.... And when you wake up you see it. It's like you've seen a dance. . . . Often that gives you good fortune. Often what you see if it's going to work he gives it to you. . . . When you perform in a show, it could even be a small thing, but someone will like it.

DR: And you say there is someone there in the dream that shows you the dance—is it always the same person?

VD: No, no, no. It's not the same person. Sometimes it could be someone like you who doesn't even dance. It's not you but maybe in the dream it appears to be you. I don't know how to say it, but . . . for us it's spirits who come to show us something. It's like you're dreaming but you actually see something and then you remember it again. . . . It could be your ancestors, who can help you—I don't know.

DR: And is there music also in those dreams?

VD: No, it's only the steps. But you know the time. The time can fall into . . . no matter which rhythm. You could do the steps slowly or rapidly; that depends upon you. No matter which rhythm, if it's slow or hot, you will know. That person could show it to you slowly but if you want to do it quickly you do it quickly. That depends on the beat that you put to it.

DR: It's very interesting because I dream melodies—

VD: So I am not lying, am I [laughs]? I also dream of people singing in my head. Those are your ancestors who are giving you that. You don't know that [laughs].

I find this interview passage fascinating not just because of what it says about the importance of dreams as a creative source and as an opening to the spirit world but also because it is an example of the fascinating interactions that can happen in ethnographic fieldwork. Twice Vado alluded to aspects of my world as a means of helping me understand his. Dreams are like research, he artfully analogized. You seek out the source—someone or something that can give you what you seek–an answer, an idea, inspiration. Meanwhile, in a moment of utter fascination, I realized that both he and I receive creative material from dreams—many of my favorite songs have in part originated from them.

Looking back, I think of this moment as comparable to Tony Seeger singing his Uncle Pete's folksongs for *Suya* people in Brazil (Seeger 2004, 20). Like Seeger, I find that offering our own "culture" for our consultants' inspection deepens relationships and provides connection of a kind that I know no other way to achieve. Such moments of genuine reciprocal exchange are what ethnography is all about, as we come to *know* one another on deeper levels. Furthermore, such moments at least temporarily level the power differential inherent in fieldwork, as the ethnographic gaze is turned on the "researcher." Authoritatively yet playfully, Vado interpreted my culture: "Those are your ancestors." I researched his dreams, so he researched mine. That this moment occurred four years into the research after Vado and I had spent significant time together and knew each other well, is also surely no accident but rather testimony to the value of long-term ethnographic research with individuals.

And what does this passage tell us about Vado and his life? First, that Vado receives creative inspiration from spirits in dreams adds choreography to the list of art forms involved in human–spirit dream communication in the literature on masks and mask performance in western Côte d'Ivoire. Second, that such communication continues in the immigrant setting is illuminating. Just as Vado uses cell phones, airplanes, and sacrifices to stay connected with Mau and other Ivorians back in Côte d'Ivoire and with his sense of himself *as* a Mau/Ivorian/African, so dreams, as a channel of communication with *ginan*, maintain a transnational connection in his life.

Ballet Life

Vado talked a bit about daily life as a ballet performer, particularly during the initial training period. He and his fellow performers lived together in military-style barracks in Bouaké, Côte d'Ivoire's second largest city. Paul Schauert (2015) writes that Ghana Dance Ensemble training was explicitly compared to military training. Likewise, Vado likened his to boot camp. Describing the training and discipline required to learn the repertoire, he said, "It was like the military. It's like they were going to take you to fight in the war. When you are there, you have to be strong. Some came, but couldn't handle it, so they left, returned [to the village]. But we who were left, we learned everything they wanted us to do."

In 1976, two years into Vado's training, the first performance took place—an unveiling for President Félix Houphouët-Boigny at the swanky Hôtel Ivoire overlooking a lagoon in Abidjan's upscale Cocody district. Ballet performers understood that this was their first test, so they felt a sense of relief and accomplishment when the president approved their representation of his nation and then approved their first international tour. Prior to embarking on the tour, however, they returned to Bouaké to spend seven additional months preparing. Ballet was Vado's ticket to his first experience away from Africa, dancing across Europe—Italy, both East and West Germany, Yugoslavia, France, and England. This and subsequent tours provided him with yet more experience that he would draw on in his future. Traveling transnationally, he became more and more comfortable in foreign contexts and increasingly more fluent in cosmopolitan cultural ways (Turino 2000). On stage, night after night, he also built up incredible endurance and toughness. In this way, in addition to training in the performative aesthetics of staging Ivorian traditions, the BNCI also, unwittingly, provided performers with skills they would later employ in their daily lives as immigrants.

Vado's choreography and performing during his tenure with the BNCI were very much informed by the philosophy and methods of the ballet. National ensembles by definition have dual missions—representing and promoting a national vision to the world via international tours and representing and promoting a vision of a unified nation. In pursuit of these goals, the BNCI traveled both transcontinentally and within Côte d'Ivoire. During its early, formative period, it toured villages to learn dances, filming them as source material in much the same way that Bartók transcribed Hungarian folk songs as sources for his compositions. Once a choreographed version of a dance was completed, it would be performed on tours of Côte d'Ivoire. Vado remembers that in those early days the BNCI traveled widely in country, visiting "Korhogo, Suéguéla, Daloa, Man, all over—Bondoukrou. . . . We went to Issia, Gagnoa, San Pedro—everywhere. Katiola, Boundiali." The cities and towns Vado recalls are all over, east to west, north to south, showing that the BNCI showcased its nationalist vision throughout all regions and to as many of the country's sixty ethnic groups as possible.

It was Houphouët-Boigny who paid for these dances. And in terms of the national ballet as a means of nation building, no event was more important to him than Festimask, a huge event that took place in a stadium in the capital city of Yamoussoukro in 1985. Discourses of how a nation should be staged, discourses of a postcolonial Africa, genres of performance, and performers such as Vado—all were circulating—across Côte d'Ivoire, transnationally, and transcontinentally. Motivated by the desire to communicate in music and dance using the power of these forms, people and ideas spread around the world. Thus began the development of Vado's universalist vision, one element of which in the BNCI was a belief in interethnic interaction and cooperation.

Interethnicity

As far as we know, ethnic groups in Africa have interacted extensively throughout history, sharing ideas and practices in many domains of life, including music and dance. Colonial administrators, ethnographers, and others have, for various strategic reasons, been known to emphasize, exaggerate, or even fabricate ethnic difference (Waterman 1990). Ethnographic literature focusing on single African ethnic groups abounds, while studies focusing on interethnic interaction, or "frontiers" between groups, remain rare a full quarter-century after Igor Kopytoff (1987) made his plea that we rethink the historical construction of African ethnicity. And yet even though interethnic interaction has been the norm throughout African history, the sharing and/or interweaving of ethnic traits has undeniably increased in frequency and scope in the postcolonial era. Ballet culture has been one engine driving this change, which is ironic given that interethnic interaction in ballet generally serves to represent traditions as inherently ethnically marked.

Here again we see the interesting dance of postethnic expression mixed with ethnicity reification that marks the ballet genre. This tension, and the notion of interethnicity, substantially influenced Vado's artistic vision. However, Vado's life story reveals that in some ways interethnicity was a presence in his life long before his BNCI audition. Prior to his involvement in the ballet, he had experienced interethnic interaction in performance, particularly in his performance of Gue Pelou. Again, the stilt mask spirit genre originated among the Dan people and was adopted by the Mau, a fact that Vado and other performers routinely cite to explain why Gue Pelou speaks and sings exclusively in Dan. Such interethnic interactions are commonplace in Africa, but for Vado the interethnicity in training, rehearsal, and performance went far beyond anything he had experienced previously.

Formally, of course, the BNCI was interethnic to the core, featuring dances from each region of Côte d'Ivoire sometimes reconceived for the stage but presented as bounded ethnic traditions, and sometimes deliberately interwoven into dance dramas or simply new interethnic combinations. Achieving such a formal result required social interactions that took interethnic interaction in new directions. The teaching and learning in rehearsals, for example, emerged as intensive sharing of ethnically marked traditions, with one performer from the ethnic group or region where the dance originated teaching the others. Sacred masks were the only exception to this practice because only an initiate of a mask had the authority to dance it. However, many secular—or at least minimally sacred—masks were danced by anyone. Vado recalls that these included the Senufo panther mask Bolohi and the popular Guro mask Zauli. But Gue Pelou and the Senufo Wambele masks were reserved for initiates of those traditions, who were, by definition, of the mask's ethnicity.

Ethnicity was not the sole factor determining the authority to perform a tradition. Skill could be equally important and at times overrode ethnicity when it came to deciding who should perform. For instance, one of the original members of the troupe was a Dan drummer, but his sole skill was playing his five-headed drum to accompany young women dancing the well-known Dan girls' *tématé*. Two members of the ballet, though not Dan, could drum the *tématé* more skillfully. As a result, the Dan drummer did not last long in the ballet. This points to something important about Ivorian Ballet culture—while unity might have been an expressed goal of politicians and administrators, interethnic interaction was often less cooperative or collaborative than it was competitive. "You have to be able to do what you do better than anyone else or else they leave you behind," Vado told me. "So that must inspire people," I replied. "Yes, that which you knew, it had to be magnificent!"

Vado did not seem to mind competition, as he always talked about it confidently and matter of factly as a given in his work. He rose to prominence in the

Ivorian traditional dance scene at such a young age, and then so quickly to a leading role in the national ballet, that it stands to reason that he is confident. But his time spent in the BNCI fostered his growth not only as a performer but also as a choreographer, a manager of sorts, and perhaps most important as a leader. Again, ballet experience fostered the development of skills that would prove useful to Vado later in life.

Kotchegna

After fifteen years, Vado's dissatisfaction with his role in the ballet was increasing. Like other original or early members of the troupe, he had multiple complaints. As hard as they trained and toured, it might have been expected their pay was good, but "The pay—it's not like it was sufficient. It could not pay the rent, it could not pay to feed my children." Feeling routinely tired and underpaid, Vado began contemplating leaving. It was an injury, however, that finally prompted him to make the move.

> VD: At that moment my feet and my knees were already badly worn. . . . And so I said to the director that I had to take time off to heal for three months in the village. He said, 'No you cannot go. You must continue your work.' I knew that if I continued to work, my knees would be ruined. So I said, 'Is there no small amount of money that you can give me so I can be cured?' He wouldn't do it. . . . After that, I left, I asked to resign and I left for the village.

Because of his injury and minimal salary, Vado was forced to return to Toufinga to recuperate, with little to show for all his years in the BNCI. The pressure to be seen as a "Big Man"—someone who went away, achieved great success, and returned home with gifts and money for his family and friends—was great. As Vado remembered, going home "without something—they'll say that I left with [the Ballet and went] to Europe, that I have a house in Abidjan. . . . I cannot go back there and just sit down like that." Furthermore, after all those years in cosmopolitan Abidjan and in international touring, Vado knew that he no longer belonged in his village, that his place was in the city.

Vado began to visualize options. Once cured, he returned to Abidjan and looked up others who had left the ballet, including his friend Zagbo Martin—a Bete man who sings and plays the musical bow and, like Vado, had developed skills as a choreographer and leader. The year was 1989:

> So, I asked Zagbo Martin to come help me form a new group. "We're going to do it together," I said. He said that since it was I who was the elder, and because I was [in the ballet] before everyone else, that it would have to be me that would choose the name, [and] create a group. So I chose the Mau name

from my region. I said, "Kotchegna [messenger], Kotchegna." "That's good," everyone said. . . . I had spent a long time in Abidjan, and I knew what it took to form a group.

Vado's confidence, experience, and skills, all honed in the BNCI, positioned him to take the leadership role Zagbo envisioned for him. Vado told me that it was ultimately respect for his age and stage experience that motivated his colleagues to accept his authority.

Vado did not disappoint them. In the national ballet, he had gained a great deal of experience dancing and eventually choreographing complex dance dramas that interwove various ethnic traditions. These dramas generally told stories about village life and were often moralistic, designed to educate audience members about the value of traditional Ivorian lifeways. Two pieces choreographed by the ballet's second director, Louis Akin, exemplify the form. "The Vampire," for example celebrates traditional medicine's victories over sorcery attacks that Western medicine is powerless to treat, while "The Hunt," about a hunter entering the wild, dangerous forest on a day when such entry is forbidden, stresses the importance of following the rules. Structurally both pieces typify the form. The first half tells the story through dance, reaching a happy ending that calls for celebration. The second, celebratory, portion features dances showcasing traditions from around the country and sometimes goes on longer than the narrative. The dances are always polished, choreographed, and in general filtered through the ballet's transformation of village-based dance/musical traditions.

Vado recognized that what his new group needed first was a piece to dance, so, relying on his national ballet experience, he created his first original dance drama, "The History of Mahou Masks," about the cosmological myth of masks among the Mau people. Creating this piece marked an important milestone in Vado's career and began establishing Kotchegna as a leading ensemble in the Ivorian arts community. For Vado, creativity was one of the most important factors enabling him to strike out on his own, first in Abidjan and later in New York.

Because of Vado's connections established during his time with the national ballet, things developed quickly for Kotchegna. Just two months after their debut performance, in the Ivorian port city of San Pedro, an Australian friend of Vado's arranged for their first overseas tour—a three-month series of dates in Australia. From its beginnings, Kotchegna was a transnational group, building formally on transnational state ensemble traditions and circulating transnationally on tour.

Despite this auspicious and illustrious beginning, things were not so rosy when Kotchegna returned, exhausted, to Abidjan. Laughing in an exasperated way, Vado said, "No one had work. The group [Kotchegna] was not working well. . . . When we had a little show, I had to pay for the room each time. We arranged to rent a performance space for five thousand CFA—that's not a lot of money, but we weren't earning much." Daunted by the expense of renting space, the group rehearsed and performed less and so were prevented from building their reputation and making the money they needed to continue. Vado was thus forced to look elsewhere for financial support.

Ironically, while Kotchegna struggled to find work, individual ensemble performers made ends meet by dancing in offstage, community environments, which Vado labeled "traditional." This was the only reason, he told me, that he could afford to pay for rehearsal and performance space for the ensemble and feed his children. "Sometimes people came to hire the long mask to dance traditionally, which happened a lot, and which paid for the room." In contrast, the Ghana Dance Ensemble (GDE), according to Paul Schauert, forbade its members to pursue outside work, though many risked their GDE jobs and pursued such work anyway (2015, 129ff). Vado had actually obeyed this rule while with the BNCI, but he recognized that for Kotchegna to remain viable he had to allow moonlighting.

Just as there was fluidity between staged and community performances for individual performers, there was fluidity between professional groups. Another original BNCI member, Senufo xylophone master and dancer Seguenon Kone, left the national ballet around the same time as Vado to form what became a celebrated professional ensemble that performed regularly at the Hotel Wafou in Abidjan. On occasion he hired Vado and others as extras. This fluidity has been replicated in the American context, with many performers—Vado, Sogbety, Samba, and Djo Bi, as well as Seguenon, Bi Bo Ti, and others—having their own groups but using leaders and members of other groups if the pay allows. Working together, as immigrants do today, was first established in Abidjan and is another way in which ballet culture and experience in Côte d'Ivoire set the stage for immigrant performers in the United States.

Lest I imply a linear progression from "traditional" to staged to touring, I should say that performers tended to move back and forth between community and stage. Furthermore, lest I err in characterizing a career with the national ballet as "selling out," I must reiterate that it was the traditional performances that were the more lucrative. Vado and company's experience of modernity did not progress from highly localized, unmediated live to staged, mediated, reinvented, "modern"; rather, these performance options existed simultaneously, offering performers different kinds of payback—more cash for traditional work but more opportunity and training for future migration on the stage.

The Decision to Emigrate

Despite the accolades Kotchegna was receiving, money remained scarce. In a voice that still betrays frustration, Vado said, "There was nothing. I had four children, I didn't have enough money to feed them, and they were in school." The cost of uniforms, supplies, and tuition prevents many Ivorian families from educating their children. Vado desperately wanted that opportunity, but "when we had a show, which we had a lot, there was no money to be had."

Still, it was his health that ultimately led Vado to seriously consider emigrating. For years, he had suffered from jawbone degeneration.[11] "I don't know the name, but in Mande, we call it kɔrɔ; it's the bone."[12] He explained why they call the disease "bone": "When they fix it traditionally, they take the bone out and a creature comes out with it. But we say bone because something bad comes [out] with your bone. . . . They cut out the bad part or else it spreads and becomes a tumor in your head."

Whatever the malady was called, it caused Vado to suffer greatly and resisted multiple attempts at treatment:

> I think it started in 1979; it was when I was in the ballet. It was not during our first trip [tour to Europe]; it was the second. . . . We went to Europe. . . . Yes, 1979. It was there that it began. It began when I was in Paris. . . . We were there for three months, we toured. When we arrived back in Abidjan, it was a bit serious. I had a friend who was at the hospital, who worked there. They looked at it and they said they could remove it . . . so they removed some bone from inside, from next to my teeth. My incisors there. They discovered that and they removed it. They did not take my teeth at first. After they removed it, two years passed and then it returned. I went three years with it there. I went back again to the same place. They said they should remove it again . . . so they removed it and two years later it came back again. . . . A third time. . . . I was no longer in the national ballet, and I did not have money to have it removed again.

Following three operations, each of which was only temporarily successful, Vado decided to give traditional medicine a try, making a move very common in Africa, where Western medicine and traditional medicine operate as two paradigms that are fully distinct but interwoven in the lives of people seeking cures to sometimes intractable conditions.[13] Refusing a recommended fourth surgery, Vado tried many traditional practitioners and even tried to treat himself, but nothing worked. "I know how to heal people with this, but for me it would not go away."

One of the reasons that Vado thought traditional medicine could heal him was that he attributed his affliction to a sorcery attack. I asked, "Do you think the origin was in the village like the other sicknesses?" "Yes, because each time I'm behind the mask, they make medicine that will cause illness":

> When you dance in Côte d'Ivoire—among us, the Mau, when you do something that makes everyone start talking about you, they throw, they throw medicine at you so that you fall. . . . It's serious. Here [in the United States], we call it voudou. You throw that at a man to ensure that he doesn't gain anything.

> That's how it is—it's jealousy! . . . When you dance in Africa it's like that. Yes . . . if you are not careful, you don't know where you will end up.

Vado did not reveal who victimized him or why, but the fact that sorcery caused his ailment is a given:

> And now if they talk about you all the time, then everybody becomes against you. If you have some medicine you use it against the person who is powerful. If you can do something against him, that shows that your medicine is powerful.

Adding insult to injury, as the ailment progressed and his cheek and jaw became swollen, people began to ridicule Vado:

> VD: Everyone mocked me. Women in Yopougon [the Abidjan neighborhood where the majority of Mau immigrants reside] began chanting my name. . . . In Abidjan . . . the Mau are my ethnic group. We dance with them. But my mouth was like that [holds it] all the time—a huge growth—like that. So they would sing my name: "Vado Lamakou." That means Vado has a lump on his mouth. So they made a song with that. They didn't sing it when I was there, but I heard from people what they were saying [laughs].

By early 1994, because he had suffered for fifteen years, through three operations, and his condition was only getting worse, Vado turned to a trusted source of healing, advice, and power: Gue Pelou.

> That's when I made a sacrifice to my mask. I gave a kola nut to the mask. I said, "You have to get something for me to make this go away," because I have done everything, I don't leave the mask anywhere I go, I'm with him. So he's supposed to find some way to make it go away. "And fix this. . . ." I said "I'm here and I'm not doing well. . . . Look at me. You must help me, so that I can leave Abidjan."

The mask spirit's response was swift. Soon Vado had an offer.

> That's when they came and told me they needed lots of dances from Côte d'Ivoire to come here [the United States]. That's when they asked me to come be part of it. . . . Zagbo Martin, who was in the national ballet—we were there together. . . . One day I saw him coming, saying "Vado, Vado!" I said, "What happened?" He said, "They have something—we're going to go to America. They want the long [stilt] mask. They want four long masks. They found one in Man, and they want three others." So they put the Kotchegna name in it. I took Sogbety and Moha and we all came.

"They" referred to Vado's old employer, the BNCI. A festival in the United States—Memphis in May—planned to feature Côte d'Ivoire for its 1994 event.

The Ivorian government, the primary contact and organizer, gathered over one hundred performers to represent the best of Ivorian music and dance, and naturally the national ballet was the first source it tapped. However, ever since Vado's departure, it had lacked the iconic stilt mask of the western region, so it came looking for him. Vado remembered the sacrifice to his mask and exclaimed, "God is great. He helped me. I came here."

Deciding to Stay: When Tour Becomes Immigration

By the time Vado arrived in Memphis, in May 1994, his cheek had become extraordinarily swollen:

VD: That's why I looked like I did, with the big growth like that. You saw the photo yesterday. That's what I looked like when I arrived here. . . . So when I got here, I said, "Maybe I can find something for myself." I said, 'I'm going to stay here. Going to stay here to cure this (points to his cheek). Once it's healed, if I want to return I can return. If I want to stay I'll stay."

DR: So that's the reason you stayed?

VD: Yes, that was it.

Vado's motivation was better health care; his means can be summed up in one word, ballet. His training, skills, and experience, including aesthetic approaches and repertoires associated with the staging of Ivorian music and dance, drum repair, stilt mask spirit performance, worldliness and comfort abroad—these bought Vado his ticket to Memphis.

Making the Transition

Vado was "the boss" of the stilt mask quartet that performed at Memphis in May, dancing in front of the other stilt mask spirits. As I did, Vado found the experience surreal but for different reasons. Not understanding the English narration, he had no idea that he and his fellow Ivorians were effectively playing evolutionary forebears of the musicians following them in the program. For Vado, what was surreal was that the festival had paid so much money to bring the Ivorians all the way to Memphis only to limit their performance to twenty minutes. The discourse of the script—fortunately, I would argue—went over his head.

What did not go over his head was the opportunity to remain in the United States. From Memphis, Vado made his way to New York to find Ivorian dancer Mamadou Dahoue, who had immigrated several years earlier. Because Dahoue did not yet have his papers, he was reluctant to have Vado stay with him. Instead, he connected Vado with Djoniba, a Martiniquan who runs a well-known African dance and percussion studio in the East Village neighborhood of lower Manhattan. Dahoue introduced Vado to Djoniba as a dancer and drummer, hoping that the latter would offer Vado a teaching opportunity. Instead Djoniba said, "I need someone to make drums." Vado did not consider himself a drum maker and never would have back in Côte d'Ivoire. Fortunately, though, leading his own company had broadened his experience in numerous ways. The BNCI had professional drum makers and maintainers, but running a small company required Vado to take on many tasks, one of which was making and repairing drums. In this case, his experience related to ballet was not with the BNCI but with his own Kotchegna, where the *jembe* maintenance he learned proved critical at the dawn of his new life as an immigrant:

VD: When I was In Abidjan, when my drum broke, I would fix my own *jembe*, but not someone else's and then charge money.

DR: So it was here that you began this work?"

VD: Yes, there were others who did this in Abidjan but they were not many. Since I had a group there with lots of drums. If they broke, I would do them. It was because of that that little by little I became skilled at repairing drums.

Djoniba not only hired Vado but also found him a place to live at the bargain basement price (especially for New York) of $100 a month. In his tiny studio apartment, Vado worked and lived surrounded by drumheads, drum bodies, and sundry parts. He was paid by the drum. "If I made five *jembes*," Vado explained, "a hundred dollars. If I made one, twenty dollars. . . . If I made a drum for someone else who was not Djoniba . . . one *jembe* was seventy-five dollars. But I still just made twenty, and Djoniba took the rest." Vado gave me the impression that he appreciated the Martiniquan's help and generosity but felt mildly exploited by him. As time went on, however, Djoniba proved to be extraordinarily useful.

Dance and Drum Classes: Expectation and Adaptation

Gradually Djoniba began allotting space in his business for Vado to teach dance classes, which supplemented his drum-making income and the small amounts he was beginning to make performing. In his teaching, Vado began to see that, while ballet traditions from other West African countries—especially Guinea—were well established in North American drum and dance class culture, Ivorian traditions were virtually unknown. A discourse identifying African music and how Africa should be represented in performance—with a Guinean *jembe* repertoire at its center—predated Vado's arrival. As a result, to meet market demand he had to adapt by teaching Guinean dance. Most of the drummers available to accompany his classes were either Guinean and/or had studied with Guinean drummers, which was yet another practical factor encouraging Vado to teach Guinean dance.

But Vado wanted to teach Ivorian dance and stubbornly began doing so. Given the great ignorance of Ivorian traditions, he was still forced to compromise, using recorded drums: "When I wanted to dance Ivorian, I used my little brother's cassette." Here Vado was referring to his brother Kossa, who lives in Norway. In using recordings, Vado can be seen as avoiding the prevailing discourse of African music and dance in mid-1990s New York City. He can also be seen as showcasing layers of transnational mediation: a commodity produced by an Ivorian in Europe circulated to an Ivorian in North America for teaching music and dance using repertoire and aesthetics based on the transnational Ballet genre and transmitted to young New Yorkers.

Roughly two years after his arrival, Vado grew tired of his cramped quarters above Djoniba. His experience in this room, while difficult was also fortuitous in that in 1996 he took in a roommate who would influence his career. Punctuating his words with occasional laughter, Vado reminisced:

> When it rained, I had to put up plastic. When it rained, it rained right into the room. . . . And it was a little bed. . . . One day, a guy arrived at Djoniba's by the name of Madou Dembele. He's a good drummer who can play Ivorian beats. . . . He's from Côte d'Ivoire. I was happy–I said, "Ah. . . ." I didn't have a drummer [who knew Ivorian rhythms]. So [Madou] moved in to my place. Two people in that little bed, for a long time. . . . Then Madou got a girlfriend . . . and he left. Same thing for me. . . . I had a Japanese girlfriend and I moved in with her.

Madou Dembele's arrival was a major influence on the development of Vado's career. Though originally from Mali, Madou grew up in Côte d'Ivoire and knew some Ivorian rhythms. "You didn't have a drummer who could do Ivorian rhythms until Dembele?" I asked. "Even he couldn't do them all," Vado replied. "He does only Mande—he does not know how to do other things. So I danced the rhythms *soliya* and *Mandiani* and I danced *kuku* steps as well. I had to do something."

Conforming with expectation and relying on available resources not only led Vado to adapt his dance practices; it also forced him to draw on his experience and diversify the work he would do. For example, although his expertise was in dance and he had drummed little since leaving Toufinga for Abidjan in his teens, to make ends meet in the United States he began leading drum classes and performing on the *jembe*. Vado's increased focus on drumming brings to mind the story of Michael Babatunde Olatunji, the Yoruba man who in 1950 immigrated to the United States from Nigeria, first to attend Morehouse College and then to earn a graduate degree in public administration at New York University. Prior to his arrival, Olatunji, who did not come from a drumming lineage, had little drumming experience. In what has become a legend, however, he not only picked up African drumming in the United States but transformed himself into an iconic figure whose recording *Drums of Passion* became a defining text of African music in the American imagination (Charry 2005, 2–3). There is less irony in Vado's story. He did have drumming experience prior to immigrating, and he was clearly defined as a performer, albeit a dancer, already accustomed to representing Africa on stage. The subtle connection, however, is that like Olatunji Vado strategically adapted to his American context by conforming to a common discourse—the stereotype of the African drummer—which by the 1990s would be most perfectly met by playing the iconic *jembe*.

The division of labor in a large ensemble like BNCI, which was big enough for performers to specialize as drummers or dancers, and which had technical staff for tasks like drum repair, was not replicated in Vado's Ensemble Kotchegna. "In the BNCI I did not play drums," Vado explained. "I let it go and I only danced there. But when I left to create a group for myself, sometimes the drummers would not be there, and I was obligated to play." In this sense, it was his post-BNCI experience of leading his own ensemble, that filled out Vado's skill set in a way that would prove useful in his immigrant life. Profiting from the *jembe*'s increasing popularity, Vado has continued setting up and repairing *jembes*, most frequently working with an importer named Aristide. This provides him with a significant portion of his income. Teaching *jembe* classes also remains important. "I can't let work be left only to work involving dance," he said, indicating that without his *jembe* work his dance income would not be sufficient to his needs. The popularity of the *jembe* thus has helped Vado lead a successful life as an immigrant. Repairing, tuning, and setting up *jembes* is Vado's most consistent work.

Healed

Relying heavily on Djoniba in his early years, Vado was able to make use of his ballet skills, if not to thrive, then at least to survive, in his new immigrant life. Survival, however, continued to be threatened by the illness that initially drove him to stay in the United States. Several months into his stay with Djoniba, the degeneration of his jawbone and the swelling of his cheek continued to worsen to the point that something had to be done. Djoniba's wife offered to take Vado to the dentist, but he was afraid that lacking papers and insurance would put him at great risk. Djoniba suggested that Vado create a pseudonym and with this solution in hand, to the dentist they went.

While he did not admit to this at the time, the dentist who examined Vado later confided in him that he had never seen anything like the combination of symptoms Vado was presenting. He told Vado to go to New York University's Bellevue Hospital, where he worked. There it was concluded that a major operation was necessary. The dentist told Vado, "You have to cut out a piece of your jaw, and if you do not do so you won't live more than another five years."

A series of office visits ensued, each time the dentist accepting payment of just $20, in preparation for the operation. He was willing to operate only if Vado had someone who would take financial responsibility in case anything went wrong. Djoniba, Vado fondly remembered, was willing to take this responsibility to help his friend.

Vado showed me with his hands how the surgeons did the operation, first cutting across the bottom of his jaw and peeling back his face and then replacing many of his teeth with someone else's. I listened wide-eyed, unprepared for what was coming next. "You know the chain on a bicycle? They put that right here," Vado said as he pointed to the hinge in his jaw. Three months later, he was back under the knife. "In the second operation . . . they took bone from back here," he said as he pointed to his lower hip, "and put it up here in my jaw. And they put [these two bones] together. . . . [Later] when they put the bone in, they took the chain out." When Vado woke up, he did not know whether it was the same or another day. Djoniba came to visit, followed by Mamadou Dahoue. "When I saw Mamadou, he started crying like a baby. He started crying, and that scared me too," he said.

I listened raptly as Vado told this story. Most amazing to me was the good humor with which he recalled such a painful, trying period. As with so many other health challenges, he seems unfazed by the threats to his body. I had always noticed that Vado's jaw seemed a little uneven. At this point in our conversation, he showed me exactly how the shape of the reconstructed part juts out a bit and doesn't quite look the same as the other side. He also showed me the graft they used with skin from his leg to cover his new jaw. My admiration for him grew even deeper with this conversation.

According to Vado, "This all took place between 1994 and 1998. For four years, I had no teeth on the bottom. I ate with these four teeth (on his far left side). Four years." Finally in 1998, the hospital called to schedule the final operation, replacing his teeth. Again someone had to take financial responsibility; this time it was his girlfriend. The operation took place, and it seemed that Vado was finally in the clear.

Amazingly, Vado worked throughout the period of his bone illness, not only repairing drums but also teaching drum and dance classes and performing. Gue Pelou was becoming especially well known in many quarters of the New York dance world, seen regularly not just with Kotchegna but with other groups such as the Mask Dance Company. The week following the last operation on his jaw, Vado had a show at the Brooklyn Art Museum, in a series called *Dance Africa*. While performing he suffered an injury that would force him to take a break. "At *Dance Africa*," he said in a high falsetto, "I broke my Achilles! They fixed my teeth, and now I have no leg!" Our ringing laughter filled the room. I distinctly remember that moment as one of many in which Vado's personal character moved me; he truly is a model of persistence and transcendence of physical challenge.

And yet, while he manages somehow to keep his sense of humor about this injury, losing income is a serious issue for Vado, affecting not only him and his wife Lisa, who struggle to afford life in expensive Manhattan, but also his family back in Côte d'Ivoire:

> When I broke my Achilles, I had to take several weeks off. But I could still play drums and with that I could still pay for my children's school in Africa. ... If I had left it like that I could not work and that's not good. I have to earn something to feed my family and also I pay for my family's house in Africa [in the Abidjan neighborhood of Yopougon]. I pay and my children live there.

"That's Africa": Family and Money

The time that Vado and I spent together was punctuated—indeed, constantly interrupted—by his cell phone ringing. I commented on this phenomenon in my field notes:

> 11-24-08. Vado's cell rings seemingly constantly. While he has had calls from a sister in Africa (like Djo Bi, when it's one of those calls coming in, he says, "C'est l'afrique" [It's Africa], as if the whole continent is calling him, and they both react the same way—often not answering, and commenting, "Toujours l'argent." [Always money]), and African American drum purchasers, almost every call seems to be from another Ivorian immigrant, most of whom are not local. Eric called from Florida. Some woman called from Syracuse requesting a phone card so she could call an ill relative [back in Côte d'Ivoire]. Aristide called to drop off some drums for repair. The cell phone emerges as a terribly important means of community maintenance for these far-flung folks (field notes, 24).

Ivorian performers use cell phones to maintain community not only as immigrants but also as part of a larger transnational network, including family members back home, with whom they regularly communicate. A great many of these phone calls have to do with the flow of cash through the transnational Ivorian community. When the phone rings and Vado sighs, "Eeh–c'est l'Afrique!" he is sharing an experience with other members of the Ivorian immigrant community. Transnational beings, they inhabit their new immigrant world and their old home country simultaneously. Many make regular trips home and financially support their families.

At every turn Ivorian immigrants encounter expectation: discourses of what Africa is and how it should be represented on one hand and social pressure to succeed and share the fruits of success on the other. All of the immigrants I know send money home regardless of whether they can afford their own expensive lives in the United States. The importance of remittance in Vado's life, and in the broader transnational Ivorian community, cannot be overstated.

Vado not only sends money regularly but also arranges for family members to join him so that they can help him with his financial responsibilities. His "C'est l'Afrique!" uttered with a sigh and a slight grin, somehow captures both the comedy and tragedy of his impossible fix—struggling to survive in New York while sending home money that he can little afford but that, from the family's perspective, is never enough.

Reprisals when family members believe money is being hoarded in America frequently take the form of sorcery attacks. I once asked Vado whether everyone back home was content with the fact that Gue Pelou was in New York:

VD: Many people are not happy. That's why they always attack me. Always voudou.

DR: Even from Côte d'Ivoire?

VD: Yeah . . . my family—eh!—they think I make a lot of money here and I don't give it to them! But I don't get anything here. Anything I get here, it's a bill, to pay a bill!

DR: I know, it's like that in the United States!

VD: But the little I give to them, they think I have a lot but I give them only a little. . . . It's hard! I've got my kids, they are going to school. Thirty, twenty-five, nineteen, seventeen [their ages]. . . . My seventeen-year-old plays soccer. . . . My girl who is nineteen is in secretary school. . . . All that is expensive.

As Geschiere writes of Cameroonian families who become spread across multiple continents, those who remain at home *expect* to profit from the success of those who emigrate. This can then extend fear of sorcery, or witchcraft, across continental borders. Geschiere writes, "This stretching of intimacy dramatically increases the scope of witchcraft fears. Disappointing the family remains extremely dangerous, even if one is a great distance from home" (2013, 62).

When Kossa, Vado's brother whose recordings allowed Vado to teach Ivorian dance, came to the United States, he met a Norwegian woman who invited him to Norway, where he now works as a drummer and, like Vado, sends money back home (another brother has since joined Kossa in Norway). As for increasing the cash flow to Toufinga and Abidjan, it was in part with this in mind that Vado worked hard to bring his nephews Sogbety Diomande and Moha Dosso to the United States in 1997. Dosso had assumed the directorship of Ensemble Kotchegna in Vado's absence, and Sogbety, though just a teenager, had become one of the ensemble's featured performers. Vado knew they were ready for North American stages, and he desperately needed relief from the burden of his family's support:

VD: Like Sogbety here and Moha . . . you have to get someone near you. Because Sogbety's father is my big brother, we are of the same mother, same father. I was doing everything [I could to support my brother]! [It's as if they think] I can't do anything good here. "Send me money! Send me money!" I stopped everything; I took three months. Finally I got Sogbety here, and [then I thought] "Maybe I will rest a little bit. . . ." I saved money to pay for Sogbety, to get his visa and everything . . . now [that] Sogbety [is] here . . . I don't pay anything for [my brother] anymore. Sogbety's supposed to do that. So that's why [these past] ten years have been good for me, now.

    Moha [is] helping [on the] other side, too! Moha is my big sister's son. . . . That's why it's good when they are both working, doing well. If I have a problem . . . they help me, too! When I was sick, they came in . . . that's good.

DR: I hadn't understood that before, that when you invite family members here, they can help you support the family back home.

VD: Yeah! If everything is on you, it's no good. You have to support yourself, you have to support your people, your parents' people—it's a lot! Because when you are somewhere [far away], everyone wants something from you.

In Vado's family, economic concerns drive artistic and religious practice, exemplifying the "relationships between aesthetic production and economy" that Paulla Ebron urges scholars to better track (Ebron 2002, 20).

For Vado's family, economic concerns drive artistic and religious practice. Both Sogbety and Moha are trained stilt mask spirit performers, having been initiated in Toufinga and then trained in ballet-style stilt mask while with Kotchegna in Abidjan. After spending several years in New York, the nephews moved to the Midwest, Sogbety to Mansfield, Ohio, and Moha first to Cincinnati and eventually to Scottsburg, Indiana. From these locations, one might say, they are able to increase Gue Pelou's audience and market range. With Vado at the helm, all three dance the "same" mask, again reinforcing that the mask and the costume are not the *nya*, or mask spirit; rather, the *nya* is the spiritual power at the base of the performance. Trained in the staged version of this religious tradition, Sogbety and Moha have been able to take advantage of economic opportunities that in turn ease their Uncle Vado's burden.

For logistical help in raising money for his nephews' immigration, Vado approached a New York ensemble that he had danced with early on, the Mask Dance Company. By definition Ivorian, the Mask Dance Company, led by founder/director Bley Zaguehi, regularly featured professional musicians, dancers, and mask performers from Côte d'Ivoire. However, although it arranged visas and transportation, it did not pay for them. "You pay them, and they arrange for people to come," said Vado:

VD: I didn't have enough work.... I was only doing *jembe* repair. Dance classes weren't working because there were no drummers, and people didn't know Ivorian [rhythms].... Everyone back in Côte d'Ivoire thought that I had lots of money. That's why I cut off all the things I was doing for Moha's father. We had a big argument. Once [Moha] was here, he could [help his father]. I stopped all the things I was doing for [Moha's father] after two months. We had a big fight.

The months of hard work and sacrifice required to procure Sogbety's and Moha's invitations to perform with the Mask Dance Company, including raising money for visas and plane tickets, were little appreciated by some of Vado's family back in Toufinga and Abidjan.

Anthrax

Once Sogbety and Moha were settled in and finding somewhat regular work, and Vado had recovered his investment and regained his health, a period of several years began that might be considered Vado's heyday in New York. His reputation spread as Kotchegna began securing more regular "traditional," ballet-style work and he began innovating, stretching the boundaries of mask performance by collaborating with a variety of artists, from tap dancer Tamango (an immigrant from French Guiana via Paris) to jazz artists to a *capoeira* group in which Gue Pelou danced to *berimbau*. Gue Pelou graced the pages of the *New Yorker* (Karlsson 2001) and the *New York Times* (Kisselgoff 2001), and at turns Kotchegna and Vado alone began performing more regularly in New York and touring more widely. Locally Vado was dancing at venues such as Joe's Pub, the Guggenheim Museum, The Kitchen. Lincoln Center, the African Museum, and the American Stock Exchange. Touring took him to Disney World, the Kennedy Center, and the Georgia Dome, as well as to Summerdance in Santa Barbara. Increasingly, he was performing internationally, from Montreal to Monterey, from Greece to Guyana.

While Kotchegna, being a large ensemble, was less nimble in international travel, it became ever busier with shows all over New York. Out-of-state shows were also picking up, and by 2005 the troupe had performed at universities and festivals all over the country, including Massachusetts, Minnesota, North Carolina, Florida, Ohio, Pennsylvania, and Maine. Vado's dance classes were becoming more popular as well, and, aside from his regular classes at Djoniba, he began teaching at the illustrious Alvin Ailey American Dance Theater. He continued teaching *jembe* and setting up and repairing drums, which remained his most regular income.

Depending on whose story you believe, it was working with drums that either directly or indirectly led to Vado's next major crisis. On February 16, 2006, while dancing on stage with Kotchegna at Mansfield University's Steadman

Theater in Mansfield, Pennsylvania, Vado collapsed.[14] Emergency officials transported him to Soldiers and Sailors Memorial Hospital in the nearby city of Wellsboro. Two days later, following extensive blood tests, he was transferred to Robert Packer Hospital in Sayre, Pennsylvania. On February 20, officials identified signs of anthrax in his blood samples, which were promptly sent to the Pennsylvania Department of Health for more extensive testing. After state officials confirmed the diagnosis, a public health investigation and eradication process began. The New York City Department of Health and Mental Hygiene, the Centers for Disease Control and Prevention, and the FBI began coordinating efforts to deal with "the first case of naturally occurring inhalation anthrax in the United States since 1976" (Chan, 2006). To state that it was ironic that Vado—who had immigrated to the United States for access to better health care and better health—was the victim of this historic, life-threatening illness would be a gross understatement.

Anthrax. The word itself inspired fear, and the story was quickly picked up by the national press. The *New York Times* ran a retrospective article about the anthrax attacks that occurred in the aftermath of 9/11. The television show *Animal Planet* featured the story in its sensationalistic series *Killer Outbreaks*, in which Dr. Nche Zama, one of Vado's surgeons, "says starkly, 'His lungs looked what I would describe as angry,'" (Genzlinger 2011). Although it was quickly recognized that Vado's case had nothing to do with terrorism, fear of biological warfare and the rarity of naturally occurring anthrax kept this story in the headlines with Vado at its center.

But how did he contract anthrax? There are at least two answers to this question: one that involves mainstream, first-world health paradigms and a second that involves a West African model of health care that accounts for profound interactions between living bodies and spirits. According to the official story, investigators placed the blame on unprocessed animal hides that, they claim, Vado brought into the United States when he returned from a trip to Côte d'Ivoire on December 21, 2005, and stored in his storage space/workshop in a building near the foot of the Manhattan Bridge in Brooklyn. On February 15, 2006, Vado "processed" the skins, removing their fur with a razor blade, which released the anthrax bacteria into the air. This highly contagious agent, having contaminated the space, lodged itself in his lungs, causing his near fatal collapse the next night in Pennsylvania.

Vado confirmed parts of this story. "I went to Africa to get new stuff to bring back," he told me. "New drums, and two skins I came back with." Here, however, his explanation diverged from the official account. Vado insisted that in December 2005, just after returning from Côte d'Ivoire, he set up two drums using the skins he brought with him which he subsequently played in various settings.

VD: I have fixed drums like this many times.... It was in February, when I took skins from those people in Queens here that my problems began. They say I brought skins from Africa with anthrax on them. But these skins I didn't have a problem with because they cleaned them already [before] I got them—they put them under the sun in Africa.... So this time I went to pick up skins from those people in Queens. American skins. They say the two skins I brought from Africa ... made me sick. But two months passed already after I fixed drums with those skins. I didn't have any problem that time.

DR: Did you say that to—

VD: Yes I told them [the FBI] that.

DR: What did they say?

VD: They said that's not true. But when I [arrived back in New York from Abidjan] they checked everything at the airport.

DR: So you think there was some other cause?

VD: Yes. When I came from Africa I think maybe African people did something to me to make me sick. That's what I was thinking. Because people don't like when you go far away, they don't like you. When you're going somewhere better than them, they don't like it. They want to do something to bring you down. That's what I was thinking.

Vado's explanation involves the common West African belief and health discourse that people are vulnerable to malicious "attacks" that can involve pharmacological use of plants and other natural phenomena and/or the negative use of spiritual energy, or sorcery. His success makes him vulnerable to such attacks, which he unequivocally believes was the cause of his anthrax.

Given the number of times Vado believes he has been attacked and consequently made gravely ill, I found it remarkable how unfazed he seems. While not denying that anthrax nearly killed him, he told his story with a smile that seemed both serene and playful; he seemed existentially detached from the constant threat of harm. Moreover, he believes that his mask spirit keeps him safe, and he takes comfort in the fact that, despite many attempts, jealous competitors have not been able to bring him down. He stays one step ahead of them in his own spiritual preparations before each trip to Côte d'Ivoire, but he holds the somewhat fatalistic view that when it is time he will go.

Friends have advised Vado to stay away from Africa altogether because "When I go to Africa, something happens," he says. However, he returned unscathed from his trip home to make sacrifices in 2010:

VD: Only this time when I went [nothing happened]. People told me, don't go don't go! But I said, if I don't go to my home how ... I don't want to stop going to my country because they can make me sick. If it were time for me to be dead, I would be dead. If it's not time, then they can do everything, and I will be back. Yeah [smiles]. So that's why I went this year, to make a sacrifice. I went everywhere. If I want to go, I go there.

DR: And this time you didn't have any problems?

VD: I went and I'm here.

DR: And I imagine that you did some preparations before you traveled?

VD: Yes. . . . I did some here and I did some there when I arrived.

DR: And so that worked?

VD: I believe it worked.

I find his answer to my last question telling. When I asked whether his advance preparations had worked, he might simply have said yes. Instead, he invoked belief—"I *believe* it worked"—underscoring a key element of his health care model. I had encountered this before, multiple times, in my research in Côte d'Ivoire. For example, when we were in the middle of some relatively dangerous research involving a sorcery-catching mask in the western region in the 1990s, my research assistant, Biemi Gba Jacques, told me that his Christian faith rendered him invulnerable to sorcery; in other words, he didn't *believe* in sorcery, so it could not affect him (Reed 2003). Clearly Vado believes he is vulnerable because he attributes many health problems to sorcery, but just the same he believes he can fend off the sorcerers' ultimate aim–to take his life.

Anthrax might not have killed Vado, but it was devastating to his then thriving career, halting everything, as he painfully recalled: "From 2000 to 2003, that was a good time—we were doing lots of things. A lot of good shows during that time." Kotchegna had so many bookings that they needed no rehearsals to maintain a high level of performance. Then came anthrax. "Did you lose students then?" I asked. "Oh, yes, a lot!" he said. "Those who were in my company, I lost some of them, but those who [were] not in my company but just took classes, I lost many of them." Amazingly, though, Vado returned to work quickly. "After one month I began dancing and I did shows. When you do shows, you have to be at your best. But when you do classes, you don't have to be in such great shape."

More devastating than losing students and performers was losing all of his earthly belongings. Vado's apartment in the East Village, his space in Brooklyn, and even his friend Justin Kafundo's apartment, where Vado had been recording a CD, were completely emptied out and decontaminated. Everything Vado and his wife Lisa owned was carted off and destroyed, without financial compensation. The *New York Times* described the cleanup:

Workers in hazardous-materials suits are passing high-efficiency particulate air-filtered vacuum machines over floors, and soaking hard surfaces with a bleach solution and rinsing them off, usually after an hour, with soap and water. Workers are also collecting hair and dust samples in petri dishes and waiting to see if spores develop after 24–48 hours. Some materials that cannot be cleaned, like certain carpets, will be wrapped in plastic, sprayed with bleach, boxed, sprayed and then incinerated (Chan and Moynihan 2006).

Vado was nearly finished with a new CD he had been recording at Kafando's apartment, which was located in the same building where Vado and Lisa lived. He had dedicated months of work to this project. Recalling, Vado said, "This was around the time that I had hurt my leg and the doctor said you can't dance. So I worked on my music at that time since I could still sing and drum. If I cannot dance, I must sing."

Replaceable and irreplaceable things were destroyed. Vado especially mourned the loss of his CD project, including the original tracks and the recording equipment:

> When I became ill, they said [Justin] had come into my place to get my tracks and take them into his studio [so they also] took all of his things. They took all of my things and all of his things and burned them. It cost him two hundred thousand dollars or something. They burned everything. . . . That was four years ago and he's still in the process of suing. They took all of his things, they took all of my things . . . they took all of my things from my storage . . . they said there was anthrax on everything. My CD—there were a thousand copies in a box. They said there was anthrax on the CDs. No clothes. Nothing left inside. They took everything and said they had to burn it. All my stuff.

For eight years, Vado and Lisa have worked hard reconstructing their lives. As of this writing, in 2014, he is back teaching at both Djoniba and Alvin Ailey; Kotchegna does its annual *Kekene* concert and tours to festivals and colleges in the Northeast; Lisa, whom Vado married in 2001, has become his dedicated manager; and Vado keeps on making *jembes*. His world is transnational in many respects—social, professional, familial, and spiritual. He must continually propitiate ancestors who have the power to injure him or make him ill. According to folklorist Bonnie O'Connor (1994), culture and belief are often key factors in health care choices for people living in the United States. Although her focus is the so-called alternative health community, her thesis resonates with Vado's perspective. An understanding of Vado neither as performer nor as immigrant is complete without an understanding of his beliefs. All of these are inextricably linked with his views on and experiences of illness and health.

These days, Vado's knees, having supported his dancing for nearly sixty years, are suffering. Ever the optimist, he nevertheless recognizes that his time as a regular performer is on the wane. Of course, that means that his ability to support his transnational family is nearing its end as well. And it should come as no surprise that his solution to this state of affairs interweaves performance, immigration, family, and health. He is working on obtaining visas for two of his children—a daughter and a son—who are professional performers. If he is successful, the Ivorian immigrant community will be "renewed" on North American stages for another generation.

ACT II
SAMBA DIALLO

5 "Culture Brings Everybody Together"
Samba Diallo's Ayoka

A STEAMY AFTERNOON in suburban Atlanta, late July 2010 (PURL 5.1). A crowd of around one hundred people took seats in an air-conditioned space inside the Smyrna Cultural Center in anticipation of Samba Diallo's annual showcase, *Ayoka*. Samba danced in to the right of the audience followed by four female African American dancers in matching handwoven outfits. "Soma sa sa ngole na woyo ye ke" (The morning rain comes gently) sang Samba in Mauka; the dancers responded in kind. All five danced past the seated drummers, who began to play the Maninka rhythm *kuku*. The dancers took position on the stage, with Samba in front, ready to lead the group through a predetermined series of breaks.

Walking toward the dancers, lead drummer Papa Diarra signaled the first break with his *jembe*. Extraordinarily creative, Papa often varied the standard signal (usually played x•xx•x•xx•xx•x) to mark each dance transition. Even his first signal was altered—the stock phrase surrounded by improvised ornaments. After several fairly standard transitions, Papa played a more cryptic version, leaving out several beats of the phrase, but the dancers were tuned in and followed his lead. From that point on, Papa modified each transition signal with inventive improvisations. He always retained enough of the integrity of the phrase for it to be recognizable, which is crucial in ballet-style performance. In sync and smiling, the dancers moved through seven or eight breaks before Samba led them off with *kuku* still sounding.

Then, ducking under the doorway and dramatically dancing past the audience to the stage, the Mau stilt mask spirit Gue Pelou arrived. As the drummers continued *kuku*, the stilt mask spirit unleashed his characteristic falsetto scream. With Gue Pelou now center stage, Papa turned toward the drummers and played gradually quickening, evenly spaced slaps—the most common technique for speeding up the tempo. The drummers responded, and the tempo became hotter in preparation for Gue Pelou's demonstrations. Papa and the mask spirit joined forces for a very long break featuring coordination between drum strikes and the mask spirit's arms and hands, accentuated by fly whisks, or his rapidly moving extra-long legs. Several shorter breaks followed until the end of the segment.

Samba's interweaving of difference that characterizes ballet and is fundamental to the ballet discourse of unity was in full flower here. A Mau mask spirit from Côte d'Ivoire danced to a Maninka rhythm from Guinea played on Maninka instruments by Guineans, Ivorians, African Americans, and Liberians in suburban Atlanta. Simultaneously expressed was transnationalism and nationalism, the latter unmistakable in the huge backdrop featuring the colors of the Ivorian flag.

Each year Samba Diallo produces *Ayoka*, featuring his dance troupe Attoungblan along with members of the Ivorian immigrant performer community, other West Africans, and Americans. This event exemplifies Samba's performative and promotional strategy, which I see as a discourse of unity. Just as with Vado Diomande's discourse, however, Samba's is complex, simultaneously nationalist and transnational, universal and particular, and in its pursuit he engages other, supporting discourses. For example, in his promotional materials, he strategically employs terms such as *history*, *culture*, and *tradition* to tell us that his work is anchored in a kind of ancient wisdom that attracts some Americans to African dance.

As with Vado's *Kekene*, I approach my analysis of Samba's *Ayoka* in two parts: printed, verbal discourse in the form of posters, business cards, and the like; and performance, including instrumentation, rhythm, repertoire, performers, and performance speech. Ultimately all of these are informed by Samba's beliefs about culture, influenced by his experience in the Ivorian ballet. As Samba said at the end of the 2010 *Ayoka*: "Culture brings everybody together." Explicitly challenging a racialized discourse of Africa, he said that "music is a door through which we see through the color, we see through the race." Interestingly, both his universalist and nationalist discourses are in some ways more extensively articulated than are Vado's. Performance serves as a space in which seemingly incompatible extremes can coexist, rendering Samba's *Ayoka* a complex, polysemic phenomenon.

Verbal Discourse

What's in a Name?

As for Vado, naming for Samba is an exercise in ballet-style interweaving of difference. For performances Samba gathers his best students under the name Attoungblan—the Baule name for the famous "talking drums" of the Akan linguistic and cultural family (of which the Baule are one group). *Attoungblan* is a distinctively Ivorian reference for these drums (which in English are better known by the Asante name *atumpan*) and is furthermore an explicit link to the Baule, the most powerful Ivorian ethnic group, who dominated Ivorian politics from the late colonial era through the first forty years of independence. The late Félix Houphouët-Boigny, who served as president of Côte d'Ivoire from 1960 to 1993, was Baule, which as a reference in certain contexts can be read as a nationalist positioning. For Samba there is also a sense of the personal in his choice of name, given that his mother was Baule although he did not grow up in a Baule environment and does not identify as such. Fond of taglines, on business cards, posters, and the like Samba describes Attoungblan as "Ivory Coast Dance Theater," and/or an "Educational Cultural Art Entertainment Group." The first stresses entertainment and performance; the second clearly emphasizes cultural education. To a greater extent than my other consultants, Samba sees education as part of his work; indeed, his business card calls him a "cultural art educator."

To name his annual concerts, Samba borrowed a word, *Ayoka* (thank you), from the Bete language (one of the sixty Ivorian languages he does not speak), explaining his choice this way:

> The whole word [*ayoka*] means "Thank you very much." When someone gives you something and you are happy, [you say], "Eh, *ayoka*." I chose the name because it's a day for knowing African culture, Côte d'Ivoire, here in America. "We are grateful [to you] for bringing African culture here—*ayoka*."

Having grown up in multiethnic urban settings and later trained in ballet, not to mention his personal, postethnic identity, it was natural for Samba to label his shows using a language he does not speak; arguably, Samba can identify equally with any Ivorian language.

Printed Promotional Discourse

Samba thinks carefully about his verbal representational choices. I asked him why he chose the label *African* for his *Ayoka* poster, "An Evening Celebrating the History of African Art and Culture through DRUMS MUSIC SONG DANCE":

> Even if the emphasis is on Côte d'Ivoire, it should include all of Africa. Here [in the United States] in particular people know Africa. They don't know Guinea or Côte d'Ivoire [but] they know Africa. So when you say "African culture," they know that. But the culture of Côte d'Ivoire? What's that? Côte d'Ivoire? . . . We celebrate African culture . . . Everything is based on Côte d'Ivoire, but we may have guests—[maybe some] from Ghana, some from elsewhere. So people are going to come and they will say, "You are talking about Côte d'Ivoire, but we see a Guinean dance there!" But all that is Africa.

In Samba's performance-defining discourse in names and taglines, he strategically considers his audience, which, he reasons, will be more familiar with and respond more readily to "Africa" than to a particular African country. For the few Americans who are more educated about African music and might recognize elements from multiple countries, he employs "African culture" in defense of his representational choices. Once again, while it is tempting to assume that epistemologically the generalized "African culture" might only appear in the context of immigrant America, in fact this sort of transnational, continental identification occurs in Côte d'Ivoire as well. As Samba said, "Even in Côte d'Ivoire, when we have a presentation, it's normal to invite people from other countries to be part of it." However, on the same poster advertising a performance of "African culture," one finds "Ivory Coast Exposé." Just like Vado, Samba promotes his performances in both general terms ("Africa") and nationalist terms simultaneously.

In addition to interlaying nationalist and universalist discourse, Samba strategically crafts promotional language that he believes will appeal to North American audiences. His brochure for the "Ivory Coast Attoungblan Dance Theatre" describes his group like this:

> *Attoungblan* are the sacred and powerful twin messenger drums from the Akan tribe of Côte d'Ivoire (known as the Ivory Coast). The Attoungblan Ivory Coast Dance Theatre represents these sacred messengers, bringing you an exciting experience of this culture through dance and drumming.

Such a description typifies in some respects the discourse used to promote West African music and dance in the United States. Certain keywords—*sacred, powerful, exciting,* and *culture*—are ubiquitous in African performance promotional discourse because they strike the right tone for luring in American audiences hungry for experience of the exotic.

Images

By far the national receives greater visual emphasis in Samba's posters, flyers, business cards, and even my laminated *Ayoka* "press pass." Without exception the orange, green, and white of the Ivorian flag make up the color scheme, and nearly all of the advertising centrally features a map of Côte d'Ivoire. The *Ayoka* promotional poster in figure 5.1 serves as a case in point.

Discourse on Stage

The 2010 *Ayoka* was smaller than subsequent versions, which took place in larger venues and featured more Ivorian performers. The budget was small in 2010; Samba paid out $2,000 for the event, including $200 for every performer except for master drummer Papa Diarra, who received $300. The show brought in just $675, prompting Samba's family/sponsors to vow support for future shows.

The audience of about seventy was roughly half of African descent and half European American, and the performers were exclusively of African descent. Still, Samba's promotional discourse was all about unity—explicitly including racial unity—and it was prominent in the speech he delivered at the end of the performance. *Ayoka* is profoundly influenced by the discourse of ballet, bringing together people, genres, instruments, and traditions of disparate origins in the service of a larger ideological goal.

Figure 5.1 *Ayoka* 2010 poster.

Instrumentation

Samba follows the ballet norm by performing all Ivorian music on *jembes* and accompanying *dundun*. While the Maninka *jembe* rhythm *kuku* was featured at nearly every Ivorian immigrant performance I attended during my research, never had it dominated a show like it did the 2010 *Ayoka*. One of the most common *jembe* rhythms in North America, *kuku* is somewhat of a fallback for Ivorian immigrants, who at times substitute it for less familiar rhythms that fewer drummers, dancers, and audience members may know. Whether in *jembe* classes taught by Guineans or Ivorians or in drum circles in Midwestern meadows or on California beaches, *kuku* is one of the rhythms most likely to be heard. Having studied with Ivorian immigrants for nine years as of this book's writing, I no longer find it surprising that a mask like Gue Pelou dances to *kuku*. Even so, back in 2006, when I was first introduced to sacred Mau stilt mask dancing to a popular Maninka *jembe* rhythm associated with leisure and celebration, I was astonished. This broke every rule I had been taught about what music is appropriate for the sonic manifestation of a mask spirit. I learned that ballet operates by different rules.

One would expect nothing but *jembe/dundun* (and perhaps other drums commonly played with them, such as the *bugarabu*, *sangban*, and *kenkeni*) to accompany *kuku*. But for non-Maninka rhythms, *jembe/dundun* replaces single-stringed harps (e.g., for the Senufo Bolohi) or other types of drum ensembles (e.g., Mau Gue Pelou and Guro Zauli). Transposition of these and other rhythms is a standard ballet practice.

For some of the *Ayoka* 2010 dances, Guinean *jeli* Kierno Diabaté added his heptatonic wooden xylophone, or *jelibala*, to the mix. The addition of the *jelibala* often represents not just an interethnic mixing of instruments but also a blending of disparate musical and social systems. It would be highly unusual, for example, to see a Maninka *jeli*—a hereditary role that is part of the Mande occupational caste system—playing a *bala* along with noncaste drummers for a mask spirit performance in a Mau village. The ballet stage is where such mixing has become the norm. At *Ayoka* 2010 Liberian women added another dimension—gourd rattles with beaded string nets, which are common to Liberia and western Côte d'Ivoire. The result was a mix of instrument traditions from at least three countries in a new transnational ensemble formation.

Genre/Structure

In contrast to Vado's *Kekene*, Samba's *Ayoka* does not include a choreographed drama. Instead, it showcases non-narrative dances, including both those ethnically marked and those choreographed by Samba. Again, Samba makes heavier use than do his colleagues of *kuku* for his choreographed dances, and in some cases *kuku* is substituted for the usual rhythm accompanying an ethnically marked dance. This is not unusual, particularly when the drummers' knowledge of Ivorian rhythms is limited.

Being a dancer, Samba emphasizes choreographed dance pieces. In this, *Ayoka* is similar to *Kekene*, just *sans* narrative. In terms of dance genres, *Ayoka* is standard Ivorian immigrant ballet with some exceptions. In 2010 three Ivorian masks—Bolohi, Gue Pelou, and Zauli—were featured along with the Soli Wule mask from Guinea, which is commonly included in Ivorian immigrant performances in the United States. Like Gue Pelou, Zauli danced not to the Guro *zauli* rhythm but to *kuku*, which is further evidence of the strong Mande influence on Ivorian ballet, resulting from the dominance of Guinean Mande traditions (PURL 5.2). Also featured in the 2010 *Ayoka* was the harvest celebration rhythm *sinte* from the Boké region of Guinea. While I do not recall *sinte* in other Ivorian ballet contexts, its inclusion is not surprising given that it is relatively standard in the Guinean *jembe* repertoire—despite *Ayoka's* tagline "Ivory Coast Exposé." As Samba said to me, "We all come together" through music and dance, and he is not the least bit troubled using traditions from outside his country in his deliberately pan-African representations of Ivory Coast culture. Besides, he said, Guinea, Côte d'Ivoire—"all that is Africa."

After the six Attoungblan dancers finished yet another series of choreographed breaks to *kuku* during the 2010 *Ayoka*, Tia Webster, a young African American woman from Cincinnati, took the stage for a solo showcase (PURL 5.3). Tia had studied extensively with West African dance instructors, mostly in the Guinean *jembe* dance tradition. Papa began striking his *jembe* more forcefully, increasing its volume, while stepping toward the dancing Tia, raising the energy for a series of breaks. Tia is an extremely skilled dancer, and Papa is a giant talent on the *jembe*; yet their coordination at this moment felt looser and less precise than when Papa drummed for the troupe as a whole. More than likely, this lack of precision was due to Tia's training in Guinean dance in contrast to Papa's Ivorian ballet training and expertise.

During certain interludes between choreographed pieces featuring Attoungblan or mask dances, the musicians improvised and the Liberian women came forward. The music during these passages varied from standard rhythms such as *kuku* to what sounded to my ears like improvisatory riffing based on typical patterns. Kierno Diabate in particular kept the music flowing to avoid "dead time" between dances. During one interlude, he improvised a *jelibala* pattern on his xylophone, which Papa supported with an improvised pattern using a *jembe* and one of the *dundun* drums, both of which he played with his hands. First Gayle Fangalo and then Multhee Randall came forward to dance. Papa signaled changes in dance pattern with the standard call, and the crowd began responding with claps and cries of encouragement each time the dance shifted. Then

Kierno playfully altered the melody he was improvising and began the chorus of "Waka Waka (This Time for Africa)," the popular theme song by Colombian pop star Shakira from that year's FIFA World Cup, which was taking place that very summer in South Africa. Picking up on Kierno's cue, first Papa and then Moha, Hamidou, and several others began singing:

> Tsamina mina, eh eh
> Waka waka, eh eh
> Tsamina mina zangalewa
> This time for Africa

"Waka Waka" quotes a internationally popular song in the *makossa* style from 1986, "Zangalewa," by the group Golden Sounds from Cameroon. Again, ballet-style interweaving was taken to new extremes in this moment: a Guinean Maninka *jeli* and an Ivorian Bobo descendant from Burkina Faso singing a Colombian pop star's hit about the South African World Cup which itself was based on a Cameroonian pop song. While "Waka Waka" had stirred controversy in South Africa, with some complaining that local culture was not foregrounded in the fanfare surrounding the World Cup (Dugger 2010), in *Ayoka*'s "celebration of African culture" and its "Ivory Coast Exposé" it drew not protests but cheers from the few in the crowd who caught the reference.

Images

Just as *Ayoka*'s repertoire is dominated by Ivorian dances and masks, so its visual choices favor Ivorian imagery. Behind the performers throughout the 2010 show, a large cloth backdrop dyed in the Ivorian national colors of orange, green, and white served as a constant reminder that the show was primarily an Ivorian expression. In several dance showcases, the Attoungblan dancers wore orange, green, and white outfits (see figure 5.2). When it comes to visuals, from business cards to costumes, Samba consistently frames his work as Ivorian.

Performers

While visuals and repertoire might lead one to think that *Ayoka* is simply a performance of Ivorian nationalism, a look at the performers' demographics reveals a very different picture, one of transnational diversity but featuring only peoples of African descent. Table 5.1 lists the 2010 performers' countries (or US cities and states) of origin and their ethnicity, race, or nationality. Of the fifteen performers, only three, or 20 percent, were Ivorians. The lion's share, five, were African American (33 percent); two were Nigerian immigrants and two, Liberian immigrants; one was a Liberian American born in the United States; and two were Guineans.

"Culture Brings Everybody Together" | 137

Figure 5.2 Attoungblan dancers at *Ayoka* 2012 in Atlanta. Photograph by Christy True.

The dancers alone are a study in mobility. Every one of them but Tia Webster currently lives in Atlanta (Tia traveled to the show with Hamidou and Moha from Cincinnati), though only Raquel Clark is originally from there. The remainder of the African Americans are Atlanta transplants from elsewhere in the American East. Rounding out the group are four African immigrants, one of whom, "Michelle Nigeria," grew up in Italy. Five of the six drummers are African immigrants, and even among those five there is considerable diversity. Papa, though he grew up in Abidjan, was born of parents from Burkina Faso. In the Ivorian context, and even among Ivorian immigrants in the United States, he is regularly called a Burkinabé. Samba is "the exception" I call "postethnic," being the only Ivorian I have ever met who does not consider ethnicity his primary identity. Of the two Guineans in the troupe, one is from the forest region and the other is a northern Mande *jeli*. Von Valentine, just a teenager in 2010, is dancer Multhee Randle's son, of Liberian ancestry but born in the United States.

Samba explicitly asserts that through dance we "see through the color," so I found it noteworthy that the performers in the 2010 *Ayoka*, unlike those in Vado's *Kekene*, were all of African descent. Was this an intentional move toward kind of diasporic sensibility? I asked Samba, "In your performances, are there always only blacks?"

Table 5.1 *Ayoka* 2010 performers

Artists	Country of origin and/or US location	Nationality/race/ethnicity
Drummers/musicians (all male)		
Papa Diarra	Côte d'Ivoire; New York, NY	Ivorian; Bobo
Moha Dosso	Côte d'Ivoire; Scottsburg, IN	Ivorian; Mau
Samba Diallo	Côte d'Ivoire; Atlanta, GA	Ivorian; considers himself of both his mother's and his father's ethnicity: Abidji and Jula/Baule, respectively
Kierno Diabate	Guinea; New Orleans, LA	Guinean; Maninka
Hamidou Koivogui	Guinea; Cincinnati, OH	Guinean
Von Valentine	Liberia; Atlanta, GA	Liberian American
Dancers (all female)		
Gayle Fangalo	Liberia	Liberian
Multhee Randall	Liberia	Liberian
Tia Webster	Cincinnati, OH	African American
Ingrid Chiles*	Greenville, SC	African American
Nicole Jackson*	Dayton, OH	African American
Bridget Shelton*	Tennessee (city unknown)	African American
Raquel Clark*	Atlanta, GA	African American
Nkoyo Iffong*	Nigeria via Utah	Nigerian
Michelle Nigeria (stage name; née Michelle Giuggia)	Nigeria via Italy	Nigerian

*Member of Attoungblan.
Note: The categorization in the right-hand column is admittedly problematic in that it conflates nationality, race, and ethnicity. Given that this show was framed as a performance of Ivorian music and dance, my point is simply to demonstrate to some extent the diversity of the performers' identities. For African performers, I note how they identify in terms of nationality and ethnicity when I know both; performers who identify as African American are listed as such.

SAMBA DIALLO (SD): In the beginning, I would sometimes use white drummers, but some people hiring the group would complain that they wanted "authentic" and/or "traditional" African dance.

DANIEL REED (DR): But since you did sometimes perform with whites, does this matter to you—is it all the same?

SD: Yeah, I don't care. If they dance well, play well, that's what I care about . . . [but] African Americans want black people on the stage, even if it is African Americans, but not whites.

DR: What have they actually said in complaint?

SD: There is a complaint about white people having the means to come in and steal our culture and furthermore make a business and make money out of it because they have the financial means to do so. [African Americans] want whites to come to their classes. But when, after two or three months of classes, they see whites on stage, they feel that [the whites] have come to take their work. So there is that tension also.

Samba and I then discussed the legacy of colonialism as historical context for these tensions. Like Vado, Samba encounters resistance to his unity-centered discourse along racial lines. In this instance—the 2010 *Ayoka*—he made the decision to limit his representation of unity to people of African descent in order to cater to audience members' expectations of Africa on stage—expectations rooted in a diasporic sensibility. However, in the 2012 *Ayoka*, he did include white drummers (and a white ethnomusicologist—me—giving a lecture on West African masks).

In any case, far from just Ivorians, the demography of this Attoungblan reflected the interweaving of difference for a larger ideological purpose that is at the core of the notion of ballet. That larger purpose came through loud and clear in a speech Samba delivered at the end of the show.

Verbal Discourse on Stage

At the end of the 2010 *Ayoka*, Samba stood before the crowd and, in an entertaining manner, made clear his primary motivation. He views his purpose as a cultural educator not just to expose American audiences to African culture; rather, his larger purpose is bringing people together across ethnic, national, racial, and any other lines that divide us. He believes that the work he does has a universalist mission of making the world a better place (PURL 5.4):

> You see that we come from lots of different places—Ivory Coast, Georgia, everywhere. So we want to share the culture because we believe that through culture we can achieve beauty. Because those drums speak the same language. We don't say, "Oh, this is white, this is black." We don't say, "When the drums

Figure 5.3 Samba Diallo leading audience dancers at *Ayoka* 2010. Photograph by Christy True.

play, you are white, you're black, just feel the beat [dances in a humorous way]." You don't even know why you're moving [dancing]. It's very important—the beat. So you see, music is a door [through which] we see through the color, we see through the race. Culture brings everybody together, so we are glad that you are here today.

Then Samba surprised his friends and the crowd by announcing publicly for the first time that he had become an American citizen. Mary and Curran Rau, who had sponsored his citizenship, joined him on stage for an emotional hug. He then returned to his mission of uniting all people. Declaring that "in Africa there are no spectators," he actualized his belief that culture brings everyone together by inviting the audience—black and white—to join him on stage, where he led them through a series of dances (see figure 5.3). At this moment—the finale—Samba's verbal and performative discourses were aligned as he drew on and expanded the discourse of ballet, uniting difference not just across ethnic lines to unite a nation but across any lines that divide people to unite a world.

6 "I'm Happy Because I'm Different"
Samba Diallo and Exceptionalism

DANIEL REED (DR): Why do you dance? What do you love about dance, and why do you continue to dance here in the United States?

SAMBA DIALLO (SD): For me, it's a form of rejoicing. Through dance, I feel happy. Through dance, I feel better. Through dance, I feel relaxed. Through dance, I relieve stress. It's a way for me to combat all sorts of problems.... Here in the United States, when I teach dance, not only am I teaching people dance—corporal expression—I myself am also exercising. Dance also is mental. It heals.... I dance because it's something I find in my blood. I need to move. It's in my blood.... Dance removes all worries from me, and I don't have any feelings but joy.... When you watch a friend do a solo, it's like a competition, but it's a friendly competition. It's a competition that is cultural and brotherly.... It's through dance that we Africans, who are foreigners, rejoice. It's through dance that we come together, we see our friends who live in different states. When they come we feel joy, we remember our country, we dance, we smile. Really that's what it is. Dance—it's joyous for us, too. Without dance, without what we do here, many of us would be stressed because we all have problems.... When I know I'm going to teach this evening or tomorrow, I feel pleased that I will be around people. We meet up, we communicate, we dance.

Ivorians like to hold hands as they walk—not just romantic couples, not just parents walking cautiously with small children. Friends, young and old, hold hands; sometimes even new acquaintances hold hands. So I was not surprised when, on the first day of Sogbety Diomande's 2006 West African Celebration near Mansfield, Ohio, Samba Diallo took my hand. It was shortly after my lecture and after having just met; we were chatting as we walked down a dirt road on the grounds of the Mohican Outdoor School. "Come to Atlanta and do research with me," Samba said as he gently slid his hand into mine. This was a pivotal moment. I had accepted Sogbety's invitation in part because I saw it as an opportunity for ethnographic reciprocation (in a general sense by giving the talk itself; more concretely I hoped it would allow me to help Ivorian performers find more work), and in part because it felt amusingly novel to be invited to give a talk at my dad's school in my hometown by an Ivorian from one hundred kilometers north of where I had lived in Côte d'Ivoire. Naturally, though, I had also thought that research might be possible. When Samba took my hand and asked me to come to Atlanta and study his life, I realized a new field project had chosen me. I had only to say yes.

From the moment of our first meeting that late summer day in Ohio until the time of this writing, Samba (see figure 6.1) has been an extremely welcoming, generous collaborator, and being a researcher himself he clearly "gets" the value of research. He has enthusiastically agreed to every interview request and has regularly invited me to Atlanta to give lectures at his festivals, attend and film performances, and spend time with him—at his home, at the studio where he teaches dance, and at his favorite Indian restaurant. A warm, amiable presence, Samba shares with me many values and goals regarding the potential of research on and teaching performance to promote cross-cultural understanding. He defines himself as an educator. An exceptionally virtuosic dancer, Samba's life story portrays him as exceptional in many other ways as well, from his unusually ambiguous ethnic identity to his upbringing in pluralistic settings to his immigration and settling in the United States.

Figure 6.1 Samba Diallo teaching dance at the 2008 Lotus Festival in Bloomington, Indiana. Photograph by author.

Childhood

Unlike Vado, Sogbety, and Dr. Djo Bi, Samba was born in the city. When about to give birth, Samba's mother traveled the seventy kilometers from home in the small city of Sikensi to Abidjan so that she could have a hospital birth. The hospital was in Treichville—a popular neighborhood in Abidjan located on the Ebrié Lagoon just across a bridge from the downtown Plateau district—a place that would be important in Samba's future. After some recovery time with family in Treichville, Samba's mother took him back home to Sikensi.

A small city of about 10,000 residents on one of the major highways northwest out of Abidjan, Sikensi was just beyond the orbit of the huge commercial capital. Typical of many small southern cities, it had grown around state-owned, large-scale agriculture—the fuel that drove economic prosperity from independence through the early 1980s during a period known as the "Ivorian Miracle." Large agricultural plantations were established in deforested areas across southern Côte d'Ivoire throughout the colonial and postcolonial periods. They required a large labor force, and Félix Houphouët-Boigny, during his thirty-three years as president, actively encouraged migration from northern Côte d'Ivoire and neighboring countries to meet demand. Sikensi was a case in point. Technically in the ethnic region of the Abidji or Adjoukrou, it was in fact a multiethnic city, as Samba described:

> There [were] lots of foreigners, especially Jula.[1] There was a big kola nut plantation there. Things were transported to Mali and other places. It was a big commercial center. It was an Abidji village but there was everyone there—Jula, Bete, people from Burkina Faso.... There were Dan... Guro, Senufo.... There were many different ethnic groups there.

Samba's parents met and were married in Sikensi, where his father worked as a civil servant at the subprefecture. As for many Ivorian families, especially those of some means, Samba's childhood home was occupied not just by his parents and siblings but also by others in what Americans would call his "extended" family. The oldest of four boys, Samba grew up not just with his brothers but also with several cousins. His mother was of Abidji ethnicity (like Adjoukrou, a Kwa subgroup) and was originally from Sikensi.[2] His father was not from Sikensi, however, and his ethnicity is somewhat mysterious. He was born in Grand Bassam, the original French colonial capital just southeast of Abidjan, to a mother originally from Toumodi, a town in the middle of the Baule ethnic region of south central Côte d'Ivoire. He did not know his own father, who died when he was young, and he always said that Samba's grandfather had been born in Mali and that he had immigrated to Toumodi.

Because of his father's ambiguous heritage, Samba does not identify clearly as one or another ethnicity. I found this surprising and asked him about it:

DR: This is very interesting to me because . . . in my experience in Côte d'Ivoire, with sixty ethnic groups and lots of difference between people, I think that every person I know identifies as one particular ethnic group. And I think that whether in the village or in Abidjan or here in United States, one of the first things you say when you meet someone is "He is Senufo," or "She is Bete."

SD: Voilà—exactly.

DR: But you are exceptional?

SD: That's right.

DR: You think you are exceptional in the domain of ethnicity?

SD: Yes. I feel like that because those whose parents are both Bete are automatically Bete and those whose parents are both Senufo are automatically Senufo. But for me it's different. . . . If my father had been from Mali or Guinea—even if he had come to Côte d'Ivoire and married an Ivorian—automatically I would be considered Guinean or Malian because of my father. But my father was Ivorian, and it was my grandparents who were from Mali. . . . Myself, I'm happy because I am different. I grew up in a context, well, my mother is Abidji, my grandmother is Baule. My great grandparents are Jula. So I am a little everywhere.

Given the large numbers of immigrants who live in Côte d'Ivoire, where it is estimated that around 25 percent of the population is foreign born, I was surprised that I had not met more people of mixed ethnicity like Samba. "For people from the city, it's starting to change a little," Samba said, "but by far the majority marry among themselves, [and so] people identify clearly as one ethnic group." That Samba's own identity blurs ethnic lines is but one aspect of his life experience that almost seems to foreshadow a career that would foreground the blending of ethnic difference.

Seemingly consistent with his partial northern heritage, Samba's father was Muslim, but of his two sisters (Samba's aunts), one was Muslim and the other Christian. This confused Samba when he was young: "Normally, if you're a Muslim, all of your children will be Muslim." He was led to the conclusion that his father was Muslim not by heritage but by choice. Of his own nuclear family, Samba said, "We were not forced to become Muslim." "Including your mother?" I asked. "That's what is bizarre," he answered. "She was Christian! It was all of these aspects that gave me the courage to think. Because usually if a man is Muslim, his wife is Muslim, too. Or if she were not Muslim, she would automatically convert.

But my mother was never Muslim. She goes to the church; she is a Christian." While Samba's family was unusual in this sense, it was not unique; he recalled that during his childhood he knew a few other families whose members were divided between Islam and Christianity.

Samba points to his family's approach to religion, at least in his youngest days, as influencing him to think for himself. In a country in which religious difference has been politicized, polarized, and prejudicial (playing a role in the lead-up to the civil war), such tolerance within a family, while not unusual in and of itself, was something Samba appreciated about his upbringing. I asked if religion had been a point of conflict in his family.

> No, everyone lived in joy. Even my father said to me, "Samba, you must pray. You can be Muslim or Christian, or whatever religion you want to follow. The point is you must believe in God." That surprised me! Because the son of a Muslim must be Muslim automatically. Right behind our house in Sikensi there was a Qur'anic school. And so each time they did the call to prayer, we heard that at the house. But our father never forced us to go there. We had a choice.

In this way, Samba's early experiences taught him that, like ethnicity, religious identities can be fluid and dynamic.

Learning to Dance

When Samba was young, his parents divorced and his father remarried and had another three children, all daughters, with Samba's stepmother. Now Samba was the eldest of eight. His family compound was also home to a male cousin, making nine in all. Given the ease with which he dances, I was curious whether his family had been involved in music and/or dance. Samba told me that his maternal grandfather had been chief of his village and his mother's family included many "nobles," some of whom were musicians. He added, "Some of my siblings played music—guitar and what have you. But it was only one younger brother who followed me into dance. He was great at contemporary dance—dances like smurf [break dancing], disco, and funk—but he fell into a life of drugs and these days he's living on the street." While there is some artistic ability in his family, Samba does not locate the source of his talent in his ancestry but rather in God and the context in which he grew up:

SD: I could say that it was a gift. In the town where I was living, I would just watch music and dance all the time and learn that way. When I watch, I learn a lot. When I watch, I imitate, and I learn easily. That's why I say it was a gift. So it was from there that I began to dance and to create dances.

DR: In your opinion, where does that gift come from?

SD: I believe in God because that gift—it comes from God.

Sikensi proved to be fertile soil in which Samba's God-given gifts could blossom. Fascinated by his descriptions of the multiethnic music and dance he had grown up with in Sikensi, I asked him to tell me more:

SD: In Sikensi, there were Jula and Bete and other ethnic groups. At every celebration, every ethnic group would come out and do their traditional dances. . . . If the chief of the village was happy and wanted to see a celebration, he would send [money] and hire groups from around the village. But the majority of the time it was a festival like, for example, [Ivorian] Independence Day or Christmas or Easter. People [would] gather together in community. Since there was not a big theater, this would always take place in the marketplace. . . . The different ethnic groups would dance all around the marketplace at the same time. Especially Tabaski[3] and Independence Day and Ramadan. . . . The majority of the Dan would dance at their chief's house. That's where I saw the [stilt mask spirit] for the first time. Because our neighbor was a Dan [Yakuba] chief . . . whenever he was happy, or wanted to celebrate life, the long mask would come out and perform for the neighbors. . . . But it was usually in the marketplace—an open space. So that's where you could go and see lots of different types of dances, and when you returned to the house, you would imitate them a bit. . . . Even if you [were] not from that ethnic group you [could] still come out and dance.

I noted the similarity between the interethnic sharing of music and dance in Sikensi and in the Ballet National de Côte d'Ivoire (BNCI):

DR: That's a very interesting context, because if you imagine, for example, the ballet, where they mix dances from different ethnic groups, you grew up in that context.

SD: Exactly. . . . When I got involved in the ballet . . . I felt at ease because I learned the movements rapidly. . . . You can't learn when you're afraid. When you're afraid you make mistakes. It was good for me because I learned easily. . . . Take for example the dance *abodan*. I had not learned that before, but when I arrived at the ballet, they taught me that dance. . . . Some members were so happy to see me execute the movements smoothly. The one who was Akan even said, "You're really good at that!" And the guys asked, "Are you Baule?" While I am part Baule, I did not learn the dance typically.

Ivorians describing indigenous forms of music and dance in French often use *typical* to denote "belonging" to a particular ethnic group. Such dance forms epistemologically are the stuff of tradition, learned through acculturation and/or initiation—indigenous, experiential education through which the young learn how to behave as adults in their ethnic communities. Had he grown up in Baule country, Samba might have been introduced to dances such as *abodan*, *adjoss*, and *kotou*. But he did not undergo Baule initiation or initiation in any of the other ethnic traditions that make up his mixed heritage. His skill in dancing *abodan* was not a question of his ethnicity, as his response makes clear, but of his childhood context—a rich, multiethnic, *informal* experiential education in multiple forms of music and dance.

Teen Years: More Schooling, More Dancing

Very commonly in Côte d'Ivoire, children whose families can afford to do so leave home when it comes time to attend "college," the rough equivalent of junior high school. Samba did exactly that, leaving Sikensi when he finished primary school to go to the small town of Azaguie, near Agboville in southeast Côte d'Ivoire. He was sent to live with a friend of his father's, a man named Feu Soumahoro Faby. Samba's father had appealed to Feu not just to house Samba but to also act as his tutor, so Feu took Samba under his wing. A Muslim, he was concerned that Samba's approach to religion was far too casual. Samba does not enjoy his memories of this period:

> [Feu] demanded that I pray. I said, "But I don't know the Qur'an!" "You're going to learn it!" he said. He bought a translation of the Qur'an in French. I didn't want to, but he said, "You're going to pray before eating with everyone."

Then one day his tutor asked him to pray in front of the family. "Everyone was there together and the hour of prayer approached":

> I was uncomfortable. He forced me. He said, "Come pray! I said, "I don't know how to throw" [the water]. He said, "You're going to learn!" And that really made me feel bad. So I did it but I didn't really understand what I was doing. From that time on, if I was there and everyone was praying, I would pray too.

Nominally a Muslim from that point on, Samba never did feel that the shoe fit. He could not understand the prayers he uttered. He resented being forced to pray and felt little connection to Islam as a result.

Nonetheless, Samba spent several years living with Feu and his family while he moved through college. When he was in his late teens, he began attending *lycée* (high school) in Agboville, leaving behind his tutor's repressive environment. After a couple of years, he began attending a professional school in the center west city of Daloa to earn a certificate in industrial electricity. All through this period—from his midteens to his early twenties—Samba spent every school vacation in the big city of Abidjan, specifically the neighborhood of Treichville, with his grandmother. A mostly working-class neighborhood, Treichville is famous for its live music, its huge lively market, its port, and its train station connecting the Ivorian coast to points inland all the way to Ougadougou in Burkina

Faso, 660 kilometers north. In Treichville, Samba felt free to be himself. He came of age during these vacations, spending time with friends, dancing at parties and clubs, and enjoying the excitement of urban living.

Becoming a Christian and a Competitive Dancer

Samba had joined the Boy Scouts prior to moving to Abidjan, and his troupe was associated with a Catholic parish in Treichville, Jeanne d'Arc de Treichville. Through Scouts he became increasingly familiar with this church where he felt very welcomed by the priest, sometimes attending services, It was here that he met a young modern dancer named Max Quao Gaudens, and the two became good friends. "Every Saturday we would go to his house, and there would be instruments, and we would dance. And he was really a devoted Christian. Everything we did we had to pray," recalled Samba. These weekly dance sessions gradually evolved into more formal rehearsals, and Max and Samba formed a dance group named Jeanne d'Arc de Treichville. This was as much an exercise of faith as an exercise of the body. "Everything we did, we did in prayer. And this friend, my brother Max, every time he went to church, he prayed a lot. And he would bring the whole group, and we would pray."

His experiences with Max and with Max's church and its dance group eventually led Samba to convert to Christianity, with which he felt more comfortable than he had with Islam:

> From that time—[while] I can't say I'm a good Christian—I [began] believing in Jesus Christ. . . . I became a believer in God. I only became Muslim because my tutor made me. It's not that I detest[ed] Islam, but I did not feel at ease, I didn't feel in my own body. When I would pray to God, I didn't even know what I was saying. That didn't inspire me to learn more. I feel at ease when I read the Bible because it's clear, because it's in French and I can understand it.

As the dance group improved, it began to compete. In 1988, when Samba was about twenty-four, he caught wind of a national dance competition, Varietoscope, that piqued his interest. Varietoscope had two categories—traditional and modern, though theater was added later. Initially, twenty-five groups selected from throughout the country competed—five each at five regional competitions. The regional winners then competed in the final rounds in Abidjan. A major event, Varietoscope's final rounds were televised on Saturdays on state television.

When Samba heard about Varietoscope, he immediately formed a new, competitive dance group out of his church association, again named Jeanne d'Arc de Treichville but now representing not just the church but the "commune" of Treichville (similar to a district). Some members were involved in choreography, but the group now consisted of just three male and three female dancers—Samba, a Togolese woman, and four others each from one of the Akan subgroups in southeastern Côte d'Ivoire. "We were a new group, but we really worked hard. We rehearsed every night for four hours," he recalled. It paid off. "Our first time we made it to the semifinal," he said, smiling proudly. "It was good. It was good. Because at first nobody knew who we were.... We lost to a group that had been competing for years but everyone was saying, 'Who are these people?'"

The music for the competitions, preselected by Varietoscope's director, included one traditional and one modern piece. In Samba's first year of competing, the traditional piece was based on the Baule rhythm *goli*, featuring what Samba called modern instrumentation consisting of gourd rattles and a cow horn, along with guitar, bass guitar, keyboard, and drum kit. The modern piece was a 1988 hit song, "I Call Your Name," by white South African pop star Johnny Clegg and his band Savuka, which, though it consisted of Zulu musicians and was known for its use of Zulu elements (see Taylor 1997), was clearly defined in the dance competition as a modern band. The *goli* piece featured instrumentation just as "modern" as Savuka's but, presumably because the piece was built around the well-known rhythm of the Baule mask of the same name, it was defined as traditional.[4] In each case, the dance groups were judged on the creativity of their choreography and technical skill.

Having risen to the level that Jean d'Arc achieved in its first attempt, the group found itself in the spotlight. Samba took this opportunity to audition for the BNCI. "I went for an audition and I got into the ballet. After that I did several months there. But then the [Varietoscope] competition started back up and I disappeared from the ballet." I asked him why he had so quickly given it up. "The ballet," he replied, "was good, but I was happier with my little group. And it was a national competition and I did not want to miss it."

Before returning to competitive dance, however, Samba spent some time with a theater troupe known as Union Theatre de Krindjabo (UTK, or the Theatrical Union of Krindjabo, a town in the Agni ethnic region). With UTK, Samba benefited from the expertise of principal actors Kablan Patrice (now working in South Africa) and Adje Maurice, from whom he received excellent training in theatrical arts. With experts of this caliber, Samba says, he became a more complete performer. Certainly, in the range of dramatic dance pieces in which he has appeared in the United States, acting has been required. Samba's first love, dance, kept calling him, however, and he returned to Jean d'Arc. He found that the group had become full of tension due to the attention and pressure created by its initial success, which ultimately led the group to fracture:

> We had disagreements and we split in two. Some of us left and formed another group based in another commune ... Jacquesville [a village on the coast just west of Abidjan].... We took the name Etchue Wuehoun, or The Children of Jacquesville.... With that group we made it all the way to the final. But we did not win.... It was after that that I went back again to the [national] ballet

rehearsals. When the director saw me, he asked an assistant, "Who is that guy? I remember him!" I did not want to tell him that I quit because of the competition. He motioned for me to come talk to him and began giving me a really hard time. "Where were you?" he asked. . . . I made up a story and said, "I was traveling." He let me back in the group, but he impressed upon me that I should not quit again.

Samba could not resist the temptation to make a third run at the Varietoscope, though. He remained with the BNCI, but surreptitiously regrouped with members of his Treichville group to begin training for a third year. Back in its original location, the members found that there was simply too much talent and too many dancers for one team, so once again they divided in two. The best dancers, including Samba, were again selected to represent Treichville under the name Rosaire de Treichville (Rosary of Treichville). The rest became a kind of secondary squad training under Kablan Patrice and a superb Nigerian dancer named Jimson. They were recruited to represent Aboisso—a commune in the Agni region just northeast of Abidjan.

As he rehearsed with Rosaire, the BNCI began preparing for a tour of either France or Spain—Samba could not remember which. But he did remember that he didn't want to go: "So I just didn't show up. . . . I wanted to stay for the competition." Still, while the ballet dropped him from the roster for that tour, they did not bar him from returning later. In their third attempt, this being the 1993 Varietoscope competition, Samba's group finally prevailed: "This time it was the Rosaire de Treichville that won the cup. The mayor of Treichville was very happy. To encourage us, he and his youth representative . . . visited us often because we were representing the commune. So it was like the whole commune had won together."

Dancing onto the National Stage

By dancing for three years in the final rounds of the high-profile Varietoscope and finally winning the cup, Samba not only had gained considerable skill as a dancer and choreographer but also had developed a reputation among professional dancers in Abidjan. During this period, he got to know Ivorian popular music star Meiway, who offered to send him to Rose Marie Giraud—director of perhaps the best-known private ballet-style school and touring group in the country, les Guirivoires. Samba spent some time with Giraud's prestigious program in the upscale Deux Plateau neighborhood of Abidjan, but began to feel that he could learn more at the BNCI. Shortly after rejoining the national troupe, he was on a plane to Kenya to perform at an international dance festival. Unlike Vado, who was a soloist and choreographer with the national troupe, Samba was a member of the chorus.

His competitive groups had been fun, but now Samba felt the honor of representing his nation on the world stage alongside groups from other African countries.

SD: The ballet was different because it was a professional thing. People were paid and were well treated. With my [competitive] group, we danced for love and joy. If someone came along who wanted to pay us for a show, that was great, but we did it for joy. Our objective was to become professional . . . But we lacked a rehearsal hall. . . . There were a lot of obstacles that made it so that we could not evolve. The dancers were very devoted . . . they would dance in someone's courtyard every Saturday. The mayor's office needed us a great deal during the time of the competition. But after the competition they didn't care about us. . . . They wouldn't even provide us a rehearsal space. . . . All we wanted was a rehearsal room. . . . It was very difficult.

DR: So it was discouraging and now the ballet is there, [a group] that could pay you for doing what you want. . . . Were you the only member of the competition group that went on to the ballet?

SD: Yes. Some had other jobs. Some were in school. When you are in the ballet, you cannot be in school. One guy was a great dancer. He went to France, where he ended up in a magazine and a lot of TV commercials. He was really good. . . . He became a ballet dancer. . . . Another guy, Tony Kouad, went to France and became a great singer. Now he's in Seattle.

Samba's days of relegating dance, and living in Abidjan, to school vacations were behind him. His grandmother now deceased, Samba lived with his good friend Max Quao's family in Treichville. Migrating to the national ballet was a move forward in numerous respects, including the development of skills that would serve him well in his future. Part of his training occurred at the prestigious Institut des Arts et de l'Action Culturelle (Institute of the Arts and Cultural Action)—the arts campus of the University of Abidjan—where he enrolled in dance classes. While his Varietoscope ensembles had nurtured his dance technique and choreographic skill, the repertoire and overall performance practices of ballet discourse that the BNCI would teach him were to prove especially useful down the road.

DR: You talk about the training you received in the ballet. What exactly do you mean by training?

SD: Those who grew up in the village, they . . . learned their traditions, their culture of their country or their village, their history. . . . When you become a member of the [BNCI], they train you further there. In your village, you are well trained but limited to the dance of your village, or the dance of [that region]. But when you are a part of the [BNCI] . . . you learn dances from the West, from the North, from the South . . . so your experience opens up. The knowledge that you had is augmented. You're from the East, but you do dances from the West. You might do a dance from the North, and they [would] say, "How do you do our dance so well . . .? It's because of your BNCI training. . . . You receive an education [from experts from all the different regions] that is very typical [i.e., traditional]."

In addition to dance traditions from around the country, Samba learned choreography created by the BNCI itself that was part of its own tradition and discourse. Samba described the importance of training in set, choreographed transitions between dances:

The [BNCI] has many different dance steps. And [some] are created [by the choreographers], and others . . . are traditional. Because, in the tradition, it's done the same way always, and we have to respect that. Now, to create the transitions from one dance to another, you might put in a song with a dance. Say you have ended at a certain place on the stage and need to get to another. You have to create a dance that walks, you must add some movement of the hands. All that is to create a transition so you can start the [next] dance.

I asked Samba if he could imagine what it might be like for an immigrant performer *not* to have such experience; in other words, what might it be like to arrive straight from a village onto a North American stage.

I think it would be difficult for someone to come directly from the village. . . . Dance in the village is pretty much just going forward, then returning, going forward, then returning again, because people are [in a circle]. The circle is the symbol of unity, connectivity. . . . To succeed in America, people need to know the stage. . . . You might dance well, but [if] you cannot do a simple choreography, then [you will have trouble].

Skills and knowledge derived from ballet training were regarded by some performers as training for a migrant labor market abroad. The BNCI served as a platform for performers to prepare for emigration. In 1993 the Ivorian Miracle was a fading memory. President Houphouët-Boigny died in December of that year, and the leader of the National Assembly, Henri Konan Bedie, took his place. Then, in January 1994, the CFA—the currency used by nearly all francophone African countries—was devalued by half. Overnight salaries were worth 50 percent what they had been. The Ivorian economy was tanking, and the incentive for people who could to flee the country for work elsewhere was great.

Furthermore, some performers believed that the BNCI was taking advantage of them. "Many believe[ed] this," Samba said. "Many had toured the world with the ballet and come back home. But when you start to use or mistreat your team, you lose many." It was no secret that BNCI performers were looking for opportunities to emigrate, which created tension and mistrust, especially during the run-up to selecting members for any given tour:

> When they were [choosing] who would go on a tour, everyone behaved well so that they would not suspect anything. If they suspected that you might flee, they would not select you. They even had spies ... who would try to determine if you might flee and plan something with you as a trap to see what [you were] thinking. Then they would inform the director. When they made the final list, your name would not be on it. So no one trusted each other. If they had the smallest inkling ... that you might leave, they would not take you. It was really hard on people.

Such a cutthroat environment was one more example of the intense competition that I had been encountering in my consultants' stories. From the village to national competitions to private and state ballet groups, and between performers in their new settings in America, fierce competition was ever present. According to Samba, "There were around twenty-five of us, and when we had a show, they selected who would perform. So everyone was always battling. . . . You would dance with as much energy as you could so they would select you." "What percent of the group was selected for each show?" I asked. "It depended on the show. For little shows for journalists or some kind of gala, they might take only twelve or fifteen people. But if there was a big stage, they would bring along a larger group. If for example they were going to China, they [would] make a larger selection."

The director and his staff weighed many factors in their selections. In general, BNCI administrators discouraged members from forming their own, smaller ensembles on the side (Schauert 2015). "If [performers] had their own group, [BNCI administrators] would see that as competition. . . . They would not be selected because the BNCI feared that they would flee. So sometimes the very best dancers and drummers were not selected."

Despite the intense competition and the distrust and suspicion it created, many performers continued to jockey for slots on tours to Europe or North America, which would give them a chance to "disappear." "As for me," said Samba, "my objective was to come [to the United States]." His chance came when the BNCI made its selection for a trip to Memphis in May 1994.

Immigration

Memphis in May

DR: What was it like for you to perform in [Memphis in May]?

SD: At first, we thought it was something fabulous, really important. We were happy because we had come to America to dance. . . . But then we saw that we could not dance our choreography . . . People all had their places for their groups, with the result that they had to cut each dance short because there was another group [waiting to follow]. We thought we [were] going to come and do *our* ballet. . . . We did not think that they would cut us off. So we danced, but we didn't see it as hugely important. We knew it was a great celebration, a great festival of different groups [and] that really pleased us. But [the audience] did not see. . . . If it had been the ballet, it would've been different. But they cut us off quickly. It was like each group had two minutes . . . so it was good but we didn't feel [what] we wanted to feel about it.

DR: It was bizarre because they paid for how many people to come? Over a hundred people all the way from Côte d'Ivoire . . .

SD: For five or ten minutes—you see? [laughter].

DR: Did you do other shows also or . . . only that huge performance that I saw?

SD: I think it was only that one performance. . . . We were there for one week—I think it was just that one show."

So Samba had finally made it to the United States, to a huge performance arena on the shores of the Mississippi River, but he was denied the chance to perform to his full ability. Like Vado, Samba was not at all focused on the grand narrative threading the dozen or so groups together in Memphis. He was just confused. After hearing his version of the story, I asked him directly, "Did you understand the story that they created?" "My head wasn't there to read, you know," he replied. "I was there for the big meeting, to meet people, look at people . . . I was not concentrated on their story."

Deciding to Stay

Samba himself said it: he was in the United States to meet people. He was honored by the invitation to be a part of the tour, to show America what the Ivorian nation had to offer in music and dance. Denied all but a truncated version of their show, suffocated (unknowingly) by the weight of the heavy-handed social evolutionary discourse and not understanding why, his mind turned to his mission. Meeting people. Finding a way to stay.

Samba had taken some measures to ensure that, if he should decide to stay, it would be possible. Before the group had even left Côte d'Ivoire, he approached an assistant director to ask for what he called a certificate of education:

> I asked Coulibali Zie, the assistant director, for a signed certificate of education, affirming that I was a part of the [BNCI]. He said, "But, why?" I said, "To prove that I am in the [BNCI] and that I had a solid education and training." If I had asked Akin [the director], he would have been suspicious, but Zie did

this for me. He signed two copies . . . [and] when I came to the US, I brought them with me.

While he had made the case to Zie that a certificate might be necessary for entering and exiting the United States, in fact he wanted to have it in case it might help him find work after the ballet left and he remained.

When Memphis in May had drawn to a close and the departure date approached, Samba began seriously considering staying and started talking with others whom he could trust not to inform the director:

> After our show. . . I crossed paths with a woman named Joanne. She had enjoyed seeing us perform and hoped there might be more opportunities to do so in the future. I said to her, "I want to stay," but she responded, "You should not stay." She said, "Go back home with your company, and I will help you return." I said, "Really?" She said, "Really. You must believe in God—I will arrange for your return." I didn't really believe her, but nonetheless I said to myself, "I'll go back home." . . . I called my cousin back home, and he said, "You are coming back? Are you dumb? You could live in the United States. You should stay!" So I thought and thought and thought. "I don't know anyone here!" But my cousin gave me the number of Abou Soumahoro, a guy whose father had married my aunt. Abou lived in Gaithersburg, Maryland. . . . I called him. He said "What are you doing?" I said, "I am here with the [BNCI]. In the morning I am going back home." He said, "You are going back home? What, are you crazy? You are here in the States and you are going back? What are you going to find back there?" I said, "No, I have my group back there, and—" He interrupted: "Listen. Let all that go." He motivated me to stay, but when I got off the phone, I said to myself, "I am not sure about this. I want to go back."

As the hour of departure approached, Samba continued to agonize over what to do. Word began to spread of others who had already fled. One of Samba's friends, a dancer named Fanzie Mongueï, approached him, saying, "Can I confide in you? I don't want to go back." He told Samba that he had two other friends who wanted to stay as well. Samba mentioned his conversations with his cousin and his nagging uncertainty.

Finally, the time arrived for everyone to gather to board buses for the airport. Fanzie and his two friends stood next to Samba. "If you aren't coming, then give us your cousin's phone number," Fanzie demanded. Samba still hesitated. As the bus approached, Samba crossed paths with an elder, a former dancer named Dagobert who had become a costume designer. Samba found the words, "I'm going to stay here." Dagobert embraced him and said, "Good luck." Samba looked up at the bus as it pulled up to the curb. At that moment, one of his three friends hailed a taxi. Instinctively Samba picked up his bags and followed them into the cab. "Where are you going?" asked the cab driver. "Just go—let's go!" said Fanzie.

As Samba told the rest of the story, he became especially animated, as if it had happened the day before:

> The instant we began driving off, the directors of the group arrived on the scene. When we saw them, immediately we ducked down and hid. We passed right by them. If we had not left at the moment when we did, we could not have gotten away. It was a narrow opportunity like that. So, we disappeared.... We went directly to the Greyhound bus station and bought tickets for around a hundred dollars for Washington, DC. From there I called my cousin in Maryland, and he came to get us.... We began living with him. I did not call home for the first month or two.... I was afraid since the director had warned us that if we fled, he would call the FBI to search for us. So we were all afraid! Whether it was true or not, we did not know! Every time I heard a siren, I thought it was the police coming for me so I would hide.

After a couple of months, Samba finally mustered the courage to call home. He told his family he had stayed and was living in Maryland. His family told him that an American woman kept calling them asking for him—a woman from Memphis. Figuring it was Joanne, Samba called her. She told him that he should come back to Memphis so that she could help him get on his feet. "But I am with three friends," Samba replied. "Come, all of you, just come," she replied.

As Samba recounted this next part of his story, I barely uttered a sound other than occasional sighs or exclamations. The long narrative that follows is Samba's recounting of his difficult return to Memphis:

> We were not sure what to do, but we decided to go back and see what was possible. So the next day we left to return to Memphis. [Joanne] received us all, and then rented a place for the four of us to live. She took us to the store and bought us clothes. She took us to church every Sunday. Every Sunday we went to church. She bought us groceries.... She had two daughters, about eighteen and nineteen years of age. Her daughters began to complain that she was taking better care of us than she was them.... They then went to talk to their grandmother. One thing led to another and the grandmother came to our place and told us that if we did not get out of there, she was going to call Immigration.... We were really afraid. A week or two passed. Joanne took Fanzie and me to a park with a swimming pool, and he and I were swimming. I saw these guys who didn't look normal. I said, "Let's go back to the house." Fanzie, he wanted to keep swimming, but I sensed that something wasn't right. I was watching these guys. They were smoking on the other side of the fence, and I was not at ease.... I said, "Those guys are up to something." Fanzie said, "No, you are too scared! You are too scared!" So there we were. Ten minutes later, those guys shot a pistol. Three times. PA! PA! PA! I saw a big heavyset old man fall. Then I saw Fanzie fall to the ground. I said, "What!" He said, "I have been shot by that gun." He lifted up his swimsuit and on the side of his leg, I saw a hole! I panicked. I said "I told you we should go! I told you!" He was there, crying.... People called

the police. The police said to [Fanzie], "Who are you here with?" I hid because I didn't want them to send us back home. So I called [Joanne], and I told her, "Come! come! Fanzie has a bullet in him." When she came, I came out of hiding and said, "He is with me." So we went to the hospital and the police followed us. At the hospital, they took down our information, and there was a woman who said, "Oh, you are the young guys from the Ballet, huh? People are looking for you! They said you had fled!" When I heard that, my heart pounded! That night, they asked for someone to stay with Fanzie. I said, "No, I am not going to stay." I was afraid to stay! So I left for the house, and the next day we went back and got Fanzie and brought him home.... They did not even remove the bullet. No.... From there, [Fanzie] left for New York. He called up these other guys who had fled.... At first, we thought it was only five of us who had fled ... but then we heard that there were fourteen total! After us, a whole bunch of others had disappeared! About this time, those guys were calling us. "Come here to New York!" I didn't want to go to New York, because my comportment is different than theirs—I am a little different.... I said to myself, "No, I don't want to go to New York."... I decided to call my family back home. They told me about a cousin I had here in Atlanta, so I called him to see if I could come there with my friend. He said, "No, you come alone, or you stay there!" That was when Fanzie left for New York and I came here [to Atlanta].... Otherwise, Fanzie would have been here with me in Atlanta.

Atlanta

In 1995 Samba moved in with his cousin in Atlanta. "In the beginning, everything went well," he said. His cousin worked for Amitech,[5] a company that made car parts—buttons, door handles, and the like—and arranged for Samba to work there. His cousin and he agreed that at the end of the year, Samba would pay him a fee to help with the rent and other expenses. He worked for six months with no problems, excited to be saving money.

During this time, he began writing to dance schools trying to find work. "I wrote to black dance schools and white dance schools—everyone—and no one responded." But one person finally did—a middle-aged white woman living in the suburb of Kennesaw named Mary Rau:

> I said, "You have a school?" She said, "Yes, but you are a black man. I think you will have more opportunity downtown with all those black studios. I know nothing about black dance, but it is your best bet. African dance here, I don't know—"

Mary was hesitant to take him on, concerned that there was no market for his skills among her school's clientele, but Samba begged her: "Try it. It will work! It will work!" Mary told him that she knew a Haitian woman named Rose whose daughter was taking a ballet class at her school. "Come and I will introduce you to her," she said.

The three of them met, and Samba began by appealing to the Haitian woman in French to help him convince Mary Rau to give him a chance. When they finished, Mary turned to Rose. "What do you think, Rose? Is this a good idea?" Rose said, "This would be a new thing. If you try it, you will see lots of blacks come to the school. It could be good!" On Rose's recommendation Mary decided to take the risk and Samba began teaching at her dance studio.

> But she didn't know I didn't have papers yet. . . . After one month, I began to see young people of African descent. [Soon] I had twelve. Then their mothers began taking the class. It was happening! . . . One day, [Mary] wanted to pay me. I said, "I can't take a check. . . . I don't have my papers." "But how did you get here?" she asked. "It's a long story, but I am looking for a sponsor." She said, "How do you do that?" I said, "We have to get a lawyer and start an application." . . . For her, it was easy. We went to see a lawyer. But her husband was a little—he was suspicious. [He said to her], "Are you sure he is trustworthy?" . . . I understand—it was the circumstances.

Despite her husband's misgivings, Mary agreed not just to let Samba continue teaching but also to act as his sponsor. It was the beginning of a long process, but it gave Samba a touch of optimism that perhaps his situation could improve. In the short term, however, things got worse.

In April 1996, the time arrived for Samba to pay his cousin the fee they had agreed on. But the cousin insisted that he pay a much larger sum. After several calls back home to Africa in an effort to resolve the problem, Samba finally paid what his cousin asked. But the very fact that he had questioned the amount enraged his cousin, who then told Samba to leave. Samba did not want to leave. "Leave, or I will call the police," his cousin threatened. "But what am I going to do?" Samba asked. "I don't care" was his cousin's cold reply.

"I stopped going to work completely," Samba recalled, but he had been a reliable employee so his supervisor called to find out why he hadn't been coming in.

SD: "I had to go back to Africa," [I told her] I didn't tell her I had no papers. She called me again and again. This began to bother me. . . . One day I just went into work and [said] "Look. I like this job, and I like the people here. But I have a problem. I don't have my papers yet." She said, "How have you been working, then?" I just smiled. I [had been] hoping that she could help me. I said, "I want to ask if the company will sponsor me, because I like my work, but I have no papers."

DR: That took a lot of courage!

SD: [Smiles]. It took all of my courage, but I had no choice! . . . [my supervisor] said, "I have to talk to my boss." My heart was so [heavy], but she reassured me. She came back and said her boss could not sponsor people, that the company could not—something like that. So, I went back home because it didn't work! There I sat.

When the end of the month came and the rent was due, Samba's cousin came looking for it. "But I have no work!" Samba cried. Again his cousin said he that did not care. "I cried like a baby! I didn't know what to do! He didn't care! At the end of that month, he kicked me out. "But where am I going to go? I have no money?" "I don't care," came the familiar reply. "If I see you at work, I am going to call the police." "So I packed my bags."

A middle-aged Ivorian man who lived next door took him in. The neighbor had heard the cousin's complaints and seemed to take his side. "You are wasting time," he said to Samba. "That woman [Mary Rau] wants to help you. *A white woman wants to help you!* . . . Go to New York! You have friends there." But Samba was still reluctant. After a short time, his neighbor, too, showed Samba the door:

SD: One day he said, "You have to leave." I said, "But where am I going to go without papers?" "Go to New York! Your friends are there! Go and play around there!" I was so angry with him. . . . He told me there was a shelter that perhaps could help me.

DR: In Atlanta, or . . .

SD: No, in Marietta. . . . He took me, with my baggage, and he left me at the shelter. . . . He said, "Goodbye" [gestures a light half-hug]. . . . So now I am there. I don't know what to do. I am confused. I see these guys from that walk of life, people who drink, who are drunk, all that. And I just sat there. I had two suitcases and one guitar. I gave the guitar to one guy and one suitcase to another because I could not walk around with all that! So I was there—

DR: For how long?

SD: No, at this shelter there was not even room for me! The guy told me that at six p.m., when those people who were living there came back, he would see who had not returned, and then I could register. . . . When the people started coming back, I said, "Ohh . . ." [shakes head]. . . . Then, I thought, you must call your sponsor. So I called [Mary Rau] and said, "My friend threw me out, and so I no longer have a place to sleep. God himself made me think of you." She said, "Well, I have a young girl here at home [her daughter]. Let me talk to my husband." Well, her husband wasn't too thrilled. Then she added, "But you could go sleep in the dance school." . . . She picked me up and took me to the studio. . . . I spent a month there. When there was a class, I would leave, and when the class was over, I would come back. I would sleep. I'd get up in the morning and clean the studio.

160 | Abidjan USA

After a month, she brought me a bicycle, [she said] "so you can get yourself to our house." I would go there and bathe and then ride back to the studio. After two months, they took me into their home.

An American Family

Samba's process of becoming legal and eventually a citizen is yet another way in which his experience was exceptional relative to that of my other consultants. Mary Rau and her husband Curran, pictured with Samba in figure 6.2, are the most important parts of this story. Originally from Minnesota, the Raus had moved to Georgia long before they met Samba. It was Samba himself who wanted me to meet the Raus, because of their importance in his life story, particularly the Atlanta chapter. One day in 2010, Samba, my wife Christy True, and I visited Mary and Curran in their Kennesaw, Georgia, home. Following is a passage from my field notes written on July 28, 2010, about this visit:

> Yesterday we went with Samba to the home of what he calls his family—the home of Curran and Mary Rau in Kennesaw, a suburb in the northern part of the Atlanta metro area. This was a case of allowing a consultant to dictate the direction of research. While meeting them sounded interesting to me, because

Figure 6.2 Samba Diallo with Mary and Curran Rau at the Raus' home in Kennesaw, Georgia in 2010. Photograph by author.

we have had so little time since I arrived in Atlanta for interviews prior to yesterday morning, I was concerned that I would not manage to get enough interesting information from Samba himself before departing. I still have many questions and whole areas that I want to cover with him that we've not even begun. But it was clearly really important to Samba that I meet this couple. I decided not to fight it, and chose losing the morning of interviewing him and going with what he saw as important. . . . I now have a better understanding of Samba's life here from other perspectives. Just the simple fact that he thought it was so important that I meet this couple says a lot about him. . . . Kennesaw, Samba told me, was an important battle site in the Civil War, and is a markedly conservative place, where he said racism is still very strong. For a white couple to take an African into their home in this context was incredible to Samba. I captured much about their relationship and the Raus' version of the story on video. What's not on video is the context. Kennesaw feels more rural than the other suburbs, such as Smyrna, where Samba lives. I'll have to look on the map but it must be more of an outlying suburb [it is in fact on the fringes of the massive Atlanta metropolitan area, near the northwest corner of Cobb County]. There is a large Civil War memorial and park on the mountain that shares the town's name. The actual neighborhood where Samba's family lives consists of modest split-level and ranch-style homes, with no sidewalks and a fair number of trees. The house itself is pretty small. We gathered around the dining room table, just off the kitchen. They call him "Sam." . . . This interview with [Samba's] sponsors underscored the issues I've been grappling with regarding life story. While the formal interviews establish a skeleton, a timeline and some details, much rich detail is added in other ways, in experience spending time with Samba, talking about other things, etc. I learned really important things about him through talking with Mary especially.

The first thing that struck me was the obvious warmth and affection Samba, Mary, and Curran had for one another. The Raus considered "Sam" their son and explicitly stated so. They talked about his early struggles and later successes with the same agonizing concern and beaming pride that I would expect to find coming from any biological parents. I asked them why they had taken such an interest in Samba. Mary replied, "Probably because of his persistence. . . . We didn't realize how bad his situation was. He had to teach kids for free because he didn't have a green card."

CURRAN RAU (CR): Originally he was not going to come here [to live with us]. He had family he was living with . . . but for some reason it didn't work out and he had nowhere to go.

MARY RAU (MR): And so we had talked to him about teaching classes, and in the end he ended up living here because he didn't have anywhere to go. . . . He couldn't work because he didn't have his green card, so he had no money and he didn't know what he was going to do. We had already talked with him about dancing but when he didn't have [anywhere] to go, we said, "Come stay with us."

DR: How long had you known him before you invited him to stay here?

MR: Oh, just a couple weeks [laughter]. We had worked with people from other countries through the Friendship Force. It's a chance that you take with anybody. You know you don't know if they're going to take everything you have the minute you go out of the house, but . . . I could leave a hundred dollars out on the table and not a penny would be touched. He was the most honest—

CR: They all were—

MR: . . . I could just trust him one hundred percent.

CR: You know you just have faith and trust in people—

MR: And it works out—

CR: . . . You take a chance. . . . It's a two-way street.

MR: It all worked out. Now I have another son.

CR: [Sam] stayed the longest. He's like a son [laughter].

At this point—indeed, *every* time Samba, Mary, or Curran made a comment about the familial nature of their relationship—they all smiled. I asked, "Maybe you could speak to that. How did your relationship evolve from one of collaboration [at the dance studio] to one of ultimately helping him gain citizenship?"

CR: It was almost right away because [choking up; gestures to Mary].

MR: We didn't realize that Sam was going to be here as long as he was. And he didn't either. We were figuring six months, a year, two years—he'll get his green card and then he'll move on and do what he need[s] to do. . . . And it ended up being four years—

CR: Five years—

MR: . . . So it's just like living with someone; pretty soon he's part of the family.

CR: And he had a lot of sad moments because in his country [choking up], people were dying.

MR: His mother died when he was here, and that was sad. And they were fighting over there . . . and the fact that he couldn't go home . . . that was the sad part of him being here. . . . If these people don't have a sponsor when they come here, they just can't make it.

So far, the conversation was flowing easily and the warmth and emotion in the room was palpable. Tears and smiles came and went as the three recalled their years together. The energy in the room shifted, however, when I asked my next question. Samba had said something to me earlier about one of the Raus' children who had been living at home while Samba was there. Innocently I asked, "Did you have other children in the home when Sam was living here?" Mary suddenly looked uncomfortable, then tersely responded, "My daughter and her son were living with us when Sam was here." Kicking myself for having obviously touched a nerve, I broke the silence with another question about the Rau's experience with the Friendship Force. They then turned the conversation back to Samba, explaining that hosting foreigners had surely influenced them to be so open to Sam. "You just take a chance. You don't even think about it," Curran said.

Feeling the good vibes return, I said, "Clearly for all of you, you are family now. [Samba] talks about you that way." Mary followed my lead: "If we haven't spoken for two or three weeks, I call and say, 'How are you doing?'" She went on to say that she asks Sam to let them know when he leaves town for dancing work so that they can be there for him if need be. "In this life you have to have someone you can call, who can be there for you." Curran, however, then said, "Everything is not always peaches and cream. It never has been with any of them." The nagging tension had returned.

Only later, when Samba spoke to me while driving back to Smyrna, would I understand the tension I had felt at that moment. While it was extremely important for him to have been effectively adopted by the Raus, he told me, as in any family there were times of friction. Samba's unplanned, extended stay with them, along with the many cultural differences, sometimes led to frustration and misunderstanding. According to Samba, Curran had initially been reluctant to bring him into their home; only later, once he had gotten to know Samba better, was Curran fully on board with welcoming him into the family.

Despite such difficulties, Samba's appreciation for all that Mary and Curran have done for him, as well as his deep love for this couple, cannot be overstated. "In every family there is bad and good—that's life.... I did not let this bother me. Mary was always there for me in time of distress, sadness, and sickness. She was always worried about me [and] my well-being. She is a special woman that God sent my way. I would do anything for her without regret and hesitation." When he was completely down, with no work, no legal papers, and no place to live, it was Mary who encouraged him:

> I was crying! She said, "No, you must have faith. Things will get better. It's nothing!" I said, "No, I want to work." She said, "Everything happens in its own time. You must believe in God." They gave me a key to their house and to their studio. They said I could go there whenever I wanted. I would go there and take a shower. I sometimes slept there.... I mean, a white woman, whom I don't even know, and vice versa, is helping *me*, a stranger from Africa? Despite all the racism and stories about Kennesaw—the place where the Civil War

> battle took place? A place where lots of racists still live? Many of my friends and people I meet always tell me that they would never [stay] in Kennesaw and that I should be careful there.

That the Raus adopted "Sam" as a son and welcomed him into their home, where he lived for five years, continues to astonish him to this day.

Since Samba had so often made reference to race in Kennesaw, I asked the Raus, "What did your neighbors and your family think of you having Sam living here with you?" Curran said that he did not really care what they thought and that, because they were in a mixed neighborhood, he didn't think that anyone cared. Mary interrupted:

> MR: Maybe some of the neighbors [were accepting of Samba] but there still was this thing that Sam was black. And we did have people leave the studio after the first show [featuring Samba's students]. But you are in the deep South. This probably wouldn't have happened up North.
>
> CR: She never told Sam that.
>
> SD: I never heard her say that until right now. [shaking his head]
>
> CR: It was over twenty percent!
>
> DR: Of people who left after that first show?
>
> CR: Yes.
>
> MR: Now, there was prejudice on both sides—
>
> CR: Yes.
>
> MR: Some people left the studio because we had Sam there and he was black. But there were other black people who were at our studio that were very upset because we did our recital on *Song of the South*.

Song of the South? This, Samba had not mentioned. His first performance as an immigrant had been in a dance recital based on a racially controversial Disney film from the 1940s? I could hardly believe what I had just heard. At another point in our conversation, Mary elaborated:

> He was teaching kids African dance for free, and we were coming up on our recital, so I said go ahead and teach them a number and we'll use it in our recital. Our recital was *Song of the South*, so it just kind of fit in to do something African. And then Sam played the part of Uncle Remus, and I had my grandson, who's grown up now, play the part of the little boy, and a niece [played] the little girl. . . . I was just thinking about that, Sam, the other day. Yeah, he was our Uncle Remus. [to Samba] I don't know if you even know who Uncle Remus is.

Samba shook his head no.

Northerners move to the south, open a dance school, and produce a ballet of *Song of the South* starring an African man as Uncle Remus. In the 1990s. A man who knew nothing of Uncle Remus or what he represented, who knew nothing of the show's outdated, stereotyping dialects and characterizations of happy slaves. It was Memphis in May all over again. And yet how was I to reconcile my political and cultural distaste with the familial affection before me? These were, after all, the people who had rescued Samba from a homeless shelter, adopted him as their own, given him a home and a *job* dancing and acting. Still, by the 1990s *Song of the South* had been widely criticized as racist for decades—so much so that, despite its popularity (the song "Zippity Do Da" won an Academy Award) Disney has never released the film on home video. My stomach cringed at the idea of Samba playing Uncle Remus. However, his loving family had produced the show in the shadow of Kennesaw Mountain, site of one of the most important battles of the Civil War. As in Memphis, Samba had unwittingly represented someone else's discourse or, more accurately, something that placed him at the center of a decades-long discursive controversy about race in American life.

It was with good intentions that Mary had chosen this theme for her recital and offered Samba the role, and she was caught off guard by the response.

MR: I said, "How can you be upset when the whole story is about a black man who befriended these children when their parents did not have time for them?" Their white parents did not have time for them. But [people] were upset. They didn't think we should use that, [here in the] South, as a recital piece. . . . I never thought that I was offending people, but I guess that I was. And there was one person that [said] this. Now, he was in his seventies, and he had a lot of this "black issue." . . . He said, "Mary, I can't believe you're having a black person teach African at your dance studio. . . . My father would turn over in his grave if he knew. . . . He is a wonderful educated man, a professor here at Southern Tech.

CR: I don't go into too much detail!

MR: But you know what I'm saying, that was the old, old South. So this is some of the stuff that people still have to live with. . . . Until, sadly to say, all of these people die, some of this stuff will not be forgotten.

CR: We had friends who were in the pro and con [about hiring/living with Samba]. We just—[shrugging]—I just didn't care.

MR: That really wasn't their business. Although Sam never mentioned it to us, I'm sure . . . a lot of his black friends or African friends . . . made some comment about him living with us [Samba nods]. Although Sam wouldn't tell us, and we wouldn't tell him anything—

CR: There are two sides to everything.

MR: It's the truth. It's not going to hurt Sam at this point [to know]. He's been here long enough at this point, on this black-and-white issue. . . . to see both sides (Samba gently shakes his head).

As I later noted in my field notes during the car ride to Smyrna, Samba reflected on what he had learned in our conversation with his American family. Given his now abundant experience of racism in the United States, he said that he was not so hurt to learn, after all these years, that parents had pulled their children out of the school because of their prejudice toward him as a person of color. However, he was troubled not because of racism but because Mary, who had helped him so much, had lost business as a result of inviting him to join her staff. This reaction was moving to me, in what it said both about Samba's love and concern for his sponsors and even more so about what it said about his depth of character.

After Remus

Following his American debut as Uncle Remus, Samba continued to teach and perform at Mary's studio and at other venues as his reputation and connections grew. Despite the white flight just described, Samba's classes became extremely popular and attracted more and more students. For end-of-term recitals, Mary continued to select challenging material, once a localized version of Tchaikovsky's *Nutcracker* in which the famous dream battle scene was set "not in Paris or Russia," Curran said, "but in the Civil War, on Kennesaw Mountain."

CR: It was like the ballet except we set it on Kennesaw Mountain [with] a southern belle and a southern mansion. Instead of having the mice and the soldiers fighting, we had the Civil War and the Yankees fighting. And that, too, was a problem for some.

MR: I said, "Well, why would it be a problem . . . when they [are] all killed in the end? There wasn't a winner, so it's not like [we were saying] "Yay! yay for the Yankees!"

SD: Like she said, everyone is killed in the end. We were trying to show that war is not good. In war people die.

DR: You are brave for taking on these issues in the South, where there is still strong sentiment in support of the rebel side.

CR: Very strong. Especially then. Since that time so many people have moved in from the North that Atlanta is as much Northerner as it is Southerner now.

Becoming Legal

Samba's early days at Mary Rau's dance school allowed him to feel more comfortable in his new life as an immigrant. He was making use of his training and skills, he had a place to live and a loving and supportive family, and, despite the racism and controversies engendered by his classes and shows, he was feeling positive about his life. Also, he began to make connections and find additional work, diversifying his performances and venues. In early 1996, he crossed paths with a young American *jembe* drummer and joined his Atlanta-based group, Fusion Production, which explored connections between African and American dance such as the Charleston and the Lindy Hop.

With Fusion Production, Samba toured universities, which led to still other opportunities, such as dancing at the opening and closing ceremonies of the 1996 Olympic Games in Atlanta. Meanwhile, he occasionally traveled for work with his Ivorian immigrant friends, performing in ballet-style shows that allowed him to draw directly on his training and experience. He continued to develop as a ballet performer and gradually extended his talents into new performance domains. Things were going well. Still a low-level, background stress persisted about his status as an illegal immigrant. Increasingly he was becoming known in Cobb County and the broader Atlanta metropolitan area, and he feared the police and deportation. According to Mary, "It was really a good time and a bad time for him when he lived here. Because he never really knew how this was going to turn out, [it] was hard for Sam . . . he was afraid he was going to be sent back."

From the moment that Mary became aware that she could not legally pay Samba, she began her efforts to secure him a work permit and then a green card. She was able to act as his sponsor because she was his employer. However, Mary's lawyer, who was not a specialist in immigration law, made mistakes in filing Samba's application, so the process dragged on for years. Once the application was finally submitted, the INS sat on it for two years and then denied Samba's case. "It could have all ended there," Samba said, "with me being sent back to Côte d'Ivoire. . . . They said that [after you're rejected], one month later you have to [leave the country]. So I was sad." But Mary Rau was determined and decided to take Samba's case to her congressman, John Lewis. "John Lewis!" I exclaimed. "I know him! He became famous in the 1960s in the Civil Rights struggle!" "Yes, that's him," Samba said. Mary and Samba went together to Lewis's office in downtown Atlanta and were warmly received. Lewis's staff assisted them as they redid his INS application.

In its initial decision, the INS had asked why Mary had decided to sponsor him, given that there was no evidence of "special talent," and it questioned whether there were American citizens who could do Samba's job. This time Mary created a description of a position teaching "traditional African dance" requiring a minimum of five years' study. As the INS rules stipulated, she ran a help wanted ad in a national publication and received three applications, including one from a woman with a master's degree in dance whom Mary decided she must interview. "I told Mary," said Samba, that in the interview she should ask [the applicant] where she had received her education. Was it full-time or . . . had she done a dance conference here and there?" The applicant's responses made clear that she had not had continuous, long-term education in African dance, and so Mary was able to eliminate her. The other applicants were also clearly unqualified, so Samba could claim his qualifications to be unique. This search for a teacher was included in the new application and according to Samba, "helped us a lot."

The first victory came in October 1999 in the form of a work permit, and with it a huge weight was lifted from Samba's shoulders; he no longer had to fear the sounds of sirens or the sight of police. Ever practical, one of the first things he did was return to the factory where he had first worked with no papers under a false name. Because he had been an excellent employee, the company was happy to take him back, and as of this writing he continues in this job full-time, which frees him from having to rely on dancing for a living. He told me that to this day some of his co-workers still call him by the pseudonym he used when he first arrived in Atlanta.

Less than a year later, a letter arrived in the mail which Mary opened, deciding to surprise Samba with its contents later at a dance studio performance. Samba recalled this joyous moment:

SD: We were at a show, and [Mary] wanted me to dance in [it]. She said, "I have your letter of invitation [to dance in the show]. Open it." I said, "This show is not a good show." She insisted: "Open it!" So I opened it, and there inside was a green card. I jumped in the air. . . . I didn't even have to go to an interview. When I told people I had my green card, they said, "You didn't have an interview?" "But you have to go to an interview!" When I said, "No, it came right to my house," they were astonished because people are afraid of those interviews. . . . Everything came to me right at the house! Aah—really, I was lucky. It was a blessing. . . . So I decided to stay here. . . . God really saved me.

Even years later when he recounted this story, Samba smiled in a way that betrayed a deep yet complex array of emotions—joy, relief, and a tender lovingness toward his sponsors. "Now I understand why you call them your family, because they went beyond what you could have expected—" Samba jumped in:

Yes, I was there, and I ate their food and I wasn't even working yet. You see? And . . . I lived there with them! If it had been someone else, they would have said, "You have to start paying now!" But . . . they really helped me a lot. When they introduced me to someone, they would say, "This is my son."

The Raus did not stop with a green card. They continued working with John Lewis's office until they succeeded in reaching Samba's ultimate goal—becoming an American citizen. At his 2010 *Ayoka*, Samba made the public announcement that he had become a citizen so he could thank Mary and Curran in public. "Everyone was happy," he told me. "When I cried, my sponsor . . . started to cry. . . . She helped me because I had no one here! I came and got a green card and US citizenship? . . . They just helped and helped and helped me! You see? So I say, this family I cannot forget. This is my family here! It touched me deeply."

Samba prefers not to tell his Ivorian immigrant colleagues about his citizenship because some of them have badgered him about his legal status for a long time. He wants to surprise them with the news.

> My friends in New York . . . say, "Why are you waiting? You have to get married! I say to them, "No, God will help me." And they say, "But you've been here how long? Five years?" They want to denounce me. But I tell them, "It's a process [for green cards and citizenship]. I have to wait. God will help me." If I had gone to New York, I might still be there suffering. . . . One day, I will be talking with one of them and he will say, "I became a citizen one year ago." And I'll say, "I have three years" and surprise them! . . . They strut around and make noise, and I just sit here tranquilly [laughs] . . . Since my sponsors were there [at his show], I felt obligated to announce it. But even though I announced it, some of them didn't really understand what I said because they think it was just a green card. . . . "But you are an American citizen?" Tia [an African American woman from Cincinnati who had danced at the show], she understood and . . . said something. But Moha [Dosso, Vado Diomande's nephew] was right there, and he didn't understand a thing!

The theme of competition returns in Samba's careful management of the news of his citizenship. Playful on the surface, underneath his decision to keep this "victory" close to the vest speaks to one of the fiercest competitions of the early twenty-first century—the competition among millions in the global South for highly coveted legal status in wealthier countries such as the United States. This is why Samba's gratitude toward Mary and Curran Rau for helping him reach the ultimate goal of citizenship is boundless.

Hardships of Immigrant Life

Because I knew that in 2010 Samba had been teaching at other venues, I asked if he was still teaching for Mary. As it turned out, in 2009 Mary had closed her studio because of dwindling enrollments she attributed to the Great Recession. Fortunately for Samba, by that time his application for citizenship was already in process. The studio's closing did present difficulties, however. Mary had allowed him to keep a key and use the studio for rehearsals and performances, but now, like many performing artists, Samba had to rent space.

Even a relatively modest show like the 2010 *Ayoka* is expensive to produce and tends to fall short of breaking even. Samba was deeply moved when Mary approached him after that performance and asked, "How much did you spend?" He replied, "About nineteen hundred." Ticket sales had grossed just $675. Mary said, "Where did you get that kind of money?" "I work, that's all . . ." he replied. Mary then committed herself to helping underwrite next year's *Ayoka*. Subsequent editions have taken place at bigger and better venues, such as regional theaters of the Atlanta Ballet Theater. Still, putting on an annual show, including the logistical and financial challenges of bringing in performers and integrating them into his local dance troupe, is difficult to do.

The challenges of producing performances are not the only ones in Samba's life as an immigrant performer. Another is the differences between life in Côte d'Ivoire and the United States. In West Africa, people greet one another when they pass on the street, enter a room, step into a taxi or minibus, or what have you. Even if you do not know someone, it is considered very rude not to at least say hello. If you run into someone you *do* know, the expectation is a substantial conversation about family, health, shared friends and acquaintances, and other topics. For Samba, daily American life feels cold in comparison. "There is no joy. You go from your house to work. People don't talk to each other here, or greet one another without suspicion."

As a dance teacher, Samba feels he is not given the respect he would receive back home. Particularly as he ages, he feels he is under a microscope, so much so that he conceals his true age.

> Being an artist, when you associate your image with your age, people automatically judge you. . . . When you dance, if you make one small error, people say, "Oh see, he's old." That's why I don't tell my age. . . . Even my dancers in Atlanta . . . always want to know how old I am. I ask them, "How old do you think I am?" . . . Here it is very different because in Africa or in other countries age is very important. . . . People must know your age [and] then they respect you. But here, despite your age, you get no respect. . . . If I tell [someone] I am fifty years old, [they're] going to treat me like a two-year-old—like Michael Jordan when he was playing toward the end of his career. Anytime he made a mistake, everyone would complain: "See, he is tired. He's too old." So people began to kill him a little bit at a time. It's psychological. . . . Even Africans who are here ask your age and won't respect you because they've been influenced by the culture. And the day that I'll be old will be when you see me walking with a cane. As long as I'm dancing . . . take me as you see me.

The disrespect that, according to Samba, Americans have for one another in general is hard for him. Africa's strong social expectation that a person always treats an elder with respect created expectations in Samba's mind that he finds sorely unmet in this country.

But by far the inability to easily go home is the hardest part of Samba's life in America. One day he and I were discussing politics, which prompted me to ask him about Côte d'Ivoire's civil war and subsequent division—a reality that had lasted eight long years at the time of this conversation in 2010. "Does the political situation [in Côte d'Ivoire] make you hesitant to return?" I asked. He replied that he is resolved to remain in the United States. "I might go back and forth for business, but one never knows what will happen over there." It was only then that I realized I had never heard Samba talk about returning to visit his country. "And you haven't been back to Côte d'Ivoire since your arrival here?" "No," came the terse reply. "Since 1994?" "No." "So that's sixteen years?" The usually loquacious Samba responded simply, "Yes." I hesitated a moment before saying, "That's a long time." "Uh-huh." "During that time, Côte d'Ivoire became destabilized." "Yes, yes." I had never seen him so reticent, even taciturn. This subject was clearly not an easy one for him, so I let it drop. In the five years since that difficult conversation, although Côte d'Ivoire had finally stabilized, Samba had still not returned to visit his homeland.

On one occasion, however, when talking about his family, the difficulties of living so far from home resurfaced. "Your father," I asked, "Is he still living?"

> No, he is deceased as of less than a year ago. And my mother died about two years before my dad. And through all that, I was here and could not go back home. . . . It's difficult. It was really hard. [For my mother], I didn't go because I was afraid I would not be allowed back in the country since I did not yet have my green card. . . . For my dad, since he is Muslim and the burial was the next day after his death, I could not get there. Also during that time, work was hard to find and I didn't have the means.

Singing his own version of the song of many African immigrants, Samba added, "If I go back, I have to go for at least three or four weeks. I can't go just for several days and return." He went on to describe the expectations that would accompany such a visit—gifts for family and friends, money for lavish feasts and help for people with medical issues and other financial hardships—and the longer he stays away, the greater the expectations. The greater the expectations, the harder it would be to go and so the longer he stays away. He finds himself caught in a vicious cycle that as of this writing has lasted twenty-one years.

Community and Family in the United States

Given the great time and space between Samba and his family back home, I was curious about his community connections in the United States. I asked him, "Beyond your sponsors and your cousins you told me about, do you have other family here in the United States?" He replied, "The one who is in Maryland is the son of my aunt's husband. The one who is here in Atlanta is the son of my aunt direct. Beyond that I have no one here in the United States." Having always heard about Atlanta's large Ivorian immigrant population, I asked if he had friends or a sense of community in Atlanta. He began his answer in a rather lackluster, uninspired tone:

> There is a big Ivorian community here in Atlanta, but I am not a part of it. They are based more in Atlanta and Doraville [a suburb]. I have friends that I cross paths with, some who come from other African countries. For example, two of my best friends are Senegalese. One is here in Atlanta, and the other was here for a long time but now lives in Florida. . . . There are two Ivorians who work where I work, whom I invited to my show. . . . One said he would come but he did not come.

I decided to try another angle, leading him with specific examples. "Does the Ivorian community here have events, restaurants, and that sort of thing, like in New York?" He began mentioning a couple of restaurants run by Ivorians he did not know. He then became energized as he unloaded a lengthy response full of alienation and critique of Ivorian class prejudice:

> The Ivorian community here—one day they wanted to celebrate Ivorian Independence Day, so they dropped by to ask my cousin if I could do a dance with children. My cousin called me, and I asked how much they were going to pay. . . . He said, "No, it will just be good publicity." So I didn't do it because I know Ivorians. They're going to . . . just look for "dancers" [gestures dismissively]. If you want my service, you should pay for it. . . . I don't have contact with them, with the Ivorian community. . . . In Africa, in Côte d'Ivoire, people say dancers . . . are low class. They haven't done the baccalaureate; they haven't done school. . . . Look back at the history, for example, the formation of the national ballet, and who [it was who] knew how to dance—it was villagers! So they went into the villages to take the natives, those people who had never been to school and live in the village! But they dance! . . . Those are the people that they took from each region to form the ballet. So that's what their mentality is today—dancers are villagers . . . just *villagers*. That mentality is still there . . . when they want a dancer—the people in the ballet . . . have not even been taught; they haven't been to university. They don't even know how to travel, and while they are doing their ballet, when they find an opportunity if they are in Germany or Spain, they flee! . . .People tend to think, "Those are just villagers." Effectively, they are right. When they formed the ballet, they went to each region and they took people like Vado from the village and . . . formed the ballet. So it's really difficult. . . . On one hand, they are correct because the ballet started like that. But nonetheless you have to open your eyes and see. We do the ballet. You should go see it! But they still have that mentality. In general, Ivorians are *blofeurs* [those who try to act like Americans and/or Europeans]. Again, they are here in America, and they have money, and they say, "Those are just *dancers*." So . . . they might call you to come and just dance with children, even if they pay you ten or fifteen dollars, because in the village you're just a villager. . . . There is no respect. So if they want me, it's my work, they have to pay me.

Fascinating, I thought, that more than fifty years after independence, the colonization of the mind most famously critiqued by Ngugi (1981) persists, even across the ocean in immigrant communities. The uniquely indigenous cultural expressions that postcolonial African rulers chose to represent their nations to the world are still viewed by some educated, so-called Westernized Africans as backward, even embarrassing.

But Samba's disaffection for Ivorians in America is also deeply personal. Now discussing the Ivorian community not just in Atlanta but all over the country, he said:

> The Ivorian artists wanted to create a small [association] to help struggling Ivorian artists. . . . [It would be] based in New York, so they can be there to offer help. Fanzy lost his mother and father, and so everyone contributed.[6] But then when I lost my parents, *no one* contributed. I informed everyone, but no one contributed for me. So I said to myself, "I will no longer be part of this association. If someone dies, I don't need to give money." . . . Not *one person* gave to me. . . . So if someone loses someone, and they call me, I will offer my condolences and send them something. I will do so, but not through the Ivorian association. It's a shame this great idea died so suddenly, but that's how it is.

A Teacher of Dance

Samba loves to dance, but even more he loves to teach dance. He understands his work, both in the studio and on the stage, as educational. He sees dance as fundamentally connected to the rhythms of life:

> In Africa we say that as soon as you come out of your mother, and you start waving your arms, that is dance. . . . As I say in my classes, if you can walk you can dance; if you can eat you can dance. The act of eating is a kind of movement; eating has a cadence, has a rhythm.

To illustrate his point, Samba moved his arm back and forth from an imaginary bowl to his mouth. This little performance was at once humorous and illuminating, as it bodily demonstrated Samba's deep attunement to the rhythms in everyday life.

Having taught for over twenty years in the United States, Samba is able to identify three main reasons that students are attracted to his classes. "There are some who dance for exercise; some come because their friends come." A third group comes for the culture. Samba consciously tries to craft his work, from promotion to class content, with these markets in mind. In a June 2014 e-newsletter about "Samba Diallo's African Dance Program," he described his dance in this way:

> We provide a variety of dance classes throughout the greater Atlanta area every day of the week. Some classes introduce traditional African dancing, complete with live drumming. Other classes offer a workout with more modern African music and dance. Thanks to Samba, you will never go a day without African dance!

His use of *workout* clearly references the exercise component of Samba's classes, and he has taken this notion one step further by naming one weekly class series Afrofit:

> This total body workout offers a fun, energetic aerobic exercise set to modern African music and inspired by traditional African dances and the warm-up techniques of the National Ballet of Côte d'Ivoire.

The newsletter describes programs and classes that "showcase the arts and culture of the Ivory Coast." It features articles on specific Ivorian dances, the mask culture of Côte d'Ivoire, and other topics designed to attract clients looking for cultural education.

During the time I was researching this book, Samba generally taught two dance classes per week, one he called traditional and one he called modern. Interestingly, this structuring echoes precisely the epistemology that informed the dance categories in his Varietoscope competitions, where Samba first began choreographing for the stage. Just as in his early competitive experiences, one of the central differences between modern and traditional in his classes is the extent to which the raw materials he draws on in his choreography—the music and the dances—are "marked" as associated with a particular ethnic group. The more marked it is, the more a dance is defined as traditional or typical; the less marked, the more likely it is defined as modern or "Afro-jazz":

> I have two types of creation. When I create typical tradition, I only mix traditional dances. I . . . take a Guinean move and a Ghanaian move and I mix them. And that remains typical. [For the] other type, that I call Afro jazz, I mix modern and traditional dances . . . to popular music like *zaiiko*. People really like that. I do that every Thursday for my classes.

Samba says that he likes traditional and modern equally, but his students generally "prefer the modern because they can dance like that in night clubs." And the two categories are far from isolable and absolute—there is considerable play between them (cf. Barber 1997; Waterman 1990; Reed 2003).

Samba employs a similar creative process for all of his choreography—one that emphasizes the integration of styles of different origins that he has experienced in both his daily life and on stages since he was a child. Often he takes two dances and "puts them together, adding a transition so the dance is smooth." Sometimes he incorporates steps that he has seen elsewhere, such as in a Senegalese dance that he likes, or he creates something "in his head." Sometimes this creative process produces a dance that he sees as a new creation and he gives it a name. Often this occurs for pedagogical purposes—that is, while he is teaching his dance students, if he senses a particular kind of movement that needs attention, he might just create something on the spot.

According to Samba, not all teachers of African dance possess such skills. He is particularly critical of those who claim the authority to teach without having the kind of ballet training and experience that he believes is necessary. He explains:

> There are many Africans who come here to the United States who are not drummers or dancers but see the opportunity to make money, so they become a drummer or they become a dancer. These are the people who bother us and create problems for us because they have not had sufficient education or training.... [in] the tradition and the culture.[7]

Samba feels deeply about teaching African music and dance in an appropriate way, which requires years of education and a great deal of dedication. He said, "You have to really love culture to continue, to remain. [former BNCI director] Louis Akin said, 'An artist never ages. An artist is always alive.' We are always moving. And we have to have creativity." In his eyes, proper training and dedication along with creativity and never ending learning make a good teacher. He continues to learn from his colleagues. For example, at Sogbety's festival several years before, he learned the Mau dance *baade malon* from Vado Diomande. He videotaped Vado teaching the dance and brought the tape back to Atlanta, where he teaches the dance now. However, in his effort to grow creatively, Samba does not restrict himself to Ivorian dance. Once at a festival in Atlanta, he saw a Guinean teach a dance that he really liked. He paid the Guinean to perform the dance and teach him its history. Again he videotaped the Guinean and studied the recording so he could add it to his repertoire. "I have an open mind," Samba declared. "I am not Guinean, but if I see a dance from Guinea that pleases me, I will learn it. I do Côte d'Ivoire, but I'm open to everything."

Choreography and the Stage

When discussing his stage work, Samba described the synthetic creative processes necessary to produce an effective performance. He stressed that experience in a large company like the national ballet is necessary in developing skills to meet audience expectations in the United States. He talked about effective timing and visual presentation working together. About both dancing and drumming, he articulated very effectively that virtuosity in and of itself does not produce much of an effect. Rather, a virtuosic drum or dance solo must be timed with great care, with appropriately placed "blocks" that break the energy. These introduce a more subtle and simple rhythm that causes the energy to shift suddenly, which consistently draws great applause and cheers. According to Samba, "You have to captivate people. You have to take [them] up on high and then descend like that. It's a matter of pausing in exactly the right moment.... It makes people crazy."

> The majority of producers are not great dancers, but they can envision what people want.... The same thing holds for lighting designers. They have to know what people want. They may say, "In this part here, we need to have light like a sunset or like a sunrise." They see what people will want, what will captivate people and also go well with the costumes. They know, and they see it, even if they are not good dancers. But they know what people want. So that the stage is beautiful.... So it's all that together that makes a good show.

Thinking about applying his ballet training to US stages naturally led Samba to the similarities and differences between audiences in Africa and North America. He stressed, not surprisingly, that Ivorian audiences are generally more knowledgeable about dance traditions—how solos tend to work, how they begin and end, what movements to expect. And he discussed audience interpretations of breaks, calls, or changes, and cuts or blocks. These are the fancy rhythmic coordinations that mark the end of a break in *gbegbe*, one of the best-known Ivorian dances originally from the Bete people:

> The *gbegbe* dance, for example. Back in the home country, people know that dance ... so the drummer, when he does the call or the change, when he cuts the end, people who know that [cut] will recognize it.... Here people don't know that, so you do the break and they don't appreciate it. Because people know the history, [they know that] in *gbegbe* at the end you have to cut it [gesturing the cuts]. If you don't do that, people in the audience will kill you ... WOO.... People automatically know. When you cut, on the same beat, the crowd will cry out at the same time. They're happy because they're waiting for that part.... But if it's a dance and you miss it, they're going to say, "But who's that? Is he a Bete or a Jula?

By Jula Samba means an ethnic group that does not know the dance.

Breaks and cuts are part of the immense knowledge and many cultural practices—the ballet discourse—that Ivorian immigrant performers must know to perform together effectively. Yet as Samba suggested, at times its fine-grained details might go over North American heads.

DR: Is it easier to impress people in the United States, even though appreciation in Côte d'Ivoire is deeper?

SD: Yes, effectively people here don't know. If you're performing a mask, for example, and you make mistakes or the mask's raffia skirt is out of place, they don't know there is a problem. They just say, "Wow!" Back in the country, if your raffia falls off, people start to *yell*. You can't make mistakes back home because people know—because they are ready to judge you.... But here there is a culture of always congratulating people even if they have not done good work.... Here they appreciate you more. Back in the country, they appreciate you relative to the quality of your performance. And they judge you by comparison because they have already seen many *zaulis* and many *bolohis*, so when they see you and if you do something spectacular, they say, "Woo-hoo! You're powerful!" [That's] because they compare you to someone they have seen. But here they appreciate you without comparison.

Speaking of a specific market niche for Ivorian performance, Samba stressed the mask:

> My goal for presenting African dance, and especially Ivorian dance, is to demonstrate the importance of the African mask because people have seen a lot of African dance but [not] the most important one . . . the traditional mask. So my goal is to promote traditional masks. . . . I want my group to be known as one that performs lots of masks. . . . What makes one group different from another? People think African masks are just statues or pieces of art on the wall. Even if it's a mask from South Africa, a mask from Japan—if it's a mask that dances to the sound of the drum, I will put it in my show. I want people to experience a lot of masks and to learn about them . . . so when I plan . . . a show, I always keep a place for the masks. I want them to see the face of Africa through the different masks.

Future Plans

Samba continues to pursue his career as a dancer and a teacher of dance with a focus and commitment that I find inspiring. He is skilled at determining what he needs to grow professionally and going after it with a calm yet intense sense of purpose. And he is a masterful promoter of his work, making use of videos, websites, email, and social media on a regular basis, and promoting his classes, workshops, and performances on Facebook. While working full-time at the factory, teaching at least two classes a week, occasionally performing, and holding workshops, Samba spent several years studying website design at Kennesaw State University, earning a certificate in 2013. Now he has the skills to promote his own work and, increasingly, the work of other African immigrant artists. He has begun marketing his web design skills, working mostly through word of mouth, and says that with his web design certificate he now has yet another tool for making a living in African music and dance in the United States.

Looking forward, Samba would like to found a school in Côte d'Ivoire "that would teach about culture and unity." He believes in cultural education as a way to bring people together and overcome differences and conflict. "I think that through culture, we can find great unity," he said, "so I would like to create a huge school of dance teaching the cultures of the world . . . so everyone who comes to the school would be at ease because they would find their culture." "Like a dance UN?" I asked. "Yes, that's it. I would like to open one here, one in Ghana and Senegal and Côte d'Ivoire." His dreams for the future build on his past in very direct and specific ways. He grew up with a mixed ethnic identity in culturally pluralistic environments; he learned how to make a living representing cultural pluralism by weaving together and unifying difference. "Culture brings everyone together" I have heard him proclaim more than once at his shows. He wants to expand on that vision by creating institutions in which people can learn about each other. "It was through culture that, for example, I got to know you," he told me. At that moment we both smiled. As I later thought back on his words, I marveled at the potential of ethnography as a means of bringing people of varying backgrounds and identities together for a common purpose. From the moment we first met that August morning at my father's school in Ohio, I had always felt something in common with Samba, a shared sense of purpose in our life's work. His statement affirmed that initial feeling, and I was thankful that our paths had crossed.

Samba's life has not been easy. His decision to immigrate to the United States has led not just to greater opportunities to transform his ballet training into an economic resource, transcend difference, and pursue visions of unity. It has also led to a life of loneliness, suffering, struggle—including financial struggle—and plenty of cultural *mis*understanding. All told, however, Samba believes that leaving his homeland to pursue life as an immigrant performer was the right choice. "I'm happy because if I had stayed in Côte d'Ivoire, I would have nothing to do. With dance, today I am here in America. . . . It's better than if I had stayed in my country. I dance and I sing, but I could have nothing to eat back home in Côte d'Ivoire. With song and dance, I can travel all over the world."

ACT III
SOGBETY DIOMANDE

7 "You Know You're in a Different Country"

Sogbety Diomande's West African Drum and Dance

September 27, 2008, Bloomington, Indiana. A crisp fall evening, the downtown streets blocked off and filled with pedestrians scurrying from one performance venue to the next, past informal drum circles, street magicians, a masked woman in silver body paint dancing like a snake, a New Orleans backline-style band of horns and drums parading. It was the Lotus Festival, and normal daily life was suspended as thousands wandered between more than half a dozen venues hosting concurrent "world-music" performances, the streets transformed into festival space. Brazilian hip-hop, Turkish whirling dervishes, and Celtic-Nordic fiddle fusion were among the many options. As the setting sun beamed in through the open end of a massive tent on the north side of the courthouse square, I, in my role as master of ceremonies, welcomed Sogbety Diomande's West African Drum and Dance Company to the stage.

Jembes, dunduns, dance breaks, spectacular solos, Gue Pelou, Zauli, Bolohi—ballet discourse. Gue Pelou opened this show, walking up the stairs on the side of the stage to the booming sounds of dunduns and striding downstage, where he stood, about ten feet tall on stilts, towering over the crowd (PURL 7.1a). His mysterious, nonrepresentational black face let out a characteristic falsetto cry. Concealed under a cream, blue, and yellow, loom-woven *bubu*, his hands gripped fly whisks as his arms flapped like wings while he glided sideways. The spirit stopped, looked around, and allowed tension and suspense to build with the sonic energy of the drums. Suddenly throwing one long leg forward, Gue Pelou began a whirling, spinning motion back across the stage, one stilt landing while the other whirled, around and around and around as the crowd roared. Tossing the flywhisks down, he screamed again and then threw his body sideways and around in a flip, landing in full splits to yet louder applause. All the while the *jembes* and *dunduns* marked out the *tindin* rhythm while a Maninka *jeli* from Guinea pounded out percussive melodies as his rubber mallets struck the wooden keys of his *bala* xylophone. Following the stilt mask spirit, or *nya yan,* shouting out encouragement and soloing on his *jembe* while the mask danced, was Sogbety Diomande.

About thirty minutes into the performance, following more masks and human dancers, Sogbety's uncle, Vado Diomande, wearing shirt and pants of deep blue-dyed indigo cloth, walked briskly to the mic. He began singing, teaching the audience a song (PURL 7.2):

> Diomande ngo
> Ce min n dor ko
> Diomande ngo
>
> Diomande (vocable)
> that's the man whose name is
> Diomande (vocable)

Following a humorous breakdown in audience response, Vado spun around to face the drummers, directing them to begin singing the song and playing their instruments. He then began to demonstrate his incredible skill at dance as Dr. Djo Bi assumed the role of lead drummer. Vado and Djo Bi launched a series of breaks, the first of which was cued by Vado signaling Djo Bi to follow the rhythm of his legs moving alternately away from his body and back toward the center in rapid succession; Djo Bi fell in place immediately, matching the dancer's movement with an identical, repeating rhythmic motif. The two veterans of the ballet stage continued through several breaks, beautifully coordinated and ending with spectacular "cuts." Despite having nearly died of anthrax poisoning just three years earlier, and suffering the pain of badly damaged knees in need of surgical repair, Vado lit up the stage with a combination of technique and joy.

About forty-five minutes in, Sogbety sat center stage, a multiheaded drum between his legs. His fingers began bouncing off the smaller, "children" heads, producing high-pitched tones around resonant slaps on the large, centrally placed "mother" drum (PURL 7.3). He was playing a "modern" version, created for the stage, of the drum the Mau call variously *yado*, *ɓaanya*, or *ɓaade*.[1] Eschewing the "traditional" *ɓaade* made of thicker antelope or red deer skin and nylon rope, Sogbety uses this "professional" *jembe* modification—goatskin stretched extremely taut with an iron ring fastening each drum's skin to its goblet-shaped body. Sogbety's instrument essentially consists of five miniature *jembes* tied onto a larger but still relatively small *jembe*. Much louder and more resonant than its traditional antecedent, this "jembefied" *ɓaade* is better suited for the concert stage. The instrument itself is an interethnic hybrid, made for ballet.

After a few seconds of soloing, Sogbety's *ɓaade* was joined by *jembes* and *dunduns*—instruments of northern Mande origin and ballet standards. Layered over the drums, Guinean Kierno Diabate played the Maninka *jelibala*—the wooden xylophone associated with the *jeli* caste in Maninka and other northern

Mande groups. Vado began a song in Mau. A Guinean on the *jelibala*, an Abidjan born and raised Burkinabé and Ivorians of several ethnicities (Guro, Bete, Mau) on *jembes* accompanying Mau drumming and song—this was a transnational, interethnic mélange.

"Ballet" discourse was present in other aspects of the piece as well. The song text extolled the value of neighborliness, a theme of community and unity. The drummers performed a playful and improvisatory *tindin* rhythm, with Papa Diarra on *dundun* keeping the main time and the rhythm in an elastic way, while Sogbety artfully varied the standard *baade* pattern by ranging around the various heads of the instrument. After a time, Vado broke away from the vocal mic and began dancing elaborate breaks in alternation with dancers Clarice Toa and Marylese Burton. Each break ended dramatically with sharp, clean cuts synchronized perfectly with the master drum. Finally, after cueing the ending, Sogbety thanked the crowd in the Jula language ("a ni ce"). This was ballet—speaking each other's language in music, dance, and words and weaving it all together.

In this chapter, I analyze the performance of Sogbety Diomande's West African Drum and Dance Company at the 2008 Lotus Festival in Bloomington, Indiana. A confluence of transnational circulations, this event typified Ivorian performance and adaptations of Ivorian ballet in the United States, and was heavily influenced by Sogbety's Uncle Vado's discourse of universalism. These influences manifested in multiple interweavings of difference. Like Vado in his *Kekene* show, Sogbety fluidly blended ethnicities, nations, and aesthetics. In contrast to Vado, however, Sogbety chose not to blend races, conforming to common representational expectations about who should perform Africa on stage. He also dispensed with the choreographed dramas so central to the Ballet National de Côte d'Ivoire (BNCI) and Vado's Kotchegna Dance Company. In Sogbety's opinion, audiences in the United States are not interested in and often do not understand them, so he staged sets of different musical and dance pieces, including mask performances, in a way that harkened back to the celebration that brings ballet-style choreographed dramas to a close.

Sogbety's adaptation of the ballet form is but one of many examples of his skill in crafting his performance strategically according to each audience he faces. Ever adaptive, he pays careful attention to representational expectations based on prevailing discourses of Africa and African music. He emerges as a dynamic and strategic performer, who, though he is the youngest of the four artists featured in this book, has seen increasingly greater success in North America. Like a world-music artist, he masterfully familiarizes Otherness, very comfortably shaping his work in response to his audience (cf. Taylor 1997).

In September 2008, the Lotus World Music and Arts Festival hired Sogbety and his group for Friday and Saturday evening performances and an afternoon drumming workshop. This is an example of the immigrant community being reinforced thanks to one performer, Sogbety, who secured a gig that paid enough for him to invite his friends from across the eastern United States to join him. The reality is that Sogbety Diomande's West African Drum and Dance Company, like most Ivorian immigrant performance groups, has an ever flexible roster that does not rehearse or perform on a regular basis. What is astounding is the extent to which its performances, which feature highly coordinated, complex music and dance, give the *impression* that the company is a regularly working group. The talent of the individuals in the community and their shared experience in ballet make this possible.

For immigrant performers, one of the greatest benefits of lucrative performance contracts such as Lotus is the opportunity to reunite. Following is a passage from my field notes from October 13, 2008:

> The weekend began with everyone's arrival Thursday. I arrived at Djo Bi's around 10 pm, where a fire was already burning in his backyard and many Ivorians were informally drumming. Also present were around 6-8 people who presumably are participants in Harmony and Djo Bi's dance classes, who generally seemed to be in awe of the drummers and greatly appreciative of the chance to be with them in an informal setting. Already several were clearly drunk . . . Samba was either tired or not in a good mood and did not want to participate (he told me he was just tired from the trip, though he might have been put off by the heavy drinking). But Vado and others danced joyously; this was clearly another example of the group making music and dance just because they love to. There is absolutely no sense of saving themselves for the show. Music for them is not just about a performance, it's their lives.

Informal gatherings nearly always occur both before and after formal performances (the only exception being performances in New York, where, according to Vado, there is no space for them), and music making is always at their center. Given the amount of energy required for the performances, and even the wear and tear on drummers' hands and dancers' knees, I am always struck by the drumming and dancing that immigrant performers engage in during their off-hours, when strategic representation and consideration of audience are nonissues. In formal settings like the stage, however, representational choices are critical.

Verbal Discourse

What's in a Name?

In contrast to my other three consultants, Sogbety Diomande chose a name for his group entirely in English. No Kotchegna, no Attoungblan, no Asafo, and, for that matter, no Côte d'Ivoire. Instead, Sogbety's name identifies his group regionally as West African. "I was looking for something that was not too long and that Americans can say quickly," he told me, explaining that if he defined his group as Ivorian, some Americans would not know what that meant. Proving the well-established axiom that identity is situational and contextual, he told me that if he were to form a group in Côte d'Ivoire, "I would probably change the name. It would not be 'West African.' It would be . . . Toufinga something. . . . something Mau." In addition to promoting his self-representation in the American market, the name suits him because he generally identifies himself not as Ivorian but as African or, more frequently, West African (see also Ferguson 2006). For Sogbety this identity shift is closely related to contextual language practices:

SOGBETY DIOMANDE (SD): When you arrive here [in the United States], everyone speaks just about the same language. . . . [When] you arrive here, you're an African; it's French that you're going to speak to other Africans, or English. You don't hear people speaking different ethnic languages here and there. Here in the United States everyone speaks one language. So you feel like that a little bit. But back there in Africa, when you're in the village, it's there that you hear lots of different ethnic groups and different languages. You might hear some Baule, and you say "Oh, that's a Baule person." But that doesn't happen here. There is one big language.

DANIEL REED (DR): So language is very important [in determining identity]?

SD: Yes, language is very important because the manner in which you speak—it's like that that you play your music.

Just as French serves as the lingua franca for immigrants from francophone West Africa, enabling them to communicate across ethnic and national lines, ballet serves as a common performative language for immigrant performers. And because the language of ballet crosses national borders, Sogbety sometimes includes non-Ivorians, especially Guineans, in his shows. This he offers as yet another justification for his group's name: he "doesn't want to leave anyone out."

In every instance since meeting Sogbety in 2006, from his festivals in Mansfield, Ohio, to local library and school shows to university-based dance and drum workshops to major performances like the Lotus Festival, I have heard him use the phrase "Sogbety Diomande's West African Drum and Dance Company." On his website,[2] his school programs are similarly framed—for example, "West African Experience," "Discover West African Rhythm through Drumming and Dance," "West African Drumming and Dance Residency." Often in describing an event, Sogbety represents himself as being from Côte d'Ivoire, but in the important act of naming he prefers to identify regionally.

In addition to its fluid identities, Sogbety's promotional language features terms that tap common discourses about the representation of Africa on American stages. Sogbety's website describes his programs and performances as "high-energy," featuring "colorful costumes," "native rhythms and dances," with "powerful, awe-inspiring" mask dances that are "exciting displays of incredible energy and talent." A performed Africa is thus colorful, native, powerful, and energetic, evoking exoticism and primality.

Images

Consistent with his naming practices, Sogbety's visual representational choices—in flyers, posters, and other promotional media—include no obvious references to Côte d'Ivoire. Instead, photographic images of Gue Pelou are nearly always prominent. His annual festivals in the Mansfield, Ohio, area exemplify this. There are no maps or Ivorian national colors on posters, flyers, or advertisements. While there may be photographs of masks, drummers, and dancers, no words or images specify their country of origin. Visually and verbally, Sogbety defines his work as West African, attracting audiences with this familiar and accessible label.

Performed Discourse

Performers

Given Sogbety's tendency to identify himself as West African rather than Ivorian, I found it surprising that his company had by far the most Ivorians of any group I have seen. Nine of the eleven performers at Lotus 2008 were Ivorian immigrants; the other two were from Guinea (see table 7.1). Clearly there is no direct relationship between naming and other promotional representational strategies and the actual demographic composition of an ensemble.

Sogbety's company is an excellent example of the role of ballet experience and training in providing a base of knowledge and practice that enables a group to appear as if they regularly perform and tour together. Talking with friends and acquaintances following Sogbety's Lotus performances, I found that nearly to a person, they were surprised to learn that these eleven performers had come from as far east as New York City, as far south as New Orleans, and as far west as Indianapolis and points in between. Some had never performed together before, although most were familiar with one another, in some cases dating back to before their emigration from Côte d'Ivoire but at the very least from previous performances.

Ivorian immigrants maintain community largely via performance. Ballet-trained performers draw on their shared culture, which includes repertoire, the ability to play that repertoire using standardized *jembe* and dundun instrumentation, and breaks, cues, and other aesthetic practices. While to some degree their ballet is distinct, enough is shared for Guineans Hamidou Koivogui and Kierno Diabate to easily fall in step with the Ivorians. Again, Guinean and Ivorian national ensembles are transnationally linked in origin, sharing instrumentation,

Table 7.1 Performers in Sogbety Diomande's West African Drum and Dance Company, Lotus Festival 2008

Drummers/musicians (all male)	Country of origin; US location	Nationality/ethnicity (all Ivorian unless otherwise indicated)
Sogbety Diomande	Côte d'Ivoire; Mansfield, OH	Mau
Vado Diomande	Côte d'Ivoire; New York, NY	Mau
Djo Bi Irie Simon	Côte d'Ivoire; Bloomington, IN	Guro
Samba Diallo	Côte d'Ivoire; Atlanta, GA	Does not identify as an ethnicity
Blaise Zekalo	Côte d'Ivoire; Indianapolis, IN	Bete
Papa Diarra	Côte d'Ivoire; New York, NY	Bobo
Moha Dosso	Côte d'Ivoire; Scottsburg, IN	Mau
Clarice Toa	Côte d'Ivoire; Indianapolis, IN	Wobé
Marylese Burton	Côte d'Ivoire; Indianapolis, IN	Bete
Hamidou Koivogui	Guinea; Cincinnati, OH	Guinean; ethnicity unknown
Kierno Diabate	Guinea; New Orleans, LA	Guinean; Maninka

some rhythms, breaks, and so forth, and what is not historically shared they can easily teach each other, just as Hamidou was taught to dance the Ivorian mask spirit Bolohi. In my Lotus field notes for October 10, 2008, I commented on this:

> The sound check demonstrated the extent to which the group was still figuring out what to do and is, like a good group of jazz musicians, always on the ready. Like jazz players, they have a shared performative language—rhythms, drum language, dance steps, cueing, etc.—that they can draw upon to give a show even if they've never seen one another before. Some of this performative language has deep and long historical roots, and is shared especially by those who are of the same ethnic groups. But . . . much of the language is more recent or updated through their shared experiences in national ensembles. Even Diabate, who is Guinean and hadn't seen any of these folks in at least three years, could fall right in and perform as if he had been with them a very long time. It's really quite amazing.

Genre/Structure

The structure of the 2008 Lotus show drew heavily on ballet while leaving aside choreographed drama. One dance followed another seamlessly with no breaks but only a constant flow of sound and movement. The genres that the group drew on represented standard Ivorian immigrant ballet: Ivorian masks Gue Pelou,

Bolohi, and Zauli; Guinean mask Soli Wule (PURL 7.4); and a host of Ivorian rhythms, including *gbegbe*, *tindin*, *tématé*, and others, as well as the famous Guinean *jembe* rhythm, *kuku*.

For a mask like Gue Pelou, some Mau and Dan rules become flexible on stage, such as what rhythms manifest the spirits (*ginan*) that transport the mask spirit to the earthly realm and what instruments play as the mask performs. Other rules, however, remain as strict as they are in a Mau village. While doing this research, I found one that was absolute and non-negotiable—that governing the mask's preparation for performance. In Mau communities, a mask spirit emerges from a sacred house, which is forbidden to all but initiates of the mask society. A challenge in arranging Gue Pelou performances in the United States is reserving a space for this purpose, as the mask must have total privacy both before and after a performance when dressing and undressing. At the outdoor tent at Lotus 2008, all three artists performing that evening were to share one tent dressing room, but Vado informed me that Gue Pelou could not appear under those conditions. I quickly borrowed Harmony Harris's car, rushed home, grabbed a large tarp and every bungee cord I had, and sped back with my supplies. Stage manager Peter Ermey and I hurriedly constructed a makeshift wall dividing the dressing room in two. Had we not done so, Gue Pelou, often considered the highlight of Ivorian immigrant shows, would not have appeared.

Thankfully, the stilt mask spirit did appear on the Lotus stage and as always was a big hit. In Vado, Samba, and Sogbety's promotional materials, Gue Pelou is identified as a god of the forest. Mau masks, *nya* in Sogbety's Mauka language, are spiritual beings who come from the sacred forest adjacent to a Mau village. When invited to join the BNCI as a founding member in 1974, Sogbety's uncle Vado brought Gue Pelou from his village of Toufinga to the concert stage. Before leaving Côte d'Ivoire, Sogbety himself was initiated into the small group of Toufinga men who perform Gue Pelou. Since 1997, Vado, Sogbety, and his cousin Moha Dosso have performed Gue Pelou regularly around the eastern United States.

There are many ways in which the staged performance of Gue Pelou differs from that in Mau communities. These include spatial rearrangement (lines of performers on stage versus a circle with the mask in the center in a village) and performance structure (on the stage a predetermined sequence consisting of a song and a *tindin* rhythm, a benediction, and then a song, usually "Ge ya yi kan" in *zikinin* rhythm; in a village, purely improvised and unpredictable) (PURL 7.1b). Nothing better illustrates the principle of interweaving of difference—ethnic, generic, national—than the music.

Benedictions—one of the most important elements of any sacred mask performance on stage or off—are blessings that the mask offers to performers and audience alike. At certain intervals, the mask interjects "A sa de" (This is your sacrifice or, idiomatically, This is my offering to you), to which all present respond in unison "Amina" (Amen) while touching the palms of their hands to their foreheads. Just as in song, the mask speaks exclusively in Dan. The assistant to the mask, played by Sogbety at Lotus, acts as intermediary between mask and people, alternately repeating the mask's words and interjecting nonlexical sounds of encouragement (e.g., "Yo!"), directing the audience when to say, "Amina" and generally ensuring that the performance accords with custom.

Following Gue Pelou's spectacular appearance, the group performed the standard genres—other masks, *jembe* solos, dance solos to *kuku*, and Ivorian rhythms like *gbegbe*. I found it remarkable that Ivorian immigrants were able to perform these genres in a similar structure again and again and yet always make them fresh, electric, or hot, a word Ivorians frequently employ to describe an excellent performance. One thing that makes routine, standard performances hot is improvisation. The ways breaks are selected and employed is one key to an exciting show. Either dancers or drummers can cue the start of a break, after which the others join in. These cues are often very subtle, but both drummers and dancers must pay close attention, remaining ever ready for the other to signal through rhythm that a particular break is about to begin. There were many examples at Lotus of such smooth communication using rhythmic language from ballet. Vado, Samba, Clarice, and Marylese thrilled the crowd with break after break, usually coordinated with either Papa or Djo Bi (PURL 7.3).

Signals or cues, similar to breaks, are also used by drummers to communicate to the group. A common example is a cue that a drummer is about to signal the end of a piece. Several times at the Lotus show, Papa used this cue, which consists of alternating tones and slaps in series of four sixteenth notes each:

TTTT/SSSS/ TTTT/SSSS/ TTTT/SSSS/ TTTT/SSSS/ ... (PURL 7.2)

Ever imaginative, Papa altered this pattern in creative ways, at times playing more slaps and fewer tone strikes. Using this cue, he captured the group's attention for what followed: yet another cue that indicated which break they would play in unison to draw the piece to a close. In this case, Papa first played the sixteenth-note pattern just shown, then two eighth-note slaps followed by two quarter-note rests, at which point the whole ensemble ended dramatically with five eighth-note strikes in unison. Ballet knowledge thus includes a number of categories of breaks and familiarity with their use in spontaneous, improvised rhythmic communication. Breaks and cues are important communicative tools that draw on the language of ballet to make performances work, structurally and excitingly.

Instrumentation

Sogbety's Lotus 2008 show highlighted what I call "jembefication"—the transposition of non-*jembe* rhythms into *jembe/dundun* instrumentation. The mask performances alone offer three examples, as illustrated in the following paragraphs.

In Guro community contexts, the Zauli mask is generally performed with a combination of drums, played with hammer-like sticks, and hand drums as well as an ensemble of single-pitched, reed flutes playing in hocket (the rhythmic coordination of pitches played successively by two or more people). The ballet-style Zauli replaces this instrumentation with *jembe/dundun*, on which the Guro rhythms are transposed. I have never seen Zauli performed in the United States with anything but ballet instrumentation, which completely loses the distinctive sound of the Guro flutes.

The panther mask that Senufo people call Bolohi is generally performed in Senufo communities with no drums but rather with an ensemble of one-string harps called *bɔlɔnye* and several gourd rattles strung with a string net threaded with beads or lizard vertebrae. A huge calabash serves as the *bɔlɔnye*'s resonating body and its curved stick neck holds the string. *Bɔlɔnye* players both pluck the string and tap the calabash, often with metal rings on their fingers to provide a loud clack (Gibson and Reed 2002). Again, a common rhythm played with this ensemble is transposed onto the *jembe* and *dundun* for ballet performances.

The musical transformation of the Mau mask Gue Pelou was described previously. In both Mau and Dan communities, a very different drum from the *jembe* is played for stilt masks spirits. *Baa* drum ensembles, producing sound that Dan *ge* practitioners define not as music but as the mask spirit's sonic manifestation, combine single-headed, goblet-shaped, and multiheaded drums (with anywhere from two to seven heads), and often a gourd rattle. Not just any drums can be used but only *baa* drums that have been spiritually prepared via sacrifice and other mystical activities in a sacred hut or in the protected confines of the sacred forest. The rhythms from these instruments are transposed for *jembe/dundun* on the ballet stage.

Although the *jembe* originated in Maninka country along the Guinea/Mali border, it is not as if it is foreign to Côte d'Ivoire. The northern Mande play it, and increasingly, as northerners migrate into southern cities, it is played in the south as well. In the forest region, I commonly heard the *jembe* called a city drum because of its association with northerners who, during the colonial era, moved south to set up trade opportunities and eventually markets next to colonial outposts, which eventually grew into veritable cities and towns. Based on my experience in the 1990s and on numerous more recent YouTube videos, however, I can affirm that performances of mask traditions like Bolohi, Zauli, and Gue Pelou continue, using local, ethnically marked instrumentation, both in villages and in cities like Abidjan. These traditions have become jembefied on ballet stages, especially in the United States.

Images

Sogbety is as consistent as Samba Diallo when it comes to visually mirroring his promotional approach in his onstage choices. But where Samba consistently represents the Ivorian nation, Sogbety favors a more general West African, regional look. Clothing is a case in point. At Lotus 2008, the only references to Côte d'Ivoire were the Ivorian colors minimally visible in dyed yarn on Sogbety's and Papa's hats and around Samba's feet. They were so subtle that only on repeated viewing of the performance video did I even notice them. Much more prominent were the matching light yellow outfits of the drummers and many of the dancers (except Vado, who wore hand-dyed indigo, and Moha, who wore a traditional Mau loom-woven *bubu*). Those few who were well informed about Ivorian masks, might have seen Gue Pelou and Zauli as visually indexing Côte d'Ivoire, but obvious references were almost entirely absent.

A West African performance is just what Sogbety Diomande's West African Drum and Dance Company promises, and it is just what is delivered. With creative reworkings of various village and urban, nonstaged and staged traditions and with ethnically marked and nationally adopted sonic, visual, and kinetic traditions, Sogbety's shows are richly layered in meaning. An artist with a singular vision, Sogbety creates his own version of ballet discourse that draws on, reconfigures, and reimagines a West Africa he believes his audience will recognize and enjoy.

8 "When You're in a New Context, You Try Things That Work in That Context"

Sogbety Diomande and Adaptability

DANIEL REED (DR): Why do you choose to work as a drummer and dancer?

SOGBETY DIOMANDE (SD): I chose it because it comes from my heart.... Each person has his/her work in the world.... People tell you, you are free to do anything. You are free! But this is really something for my life. I want to keep it. I *need* to keep it.... I am doing the mask because I learned the mask in the village, in my family.... In Toufinga, the mask comes from the Diomande family. My family owned the tall mask in the village. If you are Bamba or Kone—they are different ethnic groups ... but the Diomande people, that's us. *We* have the *mask*. So, that's what I know.... And when I came here [to the United States], when you have learned something [for] so long, it's time for you to do something with it, because you know now, God made it. If I was in the village now, I would be the number one there. I would be the best. Everyone, when they would come to the village, they would say, "Go see Sogbety." But I am not there, I am here, and I want to keep the same thing, I don't want to do something different. I could to go school, learn, get a regular job—but you know *that* life, God showed me *that* life is not for me.

One sunny afternoon in 2004 in my office at Indiana University, I turned on my computer, opened my e-mail inbox, and unexpectedly entered "the field:"

> Daniel—I was searching the web when by chance I saw your fascinating-looking book about Dan *Ge* performance. It is of special interest to me because I am married to Sogbety Diomande, a stilt-mask dancer. Sogbety is from Toufinga, Ivory Coast, which I understand is very close to Man. We are planning to go there this coming January, if all is well with the civil war going on. It will be my first trip to Africa and Sogbety's first trip back home since coming to the United States in late 1997.... Maybe you have heard of Vado Diomande, Sogbety's uncle. He has a company here in America called "Kotchegna" that features various mask dances from the Ivory Coast. Vado himself was the

Figure 8.1 Sogbety Diomande at the 2008 Lotus Festival in Bloomington, Indiana. Photograph by author.

national stilt-dancing champion for many years and also served as artistic director of the National Ballet. Vado, Sogbety, and another cousin, Moha, all are legitimate Gue Pelou masked stilt dancers. Sogbety and Vado are in NYC, and Moha lives in Florida. . . . You can imagine how thrilled and excited I was to see your book!!! WOW!!! I've seen VERY LITTLE literature about this incredible subject. Of course I am going to order your book right after I send you this email. Sogbety and I would LOVE to correspond with you!! Please write to us!! We would love to speak with you sometime!! —Jennifer Vincent & Sogbety Diomande

I responded enthusiastically and a few more messages were exchanged, but I got busy with work and life (the "not-field" parts) and, I am embarrassed to admit, let this opportunity lay dormant.

Fortunately, fate gave me a second chance. Two years later, again in my office, I stumbled back into "the field," this time in a voicemail message from my father about an Ivorian man and a woman from Mansfield, Ohio planning to rent my dad's outdoor school to produce an African music festival (I discuss this festival in the Preface). Several months later, in August 2006, I found myself in the dining room of the Mohican Outdoor School's Groveport Lodge, preparing to give a lecture on Ge performance for the small crowd of registered guests and teachers at "Sogbety Diomande's West African Celebration." I had left my *baade* drum behind the podium as I finished adjusting the LCD projector I would use to show images and videos from my research in Côte d'Ivoire. Suddenly from behind me came the familiar sounds of Dan drum patterns—those used in *Ge* performance played on my drum. For a millisecond, I was in a state of shock; I had never before heard these rhythms in any context outside of Côte d'Ivoire (with the exception of university classrooms in which I was teaching the patterns to students). I turned and saw an Ivorian man playing my drum with Sogbety, whom I had just met, looking on. We exchanged smiles, shook hands, and Sogbety introduced me to his cousin, Moha Dosso. Astonished, I told them how excited I was to hear those rhythms. "*Jembes* and Mande *jembe* patterns are everywhere in the United States," I began, "but you're playing Dan rhythms for the mask!" "For the Dan and the Mau, it's the same thing," said Sogbety. In a rhythmic pattern that embodied powerful meanings and memories for us both, a connection was made, and I knew, there at my dad's school in my hometown, I was in "the field."

That festival in 2006 was the first ever such venture for Sogbety, just twenty-six years old at the time. It was also the first of many occasions when Sogbety and I spent time together. We met for interviews at his home in Mansfield or at my father's and stepmother's farm south of the city; I accompanied him to drum workshops in universities, public libraries, and boys and girls clubs; I helped him get work, three times at the Bloomington Lotus Festival and once at the annual meeting of the Society for Ethnomusicology in Indianapolis; I traveled to his annual festivals; and from time to time found him at performances organized by other Ivorians—in New York, Indiana and Georgia. We shared meals, played soccer with my son, and occasionally caught up by phone.

Following is a life story constructed mostly from formal interviews conducted between 2006 and 2011. Generally our conversations were in French, though Sogbety, being the most fluent English speaker of the Ivorians I know—perhaps because he has lived in the United States from the age of seventeen—often switched to English out of habit. I find in him a man whose extraordinary talents are not in the least reflected in an oversized ego. Generally understated and genuinely humble, especially for a performer, Sogbety downplayed the importance of his story, which he says is limited by being solely "from [his] experience.... I can't speak too much about these things because I speak what I live." I, however, find much of value in Sogbety's story, which provides one person's subjective experience and self-reflection on the transnational, mobile marketplace of the representation of Africa on stage.

Toufinga

Toufinga, Sogbety's birthplace, is a small Mau farming village west of Touba—the largest city in the Touba region (a region is comparable to a state). Virtually all of Toufinga residents, including Sogbety's family, are active farmers, many of whom practice both subsistence and commercial agriculture. "We grow coffee, and there is competition for having the largest coffee field. Also cotton. Big trucks come from the city to purchase these goods. Also cacao. Add rice, banana, yam.... [Farming is] the focus of the village," according to Sogbety. Toufinga is in a frontier region both in physical and cultural terms. The southernmost portion of the arboreal savanna that extends north into Mali, Touba is a region in which farming and hunting have been historically longstanding. Culturally it is the gateway to the northern Mande region, whose heartland lies to northwest, near the Guinea/Mali border. The Mau are considered a subgroup of the Maninka, also known as Malinké, who, like the Bamana and the Mandinka, make up one of the largest core Mande groups. While very similar to Maninka or Malinké, the Mauka language betrays its proximity to southern Mande languages such as Dan and Tura. Likewise, the Mau region is just on the northern side of the frontier between the more historically Christian South, and the Muslim North (Launay 1992).

A very small number of Toufinga residents identify as Christians, but far more—nearly all—profess to be Muslim. Sogbety's experience growing up reflects Toufinga's location on the Islamic periphery: "The whole village . . . was Muslim, but people didn't pray. . . . There are Muslims and there are Muslims [laughs]. My parents were Muslim, but they never told me, 'You must pray.' They leave you to take care of that yourself." Some Toufinga Muslims pray more regularly and leave the village to go to Qur'anic school, but "most people in the village just work, sometimes dance, sometimes pray."

Music and (Mask) Dance in Toufinga

The "dance" to which Sogbety referred is the mask spirit dance, which from some Islamic perspectives can be controversial. The cultural trait most strongly associated with western Côte d'Ivoire (Reed 2003), mask spirit dance is prevalent among all of the region's ethnicities and is generally practiced by select families within them. Among the Mau, for example, it is specifically the Diomande family that is most associated with the *nya*, or mask spirits, that dance on stilts (*nya yan*, or "long/tall mask spirit), and being a mask family invites both fame and disdain. "*True* Muslims," Sogbety explained, "think it's not fair that [Toufinga villagers] are Muslim but also have masks." When I asked exactly who levies such criticism, he said that he had heard this opinion expressed only *outside* the village. "In Touba, for example, but everyone knows what's in the village. Everyone knows that Toufinga is a village of masks. So there's no problem in the village. It's outside the village that people think, 'No, you have the masks. You must pray.'" Because the village had no mosque, even on Friday at noon "you pray at your house." The feast at the end of Ramadan, however, was an exception:

SD: After Ramadan, the Tabaski, everyone prays together because it's a big day of God. No one goes to the fields. Everyone goes to the middle of the village. Everyone prays and they cook lots of food, and when they finish then the show starts.

DR: What type of show?

SD: We do a show! *Mask*, the mask comes out!

DR: Which mask?

SD: The sacred mask. That's the end of the year, so when the prayer is finished, then we have the mask. And the mask dances all the way until sunset.

When I asked him to clarify which sacred mask he was referring to, Sogbety replied, "The *tall* mask." From a very early age, then, Sogbety was exposed to the performative genre that would become his livelihood. While the idea of sacred masks performing at a major Islamic holy day celebration might strike some as surprising, this is not unprecedented in West Africa (Bravmann 1983). Many West Africans identify as Muslim, but practice a flexible form of Sunni Islam that does not require adherents to abandon indigenous religious practices. During Sogbety's upbringing, sacred masks were far more important than Islam, and this has remained true ever since, including in his immigrant life in the United States.

Learning to Drum and Dance

Mask spirit performance would become Sogbety's most distinctive skill later in life, but like many African boys, he was first exposed to drumming and dance. I asked him about his early experiences of these activities, which he eventually shaped into marketable skills.

DR: When and how did you begin drumming?

SD: My dad didn't play drums; he was never a drummer. But my mother danced and sang. She was a good singer and dancer. Nobody played drums in my family. I learned how to drum from friends. . . . But in my family, everybody has music inside and everybody dances. When you dance, you can sing and you can play drums if you want. When I was a little baby, I danced everywhere. Just dance dance dance dance! When I heard a drum, nobody could stop me from dancing.

The drums of Sogbety's childhood were almost exclusively those of a family associated with the Mau and their neighbors to the south, the Dan. Goblet-shaped, with skins of antelope or red deer, they have either one head (Mau *tindin*) or multiple heads—two or more smaller drum bodies tied to a larger, central one, with each tuned to a different pitch to allow highly melodic patterns. When played for a mask performance, a multiheaded drum is called a *baanya* (mask spirit drum). If accompanying the dance called *yado* taking place on the day before young boys face circumcision, it is called a *yado* (a net-strung gourd rattle goes by the same name). However, when played by a soloist it is generally called a *baade* (mother drum), a name shared by the Dan (Reed 2003).

Often lacking access to actual drums, Sogbety would practice beating out rhythms on anything he could find:

> Even that thing we use for eating—a plate—I would play it upside down. In Africa, even if they know you're going to be a drummer, they're never going to buy you a drum . . . They let you figure out how you're going to do it—whereas here, when people know a kid is going to be a guitar player, they go to the store and buy him a guitar right there. But we don't do that. You can play the table, you can play on your heart, but you're never going to get your own drum. Because in the village there are three or four drums for the whole village. It's not like one for each person—no. It's two or three drums for everybody.

Because access to real instruments was restricted, actual Mau drums were imbued with a sense of the extraordinary. Not available for everyday use, they could be played by young children only at special events and only with permission from the man who kept the village's supply of drums hanging from the rafters of his hut:

> You have to go ask permission to use the drum. If there is a dance next week, you have to go to the guy and ask, "Can I have the drum next week? We're going to do this dance...." It's not like the guy is the king of the village. He's just somebody, a special guy there who takes care of the drum.... When the guy says, "Yes, come next week and take the drum and have fun," then, oh! Everybody is happy.

Learning how to drum, then, involved a great deal of patient *watching* and taking full advantage of rare moments when he could play real drums and keep improving. Finally, Sogbety reached the point when he felt he could define himself as a drummer:

> So that's how I started drumming. You watch [another] guy and you try to do the same thing. So you go up level [by] level [by] level.... But the real moment you know you're a drummer, that's when you play for a *big* show. Everybody knows. They ask, "Who's playing? Oh, Sogbety's playing." So you are a drummer now. Before that you just play around. I don't know if you count that as "when you start drumming" [laughter].

Following Sogbety's playful meta-comment on his answer to my question, when our laughter subsided, he returned to the subject of learning how to dance and sing, which required no special equipment, just his own body:

> Of course, dance—that's me, because I started dancing first. I got that from my mom, the dance part. She is a very good dancer.... Yes, and she can sing also. She would sing lots of songs and she would listen to songs. In the village when there was a dance, she would be there singing.... But my father is a guy who is too ashamed to dance. He dances a little, but he has a lot of shame. That has made it so he is not too advanced as a dancer. But his real skill is working in the fields.... He is in excellent shape. He's a big guy. He never gets tired. He just works like a machine. It's unbelievable. So everybody knows how hard my dad works in the village. Every day he works, go go go.

Drumming and Dreaming

Sogbety's father so valued farming and hard work that he insisted that his firstborn son dedicate his life to work in the fields. But despite his lack of formal education, Sogbety dreamed of other possibilities, of other worlds:

> SD: When I was a kid, I never went to school. I thought it was a big problem, but now I think that everybody is for God. If you go to school or not, you can still have fun with your life, if you know what to do. Since I didn't go to school, I think it is a big thing, a big part of my life. I always heard you have to go to school to be somebody good. You can't come here, have a computer job, have a good job, be a policeman, lawyer—but I didn't go to school in

the village. [So] I said, "I missed that part, and I am never going to become like those people." ... Because I was from the village, and I was a farmer and I would just work and work. ... You see, I was the firstborn, so I had to babysit a lot.

DR: How many were you?

SD: We were five. My mother had five children. I was the first, and I had two little brothers and the others were girls. So I had to put them on my back [with a cloth wrap, a common means of carrying infants and toddlers in West Africa] like my mother while my mother was working. I would put them on my back so that they would go to sleep while my mom worked in the fields. After a while, they would get hungry and wake up and I would take them to my mom, who would nurse them a little and then [go back to work]. ... I did this with my little brothers and sisters. ... One day I was lying down in the village, and I was playing the drums on my chest like this—I was little! And then I saw an airplane pass high overhead, and as I was drumming my chest like that, I said to my mother, "I will be up there one day. One day I will fly in a plane like that." And she didn't believe me. She said, "Stop it! What are you talking about?" ... She didn't believe me, and we started talking about other things. ... Then one day, my Uncle Vado Diomande, who is here in the United States, he came to the village and he said, "I have a little group in Abidjan named Ensemble Kotchegna, and I am looking for a drummer to help me ... there." He is my dad's little brother, same mother, same father—

DR: How old were you?

SD: About fourteen or fifteen. He was looking for someone, not necessarily me, but someone to help him. There were two other young men who came from a neighboring village because they knew Vado was looking for someone to take to Abidjan. ... So it was me and two other guys. Three people, and Vado had to pick one. And I'm Vado's nephew. so people thought, "Oh, of course he's going to take his nephew first." ... But Vado knew that my Dad didn't want me to leave the village, so he told me, "Sogbety, I want to take you, but I don't want to have problems with your dad because your dad doesn't want you to leave the village. He wants you to stay, to work here. So I can take someone else now, and maybe next time you will come." ... But I looked at Vado and I said, "No, I want to—*I've got to*—go to Abidjan!" So he said, "Okay, what we're going to do is, we'll talk to your dad and your mom, and if they say okay, you can come. And if not, I am going to take one of these two guys." ... So I was in Toufinga with Vado and I was crying, and I said, "I have to come! You've got to talk to my dad. I want to go to the big city. I want to go to Abidjan!" . . . So he talked to my dad, and my dad said, "No, no, no. He has to stay here." . . . The next day, or two days after that, Vado was supposed to go to the big city, to Abidjan. And I was crying, crying, crying, crying, and Vado said, "Okay, you know what you're going to do—you have to hide! I'm leaving after tomorrow. You'll go somewhere. I'll give you the date, and I'll show you where I will meet you." . . . So we were there, and I was happy because I knew I was going to go for sure, but I had to be very secretive. So I talked to my mom and I said, "Vado wants me to come, but I'm going to hide from my dad. So Mom, don't talk to Dad." But my mom wanted me to go—she was happy—

DR: That was tricky!

SD: Yes, it was tricky. So my mom didn't say anything. . . . The only problem my mom had, she said, "But how are you going to go to Abidjan without me?" Because my mom is a very big thing for me in Africa. I can't go anywhere for two days without seeing my mom, without going crazy and crying. She knows I am going to go to Abidjan for years and years, and she said, "How are you going to do that? You can't even go somewhere for two days without seeing me. How are you going to go there?" And I said, "It's going to be hard, but I'll be strong." Yeah, so she was, "Okay, okay." . . . So the day came and I took one pair of pants and one set of clothes and I acted like I was going to the farm and coming back. And from there I went to Touba. And [from] Touba, we went to Abidjan. That's how I went to Abidjan. That was a very hard thing to do for me. . . . So I was working in the big city in Kotchegna with Vado doing shows. One day Vado said, "I just got a contract to go to America. They need three stilt walkers." So Vado said, "I want you to come, I want Moha to come, and I want to come." So that was three. With Ballet National of Ivory Coast. . . . We came to Memphis.

On an airplane.

The Big City

The job with Kotchegna was extremely alluring to Sogbety. Vado was by this time not just a close relative but a local celebrity because of his successful career with the Ballet National de Côte d'Ivoire (BNCI) and now with his own ensemble. Years earlier, in 1974, Vado himself, then just seventeen, had been plucked from Toufinga by the BNCI, so to be following in his uncle's footsteps was a great honor to Sogbety. Sure, he had snuck away, but Vado himself wanted him, which was validation enough. He was becoming a professional performer.

Joining Kotchegna was only part of the draw, however. Evident in Sogbety's story is the allure of "the big city." A mythic place to him, Abidjan was the stuff of stories, a place he had heard about but never seen. From the vantage point of his small village hundreds of kilometers away on the Guinea border, Abidjan seemed to exist in another world. It was the early 1990s, and the legendary "benign dictator" Félix Houphouët-Boigny still reigned as president, though a popular movement led by student protestors in Abidjan had been pressing for a multiparty democracy. The prosperous economic period known as the "Ivorian Miracle" had passed, but the crisis of the 1994 devaluation—when the franc CFA would see its value cut in half—was still several years away. A busy international port, Abidjan was abuzz with activity, full of foreign immigrants from other West African countries, Europe, Asia, and the Middle East. It was also the epicenter of the francophone African popular music industry and home to nightclubs, pizza parlors, and the sparkling skyscrapers of the downtown Plateau district. This was the beginning of a new life for Sogbety, a radical transformation that he now looks back on with nostalgia and a small bit of regret. "My siblings were all so small when I left," he said wistfully. "Yeah, they were small, and now some have their own kids."

Sogbety lived in Vado's home "for all that time, for years. Even after 1994 when he stayed here [in the United States] and I went back, I was still staying at his house." The transition to urban life was softened by the presence of Vado and other extended-family members, along with a life in Yopougon, the suburb of choice for many migrants from the west of the country. "Was it difficult to adjust?" I once asked. "No," he said, "because Abidjan is still Africa. It's still our country. There were Mauka, who speak Mau just like in the village. So . . . it was not like moving to another country. . . . When you are in the village, everyone at some point goes to Abidjan."

While certain aspects of village life carried over in the city, many things were different. Asked to describe the differences between Toufinga and Abidjan, Sogbety defined life in the city as "modern"[1] and gave examples. The moment he stepped outside the confines of his Mauka-speaking family and friends, he could not communicate. In Abidjan, he exclaimed, "You have to speak French! I didn't speak French in the village. I learned it when I came to the big city. And I didn't go to school in the big city. I learned [French] from my friends. . . . I learned French in Abidjan." Jula—a language in the same Mande family as Mau—is a secondary lingua franca in Côte d'Ivoire, but to communicate effectively across ethnic and national lines in Abidjan, French is essential. Competency in French became one of many resources that Sogbety used to position himself for participation in a transnational world.

Also necessary in "modern" Abidjan was the clock, or what Sogbety called "timing." In village settings this is essentially what might be called "social time." Clocks are rare and time is generally not tracked numerically but in accordance with natural phenomena (such as sunrises and sunsets, phases of the moon, rainy and dry seasons). Social events operate via social time—when enough and/or the right people are present, an event begins. In Abidjan "timing" is complex and context specific. Generally speaking, many events are coordinated via some combination of clock and social time. A theater might advertise a show at 20:00 (8 p.m.), but that show might not actually begin until 20:30 or 21:00. Still, some things—the television broadcast schedule and many formal governmental activities—are likely to operate in strict coordination with the clock. Learning when to observe which "timing" was a part of Sogbety's socialization into big city life.

As for performance practice, suddenly there was the "rehearsal"—a new concept that formalized the looser socialization that characterized much learning of music and dance in the village. Moreover, performances occurred at set times during the week. One of these was the weekly *nya yan*, or stilt mask, held by the Mau immigrant community in Yopougon:

SD: In Abidjan, every Sunday we had to do the tall mask. In the village it's not like that.

DR: Why every Sunday?

SD: Because it's a money thing now. When we dance, a lot of people come from everywhere.

DR: In the neighborhood?

SD: In the neighborhood, yes. We had a special place and everybody knew—"Here are the Mauka people. They have the stilt walkers here." And everybody knew the day was Sunday. You don't need to call anybody. Everybody knows what time it starts.... People just come every Sunday.... People do that not just for the money but for people to know to get together, all the Mauka people. A lot of people come from far away; they come to spend the night.

In describing this performance event, Sogbety points to another significant difference between Abidjan and Toufinga: paid performance. To be clear, mask spirit performances in western Côte d'Ivoire communities often involve economic exchange. A "price" for a performance might be any combination of chickens, livestock, palm wine, and/or money. Among Dan people, even discussing mask spirit performance is an evocation of the power of *Ge* and thus requires giving a "kola"—which harkens to the time when kola nuts were used as currency in West Africa. In Abidjan, however, Sogbety was for the first time experiencing a kind of "paid performance" for which an audience was required to pay admission. But, crucially, this weekly event was "not just for the money"; as Sogbety says, it was an opportunity for displaced Mau in the big city to reconnect and create community. He remembers it fondly.

I wondered when the *jembe* had first entered Sogbety's performances of Mau mask spirits: "For that type of show, in the street, did you use the *jembe* for that or—"

> There was no *jembe* there. That was just for Mauka, and we used only Mauka drums. Yeah, there were no *jembes* there. . . . The *jembe* players would come by and look at our drums and say, "How do they play those?" When we go to the ballet, we are allowed to play anything now. We can play *jembe* or we can play—yeah.

Thus, even in Abidjan an event defined in ethnic terms as Mau would feature exclusively instruments defined or ethnically marked as Mau as well. The *jembe*, in Sogbety's mind, was categorically not Mau but was associated with "ballet," that discourse of interethnicity and interethnic unification.

Instrumentation and Context

In western Côte d'Ivoire in the 1990s, I sometimes heard French-speaking Ivorians call the *jembe* the city drum to distinguish it from instruments they defined as belonging to their individual ethnic groups—those associated with villages in parts of the country defined on maps as ethnically marked. Certainly *jembes* are extremely common in Abidjan, and it was in the "big city" that Sogbety first began playing one. But whether or not he played the *jembe* or some other drum depended on the event. Again, even in Abidjan an event defined as Mau would feature distinctive Mau/Dan drums. In conversation with Sogbety, I continued exploring the various kinds of drums and drumming in which Sogbety engaged during his years in the city. Given the extent to which the *jembe* now dominates his music in the United States, from classes to performances to workshops, I was curious about when he began seriously playing it.

Playing music with people of other ethnic groups became a common pastime for Sogbety in Abidjan. I asked him how this worked, and what music and instruments they would play. I had wondered if the *jembe* was the lingua franca instrument for musicians of different ethnic groups playing together, like French or the Jula language in Abidjan:

> That depends on what person you were with. If the person [is] Guro, you're going to play the music from their region. If the person is Baule, he's going to teach you some of his music. . . . I learned their drums, and I taught them ours. We showed each other.

So, then, interethnic musical interaction in informal contexts in Abidjan did not necessarily involve the *jembe*. My indirect, open line of questioning not bearing fruit, I finally asked him directly when and in what context he began playing it. "It was in the group with Vado," he replied.

When Sogbety first joined Kotchegna, several drummers in the group were considerably older and more experienced than he. One in particular, a Dan, became his primary trainer. He became the master, and Sogbety his apprentice—a common form of advanced musical training in West Africa. Constantly challenged, Sogbety endured harsh treatment and punishment until he was able to meet his master's extremely high standards and expectations. As he trained, Sogbety moved gradually through the ranks, first playing the simplest accompanying parts either on *dunduns* or smaller, similar drums. Over time he graduated to accompanying patterns on the *jembe* and then was allowed to take occasional short *jembe* solos. While he continued to play the Mau *baade* and other drums, the *jembe* increasingly became his focus.

Kotchegna drummers would play *jembes* for some dances but not for others. Modeled after the national ballet, the group sampled dances from various regions and ethnicities. When performing those of northern Mande groups like the Jula, Bamana or Maninka—in whose villages the *jembe* is commonly played—the drummers would likewise play *jembes* (as well as *dunduns*, though the *jembe/dundun* pairing is an innovation introduced by early West African ballets; see Charry 2000). When playing Guro rhythms, Kotchegna drummers used Guro drums such as the *topalon*. But just as in the BNCI, Kotchegna's instrumentation did not always match the instrumentation from the region in which a dance originated. Sogbety cited a Mau example. Although Kotchegna performed the stilt mask spirit with Mau drums (which of course would change in the United States), when they performed the Mau dance *samaba*, they played *jembes*:

SD: For example, we have a dance called *samaba*. Vado brought this sound to Kotchegna. It comes from the Mau region. It's a young man's dance—it features acrobatic moves . . . For that dance, when you have a contract . . . and they say "We're going to invite Kotchegna to play here," Kotchegna comes. It's no longer a village thing now. It's a *show* that is going to happen, and you could have whites, [and] . . . people from elsewhere who have come to watch. So the manner in which you perform, it must not be like it happens in the village. That's traditional—it's a dance for the village. So when you go out [from the village], you have to be a little bit *modern*, a little bit. So now [Kotchegna] started doing *samaba* with *jembes* and two [other] drums—a high sound and a low sound [like a *dundun*]. So the sound is going to be . . . how can I say—it's a little of everything now. You must show powerful drumming.

DR: Because the sound of the *jembe* is so much louder—

SD: It's so much louder than *that* [gestures to my Dan/Mau drum]! You can't really do the whole performance like it would be done in the village! Things must move past that, little by little . . .

DR: So it's not simple, like before it was always without *jembe* and now it's always with *jembe*, [but] it depends—

SD: *Yes*, it depends.

DR: On the context and the type of show?

SD: *Yes*. It depends on what show you've got—yes. When you play Mau music like in the Mau region, it's *sweet*, so sweet . . . but you have to have [the right] sound; it depends on the [type of] contract or show.

With Ensemble Kotchegna in Abidjan, Sogbety's serious engagement with the *jembe* began. A dance he performed outside the "ballet" frame on other ("original" or ethnically marked) instruments, he might play, in the context of ballet, on the *jembe*. Sogbety points to the purpose and context of an event and to the expected and/or intended audience as factors that determined instrumentation. A Mau community event? Mau drums. A "show" for a diverse, potentially cosmopolitan audience (read white)? *Jembe/dundun*. What Sogbety wanted to "show" in the latter case was that he was "modern." What is key here is that, if a decision was made, for whatever reason, not to use the "original" instrumentation for a given dance, it was *always* the *jembe/dundun* pairing, not some other drum or drums, that became the default instrumentation. This, I argue, is evidence that the transnational discourse of ballet, well established by Guinea and adapted by Mali, Senegal, and others prior to its Ivorian instantiation, was alive and well in Sogbety's life in early 1990s Abidjan.

Memphis

In late 1993, Vado Diomande, then a veteran of the BNCI and director of Kotchegna, was asked by the Ivorian government to put together a trio of stilt masks for the 1994 Memphis in May festival. Vado recruited his nephews Sogbety and Moha Dosso, and in May 1994 Sogbety arrived in the United States for the first time. Also on that trip was Samba Diallo, and though Sogbety knew of him, there were more than a hundred performers in the entourage and the two never met. "I was really young," said Sogbety, "so we were not in the same category, and we never spoke. It was when I came to the states this time that we got to know each other."

When Sogbety said, "So, we came to Memphis," I told him I had been there. "Yeah, I heard that!" he replied. Apparently that news had already spread through the community; I had first made the connection in conversation with Vado.

> So for about two weeks we stayed there. . . . During that two weeks—I was seventeen at that time . . . Memphis was really amazing for me to see. . . . But I really—it changed my life. I didn't think I would ever see—I didn't go to school and all that, so I didn't know I was going to be able to do those things.

You had to be able to sign your name. You had to be able to read just a little bit. For some of us, that was a big problem, coming for the first time. Even to go to the bathroom, I didn't know where to go.... And ... I didn't know how to ask anybody, to say, "Where is the bathroom?" in English.... So it was hard for me.... We went to Memphis and we stayed for two weeks and we did our show. And a lot of the people—the Ballet National people—they didn't go back. They stayed here. The last day everybody ... almost fifteen people—they just disappeared. Yeah. Vado too! ... And Moha and I—I was just seventeen years old and Moha was a little older than I. And Moha said to me, "Sogbety, are you going to stay here?" I said, "I am not staying here. I am going to Africa so I can see my mom. I am not staying here, not this time." And Moha said, "Oh, I'm going to stay here!" I said, "Moha, if you want to stay here, go ahead, but I have to go back." So Moha decided to follow me. He said, "Okay, okay, let's go back." And we went back home.

Immigration

Sogbety and Moha remained in Abidjan for another three years. Moha became director of the Abidjan-based version of Kotchegna (Vado had started a new Kotchegna in New York), and Sogbety continued performing with it. Then one day, in 1997, Sogbety, along with Moha, Dr. Djo Bi, Tra Bi Lizzie, Bi Bo Ti, and others now in the larger community of Ivorian immigrant performers, were invited by Bley Zaguehi to join his New York-based Mask Dance Company. A Bete from Côte d'Ivoire, Zaguehi had been living in the United States for about twenty-five years. Sogbety and he met when the latter arrived in Abidjan looking for recruits for his ensemble. "He came to Côte d'Ivoire," Sogbety recalled, "and he talked to me and Moha, and he talked with others—lots of people, around fifteen people." The recruits rehearsed in Abidjan and Zaguehi then arranged for their visas and travel. Over a dozen Ivorian performers, many of whom had been part of the 1994 Memphis entourage, left Abidjan to join the Mask Dance Company in New York.

Although they had been forced to wait three years, Sogbety and Moha now had a chance to enter the United States as legal immigrants. Zaguehi arranged one-year visas for every one of his recruits and helped them with legal processes after they arrived.

SD: Before the one year was finished, I already had a Social Security number. It was very clean. Two or three days after we arrived, Bley Zaguehi took us all to start the process of getting our Social Security cards. Then I was able to renew [my] visa for another year. And I was already married before that visa had expired.

DR: Whoa! It's not like that for everybody!

SD: It's not like that for everybody [laughter]! I am someone who does not want to be in an uncertain situation without papers. I wanted everything fixed.

Thinking back on his arrival in the United States, Sogbety recalled fondly those first days with Zaguehi's group, despite the fact that financially things did not go as well as he had hoped:

> We came to the US and we went directly to [Zaguehi's] house. Everything was good. We rehearsed every week, and we did shows. But the shows didn't pay well. He didn't pay well, so bit by bit people started leaving to pursue their own business, and we were no longer together. We remain good friends, but we no longer work [regularly] together. We worked with him for a year or two. Often he still calls me and says, "Sogbety I have a little show," and we work together.... His group still exists, but it's not as big as before.... Before it was a big group, and we were all together.

I noted Sogbety's nostalgia as he uttered that last phrase. Being one of the most isolated of the Ivorian immigrant performers I know and certainly the youngest when he immigrated, Sogbety highly valued the sense of community he felt in those first days in the United States. I asked him to tell me more about his experience:

> It was easy for me because I knew people. Some people come here and they have to work to get to know people, but that was not my situation. Zaguehi came to pick us up at the airport and we stayed with him. It wasn't the whole group, just Djo Bi, Tra Bi, and I who stayed at Zaguehi's place for a time. But Vado was already there [in New York], so I went to his place and I stayed with him for months—maybe a year.

While his familiarity with others in the New York community of Ivorian performers smoothed his transition, the adjustment to American life was still challenging:

SD: What was difficult for me was the differences between Africa and the United States. It didn't frighten me, but it was different. There were many differences.

DR: For example?

SD: When I first arrived it was December. And it was cold. Our bodies, they change—in summer, they change. Here in the US when it is cold, your body is a little, what do you call it? You become pale, you are a little different. When I first arrived I saw people [Ivorian friends] and I thought, "Why does everyone look different?" It was cold, and especially black people, when it becomes cold, we turn white.... But after one month, I was all right.

DR: One month? That was quick!

SD: Yes, I began to change. I went out a lot with Vado, and it didn't take long before I felt relaxed. When I first came to Memphis in 1994, I didn't see much and was so young. But when I came back, it was not so difficult.

Sogbety bounced around New York City, living in various locations while he worked with the Mask Dance Company and took steps toward securing his residency:

> After that, I found my own place, on 121st St. there in Harlem. It was the apartment where a guy lived named Djoniba, a Martiniquan who has a huge dance school in New York City, [then at] 118th St. and Broadway. . . . lived there and paid him rent. . . . Then I left there and moved to Brooklyn, where I had a place with Bi Bo Ti . . . I knew Bi Bo Ti back in [Côte d'Ivoire]. He was a good friend of Vado and was in the [BNCI]. And I left there and returned to Harlem, where I lived with some friends. It was around that time that I met my wife.

About a year and a half after arriving, Sogbety met Jennifer Vincent, a professional jazz cellist and bassist, originally from Oregon, who had lived and played music for years in New York City. She introduced Sogbety to many musicians and artists, particularly in the jazz scene. The two hit it off, and not long after they met she invited him to live with her in her Harlem apartment. Less than two years after he arrived, Sogbety and Jennifer were married. Not only did he have a partner and a place to live; now he had a path to a green card and citizenship.

Try as I might, I could not get Sogbety to talk more about the difficulties of his first days, weeks, and months in the United States. His story contrasts significantly with those of my other three consultants, in particular Dr. Djo Bi, with whom he immigrated and lived at Zaguehi's place when he first arrived, and who had received the same visa and guidance from the Mask Dance Company director. Was it easier for Sogbety because he was younger? Because he had a close relative in Vado who was already well established professionally? There could be several reasons, but the more time I spent with him, the more I sensed a dedicated optimism and a commitment to be happy regardless of his personal circumstances, as well as a flexibility and adaptability that would serve him well in his developing career down the road.

Ballet Training as a Transnationally Marketable Skill

My questions about Sogbety's experiences during his early days as an immigrant bearing less and less fruit, I changed tactics and began asking him about how he had come to the decision to migrate in the first place:

> Because if you are a musician in Africa who does ballet like what we do, if you are in Africa you work hard, you rehearse and rehearse for years and years, *so that one day you can go to another country* to show them what you know [my emphasis]. That's the situation for just about all African musicians. Even here, nearly all musicians.

It may not be surprising that ballet veterans reflect on their training and reflexively point to it as a resource they could use in the labor market of African music and dance in the United States. Sogbety's comment, however, goes further. It suggests that training in the art of representing a nation is strategically and self-consciously *pursued* by performers who wish to use it as a ticket to the transnational African performance marketplace (Schauert 2015). Sogbety continued:

> When I got to Abidjan I saw that it was there that people worked really hard to get themselves to another country. So I *worked* in Kotchegna, saying to myself, "One day maybe I'll go to France, or Greece, or who knows where." But I did not know where. I did not know if it was going to be the United States or where. But God made it so there was here.

Though ultimately Sogbety attributes his fate to divine guidance, he knew that God might provide the opportunity but he had to work hard to take advantage of it. Sogbety's comments reflect an ironic reality for West African national ensembles: the training artists receive in staging music and dance for national purposes provides them with the tools and opportunities to pursue transnational goals. Performers know that their ballet predecessors established representational expectations in wealthy nations that ballet training can prepare them to meet. Tours provide chances to defect and/or make contacts to facilitate later immigration.

The Mask Dance Company was just such an opportunity. As Sogbety began reflecting on his early experiences with Zaguehi's company, the mechanics of the ballet process became increasingly clear:

SD: [The Mask Dance Company] was like the [BCNI]. There were lots of people in that group who had been in the [BCNI]. . . . We did the same. We played the *jembe* but we had lots of other things. You know [for] the Bolohi mask dance, you have no need of a *jembe* for that. You have the calabash [the *bolɔnye*], you have the *shekere*—it is a Senufo thing. . . . They don't need a *jembe* or *dundun*. In the Mask Dance Company, we had all those instruments, so when the Bolohi danced, we did not use drums. And when we did *tématé*, we used these drums [plays my Dan *ɓaaɖe* drum]. When [the mask] Zauli came, we had to use a little bit of *dundun* for that because we didn't have that instrument. But we had the real players, Djo Bi and Tra Bi, so we played it almost the way they played in the village.

Several interesting issues emerge in Sogbety's description of the Mask Dance Company. Of course, he explicitly cites "ballet" as its reference point, specifically, the BNCI, where many Mask Dance Company members learned the particular genre and discourse associated with Ivorian ballet. Second, he shows that the kind of "jembefication" that marks current Ivorian ballet in the United States was blooming but not yet fully in flower in this ensemble. Like the BNCI and the Abidjan-based Kotchegna before it, the Mask Dance Company endeavored to represent Ivorian traditions using the same instruments one would find in a village or other community-based performance context (e.g., Bolohi was played with the *bɔlɔnye* and *shekere* as in a Senufo village). But when such instruments were not available, it was the familiar *jembe* and/or *dundun* to which drummers turned (e.g., for the Zauli mask). Once again, lacking the "authentic" ethnically marked instrument, the *jembe/dundun* pairing was the solution—the automatic authenticator of any and all Ivorian representations on the New York stage. Likewise, when instruments were lacking, the ethnically appropriate *performer* served to authenticate the performance (e.g., Tra Bi and Djo Bi, as Guro musicians, are "real players" of the Guro rhythm *zauli*, according to Sogbety).

Cognizant, as are all Ivorian performers, of the dominance of Guinean ballet in the United States, Sogbety took pains to point out that the Mask Dance Company "was *not* Guinean dance style. It was all Ivorian dance style. That's why they call it 'Mask Dance Company,' because there were so many masks in that group." Of course, the Ivorian brand is itself fundamentally influenced by its Guinean precedents, but nonetheless the distinctiveness of which Ivorian performers are proud is the marker of the particular Ivorian *national* in the *transnational* ballet discourse. Though some Guinean ethnic groups have mask performance traditions, they are far outnumbered by the prevalence of masking in Côte d'Ivoire, where roughly forty different ethnic groups dance masks.

Nevertheless, the influence of Mande music/dance culture on Ivorian ballet in the United States is dramatic and undeniable. Sogbety asserts that the transition to performing any and all Ivorian dances on the *jembe/dundun* began on ballet stages in Côte d'Ivoire but came to full fruition in New York, where, from the 1960s on, Mande traditions were taught and where, especially in Harlem and the Bronx, an increasingly large Mande population, mostly from Guinea and Mali, resided and formed one of the most prominent African diasporic groups in the country (see Racanelli 2014).

I prompted Sogbety to comment on this standard element of Ivorian immigrant performance, in which it is now common for every rhythm, be it Senufo, Guro, Bete, Dan, Mau, or other, to be played on the *jembe*:

> They are all played on *jembe*. It was not like that before. . . . That's a change that occurred here. We don't have all the instruments here. . . . That's just what everyone does here—*jembe jembe jembe jembe*! It's the *jembe* that is here. [If you go] somewhere like a school in the US, if they see this drum [my *baadè*] they will be astonished! But when they see a *jembe*, [they say] "Oh, a *jembe*!" *Everyone* knows the *jembe*. But if an American sees a thing like [the *baadè*], they won't know if it's Ivorian or where in Africa it comes from—you have to explain it!"

Diversifying

During those first years in New York, Sogbety began gradually diversifying professionally, working in a greater range of contexts and with immigrants from countries other than Côte d'Ivoire. Ironically, though, as people and performance contexts varied, instrument choice unified, and Sogbety found himself playing the *jembe* (and/or the *dundun*) almost exclusively. The *jembe* served as a point of connection to the larger Mande community in and around New York as well as to Americans familiar with the instrument as players and/or fans. Much *less* familiar to those outside Ivorian circles was Sogbety's other major asset—his stilt mask. The *jembe* was common and enabled Sogbety to connect, but Gue Pelou was distinctive and allowed him to stand out, since in the entire country only he, his cousin Moha, and his Uncle Vado could make its performance available.

One key to the marketability of Gue Pelou was Sogbety's familiarity with the conventions of its performance in ballet contexts. Through the BNCI and Kotchegna, Vado Diomande had established a short, standardized, but entertaining, Gue Pelou set that consisted of a song in *tindin* rhythm, a benediction, and then a song, usually "Ge ya yi kan" in *zikinin* rhythm. Drummers familiar with Ivorian ballet discourse are presumed to know the "standards," which include masks such as Bolohi, Zauli, and Gue Pelou, and dance rhythms such as *tématé* and *gbegbe*. Following the conventional ballet sequence of a Gue Pelou performance allowed Sogbety to collaborate with any drummers experienced with this mask spirit. Sogbety explained, "It's not this way in the village. But here, it's the same thing each time. Because the problem is . . . it's not every day that we play together with drummers that we know."

Sometimes, however, Sogbety finds performance opportunities with drummers who know nothing of the Mau *nya yan* traditions, ballet or otherwise. A very large Senegalese community lives in New York, and Sogbety occasionally performs with drummers who play *sabar*—a Wolof ensemble of drums that is well-known in places like New York and Boston.

> Often the Senegalese call me because they need the long mask. "Yes, we have a show, can you come dance?" "Yes!" So I come to dance, [but] I can't bring along my drummers because they can't pay them [and] because they only need the mask. So I go, and if it's *sabar* that they play, I dance about fifteen minutes and then it's done. . . . That happens in New York and sometimes in New Jersey. . . . It's not easy to quickly teach someone [Mau] rhythms and then do a show. So often the mask dances to *sabar*. . . . It's for the money and it's for the job.

Again, Sogbety's flexibility and adaptability serve him well, allowing him to diversify and meet an increasing range of market demands with his skills. Sogbety once danced Gue Pelou in a jazz club.

> Yes . . . in New York with jazz musicians. . . . They did a concert, [and] the guys played during the night. . . . They played guitar and were singing jazz. So one song, they wanted tall mask to come, like something scary for just five minutes, so I did that.

His description of dancing the mask in a jazz club to make a song feel "scary" struck us both as humorous. "It's a job," I said. He replied, "It's work. In Africa, you cannot, you would not, find someone who would call you for jazz and then also [ask for] the mask." He repeated: "The mask can dance to any type of music."

Sogbety dispassionately and frankly states that he makes these decisions "for the money" and just as dispassionately describes how he sees the reality of working as an immigrant mask performer:

> It would be good if it happened all the time the way it does in the village, but among [immigrants], we can't do it [that way].... That's not why we came here. If we wanted to do things the way they are done in the village, we would not have come here, we would have stayed there. This is another thing.

Following his departure from the Mask Dance Company, Sogbety began to find more work in schools and at festivals, often working with non-Ivorian African descendants. "I started collaborating with Senegalese, Guineans, Haitians ... they would call me to come play *jembe* or to come do the long mask, so I started doing things like that." Through fellow Ivorian immigrant Yahya Kamaté, Sogbety began getting more and more work in schools through the nonprofit *Young Audiences*. "They are the people who give you school jobs. I'm with them now too. You give them your [promotional materials], and then they book you at schools.... If you go online [to their website] you will see my name—I work with them a lot."

Like all members of the dispersed community of Ivorian immigrant performers, in the early years Sogbety also traveled for work, occasionally voyaging beyond his local community and region for jobs. Sometimes those jobs involved short-term relocations and were effectively migrant labor. In the early 2000s, for example, Seguenon Kone snared a lucrative contract at Disney's Animal Kingdom in Orlando.

> We would drum and dance, five shows every day, twenty minutes each, including the tall mask. But we had to pay our hotel, and we had to pay our transportation, so even though the money was good, we had to pay for those things. So the money was not much after we [took] all those things out.... I got tired of that after a while.

Sometimes Sogbety traveled for weeklong camps, weekend festivals, or even single performances. African drum and dance camps, multicultural festivals, university workshops—the range of performance contexts continued to multiply. And yet he always felt dependent on others to create these opportunities and to direct him, effectively, as an ensemble member. All this would change, however, when in 2004 Sogbety took a rather odd job in Pennsylvania, which led to a fruitful relocation to Ohio the following year.

Heading West

Sogbety's move to Ohio, while serendipitous in specifics, is reflective in broad terms of North American immigrant settlement patterns of the past few centuries. That is, he found himself, much like the early European pioneers, going farther and farther west in search of work. While *Young Audiences* in New York provided him with somewhat steady work, the pay was terrible, most likely because of simple economic supply and demand: there are African drummers aplenty in New York. Sogbety found himself traveling more often west of the city in search of any gig, large or small. Through a chance encounter, he ended up in a place where there had not been a single African drummer: my hometown of Mansfield, Ohio.

Mansfield is a small, rust belt city of about 50,000 residents in north central Ohio midway between Cleveland and Columbus. It has yet to attract immigrant populations in large numbers as have larger Ohio cities. Although a small number of touring acts do stop in Mansfield, residents are accustomed to trekking north to Cleveland or south to Columbus for many music and arts events. In 1999 Mansfield couple Melanie Seaman and Fate Christian founded a nonprofit organization, "Highlands of Ohio," to promote folk and Celtic music in the Mansfield area. Their early efforts focused on folk traditions of the British Isles, but they have begun expanding their offerings to include *jembe* workshops with Pittsburgh-based American drummer Jim Donovan of the alternative rock band Rusted Root.

Melanie Seaman's passion for Celtic music and culture led her to related interests such as European historical reenactment, and she began attending the Society for Creative Anachronism's annual festival called Pennsic. At the 2004 festival, held in Slippery Rock, Pennsylvania, she met Sogbety:

> When I met Sogbety at Pennsic (a very unlikely place to meet an African), my only introduction to African drumming was through Jim Donovan, who is not at all African. We hosted Jim several times in Bellville [a small town just south of Mansfield], where he did drum workshops for us. So I knew what a *jembe* was, but that's about it. When I spotted two Africans (Sogbety and Aristide—an Ivorian *jembe* importer) at Pennsic, the medieval event I attend every year, I was drawn to the drums they were selling. Sogbety always says "God wanted us to meet," and I almost believe that because out of fourteen thousand people at Pennsic in 2004, his little tent ended up right beside mine. I was also a vendor, and Aristide was selling drums along the path to my camp. When I first had a conversation with Sogbety, I could barely understand him and he was probably having the same problem with me, because when I told him I lived in Ohio, he thought I said "Hawaii." He wanted to come for a visit because he had been in NYC for eight years and really needed to get out due to the lack of employment for someone with his skills. I set him up with two school shows with some teacher friends in Mansfield.

Sogbety recalled his first show in Mansfield through which he discovered a new professional direction:

> Yes, all by myself. You know what happened? You know Tra Bi? When I first came here, Melanie told me about the school. She went and talked with them with my flyer, and they said, "Okay, we're going to bring Sogbety here to do something." And then it was supposed to be me and Tra Bi doing that show. I made a flyer one month in advance, and I told Tra Bi, "We're going to go to Ohio to do a show . . ." He said, "No problem, no problem." . . . We went to West Virginia. Aristide a long time ago put together a festival, and we went there for that festival. He brought Mamady Keita, me and Tra Bi and Vado. We were there, and we were supposed to go straight from West Virginia to this show here [in Mansfield]. But then in West Virginia, Tra Bi said, "I'm not going to do it." Tra Bi said he was going to go back to New York. Despite the fact his picture was on the poster. So I let him go back to New York and I came here and I did the show by myself. . . . It was the first time I did a show by myself. And since that day, that's what I'm doing. . . . And I teach them a lot, and people love it when I do it. I had my CD player there and I had my *yado* [*baade*]. I had my *dundun*, I had my *jembe* . . . I had four other little drums for people to play with me. So everything was set. And so I did my show. I let Melanie talk first: "This is Sogbety. . . ." As soon as she finished talking, I came with my drum playing. Then [I talked] with the audience and let them talk and [I kept] playing. I talked a little bit. Then I went out and took about two seconds and changed into the panther [the Senufo mask Bolohi]. During the time when she was talking I could fast change into the costume. And as soon as she saw that I was ready, she pressed the CD player. So I came out with the panther, and danced, danced, danced. They loved it! So I danced, danced, danced, and then I went out again. . . . Melanie had to talk a little bit again to give me time to change to come back. . . . I did two or three masks, and then I told them . . . I was not going to do any more masks. A couple of people came up to the stage, they sit down, we drum and we called the teachers and talked to them. Some [teachers] dance and the students played. So that's how forty-five minutes, it went like nothing. Yeah . . . it was a good show.

Having seen Sogbety perform school shows on a number of occasions in Indiana and Ohio, I find it interesting how similar his standard school show remains to this initial experience.

Plato's saying, "Necessity is the mother of invention" certainly applies here. Sogbety quickly realized he had stumbled across a great opportunity: having a show that he could successfully perform alone meant a paycheck that did not have to be shared:

> I get to keep all the money [laughs]. I get to keep all the money! And now when you go to my website you see two things: I can do a show by myself [or] a show with the troupe. Also, I go to the classroom [and] talk about Africa. . . . I [can]

teach a whole school drumming! So you've got to choose what you want me to come do.

Sogbety's portfolio of diverse offerings, so many of which he can do alone, has been quite profitable. His story is one of constant adaptation, of a willingness to try new things—new locations, new performative and presentational formats, new contexts—and find creative ways to make them work. He has a businessman's nose for opportunity, but comes across as anything *but* crass or opportunistic. In fact, he seems jovially naïve and simply willing to go along for the ride. His talent, combined with his acumen, has led to considerable success in the marketplace of African immigrant performance in the United States.

I asked whether he had ever done solo shows during his eight years in New York. "No!" he quickly replied. "Somebody would just call me. I *wanted* to do my own thing, but I needed somebody . . . I needed support." Sogbety confessed that he lacked the skills, including organization, computer literacy, and general literacy, to promote himself. But in Ohio, suddenly, he had the support he needed in Melanie and Fate, and, for the first time, they had a local artist to which they could dedicate their time. It was a fruitful collaboration. "They put their minds, *everything*, on me, so that people came to know me here. And right now, it's very good."

Sogbety did not immediately move to Mansfield. For several years, he commuted back and forth between Mansfield and New York City, where he lived with his wife. This was advantageous because he could continue to profit from performance opportunities garnered by Vado and his many other contacts in New York while also availing himself of the increasing numbers of gigs Melanie was securing on his behalf. In Ohio he had more work, sometimes in concentrated doses; for instance, he once had thirteen library shows in one week. In New York the shows might be fewer but were generally on bigger, more noteworthy stages, such as his annual performances with Kotchegna at Lincoln Center.

Over time more work began springing up in Ohio, and Sogbety found himself spending more time there. A huge benefit, especially considering the price of housing in New York, was that Fate and Melanie provided Sogbety free lodging in a rental property near their own home in an upper-middle-class neighborhood. Sogbety shared an early twentieth-century two-story brick house with various renters over the years. The neighbors on his quiet street were unaccustomed to African lifestyles and found themselves having to adjust to changes—for example, the loud sounds of *jembes* and *dunduns* or the novel sight of Sogbety chasing escaped chickens across their manicured lawns until he caught and returned them to the pen he had built in his backyard (see figure 8.2). By 2012 Sogbety was living in Mansfield full-time and beginning the process of divorcing Jennifer, with whom he was now spending almost no time in New York.

Figure 8.2 Sogbety Diomande with chickens in his backyard in Mansfield, Ohio, in November 2008. Photograph by author.

One afternoon in 2008 in his living room in Mansfield, I asked Sogbety about his volume of work compared to others' in the dispersed community of Ivorian immigrant performers. "I have the impression," I said, "that in the Ivorian immigrant community there is so much talent, but some [people] don't have work." Sogbety sighed. "Some of them go months without a job." "It seems to me that you are working more than anyone else I know," I said. "Yeah, I'm working and it's good":

> If I go [do a show] today, I'm going to get another show out of that. I never do one place and not get invited back. People are happy and they give me another job right there. . . . It's not just the way that I do my show, it's [that] it's very professional. Melanie makes everything very clear, for people to know what I'm doing. And Fate, he's the computer guy. . . . everything I need I just tell him, and he's there. . . . Everything is clear. When you go online you see what I do, and when I bring my troupe, I'm good for the troupe. . . . People see that and they give me a lot of jobs.

Indeed, Sogbety was financially secure enough not only to regularly invite his Ivorian colleagues to join him for shows but also to pay them well.

> Why I got a good name here? Everybody that I bring here to perform with me, I pay them more than I pay myself. When I call someone up to ask them

to come work with me, they don't have to ask me, "How much are you going to pay me?" Because they know I will pay them well. No question. They just come. And they're going to go home with happiness and everything. Yeah.

Organizing and performing a show from a position of leadership is not Sogbety's favorite professional activity, however.

> I like the show, but it's a ... problem ... to get people together. ... It's very hard. And not just to bring them [from all over the United States], but when they're around, you got to control everybody [laughter]. ... That part is very difficult, and somebody can get here and they might say, "I'm not going to perform, blah blah blah" and they can give me a hard time before the show is finished, so you are not comfortable until the show is finished. Because somebody might be drunk, or somebody might fight or. ... It's really hard to deal with the troupe. But it's fun getting everyone together to do the show, and when you're sitting there watching the show, you say "Wow, that's a good show." But before you get there, [there are] a lot of problems.

Ultimately, Sogbety prefers working alone:

> I like my solo thing just by myself. Just me. I wake up, I'm already on time. That's another thing with the troupe. Everybody's trying to be late. You say "Time to go!" And that's when somebody's going to get some food. ... If you talk too much, they say, "Oh he's difficult to be with." I'm not difficult but I don't want to be late! This is my show, I call you to come, and this is the time. Why are you eating at this time?

"I Can See *Me* Now"

Sogbety's life had become dramatically different over a few short years. I was curious how he saw his life now:

DR: If you had to name one thing that has changed the most for you, from the time you left Toufinga and went to Abidjan and to New York to now, when you do your shows alone, what is the thing that has changed the most?

SD: Here in Mansfield, being here almost four years now, it has changed my life. Big-time in a good way. I did a lot of things before . . . but I can see *myself*, I can see *me* now. I can see what I'm doing now.

DR: That's very interesting. So here you can see yourself now. How? Through the music or through the types of shows you do, or how have you found that change?

SD: In New York, all the things that people do there, I see them and I can do the same thing. I am someone, I like to have things of my own. Often in New York, people would call me to go to a school show, and I see the manner in which people pay and how they treat musicians.... I say, "I know how to do this." I know how to be a boss, and I know how to control a group. In New York I couldn't do it because... I have the idea but I don't know how to get a show, I don't know how to get on the computer, make everything [organized]. I need somebody to do all that. But to put a show together, to get everybody to have the idea—I'm good at that. I can do that. So here I've been changed to do that. That's a big change for me.

Though he is glad to be on his own, Sogbety misses the community of African musicians in New York because "when we get together, we play good music. But that isn't me. That isn't going to be the life for me. It's good, but you need to have your own thing." He told me that working alone had pushed him hard:

That has helped me to learn about many things. Yes, I can do a show all by myself. I don't see any of my friends being able to do that. I don't see it.... A sitdown drum class? *Everybody* can do that. But a one-hour show in front of five thousand kids—a show—[where] nobody's going [to say,] "Yeah this is boring." I don't see many people who can do that.

Figure 8.3 Sogbety Diomande leads a parade at the 2006 Lotus Festival in Bloomington, Indiana. Photograph by Christy True.

Instrumental Innovations and Pop Star Collaborations

Performing alone or in collaboration with non-Africans has afforded Sogbety the freedom to innovate in many respects, especially in the musical elements of his performances and presentations. Solo shows are not the only contexts in which he has tried new things, however; he has also involved himself in various collaborative ventures, including some with famous musicians. Sogbety's innovative streak is at turns a matter of practical adaptation and one of playful, creative license, although it is usually some combination of the two.

Sogbety's first solo performance in Mansfield featured several mask performances, but for practical reasons (i.e., the time it takes to dress other masks), he generally sticks exclusively to Bolohi in his solo ventures. Using a CD player—a survival tactic that first time out—has become commonplace in the Bolohi portions of Sogbety's presentations. Its function is two-fold: buying him the time to change costumes, and providing musical accompaniment for Bolohi's lively, acrobatic dance. I have seen Sogbety use various CDs for this purpose—always African music of some sort but only occasionally the Senufo *bolohi* rhythm. A YouTube video shows Sogbety at an unidentified elementary school in 2008 dancing the Bolohi mask to a recording of Dr. Djo Bi's New York-based band Mecca Bodega playing their unique rendition of *bolohi* with *jembe*, drum kit, bass guitar, hammered dulcimer, and trumpet.[2]

In my research on *Ge* in western Côte d'Ivoire, Dan consultants taught me that all aspects of a Dan *Ge* performance—including drum rhythms, song, and dance—are transformed into spirit. Music, they taught me, is the primary means of mediating between the spirit world, *gebo*, and the living world. Thus, only certain music, played on certain sanctified instruments, can be played in *Ge* performance.

I have experienced live and also listened to Sogbety narrate numerous instances of musical innovations of the kind I had never thought possible during my earlier *Ge* research. On one occasion at a Mansfield school, Gue Pelou danced to music played by local musicians on guitar and flute. With Jim Donovan, Sogbety has performed this mask spirit using several different instrument configurations:

SD: We did shows . . . at schools, where he played his drum set and after awhile [Gue Pelou] comes out and dances with the drum set.

DR: What does [Jim Donovan] play?

SD: He plays whatever, anything—his thing. Sometimes he might play his drum set and I . . . come out with the Bolohi. We've done that a lot so now he sometimes will play the song of Bolohi.

I then asked Sogbety if he could compare his experience dancing Gue Pelou in Toufinga with dancing in the school accompanied by Jim Donovan on the drum set:

SD: The drums that you play are like the language. When Djo Bi plays Mauka rhythms, he's speaking our language. When I play for others like Djo Bi, it's like I'm speaking their language. So it's a different feeling. Like learning a new language.... When the mask dances, and he hears the true sound of the village [the music as played in Mau villages, with Mau drums and rhythms, call/response singing—the Mau musical language], the emotion is really deep. Your whole body feeling like a—you hear the language, and it's like a—it's different than hearing a drum set. You know you're in a different country, really. You know you came here really to look for something [laughs].

DR: And you found it?

SD: Yeah! The drum set is never going to give you the feeling of the drum. We're just doing that to get the forty-five minutes done and then you go home and do your thing.... But it's a good show for people who never have been to Africa.... It's a great idea and makes everybody happy, but it's not how things are done at home.... It's a new thing and it's perfect, especially when you're in a new context, and you try things that work in that context.

Sogbety's words convey a very important message regarding what he thinks about performing masks in the United States. Clearly his intention is not simply to preserve an a priori authentic version of the traditions he performs. Indeed, by the time he was dancing Gue Pelou in a school in Ohio, Sogbety had already witnessed and experienced multiple adaptations and readaptations of this mask spirit in several contexts. He assumes that he will adapt a performance according to context, and he came *expecting to find something new* as opposed to preserving something old. The goal is to make people happy. In doing so, he has found new ways of performing masks and in that he has found *himself*—an identity that makes him happy in his new context.

I do not want to leave the impression that Sogbety is not serious about his work—that his adaptability and flexibility respect no boundaries or that his performances, being undeniably metacultural in Greg Urban's sense (Urban 2001), lack profound meaning. Quite the opposite. As for Vado, Sogbety's performance of Gue Pelou, for one, is still very much a religious experience. Yet as Sogbety negotiates a new identity, in part via mask spirit performance, not every aspect of mask spirit tradition is negotiable or adaptable. Gue Pelou, for example, remains a spirit whose performance prescribes certain practices that both Sogbety and Vado have assured me no one may alter. Most important is the "dressing of the mask," which by definition must occur in a private space closed to everyone but initiates of the tradition. "It's the same mask, in the village or here," according to Sogbety. "If it's time to get dressed, nobody can see that. I respect that everywhere I go. It's the same mask; the same spirits are there."

In fact, although in Côte d'Ivoire in the 1990s I was *taught* that the sonic aspects of a *Ge* mask performance were by definition part of the spirit's manifestation that determined certain limitations of musical form, I witnessed that rule being broken. In *Dan Ge Performance*, I interpret these moments as youthful indiscretions (Reed 2003, 119) and/or acts of resistance (ibid, 58ff; Reed 2005). In the United States, Sogbety says, even though "a drum set [doesn't] do the same thing . . . you don't get [all] the same spirits you get from 'the drum' [Mau drums playing the prescribed music]. . . . That doesn't mean the mask is changing . . . the mask [that] comes out [is] the same one. You can dance with any music." He stresses that this would not be the case for more sacred genres of Mau mask spirits in his family, including Koman, but Gue Pelou "is supposed to be funny," which allows it playful license. For example, "If you hear . . . hip-hop music playing from [the] radio, the mask can leave the drum and go over there and start dancing to the hip-hop a little bit, and then go back to the drum; nothing changes. . . . He can dance with any music."

For Dan and Mau people, all mask spirits are sacred, but not all operate by the same rules. While this suggests a formal hierarchy that in reality does not exist, I sometimes distinguish spirits as "more sacred" than others on the basis of their having more "totems" or rules and, always in direct proportion, a more serious or consequential function. It is not unusual for a single mask spirit to be entertaining and playful and still be capable of "serious" acts such as the giving of benedictions. Sogbety's stretching of the sonic boundaries of Gue Pelou performance has at least as much to do with the nature of the mask spirit as it does with Sogbety's innovations in response to the new contexts in which performs. "Gue Pelou, it's a mask of showmen. It is a mask to show people what you can do. That's why we have that mask here, and not other masks that would not be allowed to dance here. Gue Pelou is a sacred mask. Anything I do with it here, the mask [the *nya ba*, or Great Mask Spirit that remains in Toufinga] can see." In other words, according to a Dan proverb, "The bird that passes on high—we all see each other" (Reed 2003, 83).

There is a sacred realm in which mask spirit affairs take place, and Sogbety believes passionately that if the rules are not followed, no matter where a mask resides, the *nya ba* in the village will know and there will be consequences. "When we do performances here, we still offer kola, exactly like we do . . . back in the village. And from time to time we put together a lot of money and send it back to the village for a big sacrifice. [Gue Pelou] still has the same power." Here he means a kind of spiritual power that in both Mau and Dan is called *fan*. *Fan* is a fundamental essence, a life force that must be respected through proper behavior.

The *fan* of the mask can be sensed, says Sogbety, by those who recognize its presence. He believes that among African Americans there are descendants of slaves brought to the United States long ago who were involved in the affairs of masks before they were captured in Africa. "If God has given you the mask, then you have that power within you. Even if you do not have the mask with you, that power is still there, that power God gave you."

> There are lots of African Americans, and even if we don't know each other, . . . these are people who have also come from Africa. . . . One could be some guy from my family from long ago. . . . There are a lot of them who, when they see the mask, they say, "I feel something." Yeah, that's the mask. . . . Many African Americans do that. So it touches many people. . . . For me, the mask still has the power here.

One musical collaboration of which Sogbety is especially proud is drumming on Jimmy Buffett's *No Passport Required* tour in 2000. Seguenon Kone, who secured the contract, along with Sogbety, Bi Bo Ti, a Togolese, and an African American joined forces to form a *jembe/dundun* ensemble that traveled with Buffet and his band from Massachusetts to Hawaii. On each stop, the drummers performed first in the parking lot as fans, known as "parrotheads," arrived for the show. Then, just before Buffett's set, Sogbety and friends changed costumes for a short opener filled with drumming and acrobatic dancing. "That was really fun!" Sogbety said. "A lot of flying and driving, amazing hotels where we would stay, good money. Jimmy Buffett is a good guy. Everywhere we went, when they would see Jimmy Buffett, people would go crazy. So it was a fun time."

Future Dreams

Like many immigrants before him, Sogbety in recent years has helped members of his family obtain visas so they can join him in the United States. Several of his siblings have followed in his footsteps and moved to Abidjan. Such a move was common for youth in search of excitement and opportunity back when Sogbety made his in the 1990s. However, once the Ivorian civil war broke out in 2002, dividing the country in two, life for young people became ever more difficult in the rebel-held North, where up to 50 percent of schools were closed and for years daily life was disrupted (Sany 2010). The instability of life in the north, including Mau country, led increasing numbers of youth to seek refuge in Abidjan, this despite the southern xenophobia that had been a major reason for the conflict and was only growing.

Four of Sogbety's siblings are now in Abidjan—three brothers and a sister. "My younger brother Tefini . . . dances now, which astonishes me, because when I left the village, he was little, and he was too ashamed to dance. He had gone to school, and he was not used to dancing. But now, everyone in Abidjan tells me that he is really good. Everyone says, 'You've got to come see your brother—he's an amazing dancer!'" Tefini's exceptional talent has inspired Sogbety to arrange for him to come to the United States, but he has suffered through several unsuccessful attempts to obtain a visa. His interest is motivated by precisely the same desires that led his Uncle Vado to bring him to the states: first to create opportunities for his family members with marketable, ballet skills, and second to alleviate the pressure on him to support the family back home. When an immigrant performer arranges for a relative to join him, the overall family income increases. Even more important, the new arrival becomes the primary provider for her/his closest family members, thereby reducing the number of people the original immigrant must support. The more money earners in the United States, the more shared the financial responsibility for those who remain in Côte d'Ivoire.

While as of this writing Sogbety has been unsuccessful in bringing his brother to the United States, he has succeeded in arranging for his teenage son Abou to join him in Mansfield. Fathered by Sogbety and his Wobe girlfriend when the two were just teens, Abou had been raised by his mother in the Abidjan suburb of Yopougon. After years of effort, in 2013 Abou was finally granted a visa and is now living with his dad. He attends Mansfield Senior High School, where as a freshman he nearly singlehandedly transformed the varsity soccer squad into a winning team. In the summer of 2014, Sogbety bought a small house in Mansfield, which he and Abou now share.

I once asked Sogbety whether he planned to stay here or eventually go back to Côte d'Ivoire:

> I will always be in the United States, and I will come and go. . . . I don't know in how many years, but I'm going to go back and settle in Côte d'Ivoire when I get old if all goes well. . . . That's what I'm thinking. Because [in Côte d'Ivoire], when you reach a certain age, when you become old, you have more respect . . . than here. . . . We, when we go to Africa and we see our grandparents, we treat them with a great deal of respect, and that's what I want when I get old. . . . So maybe I will found a school or a place that I can bring people from the United States. Maybe one in Abidjan, one in Toufinga, and one in Touba. A school like my festival here, where people can come learn about Africa.

As he spoke about these future aspirations, I was reminded of how often he had stressed the educational aspects of his work:

> One time I had to go to the Côte d'Ivoire embassy here. I was talking to a woman who was inspecting my passport, and she said, "So what kind of work do you do here?" And I said, "I do presentations about Africa. I go into schools and I teach children about what we do in Africa. I talk about our country, Côte d'Ivoire, for the benefit of others who don't know about our country. . . . We go to schools to change ideas about Côte d'Ivoire and about Africa. . . . We try to support our country. . . . We simply go to schools and play our *jembes*. . . . We work in schools, but we work for Africa also.

Sogbety clearly feels fortunate to have received training that enables him to pursue a specialization in the immigrant labor force, one that he believes in and that allows him to occupy a social and professional position that would be harder to occupy back in Côte d'Ivoire:

> In Africa people don't always respect people who play the drums. . . . People think you have to have work, and then you can do that on the side. There are even people who won't marry musicians. . . . Lots of Africans are taxi drivers in New York. That's a job, and there's nothing wrong with that. But I want to teach people about Côte d'Ivoire. . . . Some come here just to make money. Some say our work is not good, but to us, it's education. What we teach can touch people, and they might look at the world differently. . . . So I want to be sure to say to others that even if you aren't able to go to school, there is still a life for you. . . . School is the key to the entire world. If you know how to read, you have the key to life. Open it, and you can take anything inside. We who don't go to school don't have that key, but we have a different key—the key to life.

ACT IV
Dr. Djo Bi Irie Simon

9 "Open Village"

An Ivorian Wedding in an Indiana Cornfield

In June 2008, Dr. Djo Bi Irie Simon (Djo Bi) married Harmony Harris on a farm belonging to Harmony's family near St. Bernice, a very small farming community in west central Indiana just several miles from the Illinois border. An extraordinary event, with the name "Open Village," the wedding brought together many of the finest performers in the Ivorian immigrant community and others of Djo Bi's friends with Harmony Harris's friends and family. Most of the music making and dance that occurred that weekend, like most of what these Ivorians do in the United States in classes, workshops, and performances, was based on ballet repertoire and aesthetic practice. And just like the original ballet, which interwove ethnic groups from all over Côte d'Ivoire, Ivorians this wedding interwove performers from Orlando, Syracuse, New York City, Cincinnati and Mansfield, Ohio, St. Louis, Indianapolis and Scottsburg, Indiana, and Canada and the United Kingdom, representing six ethnicities—Guro, Bete, Bobo, Maninka, Akan, Mau, and Senufo (see figure 9.1). Also performing were a Guinean from Cincinnati and a Congolese from Ann Arbor, as well as old immigrant friends with whom Djo Bi once played in New York City: one each from India and Japan and two from Korea. Their presence further extended the difference that the performance integrated ballet-style. Joining in here and there were a few of Djo Bi's current or former *jembe* students from New York, Colorado, and Indiana. Most of the attendees from the bride's family came from the local farming community, which made for quite an interesting gathering. My wife Christy True and I drove up from Bloomington, Indiana, to the wedding site, where we literally did "fieldwork" for the entire weekend.

The main festivities took place in a tent erected in the middle of the field. A smaller canvas shelter about twenty or thirty yards away was used for everything from massages to shelter for the "sacred" housing where the stilt mask spirit Gue Pelou (see figure 9.2) prepared for its appearance in the world of humans. A friend of the wedding party from Colorado set up a huge grill, and there was free beer, wine, and hard liquor.

Both formal and informal performances took place. Generally informal performances occur in the offhours of a show and serve as opportunities for

Figure 9.1 Drummers arriving at Djo Bi's wedding. *Left to right:* Bli Bi Goré Eric from Orlando, Papa Diarra from New York, and Blaise Zekalo from Indianapolis. Photograph by author.

Figure 9.2 Gue Pelou waiting to perform at Djo Bi's June 2008 wedding in St. Bernice, Indiana. Photograph by Christy True.

immigrants "to remember who we are," according to Djo Bi. The texture, the mood, the rhythms played, the way people dress—these are just some of the ways in which these informal performances contrast with their formal counterparts. They are joyous moments of reconnection, but they also act incidentally as rehearsal time. In this they not at all unlike what happens in Côte d'Ivoire, where, in the realm of traditional performance, formal rehearsals are rare; much more common are social occasions on which music and dance are learned through socialization rather than practice. According to Djo Bi, "This is the training ground for the musicians and dancers. Something that is in your head—perhaps you try it out, you can improvise, and see how that will work." At Djo Bi's wedding, the formal performances included elements of wedding ceremonies from several traditions as well as many forms of music and dance, especially mask performances, from the ballet repertoire. In both formal structure and process, this event epitomized the interethnic nature of ballet and Ivorian immigrant performance.

While every event in this book is unique, Djo Bi's wedding is the most distinctive of all. My analysis in the first three performance-focused chapters (chapters 3, 5, and 7) centered on performance elements such as instrumentation and genre to establish the common thread of ballet discourse that runs through them. In this chapter, I emphasize aspects of the wedding celebration that are distinct if not unique in comparison with staged performances. I highlight informal performances, which are intriguing for what they reveal about immigrant life and ballet discourse *offstage*, when performers represent something not to an audience but to themselves and their close family and friends. The ritual within a ritual of the wedding ceremony—the moment of the formal performance framed as "wedding," is also fascinating in how the performers interwove various elements—from conventional ballet dances such as Zauli and Bolohi to iconic symbols of traditional Africa such as kente cloth to a reggae-influenced tune celebrating immigrant life in America. The "Open Village" demonstrates that ballet discourse, which enabled Ivorian performers to become migrant laborers, was sufficiently fluid and dynamic to allow immigrants to embody and express complex and sometimes contradictory meanings.

Informal Performance I: Friday Night Bonfire

Under a full moon at around 11 p.m. on Friday, June 21, 2008, Christy and I drove slowly onto the grass fields of the Harris farm. Dimming our headlights as we approached, we saw reflections off the parked cars and a dozen or so pitched tents lit by the moon and a huge bonfire. We parked our car and walked toward the fire, recording gear in hand, to find Africans, a few Asian Americans, and European Americans drumming, playing guitars, singing, and dancing. Although the formal wedding ceremony was not until the next day, and a great deal of energy would be required for it, Djo Bi and his friends were celebrating the rare opportunity to be together with informal music and dancing. New arrivals joined the group, first greeting their friends, laughing and hugging, then joining in a rural Indiana bonfire party embodiment of Ivorian ballet.

Jembes and *dunduns* mixed with acoustic guitars and percussive whistles; Ivorians sang and drummed and danced; European American drum students of Djo Bi's from Bloomington, Colorado, and New York played accompanying patterns on *jembes*; Indian, Japanese, and Korean immigrant friends from New York played *shekere*, guitars, and ukuleles; and the Congolese musician from Michigan occasionally played *kalimba*. Songs and rhythmic patterns from various ethnic groups and regions of Côte d'Ivoire mixed in creative and novel ways. People sang and played original songs on acoustic guitar with drummers improvising rhythmic accompaniments. Threaded throughout this mélange were formal elements of ballet such as standard Ivorian rhythms, dance breaks, and, of course, *jembe* and *dundun*. From the range of performers to the range of musical instruments and forms, these informal performances incorporated ballet in an expression of the complex, pluralistic nature of Djo Bi's life as a twenty-first-century transnational immigrant.

The gathering performed many rhythms/dances and songs until at least 2 a.m. and then off and on until after daybreak. Djo Bi seemed particularly animated when playing ballet standards with old Guro friends Tra Bi Lizzie from New York City, Bi Bo Ti from Syracuse, Eric Bli Bi Goré from Orlando, and most especially Gao Bi—one of Djo Bi's oldest and closest friends from whom he had been estranged for years—who had come all the way from London to reunite with his old friend. With others joining in, the Guros played a variety of music, some of which closely resembled, in music/dance form, standard ballet practice. The Guro funeral rhythm *zanloba,* an Ivorian ballet standard, found Gao Bi and Eric on *jembe* and Blaise Zekalo, a Bete from Indianapolis, on *dundun* while two lead drummers—Tra Bi on *jembe* and Djo Bi on *bugarabu*—played solo improvisations and breaks. A Guro woman named Irène from Toledo, who was not experienced in ballet, danced for a while, slowly and subtly gyrating her hips in time with the rhythm.

An energy shift occurred, marked by Gao Bi's loud whistle, when ballet veteran Yahyah Kamate (a Maninka from New York City) jumped in front of Djo Bi and Tra Bi, prompting a series of rapid breaks, some complex enough to be characterized by Djo Bi as "compositions," in which the drummers matched Kamate's quickly moving feet beat for beat. The *zanloba* was hot, and the ensuing smiles and shouts signaled joy from the reconnected friends. At the same time, in this informal space Djo Bi and his friends were rehearsing a ballet standard to be played the following day (PURL 9.1).

Later Bi Bo Ti grabbed an acoustic guitar, sat down by the fire, and began strumming a lilting chord progression in G major, alternating between F major and G major chords. The drummers, led by Eric Bli Bi Goré, accompanied Bi Bo Ti's guitar with another Guro funerary dance called *timo*. Once the rhythmic groove had been established, Bi Bo Ti began singing, improvising on the theme of trouble. Djo Bi provided me with a rough translation:

> It's not good—trouble.
> I am Bi Bo Ti. People talk about me.
> I say, please, you are my brother.
> If I have something [a problem] with you, forget it!
> Come back.
> Trouble is not good.
> Trouble is never good."

Meanwhile, Gao Bi sang a lower harmony, danced animatedly, and blew his trademark whistle (PURL 9.2).

After Bi Bo Ti's song, one of Djo Bi's oldest friends, a Congolese musician named Papa Titos Sompa, walked toward the fire, having just arrived with his American wife and daughter from Ann Arbor. The two exchanged loud greetings and laughter as Djo Bi took Titos' daughter in his arms. After Titos moved on, Djo Bi continued to carry the young girl and began singing in Guro. Gao Bi quickly fell in, and the two began classic Guro-style two-part improvisatory singing, which might be described as a cross between hocket and polyphony. The way their vocal lines followed one another and resulted in a continuous melodic flow suggested a hocket with significant overlapping between the end of one line and the beginning of the next. However, the extent to which the ending and beginning of each sung phrase overlapped also suggested the overlaying of independent lines found in polyphony. Such layering is reminiscent of vocal forms from the central African rainforests (see Kisliuk 1998), where even more layering of staggered melodies occurs, producing a dense kaleidoscope of sound. As Djo Bi and Gao Bi wove their vocal magic, Eric Bli Bi continued leading the *jembe* drumming, now playing a variation of the Mau rhythm *zikinin* from the ballet repertoire. Rounding things out was a minor key chord progression on the guitar by Djo Bi's friend and former bandmate Ranjit Arapurakal from New York, whom Djo Bi calls "India" (PURL 9.3).

Such was the nature of the informal music making and dancing the night before the wedding. Though tired guests began heading to their tents, the music and dancing went on for hours before giving way to Ivorian and other African pop music blasted through a high-decibel sound system by DJ Richard Gougoua, a Bete from Indianapolis. The singing and drumming continued at turns during the pop music until around five in the morning, when Richard took a break and there was a brief period of relative silence. Well before seven, however, the drumming began again and continued off and on until the formal performance began a little after noon.

Throughout the morning, as people emerged from their tents and drank coffee, more performers arrived (particularly celebrated was the arrival of a car driven by Sogbety Diomande from which Vado Diomande, Moha Dosso, and Hamidou Koivogui emerged). Informal performances and slightly more formal but still playful "rehearsals" commenced. Generally speaking, rehearsals are distinct from other informal performances in that the participants and the repertoire are those that will be in the show. Considering the complexity of Ivorian immigrant ballet performance, the extremely little rehearsing for any given show is astonishing.

Even for big annual concerts such as Samba's *Ayoka* or Vado's *Kekene* (which include complex choreographed dramas), it is not unusual for there to be one or perhaps two rehearsals involving all performers the night before and/or the morning of the performance. To clarify, in Vado's and Samba's dance companies advanced students who are selected to perform rehearse the show in their classes. However, members of the dispersed ballet community usually arrive at a performance at most twenty-four hours before curtain, when, given the depth of their ballet knowledge and experience, only one rehearsal is required. Already expected to be familiar with ballet discourse, performers use rehearsals to work out specific details such as the rhythms/dances to be performed and the order of performances. They may practice at least some of the rhythms/dances but only to warm up and coordinate each other's idiosyncrasies and preferences.

From my perspective, rehearsals *feel* much like informal performances. They are generally light-hearted, joyous, full of smiles and playful repartee, and they are clearly viewed as social reconnection at least as much if not more than preparation for a show. In that sense, rehearsals, like informal performances, blend the categories of presentational and participatory music making distinguished by ethnomusicologist Tom Turino (2008) (PURL 9.4; PURL 9.5).

The informal performances continued throughout the weekend of Djo Bi's wedding even well after the formal performance accompanying the wedding ceremony. Their significance, to which I return later, cannot be overstated.

Formal Performance

In its clothing, music and dance genres, instrumentation, and ritual—the formal wedding was ballet through and through. Djo Bi explained to me why he had decided to produce such a grand event. Oddly enough, because marriage is not customarily a major ritual among the Guro, Djo Bi grew up without observing elaborate weddings. Not far to the east of Guro country, however, at the western edge of the huge Akan linguistic and cultural region, many ethnic groups are known for them. Djo Bi discovered that wedding celebrations are also common in the United States, so for his own he chose to mix Guro, Akan, and American customs. Defining it as a Guro/Akan/American mélange, he demonstrated his view that his wedding was not a simple binary mix (as in Western and Guro) but rather a complex blending of African difference, in which Akan and Western are equally Other.

Though a mixture of Western, Guro, and Akan was Djo Bi's intention, because the participants were drawing on their shared ballet experience, the wedding performance interwove elements from far more than three sources. It simultaneously indexed very specific locales and broader discourses, from the ethnic to the national to the transnational. As seen in figure 9.3, for example, the clothes Djo Bi wore—Akan kente cloth—"would be rare in a Guro village." He continued,

> We [Guros] have our own cloth, but to find [it here] is difficult. . . . The Akan kente cloth is everywhere so there is no problem . . . and it still represents, well, something traditionally African. . . . It's Pan-African. . . . It's life in the United States.

Kente cloth, as Djo Bi defines it, works in this context because it represents traditional Africa; indeed, it has become a transnational icon of Africa (Shipley 2013) (PURL 9.6).

Djo Bi's ceremony featured many types of music and dance from the ballet repertoire, especially mask performance. Its formal component began with an appearance by Mau sacred mask spirit Gue Pelou, who prepared for his performance in a canvas tent serving as the essential "sacred house" where only initiates may be present for the spirit's ritual dressing and undressing. Lead drummer Papa Diarra, whose Bobo family emigrated from Burkina Faso to Abidjan, where he grew up and lived before immigrating to New York, initiated the Mau rhythm *zikinin* on his *jembe*. Responding to the call of the drums, the towering Gue Pelou emerged from the tent. At least ten feet tall, possibly even taller thanks to his pointed conical hat above his nonrepresentational black burlap "face," this *nya yan* (Mau stilt mask spirit) wore the famous loom-woven cloth of the western region of Côte d'Ivoire.

The initial *zikinin* rhythm was in fact a break from standard ballet practice, in which Gue Pelou performances nearly always follow the same structure (song in *tindin* rhythm, benedictions, and then a song, usually "Ge ya yi kan" in *zikinin* rhythm). Instead, this part of the performance followed Mau tradition (and more generally that of many West African ethnic groups). In a Mau [or Dan] village, the mask spirit begins by leading an entourage of drummers and possibly others, including "fathers of the mask" (elder ritual specialists), in a counterclockwise direction around the performance space. At Djo Bi's wedding, Gue Pelou danced his way around the wedding tent leading the bride and groom and the musicians—Papa on lead *jembe*, Sogbety and Vado on accompanying drums, and Yuichi Iira on *shekere*, with elder Titos Sompa simply walking along, playing the supporting role of village elder.

Figure 9.3 Djo Bi wearing kente cloth at his wedding in St. Bernice, Indiana. Photograph by Christy True.

In western Côte d'Ivoire, a space where a sacred activity is to occur is considered spiritually vulnerable and in need of protection from malevolent spirits (Reed 2003). This is provided by Gue Pelou's counter-clockwise encirclement, which is common in many West African culture groups (Stone 2000; Stone 1994). According to Vado Diomande, in Dan it means "ko fli do" (Excuse me), announcing the spirit's presence and requesting permission to perform. Both Djo Bi and Vado stressed that Gue Pelou's dance was "just like in the village" where this is precisely the way a *nya yan* typically begins. Gue Pelou's presence and his actions also represent ballet discourse in action—a Mau sacred mask spirit spatially and temporally marking as sacred a space in an Indiana cornfield for a wedding of a Guro man and a Hoosier woman. As the Kente cloth symbolizes traditional Africa, to Djo Bi the stilt mask spirit represents an African, indeed an Ivorian means (by virtue of its adoption as a symbol of Ivorian nationalism by the national ballet) of marking sacred ritual time/space.

Gue Pelou slowly led the entourage around the tent, stopping occasionally to thrill the gathering crowd with acrobatic spinning, dramatic falls, and even more dramatic slow exaggerated efforts to get to his feet. Midway, Sogbety signaled for the percussionists to stop and initiated a call:

Ge ya nu o zogon we
ka go ge ya nu o

The Ge [mask spirit] has come
Elder owners of the Ge
go see the mask has come

Vado led the response: "Ge ya nu o, o, o, ge ya nu" (The Ge has come). In this song, which is in the *tindin* rhythm, Sogbety transitioned the performance into the standard Gue Pelou ballet, effectively rendering the encirclement an introduction clearly added for the ritual protection of the wedding. At no other Ivorian immigrant show have I experienced this.[1] Now in *tindin*, the performers walked the rest of the way around the tent playing the rhythm typical of the beginning of any Gue Pelou show on a North American stage. Gue Pelou's performance followed the standard structure from this point on.

The mask spirit ducked under the roof of the large tent and led his entourage inside, where a temporary wooden dance floor, about a hundred square feet, was surrounded on three sides by chairs and tables. On the fourth side, behind the "stage," were three sets of *dunduns* on stands and at least half a dozen *jembes*. A group of drummers made their way to this space. With Vado, Sogbety, and Papa still drumming *tindin*, Tra Bi, Eric, and an Ivorian drummer from St. Louis whose name I did not know joined in on *jembes* while Blaise and Hamidou played the *dunduns*. This transition was momentarily chaotic as Blaise began a *kuku* pattern, prompting the more ballet-seasoned to add an appropriate *dundun tindin* pattern. The latter, which in Mau and Dan communities is generally played on the *baanya*, is what my Dan drumming teachers onomatopoeically called "kpi-ki-li-kpi-gblin" (Reed 2003, chap. 5). Hamidou (ironically, the one Guinean present) jumped in on another *dundun*, loudly punctuating the *tindin* pattern that Vado had been playing on *bugarabu*, which freed Vado from this central, timeline-like pattern so that he could play assistant to the mask (Dan *gekia*).[2] The sound of *dunduns* taking up the *tindin* patterns marked the transition to the sound of ballet (PURL 9.7).

In keeping with the standard structure of Gue Pelou ballet performance, the mask, following the initial dance and song, offered benedictions, or blessings. He cued the drummers to stop, at which point Sogbety took over the role of *gekia* from Vado. In a characteristic high falsetto, Gue Pelou periodically screamed "A sa de!" (This is your sacrifice). "Amina!" the crowd responded, cued by Sogbety by touching his forehead with both hands.

After about five minutes, the mask began the standard, post-blessing song, which is set in *zikinin*:

Call:
Ee ge ya yi kan bo (the mask spirit has crossed the river)
Response:
zere wa wa (vocables)

As classic ballet, the song interwove several ethnic traditions. In the Dan language (like many Mau mask songs), it has at least two meanings. First is the calling of the mask spirit across the metaphorical river separating the corporal from the spiritual world, where he lives alongside ancestors and other spirit intermediaries between the people and God. Vado Diomande taught me that it also refers to the mobility of mask spirits, who travel regularly for performance, even across the big water to the United States. Initially I was intrigued that drummers who come from all over Côte d'Ivoire know all of the mask rhythms from a small western region, but knowing them, and transposing them for *jembe* and *dundun*, is part of the ballet skill set (PURL 9.8).

Following several other rhythms/dances, some performers exited the tent to join Djo Bi, Harmony, and her parents for the formal processional. Walking just in front of the bride and groom and singing in Guro were two men from Djo Bi's Guro ethnic group: Bi Bo Ti and Gao Bi. Meanwhile, Jean Assamoah, painted white (a common West African ritual marker), led the procession waving a fly whisk (also common throughout West Africa as a symbol of ritual authority). Djo Bi chose Assamoah, who is Akan, for this role because he was "doing the wedding in an Akan way and a Western way."

Although the Guro do not hold grand wedding celebrations, they do sing at marriage rituals, and Djo Bi told me that the song Bi Bo Ti and Gao Bi sang during the processional was but one of many Guro wedding songs. The text, centered on a Guro proverb that says that we are all animals but we should not fight, was offered in the hope that the newly married couple would live together peacefully. The Guro duo sang this song unaccompanied, in neutral thirds, a harmonic preference of some southern Mande groups in the forest region of Côte d'Ivoire such as the Tura and the Goh. Bi Bo Ti and Zagbo Martin began another song, this one in Bete and again in harmonies of thirds, while they led a group of drummers into the tent. Though only Zagbo Martin is Bete, all of the performers joined in the refrain because, according to Djo Bi, "we were all in the ballet." The drummers accompanied the song with an unusually quiet and slow version of the Bete *gbegbe* rhythm.

Extending Ballet Discourse: The United Nations Band

When he lived in New York City, Djo Bi performed in the United Nations Band, which besides him comprised two Koreans, one Japanese, one Indian, and one Jamaican. When they formed in the late 1990s, the members called each other by their countries (and to this day Djo Bi addresses them this way). Djo Bi was called Africa. I do not interpret this as the common misconception among Americans that Africa is a country, not a continent. Rather, as Ferguson (2006) argues, Africans themselves in certain contexts identify in such essentialized terms. Identity is situational, and Djo Bi sees his contribution to the United Nations Band as adding "an African element" to its multinational musical discourse. Japan, Jamaica, Korea, India, and Africa: ambassadors to the United Nations, the multinational band. Like the UN, the band promoted a discourse of unity achieved by aligning difference for a single purpose and vision. By including the band in his wedding, Djo Bi extended the ballet model.

India introduced the band in French, saying that they played "everyone's genre." Then the band began playing, with Japan on *shekere*, Korea on ukulele, India on guitar, and Africa on *bugarabu*, joined by a Korean woman on melodica. Though Jamaica was absent, his presence was felt in the reggae rhythm of "Living in America" (PURL 9.9, V: United Nations Band):

> Some from Africa
> Some from India
> Some from Jamaica
> Some from the Orient . . .
>
> Living in America . . .
>
> Now we're all together
> Feeling all right
> Life is all right,
> We're still standing and dancing

Land of the free
East coast to West coast
Living in America

Ivorian guest Richard Gougoua took the microphone to offer a darker assessment of immigrant life in America: "Yeah, whatever they say, living in America is not easy. The gas prices are jamming you. Even the hamburger now is two dollars. . . . Living in America—that's the way it is." This was a somewhat subtle statement, but at that moment two starkly different representations of immigrant life had been expressed: the band's almost global village–like discourse of harmony, celebration, and "feeling all right" clashing with Richard's discourse on the immigrant's economic hardships. Even at the wedding, frictions surfaced.

The formal performance lasted about three hours in all. Ivorian ballet standards took up most of it, including mask dances Zauli (PURL 9.10) and Bolohi and a different manifestation of Gue Pelou (PURL 9.11).[3] Zagbo Martin played the Akan musical bow, using a stick to strike the metal wire passing through the resonating cavity of his mouth which, when he altered its shape, enhanced one of a range of overtones. Djo Bi and Harmony chose the Akan musical bow piece for their traditional first dance, moving up to Zagbo and then in a grand arc around the performance space, as if to offer a danced greeting to everyone present (figure 9.4; also PURL 9.12). Seguenon Kone performed a spectacular solo piece in

Figure 9.4 Djo Bi and Harmony dancing as bride and groom. Photograph by Christy True.

which he danced and spun while playing a Senufo *jegele* xylophone strapped to his shoulders. Yahyah Kamaté played a lovely, breathy solo on his wooden *file* flute, and Papa Titos Sompa played his metalophone *kalimba*. For some pieces, *jembe* and *dundun* drummers added subtle accompaniment, providing a contrast to the loud, fast, and highly coordinated rhythms of the mask dances (PURL 9.13).

Informal Performance II: "Playing . . . to Remember Who We Are"

When the formal performance was over, Harmony's family members said their goodbyes and many other guests retreated to tents or lawn chairs to recoup. The performers took this opportunity to change out of their sweaty performance clothes, but less than an hour had passed when one by one they gathered in the performance tent and began chatting and joking. A few sat down, *jembes* between their legs, and began casual solos. Eventually these gave way to a coordinated, fast-paced polyrhythm, and the *dunduns* began the *gbebge*. Several times Djo Bi signaled to quicken the tempo with gradually faster single slaps on his *jembe*. The energy began to build, and I started paying attention when a semicircle of dancers formed and one by one took center stage accompanied by masterfully coordinated breaks. Having shot a great deal of video that day, which I twice had to backup to make room for more, I thought I would record just the audio of this jam session. I captured about ten to fifteen minutes on a digital audio recorder, during which the drumming and dancing intensified and the performers became more focused and animated, although they remained relaxed, as they generally are in informal performance. Aware that this mini-event was not just clearly important to the performers but also filled with visual data such as dance and dress, I quickly pulled out my video recorder. I had thought the performances were "over." How wrong I was—this was as important as anything else that happened that weekend.

This gathering was more relaxed, exuberant—even euphoric—than the formal wedding itself, which I found incredible. After little or no sleep the night before; after music and dance almost all night; after rehearsing and playing nearly all morning; and after the ceremony—they wanted *badly* to continue performing. When we later discussed this moment, Djo Bi told me, "Before, let's say it was the wedding . . . but it's now that the fête begins. . . . You're no longer dressed [up]; you come as you are, you can even jump. . . . Now everyone is himself. It's free." Clearly, compared to the participatory social music and dance of this informal session, the "main event" was not the most highly valued aspect of the weekend for Djo Bi (cf. Turino 2008).

I touched on informal performances earlier; however, their importance demands more attention. As Djo Bi said, one of the ways in which informal and formal performances differ is in attire. So-called Western clothing—T-shirts and jeans, sweaters, jogging suits, sneakers—is the most common choice for Ivorian immigrants at social gatherings such as Djo Bi and Harmony's wedding, although it is also not unusual to see a tailor-made African market cloth shirt, blouse, or skirt. Ivorian immigrant clothing for informal performance reflects choices in their daily lives outside of the performative frame. For each other, they perform a different kind of Africa—the one where they grew up, where their clothes naturally reflected the complex, postcolonial transnational economic networks through which many goods—including clothing (Clark 2010)—pass in and out of West African markets. A Yankees hat here, a Côte d'Ivoire T-shirt there, blue jeans, sandals. Although the sound and movement of this informal session were pure ballet, absent was a self-conscious desire to *visually* represent the discourse of Africa associated with ballet and the concert stage.

Informal performances are also distinct in part because of their intent: Ivorian immigrants perform for themselves and for each other and, when I am there for the camera, not for a defined audience such as in a concert hall or a high school gymnasium. As Djo Bi put it, they play "for those who know," for their fellow immigrants, which supports the idea that, though lacking a formal audience, the music making and dancing are still performative. Performance necessitates interaction between two (or more) parties, one intentionally communicating something to another. If informal, its audience and performers are one and the same. Through movement and sound, mobile Ivorians reconnect to share not just regional, national, and/or ethnic identities but *ballet* as well.

Performers willingly sacrifice energy, sleep, meals, and relaxation to perform before and after shows because informal performances *matter*. Having spent many hours with Djo Bi over multiple sessions watching and analyzing film of the wedding in great detail, I felt Djo Bi breathe a sigh of relief when, one day at his home in Bloomington, we finally reached the post-ceremony music and dancing. "Yes!" he exclaimed. "This is just for fun." I described what typically happens at weddings in the United States: when the ceremony and the reception conclude, people might linger a little but more likely go home. At Djo Bi's wedding, the ceremony ended and Harmony's family left but the celebration continued. Djo Bi explained why:

> The fun continues . . . because this is a reunion. It's a *reunion*. There are people who came from Florida. Some came from other places. Everyone eagerly awaits each other's arrival. When we are together, we're going to play more because this is our work. But we are not playing for money here. We are playing to remember where we've come from. To remember who we are.

With the exception of Vado's Kekene shows in New York City, where the complications of transportation and lodging make it infeasible, each time I have seen Ivorians from across the United States gather for a show, informal performance begins the moment they arrive and continues after the show is over. I asked Djo Bi about this:

DANIEL REED (DR): Why is it that each time there is a formal event, people begin playing music as soon as they are all together, well before the formal work, and then often well afterward as well?

DJO BI (DB): Why is it like that? Because in Africa we play music; for example, during someone's wedding we will play all night. In Africa we don't play for just two hours or for just forty-five minutes. You have *all* the time, whereas here there is a limit. . . . At my wedding, for example, all those who had come there—it had been *years* since we had seen each other all together. When we are not in New York City, [when] we are somewhere in the bush where we can play as we wish, we will play all night. . . . There were lots of people who have known each other for a long time, but it had been maybe fifteen years since they had all seen each other. . . . So there is joy.

DR: I noticed that the feeling is more relaxed.

DB: Because it's no longer an affair of masks. Now it's like the evening in the village. The rice fields, the cassava fields. . . . The year has passed; all has been given well. So people have a drink, [and] the musicians are there. It's not a question of money . . . everyone is there and they dance till tomorrow. . . . With the masks it's more serious. We have to have a celebration. . . . Anyone can come and decide to dance or not. . . . It's more open.

I explained that I had not intended to videotape the post-ceremony playing, thinking that the performance was "over." But the feeling was so good and the playing so hot that I changed my mind. Djo Bi enthusiastically responded: "It was a special feeling . . . that's it. Even all the women and you—everyone can dance there. By this time most of the crowd had left. . . . Now it's the musicians; it's *for those who know*. For them . . . voilà! Africa is what's there."

"*Africa* is what's there." But it is not the Africa of the *stage*. Though both informal and formal performances draw heavily on ballet, in the former ballet operates as a form of shared background and affinity, more akin to an ethnic identity. Many contemporary Ivorians, at home and abroad, have established new identity affiliations that today are at least as important as ethnicity if not more so. Though ironically ballet discourse is dependent on the reification of ethnicity in its ethnically marked music and dance, ballet itself becomes, for these immigrants, its own powerful form of affinity. This affinity is also nationally Ivorian and transnational—fluid, dynamic, and negotiated in the polysemic frame of performance (PURL 9.14).

Following Djo Bi's wedding ceremony, the music making continued throughout the night. Seemingly unfazed by twenty-four straight hours of drumming and dancing, the Africans were gathered around the bonfire along with a number of Americans—students and friends of Djo Bi and Harmony—playing *jembes*, *dunduns*, and even a flute. Moha Doso thrilled with his various tricks with fire, running a burning branch across his bare arms and chest and lapping at the flames with his tongue.

Christy and I finally retired to our tent, the sounds of performance still flowing across the field. After two nights of barely sleeping—in fact, I am not sure I slept at all the second night—we packed up our tent on Sunday morning and returned home, having experienced nearly thirty-six uninterrupted hours of music and dance. Djo Bi later chided me for having left before the celebration was finished: "After you left, we continued . . . because we were not just playing for the wedding. We played like we were in the village . . . [where] we could play for three days. You are always there playing. That's the purpose. It's not a matter of the wedding only. People are . . . playing together, having fun, playing."

The community of Ivorian ballet performers, spread across the United States and beyond, has few opportunities to be together. Djo Bi's wedding was a chance to reunite, and for Ivorians reuniting is performed. In other words, the community is primarily constituted in performance. Ballet communicates unity through the interweaving of difference which at the wedding extended well beyond the Ivorians and Ivorian cultural referents to encompass people of Guinean, Congolese, Indian, Korean, Japanese, and European backgrounds and identities; an African diaspora rhythm from Jamaica; transnational iconic symbols of Africa in kente cloth and *jembe*; and more. Djo Bi and Harmony's wedding served to demonstrate that ballet discourse can be flexibly adapted, thanks to its fluid, open, polysemic nature, to different needs of Ivorian immigrants, not just for finding work in the market of the staging of Africa but also in remembering who they are.

10 "Everyone Is a Cook, but He's a Chef!"
Dr. Djo Bi and Innovation

On a warm spring day in 2007, I was walking my dogs in the woods when my cell phone rang. While I did not recognize the number, I did recognize the New York area code. I answered and heard a man's voice speaking the familiar sounds of Ivorian-accented French. "I have just arrived, and everyone tells me I should call you," said the voice. "I am a drummer. Sogbety, Aristide—they said when you arrive call Daniel Reed." The area code in the back of my mind, I continued conversing under the assumption that the caller had just arrived in New York from Côte d'Ivoire. Gradually, however, I came to realize that the things this man was saying did not support my assumption. After a couple of minutes, I pulled the phone away from my ear to look again at the phone number. Finally I interjected: "Wait a minute—where are you calling from?" "Here!" exclaimed the caller. "Here where?" I asked. "Here in Bloomington!"

I stood on the forest path simultaneously thinking back and looking forward. A year earlier this research project had begun when I received a call from Sogbety Diomande, who had just moved to my hometown of Mansfield, Ohio. Now another Ivorian musician—Dr. Djo Bi Irie Simon (see figure 10.1)[1]—had moved to my *current* town, into an apartment just a few miles south of the woods where I stood. I could hardly believe it.

The next day, I met Djo Bi and his fiancé, Harmony Harris. An Indiana native transplanted to Steamboat Springs, Colorado, Harmony had gone to an African music and dance camp in New Mexico in 2006, where she met New York City–based Djo Bi. They fell in love and eventually moved to her home state, settling in Bloomington. Suddenly I had easy access to an Ivorian performer and the opportunity for more regular contact than had been possible with other performers in my study. For the next five years, Djo Bi and I would share meals, music, conversation, and laughter. I would attend his wedding and his dance classes, film his performances, and conduct formal interviews; he would guest-lecture in my African music classes at Indiana University; I would help him find work through Traditional Arts Indiana and the Lotus Festival; we would play in each other's bands. Increasingly, one of the central sites of this multisited ethnography became my own little city in south central Indiana.

244 | Abidjan USA

Figure 10.1 Djo Bi with a friend's child at his June 2008 wedding. Photograph by author.

Joyful, mercurial, brilliant, brash—these are just some of the words I came to associate with Djo Bi. His is another story in which a deeply rooted sense of tradition that developed in a rural Ivorian village led to collaborative music making with an increasingly wider circle of musicians in Côte d'Ivoire, Europe, and eventually the United States. Djo Bi's path differed from those of Vado, Sogbety, and Samba in many respects, including that he did not spend time in the Ballet National de Côte d'Ivoire (BNCI), although he became fluent in ballet discourse in a range of contexts: churches, hotels, private ballets around Abidjan and then in Europe. Eventually he used his ballet training to immigrate to the United States.

Village

Djo Bi was born in Bangofla, "a tiny village of at most 300 people" in the Guro region of west central Côte d'Ivoire. The third of ten children, he grew up hearing a story that led him to believe he was predestined to be special. One day before Djo Bi was born, his mother and his two older siblings—the firstborn Djo Lou Gouana Martine and her younger brother Djo Bi Vié—were farming when Djo Bi Vié climbed a mango tree and, reaching for a ripe fruit hanging far from his grasp, lost his grip and fell, injuring both feet. His parents took him to a local diviner/healer who assured them that he would be cured. Relieved, his parents began preparing to leave when the diviner added, "But the child who will come after this boy will be exceptionally powerful in the family."

That next child, born in 1968, was Djo Bi. From the time he was very young, Djo Bi showed signs of the power and greatness that the diviner had predicted. Both his parents were musical, each coming from families full of musicians and artists.

> My dad was a drummer, and my grandfather was a sculptor—he made masks like that [points to the masks on my wall]. . . . My dad was the youngest son, and my grandpa had many, many daughters. And of all those daughters, there was one—Zauli Lou Kambo—[who] was a *great* singer, who everyone knows all over Guro country. . . . When I was born there was already a drum in the house . . . everyone [was] always there playing music. That was . . . the good fortune that has enabled me to make a living from [music] today.

But even among fine musicians, Djo Bi stood out.

> My father had a drum, a *topalon*, at the house, and we used to enjoy ourselves with it. At night, my father would play and afterwards we the kids would play. . . . We played the drum and people already liked the way I played. And I was better than my older brother. All the people from the village would come see.

Gradually family members began to take note of Djo Bi's rapidly developing drumming talent and his precocious skill in music perception. Before he was even old enough to go to school, he began commenting on the different approaches to drumming and singing between his mother and his father's families. One night when he was six years old, Djo Bi's mother had an experience that would prove to be transformative for the young drumming prodigy.

> When I was six years old, my mother was in the fields with my little sister, Djo Lou Bahnan Celestine, and it was nighttime. We should have been in the village but we were still in the fields. A strong wind blew, and since we were kids we were afraid. We called my mother who was in the forest. Barefoot, she ran out to see what was wrong. Suddenly she stopped, grabbing her leg; she had stepped on a *dabla*—the most dangerous poisonous thorn in the region I come from. Somehow, this affected her brain; she was no longer normal. The family took her to various doctors, but none could heal her.

Increasingly worried about the fate of her children in light of her declining mental health, Djo Bi's mother insisted that Djo Bi attend school, even though neither of his older siblings had done so, and in 1975, at the age of seven, his education began.

Around this same time, his mother began to seek a cure at a local Evangelical Protestant Church.[2] The family began regularly attending as well, and soon Djo

Bi began drumming for services. At church Djo Bi had found a new outlet for his musical skills and development.

> It was at the church that I really began developing my skills. In the village there are a lot of drummers, but [at] the church there were no drummers. My mother was already there and the priests said, "We want your whole family to come here." And so the Christians adopted me. . . . I began performing in all these little towns that my parents didn't even know about.

In addition to gaining more musical experience, Djo Bi began traveling regionally with church missionaries, which allowed him to meet people from all over the Guro region and build his reputation as an exceptional young drummer.

> From my position in the church, I visited many villages. It's not everybody who travels like me. In my ethnic group, people don't travel a lot. Everyone rests where his father is, or if your father or rather your mother is from another village, you can go visit your mother's village, but then you return to the village of your father. But I, since I was at the church and I played well, I had lots of friends. I spent time in many of the villages.

The Evangelical Protestant Church thus offered Djo Bi not just a new context in which to drum but also the opportunity to travel and become exposed to a wider range of people, music, and cultural practices than he had experienced in the small village of Bangofla. This experience would prove pivotal in offering him a taste of travel, the thrill of new places and different types of people, new opportunities for collaboration with musicians different from him, and doing the thing he loved most—drumming.

Abidjan

Kada Club

Djo Bi's travel with the church was occupying more and more of his time, and he began to feel that a choice had to be made between his increasingly busy drumming schedule and school. Finally in 1981 or 1982, when he was about fourteen years old, he quit school. "I was good," he told me. "I was third in my class . . . [That year] I left at the exam [time, so] I didn't pass that [level]. After that, I didn't return to school. . . . But by this time I was already great. I was well known all over Guro country." His reputation as a drummer well established, he decided to move to Abidjan to seek his musical fortune.

As is common, Djo Bi initially sought out members of his extended family when he arrived in the city. He first found an uncle and stayed with him before settling with his brother (or cousin in American family terms), Zewenin Matias, in Banco, a poor neighborhood on the northern edge of Abidjan. "At that time people [in Banco] lived as if they were in the village. There were few schools." "No electricity?" I asked. "Right, there was nothing. They danced like they do in the village.... Each Saturday they sang and danced a bit."

One Saturday Djo Bi got word that members of a group called Kada Club would be joining the neighborhood dancing. A professional performance troupe consisting exclusively of Guro musicians and dancers, Kada Club had gained renown in part because it featured a spectacular female dancer, Zan Lou Loua.

> Even when I was still in the village I had heard her name. Everyone was talking about her.... She was the first woman to dance [the Guro mask] Zauli.... Before it was just men who danced Zauli. Her brother was her drummer.... His name was Zan Bi Tueï Blaise. They had already traveled to Belgium and all that.

An additional reason for Kada Club's success, according to Djo Bi, was their personal connections with powerful Ivorians, particularly in the military. Kada Club's director, known as Commandant Tra, was a well-connected Guro military officer. According to Djo Bi, "In Côte d'Ivoire, if you're in the military, you do well in life."

Djo Bi and his uncle, also a drummer, watched Kada Club's drumming and dance. "Both of us were sitting there [while] people played.... I took a drum—it was an ugly drum—and I went around and played a little. And the guys said, 'Hey look at this little guy—how did he learn how to play like that?' Djo Bi clearly had made an impression.

Shortly thereafter one of Kada Club's drummers, who was also in the military, was called away from Abidjan for duty. This was the break Djo Bi needed. The commandant sent another military man to Banco to invite Djo Bi to audition for the group. Because Kada Club was exclusively Guro and performed Guro dances, the audition tested Djo Bi's knowledge of what he knew best: the rhythms, dance breaks, and general performance practices in which he had been immersed throughout his childhood. "I did an audition," he recalled. "They tested me ... but it went well."

Shortly afterward Djo Bi received a visit from one of Commandant Tra's junior officers. "You have passed the audition," the officer announced. "Commandant Tra wishes you to join Kada Club." Not only did the commandant offer Djo Bi his first professional position as a drummer, he also invited him to live with him. Suddenly Djo Bi was residing in Commandant Tra's spacious home in the affluent downtown Plateau neighborhood. With its high-rise buildings and expensive boutiques, Plateau was a world away from the urban village conditions of Banco. "So I slept in the Plateau—from Banco to the Plateau! Rapidly like that!" Djo Bi said, laughing raucously. Astonished by this rags-to-riches narrative, I began laughing as well. Clearly the invitation to join Kada Club had been more than a mere job offer; it represented a complete transformation for the fourteen-year-old drummer. As he recalled this pivotal moment in his life, Djo Bi beamed, betraying the pride that he still felt some thirty years later.

Djo Bi began regularly rehearsing with Kada Club at the group's rehearsal space in Yopougon, a neighborhood on the northwest edge of the city where many migrants from the Ivorian west—including Guro, Dan, and Mau—had settled in great numbers. Even in multiethnic, multinational, cosmopolitan Abidjan, ethnicity retained its affinal salience. On arriving in the city, migrants tended to seek out others from their ethnic region. Neighborhoods, places of worship, and business transactions were where members of the same ethnic group would try to connect. Djo Bi's seemingly easy acceptance into a Guro ensemble was a case in point.

Kada Club experienced a breakthrough when a well-known television personality—a Guro named Jacques Foua Bi—began to feature the group regularly on the state-run Radiodiffusion Télévision Ivorienne (RTI) network. Director of the news program on what at the time was the only television channel in the country, Foua Bi gave his fellow Guro performers regular exposure to a national audience, catapulting them to a new level of fame. Kada Club became a household name in high demand for performances. Not underplaying the group's talent, Djo Bi admitted, "It was because [Foua Bi] was Guro that he did this."

Leaving the Church

DJO BI (DB): I was still going to church when I arrived in Abidjan. Because people who went to [my] church . . . had talked to people in the village and they had heard my name. . . . But when they saw me drumming on the television, to them, I was no longer Christian. The next day, I went to church and they said, "You must go sit in the back and not play." Since I was playing with [Kada Club], I must not play here in the church, for God. When they said that I got up and left the church and have stayed away to this day.

DANIEL REED (DR): Why do you think they made this decision?

DB: For them, everything that you do must be for the church. You must not do things that are not part of the church. That's how they understood the church to work. Whereas here, we could dance Zauli in the church here, no problem. We go out each time, we dance. . . . That causes no problems—it's no big deal!

DR: So if I understand correctly, if you have talent then you must use that talent only—

DB: In the church! Yes. Not for the Ballet National, not for—no no no no no. So when I was at the church, before I left for Kada Club, I said to myself, "I am not going to stop. I have so much talent I am not going to limit myself to only being here [at the church]." I could do better. I could play better . . . I could learn more. . . . I envisioned that I could even go and play in Europe! Why not? Because at that moment in my head was [the idea] that I could go play with the Ballet National, where you have lots of drummers, where you have many more rhythms [to learn]! I was young and I knew that this was my career.

At this point in his story, Djo Bi cycled back to an earlier memory, when he was about seven years old and his dreams of being a drummer were still in their infancy:

> Even before, when I was still in the village, we had a "televisual school"; that was the time—when I was in school in 1975 . . . when Houphouët-Boigny had televisions installed in all of the schools in Côte d'Ivoire. And they used to broadcast the Ballet National, and I saw all those dances . . . in [preschool]. . . . I brought in a little drum, a little one like that one your son has [a small *jembe*]. I brought that in, and the teacher said that because sometimes he had seen me play, I must play a little and the others would sing a little.

From a very young age, Djo Bi had known and dreamed about drumming in the BNCI. The church had provided opportunities for him to grow musically and personally, but he began to feel that he had reached the limits of that growth. Eventually Djo Bi saw even Kada Club as stunting his musical evolution.

> Even after I came to Kada Club, I said to myself—"Listen, even this I could go beyond!" Because in Kada Club, it was only two rhythms. *gbegbe* and *aluku*, while in the Ballet National, you have *tématé*, you have *abodan*—you have all of them! So I thought that I needed to grow beyond the place where I was.

Although Djo Bi had matured well beyond his years musically, he was still naïve about the workings of professional music and dance in Côte d'Ivoire:

> I was still in Kada Club, but I wrote to the Ballet National, because I already knew how to write. I read the newspapers, and I read and I read and one day, I ran across their address. And I wrote to them, and they responded. . . . They said, "Thank you very much, but at this point we don't need anyone." I just didn't know you had to go and introduce yourself to them. I just didn't know that.

Djo Bi also got a taste of the cutthroat competition for the best drumming positions such as those in the BNCI.

DB: There were people in the national ballet who acted like it *belonged* to them. There were people who didn't want to leave, who wanted to stay because they got to travel, they had good clothes. . . . We, the young, for us to find a way in, it was a problem. So after [the Ballet] responded, I said "Okay no problem." I stayed in Kada Club. We played a lot, at many funerals.

DR: I had wanted to ask . . . where Kada Club tended to perform.

DB: It was at funerals, especially funerals . . . Guro funerals, sometimes Baule funerals. . . . Sometimes we traveled; we might play at Beoumi or other towns.

DR: So it wasn't necessarily in Abidjan—you toured around a little bit in the country?

DB: Yes, we toured a bit, to Ferkessedougou . . . to Beoumi, and other towns, including Assinie, the touristic city next to Bassam. There were several at Gagnoa, Daloa, Vavoua, and in tiny villages also. Since the commandant . . . knew people . . . we played not only at funerals. We also played a lot at parties, but more than anything we played at funerals.

DR: You played in many towns outside the Guro region, but the composition of that group was all Guro, or were there other ethnicities as well?

DB: Completely Guro. It could extend up to twenty-three people.

DR: Wow, it was big!

DB: It was a huge group! The commandant was the director, but there were other people also who were assistant directors, who directed the group. The directors came along—they were the guys wearing ties . . . who had good work, who had cars. The head customs officer, the police, the soldiers—all that. They were behind it and all of them were Guro.

DR: But you played at Ferkessedougou and those other places that were not in the Guro region. [Were your performances] for the Guro who had moved there?

DB: When we played at Ferkessedougou, for example, it wasn't for a funeral service but rather for a professional production. All those performances for Guro in Abidjan, those were for funerals. But in other locations, those were professional productions.

Young and Restless

Djo Bi continued with Kada Club, over time making more and more connections in the wider community of professional performers in Abidjan but feeling more and more limited by the musical scope and pay scale. Ever restless, he began actively looking for something better, more challenging. "I remained in that group, but I began to notice that I was getting older. So you always have to find something better." His idealization of the BNCI started to fade as he began to learn about other, better-paying work.

You know my friend who came [to my wedding] from England—Gao Bi? I knew that he worked with Wafou. It was a huge hotel in Abidjan, in Biatri, right on the beach, past Treichville next to the lagoon. It was full of tourists.... the artists who worked there got paid better than those who worked at the Ballet National.

Hotel Wafou, which is still in business at the time of this writing, is one of a handful of five-star hotels in Abidjan that cater to tourists, foreign travelers, and wealthy Ivorians. After independence in 1960, and even more so after the creation of the BNCI in 1974, these hotels—not just in Abidjan but in smaller cities such as Man and Korhogo as well—became venues for ballet-style performance. They frequently competed with the BNCI for the finest, most virtuosic traditional musicians and dancers, often luring them away with more lucrative contracts. As the Ivorian economy flourished through the 1970s and these hotels grew in number, venues began to multiply, spreading ballet and its discourse throughout the country. No wonder, then, that Djo Bi found himself attracted to Wafou, one of the most exclusive and highest-paying opportunities. But landing an audition took considerable persistence.

DB: I was still living with Commandant Tra during this time. I snuck away to the hotel. . . . I was still a little, young guy.

DR: Around how old?

DB: Something like eighteen. . . . I played with Kada Club for at least two years—maybe a little more. So I went to introduce myself . . . to the director whose name was Kourouma Moussa. [But] it was a problem for me to introduce myself to him because I was still young and already a great drummer. [At Wafou], when a tour would happen, they had to eliminate certain people. . . . That meant it was a group that knew each other and they didn't want to let someone else in. Because it's the drum that makes the dance . . . when you are young and you're a good drummer, then the director wants you so that he can show you to the whites. That gets him the contract. . . . Since I was young, I had to find someone who could introduce me to the director. I went over there all the time, again and again. This lasted a really long time.

DR: How long?

DB: A whole year!

Finally his strategy worked, and Djo Bi managed to arrange an introduction, but "[the Wafou director] said the group was going to travel, was going to . . . Europe. *That* was what interested me; *that* was what *really* interested me!"

The director wanted two groups. When one travels, the other could perform in the hotel. It was at that moment then he asked us to audition. So we arrived, and I auditioned and I got in! [But] there was already a problem for me at the audition because the drummer who was there, he had been to my church, and it was his uncle [who introduced me to the director].... Then someone—I don't know who—went and told Commandant Tra that his artists had left to go to Wafou. So he picked up the telephone and he called Kourouma ... and he said you better be careful or else I'll send the military there!

Not knowing his plan to join Wafou had been discovered, Djo Bi procured a copy of his birth certificate so that he could apply for a passport. Then one day, Commandant Tra confronted him. "I know you have joined Kourouma Moussa," Djo Bi recalled him saying. "He is a good friend of mine and I don't want there to be problems between us ... I am going to find someone else [to drum for me]; you can go ahead and move out of my house." Facing homelessness, Djo Bi promised to remain with Kada Club, but having gotten so close to performing in Europe, he became increasingly restless and more committed to realizing this dream.

Though he had decided to remain with Kada Club, Djo Bi was tired of the same old thing. Around this time, back in his old neighborhood of Banco, a new group was attracting his interest. Like Kada Club, Zomblé Gonè Club primarily performed for funerals and defined itself as a Guro ensemble, but it was different. "There are Guro, and there are Guro, and there are Guro," said Djo Bi, meaning that there are subgroups with different cultural practices. He explained:

DB: Kada Club comes from the Guros of Daloa, the Guros of Vavoua.... While those [like me] who come from Zenoula, Gohitafla, Bouafle—it's we who have Zauli. We dance more masks than they do. And now people from my region had formed their own group in the mold of Kada Club.... So one day I visited my uncle in Banco and this new group was playing.... By this time I had already been on television; people had seen me ... with Kada Club. I came, and I said to [Zomblé Gome Club's] drummer, "Let's go, I'll help you a little." When I sat down at the drum—ah—all of Banco came! So the group gave me a house. Right away! I began to leave Kada Club to return to my own tradition. And now I sought more dancers because some of the people in this group had come from the Ballet National. This group became the number one group in Abidjan. All the Kada Clubs are washed up now.

DR: What year was this?

DB: Nineteen eighty four, when the ... cup of Africa [soccer tournament] ... was played in Abidjan, that Cameroon won. With this new group, I traveled even more. It was about this time that my name became more ... [and] more [known].

Djo Bi continued to dream of bigger and better opportunities. One day he saw a television performance by Rose Marie Giraud and Les Guirivoires. Giraud, a dancer and choreographer, had founded Les Guirivoires and the dance school associated with it, the School of Dance and Cultural Exchange (EDEC) in 1973. By the mid-eighties, Les Guirivoires had toured throughout Europe, North America, and Africa, and EDEC, based in the upscale Abidjan neighborhood Deux Plateau, had become a major center of traditional Ivorian music and dance instruction. So well known was Giraud that in 1994, when I was first in Abidjan, my host, ethnomusicologist Paul Dagri, arranged a visit to EDEC. Giraud now lives in New York, where she directs an American version of Les Guirivoires.

After seeing Les Guirivoires, "the idea of Rose Marie entered into my head," Djo Bi recalled. "I said, okay, maybe I could go there." Arranging for an audition with Giraud took nearly a year, despite his growing reputation. Finally, in 1986, "[she] auditioned me, and . . . said, 'You, you're not a student. I must pay you CFA thirty thousand.' She's going to pay me thirty thousand a month?!? Wow! So I began to rehearse." At the time this was standard professional pay in Côte d'Ivoire. Not only did Djo Bi have his ticket to international touring and performance, he had, for the first time, a very good salary.

Perhaps most important, Les Guirivoires were modeled very much on the interethnic "ballet" model of performance. Djo Bi had been exposed to the collaborative interweaving of traditions found in ballet, first in church and then in informal music and dance sessions while living in Abidjan. However, his stage career had been focused on his own Guro traditions. Les Guirivoires offered the kind of rhythmic expansion, an opening up of new musical worlds and opportunities, that Djo Bi had long sought.

> We call it the ballet because when you arrive in Abidjan, to prepare yourself to travel to Europe or to go to the United States, to go all over, you have to know other people's rhythms. You have to know all the rhythms. . . . It's when we all come together, each one learns from the other.

Learning ballet, for Djo Bi, was akin to winning the lottery for a visa to go abroad. Legally, however, such opportunities remained out of reach for the young drummer, who, not yet eighteen, could not apply for his own passport. Djo Bi put his creative mind to this problem and had a new birth certificate made that showed him to be three years older. "I was *really* born December thirty-first, nineteen sixty-eight," he said with a smile. "So I changed that because in Africa it's possible to change anything [laughter]. . . . I'm really thirty-eight years old now!"

At this moment in our conversation, Djo Bi and I stopped talking and sized each other up in a way we had not thought to do in the year we had known one another. We both came to realize that he was my younger brother. Age in Ivorian relationships grants authority that must be respected; it can be abused and is often the subject of jokes, but it is a tangible element, especially in *familial* relationships. "Now I have to give you respect," he said. "Yes," I retorted, "now you have to *start!*" He laughed his loud, chesty laugh. We proceeded with the interview, although several important things had just happened. I had learned his real age and an important part of his story. More significant, however, he had called me his older brother, affirming both a familial intimacy and his junior status and thus my authority over him. From that point in November 2008 on, our interactions were spiced with me teasingly reminding him that I was his elder, and on occasion I had to adopt that role in a more formal manner, for a serious purpose.

In February 1986, Djo Bi was on his first international flight, heading to France with Les Guirivoires to perform at an African music festival and at other venues around the country. Happily, his old Guro acquaintance Gao Bi from Wafou was also a member of the troupe. The two animated, outgoing Guros spent their time off socializing and partying with French artists: "That was when we got to know each other really well. He was like a parent for me." They also had plenty of opportunities to build their musical and personal rapport, rehearsing and performing regularly in Côte d'Ivoire and occasionally in France. In 1990 Les Guirivoires performed in the United States, and Djo Bi got his first taste of the country he would later call home. This tour introduced him to fifteen states, from New York to California, and even included a visit to the White House, then occupied by George H. W. Bush.

Although Djo Bi was gaining much from his run in Giraud's ensemble in terms of performing experience and travel, he was becoming increasingly disillusioned about his income. The early days of 30,000 CFA per month had become a memory, and after the US tour, Djo Bi returned to Abidjan with just 5,000 CFA in his pocket. By this time, his experience and reputation had made him attractive to directors of many of the growing number of traditional percussion and dance ensembles in the city, so he left Rose Marie Giraud in search of better pay.

Djo Bi found a better paycheck at the Hotel Wafou of all places, where the house ensemble was now under the direction of Seguenon Kone. A veteran of the BNCI, Kone was a virtuoso on the Senufo xylophone (*jegele*) and a highly skilled drummer, dancer, and choreographer. Directing an ensemble known as L'Ivoire Spectacle, he had revived the performing tradition of Wafou, whose reputation had faded somewhat since the days of Kourouma. An active member of the community of Ivorian performers in the United States, Kone today lives in New Orleans, where he directs a stateside version of L'Ivoire Spectacle.

Despite his increased pay at Wafou, Djo Bi continued looking for work to supplement his income.

> I lived in Bobo, which is a little better than Banco but still poor. . . . I arrived there, and I was already a great drummer. And there were Guro all over, in little villages and everywhere. Wherever I went, they had [performance opportunities] for me. And I started making more money just freelancing at these Guro events, at villages, and in Abidjan, than I was making at Wafou.

Despite Seguenon's efforts to keep him, Djo Bi left the hotel to free up his schedule for Guro community events. However, along with his growing reputation came increasing financial demands. "During that time . . . family members from my village would often come see me. They have to eat, you have to pay for their transportation—all that." Struggling to keep up with his financial obligations, Djo Bi returned to the more affordable Banco neighborhood and rejoined Zamblé Gonè Club.

Facing financial hardship, Djo Bi continued playing drums and dreaming of a better future. Then, as the cliché says, fortune came knocking at the door:

DB: One day, back in Banco . . . I was sleeping. You know *koutoukou* [a very potent homemade gin]?

DR: Oh, yes.

DB: We bought some *koutoukou* on credit. We didn't have money. And now we were sleeping. It was hot. And then somebody [knocked] It was a guy who I met in Nantes, France! . . . He was Ivorian, he was an Abbé [Ivorian ethnic group]. His mother was a priestess. His name was Robi Tchimou. . . . So he came and he said, "I've come to look for you. Are you ready to go to France?" I said "What?!? What did you say?" He said that he had gone to look for me at Rose Marie Giraud's before, but they didn't tell him where I was!

Robi wanted Djo Bi to join an arts outreach group he had formed to improve the lives of at-risk native and immigrant youth in France.

> He had recruited about twelve or thirteen people, and he was now based about forty-five kilometers from Paris, in a suburb where there were many immigrants. . . . In France it's not the same thing as here. When you create a little association, the state gives you money, the mayor gives you money, and you have one day a week when you work with children . . . to keep them from becoming criminals. And they come to this for no fee. . . . It was the mayor who paid the association. They have their system there—it's not the same thing here. So the guy came and found me and I said yes. . . . He did all the visas and everything. And I arrived in France.

Immigrant Life, Chapter 1: France

Returning to France not on tour but as a resident artist, Djo Bi began life as a transnational immigrant in 1991. In Mantes-la-Jolie—a Paris suburb with a large immigrant population—he began rehearsing with the musicians Robi had recruited for his group/outreach association. "When I arrived we began to rehearse. There were many people. There were some musicians who knew how to read music who came from Cameroon, [some from] the Comoros islands. . . . There were lots of us." Comprising Africans from various countries, the ensemble operated like a national ballet in that the members taught each other music and dance originating from their respective countries. They played some non-African instruments as well. According to Djo Bi, "Some played the piano ... some played percussion using *atumblan* [Akan talking drums]. ... If we played for people, I was on the *topalon* [a Guro drum]." He spent several years with this group, most of whose members were initially Robi Kimoun's friends from Nantes.

> The guy who formed the group, Robi Kimoun, they were his friends. We had all met before in Nantes, but then everyone had moved around. Some had gone to Paris, some [elsewhere], but he gathered them all there in Nantes. ... Since Robi had moved next to Paris, he decided to create his group there and call his friends.

Over time, though, Djo Bi increasingly took on a leadership role—including writing new repertoire—despite the fact that, unlike many of the others in the group, he did not know how to read music. Gradually tensions began to build.

DB: Some of the guys said, "Hey, do you know how to read music?" And I said "No, it's all here [points to his head]." ... and ... the people began to like my compositions. These compositions were coming quickly to me. ... They [came from] an African [source], like [what I wrote for] Mecca Bodega [a New York–based group in which Djo Bi played in the 2000s], in that style. It was all his friends, and they all had their own CDs before, and they all were also singers. But they were not able to reach the performing level that I asked of them, and so some of them quit the group. But that was when I first started the group Asafo.

Though still funded by the French government, the group took the name Asafo, one that Djo Bi has used throughout his career, and by 1995 it was traveling more widely, all over France, Cologne, Mannheim, and Berlin in Germany, and even Turkey. "We went to Turkey for a big festival. Istanbul. Wow, oh, I loved that. ... I even met a woman on the airplane who took me to her mother's big restaurant—Oh! I'm telling you!" Djo Bi told me that he had loved the food, the culture, and clearly the attention he received from the Turkish people, whom he found less accustomed to dark-skinned people than were the French. Djo Bi saw the Turks' reactions to him and the group as entertaining. "When we were at a bar, everyone in the bar came to look at us. They thought we were black Americans [laughs]."

Belgium

In the endless touring, tensions continued to grow. Also growing, however, was Djo Bi's reputation. In 1996, having lived in Montes-la-Jolie for three and a half years, he decided it was time to move on from Kimoun and the suburbs and take advantage of better-paying, higher-status jobs in Paris.

> There are times when you have to advance to the next level. In France, there is just one big city—it's Paris, that's it. Here you have a lot of them. But when you are fifty-five kilometers from Paris, that's far away. Paris is where everything was happening.... When I saw that this association wasn't working anymore, I met someone who had a school—an Ivorian [Wobe] whose name was Georges Momboye. This guy had a big school in Paris at that time. I had known him in Côte d'Ivoire.... At this time, when I left, I was the best of *all* the drummers! So people really started coming around.... I went with Georges Momboye and I left those who had gotten me to France.

With Momboye, Djo Bi reached a new level of professionalism in the staging of Ivorian ballet. Momboye's tours covered Switzerland, Morocco, Turkey, and England, often in large venues. Enjoying a position as a lead drummer, he continued to develop his professionalism and his reputation continued to spread.

It was the mid-1990s, the time of what might be called "the *jembe* explosion." Having grown in popularity from the time of the first Ballets Africains tours in the 1950s, by the early 1990s the *jembe* had become an icon of Pan-African discourse (Polak 2006; Charry 1996, 2000; Flaig 2010) and was becoming increasingly popular across North America, Europe, East Asia, Latin America, and even Africa. Growing apace was the drum circle culture. In 1996 Mamady Keita was arguably the most famous *jembe* drummer ever. He was a Guinean Maninka who had been the lead drummer and director of another of Guinean President Sekou Touré's national ensembles, the Djoliba National Ballet. In Belgium he had established a school, Tamtam Mandingue (Mande Drum). Keita had caught wind of Djo Bi's extraordinary talent and invited him to Brussels to teach a workshop on Ivorian rhythms. Djo Bi subsequently recorded rhythms from the Ivorian ballet repertoire (the Dan Yakuba rhythm *tématé* and the ever popular Guro *zauli*).

That a drummer of the international renown and stature of Mamady Keita had called on Djo Bi was a strong testament to Djo Bi's own ascendancy in the transnational networks of African drumming and dance, and exemplifies the transnational circulations of ballet. The early model of LBA influenced the formation, form, and approach of the Ivorian ballet; Ivorian ballet discourse disseminated via Ivorian media and ballet culture had spread beyond the national stage and into private institutions such as hotels and dance studios, where artists such as Djo Bi absorbed it; back in Guinea LBA influenced the formation of new national ensembles that toured the Global North; Mamady Keita, after the death of Guinean president Sekou Touré and the loss of government support for state ensembles, left Guinea, eventually landing in Belgium; Djo Bi, trained in ballet with Guiraud, Wafou, and others, migrated to France, where he toured with transnational African ensembles and encountered Keita; Keita asked Djo Bi to teach him rhythms from the Ivorian ballet repertoire on *jembe*—rhythms that were only starting to be played on *jembe* on ballet stages influenced by Guinean precedent. The beat goes on.

Belgium/Museum Work

While in Belgium in 1996, Djo Bi had an experience that would in some ways reshape his future professional development. Through African music and culture networks in which Keita was involved, Djo Bi met Anne-Marie Bouttiaux, a Belgian anthropologist and specialist in African masks who was a curator at the Tervuren Royal Museum for Central Africa. Shortly after this meeting, Djo Bi found himself a member of a research project on Guro masks.

DB: We made three research trips together to Côte d'Ivoire. Buying masks, everything. It was about this time I learned how to explain things very well. This taught me that I could get to know my own culture even better because I would ask questions, and they would talk more and more. . . . During the first research trip, we collected around twenty-one masks in one month. During the second trip, we collected even more. We went to four or five villages a day. Everyone brought out their masks and danced them, and afterwards we [bought] them. . . . [We also shot] video, and I [played drums].

DR: What region was this?

DB: The Guro region, in Zenoula. Zenoula, Gohitafla—all that is the same. . . . It was during that time that I developed how to explain masks and I myself did a lot of research.

Djo Bi talked in some detail about returning from Europe to his home country and especially the region of his birth. The three research trips lasted only about a month each, but they were packed with activity. Djo Bi proudly claimed that, despite Bouttiaux's reputation as an internationally known scholar who has published on the subject of Guro masks, this project's success was due to *his* influence and connections in the Guro region.

DB: We went only to villages, and the museum provided the budget. So we had chauffeurs, we had a car, we went everywhere [laughs].

DR: And the masks that they bought, are they now on the wall of the museum?

DB: Yes, and she has also had traveling exhibitions.

DR: How did people receive you when you were a part of that research group in Guro country?

DB: Number one, she was really lucky that I was already so well known as a great drummer. In my ethnic group, everybody already knew me. . . . From my position in the church, I visited many villages. It's not everybody who travels like me. In my ethnic group, people don't travel a lot. But since I was at the church and I played well, I had lots of friends. I spent time in *so* many of the villages. . . . Before I went to France, I was already known all over the Guro region. And furthermore I had spent all that time in Abidjan being on the television, making friends. I knew all sorts of people. . . . When I returned with the Belgian woman, everyone knew it was not because of her but it was because of me. . . . It was *I* who was in charge of things. Voilà. . . . First of all, she was a woman, so it would [have been] hard for people to explain [mask information to her] . . . So they welcomed us because of me. And when I was in the village, I wore village clothes, and people said, "So that's the guy who is in France?" And why did we get lots of masks? The people didn't really care that we came to buy masks. They came to see *me play* with their masks. *That* was their object. And when the masks came out they didn't even watch them—it was *me* they came to watch [laughter]. And so after [each performance], I would go sit down with the chief, and I would say, "That mask there—we want to buy it—the complete costume. And we will buy you another one."

Djo Bi's eyes shone. It clearly meant a great deal to him to tell this story in such a way as to highlight his importance and fame as a central element of the narrative. Not a renowned scholar from Belgium, not thrilling mask performances, not even the *selling* of masks could avert the eyes of the adoring crowd from Djo Bi and his drum.

Given the long, contentious history of the procurement of sacred objects for display by wealthy collectors or museums, I was surprised not only that Djo Bi had involved himself in this process but that he seemed proud of having done so. He clarified this for me:

DB: The true mask—we don't sell that. But all of that [costume]—that is the wood [gestures around his face] that you watch and someone dances in—we don't really care about that. To make a new one, well that's just the costume. Since it's just a costume, it's like what you're wearing—when it's worn out, you get a new one. . . . But that which is the real, *real* mask where we cut the throat [sacrifice an animal] over it . . . that we do not sell. You can't sell that. . . . If you saw it, you wouldn't even want it. . . . it's not pretty, it's not well made, it's different.

DR: It's the power?

DB: Yes, it's the power that is there.

Even though the researchers were interested only in the performed mask costumes and not the sacred masks imbued with spiritual power, they still had to convince Guro villagers to take part in the project. Djo Bi recalled that they had to establish themselves in each village: "It was around the drinks that everything was arranged. *Bangui* [palm wine] is [usually] necessary for sacrifices, but today because everything is changing, beer is used even for that purpose." The team also had to offer "sacrifices"—chickens, goats, or in the most serious cases cows—to be ritually killed and eaten as part of the event. Finally, however, it was the purpose of the project that was the most important factor in persuading villagers to participate. Djo Bi had to reassure his Guro brothers and sisters that the goal "was not to make money, but it was to preserve the traditions forever."

I recalled when I had first introduced my research to him three years earlier. Then he had demonstrated a keen familiarity and experience with what he understood to be the value of research. Never once did he express concern that I was taking advantage of him, but trusted that our work together was in his long-term benefit, that it would preserve his name in posterity. The same ego that was stroked by his reception on returning to Guro country from Europe animated his wish to be remembered and known into the future as an important artist. This greatly facilitated my work with him.

England

After Djo Bi finished his work with the museum, he returned to France and resumed performing with Momboye, but work was starting to dry up. A managerial shake-up had resulted in the hiring of a new person to manage the company, which led to a successful tour of England during which Djo Bi met a famous Nigerian choreographer named Peter Badejo and the two hit it off. Concerned that Momboye's resurgence might not last and excited by another new opportunity, Djo Bi joined Badejo's ensemble, Badejo Arts, for an English tour. By this time the *jembe*'s acceptability in formal, staged representations of African music and dance was well established. A quick learner, Djo Bi and his *jembe* fit right in with a Yoruba-based ensemble led by a Nigerian director performing on English concert stages.

Djo Bi recalled that his work with Badejo was well publicized and lucrative. "It was in the papers, and it paid well, so the people I had played for in France, we began to discuss the fact that I would no longer play for them." Ultimately, however, Djo Bi's venture to England brought on problems with his legal status. The visa that he had procured for his work in France was short-term and, in fact, suspect.

> Every three months, I had to renew my papers. When Jacques Chirac was elected, that changed a bit. All those who had [short-term visas]—you began to have problems if you left [France, and] you [came] back from your home country. If you tour around Europe, no problem. But if you come from Africa, that's going to create problems for you. So two times, they deported me [to Côte d'Ivoire].... I arrived and they said "That's not you in the photograph on your passport" [smiles mischievously] even though I had been in France for

years.... People do that [use fake photos] there. But they caught lots of people. So if you're [on tour] in a group, they will get you. If you're not French, and if you don't have a ten-year visa, they will take you. I had problems like that. So I am not at all afraid of those little things because we [immigrants] know all about that. I am not afraid of that [laughs]! We young [immigrants] are the soldiers [more laughter]!

Djo Bi was deported, but although he could get another visa to return to France, this no longer interested him. London was the place he now wanted to live. He had established an exciting and fulfilling new life there, one of greatly increased financial opportunity and, most important, had met the woman with whom he was in love, Jennah Rose. An Australian also temporarily in London, Jennah was now alone and unable to get Djo Bi back into the country, so the two devised a secret plan to procure a visa, and that's where the real trouble began.

Djo Bi convinced Peter Badejo that he wanted to join his group permanently. Attracted by the opportunity to continue working with a drummer of Djo Bi's caliber, Badejo agreed to help Djo Bi get a visa to go to England directly without passing through France. All seemed in order until Djo Bi's cover was blown, remarkably, by his old friend Gao Bi.

> Then my friend, Gao Bi . . . because I know how to play well and I had lots of contracts, he wanted to take my place. So he went to Badejo . . . and he said, "If [Djo Bi] comes here, it's not to stay, it's to go on to Australia." So they did not give me [a visa]; they did not do my thing.

Gao Bi's betrayal devastated his old friend.

> We had known each other since Côte d'Ivoire! It was *he* who introduced me to many of the people in the ballet community. When I talked about Wafou and all that, *his* name was in all of that. When the ballet was in France, he hid; he stayed there and didn't go back home with the ballet. Who did he come see then? It was *me*. . . . He stayed with me then [before he went to England]. During that time, things were not so carefully controlled [at border crossings]. When I was in England I stayed with him. They even offered me a hotel, but I said, "No, I'll stay with my brother." I stayed with him—we sang, we danced, we drank, we cooked, we ate, we did things. I made a lot of money. He didn't have papers but I did, so I went to the village and came back [to London] again and again. But I didn't know he had become jealous. . . . When I had problems and I wanted to stay in England, he went to Peter Badejo and said, "No, Djo Bi is not coming to work with you. He's coming to get papers and to leave." You see, he abandoned me. . . . So I stayed in Abidjan. I said no to France. I stayed—what can you do? . . . I would have gone to England and then gone on to Australia. That was my plan . . . but . . . he turned me in. That's why I went nearly nine years without speaking to him. To [be invited to] my [wedding] festival, it was *he* who begged forgiveness from me. . . . I'm not someone who will do bad things to people, so I said, "You should come"

At Djo Bi and Harmony's 2008 wedding, I met Gao Bi for the first time, completely ignorant of this story and oblivious to any tension. The two sang, danced, drummed, drank, and seemed to be in utter ecstasy in each other's company. Throughout the weekend, day and night, Gao Bi playfully blew a whistle hanging around his neck. The two old friends were burying the hatchet in grand form. Little did I know that Gao Bi was closing a difficult chapter in Djo Bi's life, one that began with his old friend preventing his return to England and thus his immigration to Australia with his lover, which led to years of struggle chasing work as an illegal alien in the United States. What I observed at the wedding was Gao Bi witnessing and celebrating the happy ending to a saga whose wheels his betrayal had put in motion.

Djo Bi in New York

Djo Bi had no intention of remaining in Abidjan. One morning in 1997, he ran across some old friends from the ballet community—Seguenon, Bi Bo Ti, Gao Bi, Sogbety Diomande, and others—who were preparing to go to the United States. Bley Zaguehi, an Ivorian in New York and director of the Mask Dance Company there, had invited them to come on temporary visas ostensibly to perform with him. Djo Bi managed to get himself added to the list of invitees. For several of his companions, this was the first attempt to leave Côte d'Ivoire, and their passports were suspiciously brand new, lacking any proof of their viability as performers. Djo Bi, however, "had two passports attached to each other because I had so many visas." His presence, he insisted, helped the others get their visas. "They said, 'Oh, you are in this group, no problem.' This is what brought me to New York."

In New York, Djo Bi and his friends learned that in fact there was no work. Recalling this experience, Djo Bi turned dour. With lingering anger in his voice, he explained:

DB: Bley Zaguehi said to us, "Sort it out! You have to take care of yourself. You have to find something on your own." And I said, "What? There was the language—it was not even French, and we were used to the French language, and you arrive, and everyone [at Bley Zaguehi's apartment]—Tra Bi, me, Bi Bo Ti—we were spread all over the floor. Every one of us now had to search for himself [for work and to survive]. Without any money. You don't know what to do. So that's what brought me to America. When I arrived in America—because I had already done France for many years—when I saw that I was going to have to start again from zero, I thought . . . [it would be] too hard for me. It was not like that for guys like Tra Bi and Sogbety because for them this was the first time they had ever been in a white country. For them it was new; for me it was not the same thing. I had already gone past that; I could not start again from zero! That's why I did not feel good.

DR: There were how many of you?

DB: Oh, we were more than fifteen. And they even brought over more after that. There are things I won't say in front of the camera. And now we were all there and it was necessary for everybody to hustle. No papers. No food. And with all that, our families back home, for them—as soon as you have boarded an airplane and you arrive here you are a millionaire! So it was difficult, difficult, difficult.

After sleeping on Bley Zaguehi's floor for about two months, Djo Bi and Tra Bi found their first job, drumming for a dance class taught by Ivorian ballet veteran Mamadou Dahoue. They found a cheap room to share in Brooklyn, but Tra Bi quickly found a woman who would marry him and went to live with her, leaving Djo Bi alone. "Now I had to search," Djo Bi said, alluding to the Ivorian immigrant's taken-for-granted strategy of finding an American to marry to establish residency, a strategy so normalized it needed no framing or explanation. Djo Bi befriended a woman and moved in with her briefly, but the arrangement did not work out.

About this time, Djo Bi's Australian girlfriend from London came searching for him, still wanting to marry him. He agreed, although marrying an Australian did nothing to help his status in the United States. Once wed, Jennah made several trips between London and New York before both agreed that the marriage was not practical. "I said to myself, listen—[I'm] already in the United States. Why couldn't I get my papers here? So I refused to go with her to Australia. But because she loved me so much—she is straightforward—she gave me a divorce. She came here to sign the papers right in front of me." Jennah and Djo Bi remain close to this day. "She calls us frequently here," he said.

The struggle to find food and a place to sleep continued, with Djo Bi working for Dahoue and anyone else who could pay him a few dollars to accompany dance classes. Then he met Lisa Vives, a divorced Jewish journalist who worked in New York but lived in New Jersey. With Lisa, Djo Bi established a modicum of stability, in terms of both relationship and residency, but things were precarious. For eight years, from late 1997 until almost 2006, their on-again/off-again relationship endured, but ultimately it did not last.

Work was inconsistent during those eight years. Djo Bi did get occasional gigs from Bley Zaguehi, but they were not enough to sustain him:

> I remained with the Mask Dance Company for about two years. They were not very active. They are not people who look for work. . . . He brought us here and then everybody had to hustle to find their own work. . . . After a while we started to have a class here or there, we started meeting people, we began doing shows with places like Djoniba[3] [and] with other people. Private individuals would take you, [and] you might make twenty dollars, enough to eat

or buy cigarettes [or] to buy a five-dollar phone card to call your family. When we first got here, even going out in the morning to look for breakfast, you see the color of the food but you have no idea what it is. You arrive and you ask and [they say] only "Yes, yes." They just give you what [they think] you want. If there is a little meat inside it, it would be okay. We mostly ate Chinese food. Voilà. Chicken fried rice. It's made quickly and we know what it is. You have chicken, you have rice . . . you buy a beer, you come, you have your pack of cigarettes, you're in front of the television, and the day passes. And you wait.

Djo Bi's struggles to find work were compounded by his inability to speak English.

DR: Was it upon arriving here in the United States that you began to learn English?

DB: Exactly. Because [when I was] in England, I [still] *lived* in France. If you're living in France and you go to England, it's different. What [little English] you learned in school, it's different [i.e., British English].

Moreover, many English speak at least some French, which he did not find to be the case in New York. Fortunately, through the immigrant grapevine he learned of English classes:

DB: Upon arriving here, [it became] obligatory to speak English. So everybody knows there are these little schools, and we went to [them]. Even in New York, there are free schools.

DR: For learning English?

DB: Voilà. You can pay a little bit, but you have to go. To go learn how to read a little.

Language struggles. Lack of work. Pressures from home. Europe began feeling like a dream that had transformed into an American nightmare. Djo Bi felt his spirit descend into a darker space than he had ever known:

DB: At that moment, I was really, really, really down. I had smoked. . . . If you want, I can tell you everything. Do you want me to tell you everything?

DR: Tell me what you want me to know.

At this point in our conversation, Djo Bi went back through a few of the topics we had discussed earlier, adding details and a different, darker perspective on his early days in the United States.

I smoked crack during that period. I'm telling you. Yes, I was really down. When you saw me—ah! I had become really skinny. After Paris, after France, when I first arrived, I had no papers, the woman [Jennah] that I married kicked me out. When we divorced, I ended up with a Jewish woman named Lisa.... We loved each other, but I was into some bad things, and so was she, so she couldn't help me. And I wanted to be good. It was really hard for me. Everyone refused me. They gave me no work. But I had always had my power to arrange for work. To earn my own money. When people saw me, they hid. When they saw me pass by, they turned away.

Djo Bi needed help, and he found it in his friendship with a Japanese immigrant musician whom he had met in a subway station. As in many big cities, the subway is a popular place for buskers, including immigrant musicians for whom it may be the best gig they can find.

DB: At that time, I was very, very, very, very down. I played in dance class. After, they gave you five dollars. That wasn't enough even to get home. So I began playing in the subway, where I could earn two hundred dollars or I could make a hundred and eighty. So I no longer went to dance classes. That's when I met Japan. His real name was Yuichi Iida, but I called him Japan [laughter]. He had been to Senegal before. When he met me he said, "I have met many drummers, but you—your spirit is different. You are my friend." So this little guy started taking care of me. He was a student in recording arts. I went [to a studio] with [him and] his Korean friend Joe Jang. Then we started living together. Anytime I needed something, he came to my aid. Every time. That's why he came all the way to Indiana for my wedding. I paid for his car. It was I who paid for the transportation for everybody, for all those people. We put three thousand dollars on a credit card for all that. That was no problem, though, because when you're going to do something, you have to do it.

DR: So you really suffered in New York?

DB: And how. How I suffered. And I slept, I slept, I slept, and I walked around all night until it was daylight. Three days in a row, I would not even bathe.

Innovation, Diversification as Strategy

From an early age, central to Djo Bi's identity was that he was a star, so his self-esteem plummeted when he failed to obtain regular work with his drum. But if it was not staged Ivorian ballet, the subway nevertheless served as a productive space for meeting wayward musical collaborators. Previous experience, especially in Europe, had extended his musical skills across various genres, so Djo Bi was able to develop his musical creativity and flexibility. As time wore on and he began reflecting on the relationship between his present opportunities and his past experiences, he realized that he had a quality that made him stand out from others in the community of Ivorian immigrant musicians.

DB: The thing that brought me a lot of money [was that] I know how to play a lot of [different] music.... It was a part of me that I could use in New York.... Vado, for example was already there, so all that [work] that Vado has, he's not going to give it to me! He's going to give it to Sogbety [Vado's nephew] first.... So what was good for me is that I knew how to play [other types of] music.... I could go places the others could not go.

DR: Can you give me an example?

DB: For example, I played with jazz guys. If you're not really a musician you don't even know the tempo. And I played with guys in schools who liked me a lot. They already had contracts; they taught in schools, and they paid me out of pocket so that I could live.... That's how it was until I met [the band] Mecca Bodega. I had already become something, kind of big. I traveled, and I stayed in California for many months.

DR: Oh yeah?

DB: Yes, in Oakland ... with the Congolese—I was invited by a guy named Malonga.... That's where I met Papa Titos [Papa Titos Sompa, a Congolese immigrant musician] and all those guys. And the Congolese [liked] me a lot because I play their music *really well*. And that's what is different between me and those other [Ivorian] people. The others know how to play well a little Guinean and our music. For me, it's Benin, it's Haiti, it's with groups [like] the Congolese and all those who come to me and say, "Djo Bi, you must play!" So it's my musicianship that has enabled me to survive until today. Yes, each time.

DR: That's interesting. You found it necessary to be diverse—

DB: Voilà—

DR: ... to diversify the types of music that you played.

DB: That's right. Even sometimes with Mecca Bodega, those rhythms, I showed them a lot. Even when I was not there I recommended others [Ivorians] to play their gigs.... The guys called them—I don't know if they were afraid or what—but they wouldn't go. If someone came to me and said, "Djo Bi, I play with this group here. Today I have other things to do—you go." Me, I would go, because I'm confident. I would go there, we rehearse—it's good. But while I will do that, they won't do it. So there is a difference there. You know, music, artists—we are all artists—but each of us has a limit, a limit that he cannot transcend. For some people, it's just dancing. They don't know music at all, like Mamadou Dahoue, for example. And some know how to play. Guys like Vado, for example—he dances, he sings, he drums, but it's all traditional. It's square. But to be a true musician, to be able to eat from [it], you must be really—truly, it's a gift. You cannot say that you learned it. No . . . it's a gift. You're born with it. And plus you have to interest yourself in it. When you interest yourself in something, you come to know it. There are not a thousand ways to know something. You have to always practice. When you practice, you are there. So I really liked that. The base of music—I really liked that already. Because when the time comes . . . all your muscles become old, [and] you can no longer play like you can play now. But with music, you could just play a shaker but it's okay. . . . When you compose . . . that's what made [me a] more complete [musician]. And my good fortune with Mecca Bodega . . . was because I knew lots of rhythms. And they are open people. When I come with a rhythm, they just put something inside it and then there it is. We had a new thing. And all of it was danceable.

DR: So you played many types of music in New York. Was it all performances or did you do recordings also?

DB: I did more recordings than shows. In New York, you know, I made a living from that. In the beginning, at first, I was [just] playing in big nightclubs. And you know, that would end at five in the morning. Or perhaps it was three-thirty. By the time you get back to the house, it's already around seven in the morning. Where are you going to work then? When you work like that, you sleep all day. And it's for what—a hundred dollars or something.

DR: That was what type of music, jazz or—

DB: Techno. In *huge* clubs! In huge clubs, where they have stages! When you play the drums someone over there understands [hears] nothing because there are just *so* many people! There are *huge* clubs. In New York it's like that with hip-hop and all that. . . . You are there playing drums. With a DJ.

DR: There is a DJ, and you on the drum—you alone or were there others?

DB: Me, by myself. People come and pay to dance in clubs. Well-dressed people. People who drink a lot. Tra Bi did this same work. [But] I . . . don't want that because you don't play *in* the music, in the [style] the music is—no, no, no. Because the music is already *loud*!

DR: It's prerecorded music?

DB: Yes, it's music that is already recorded and that the DJ plays. You play whatever you want!

DR: So you are the only *live* musician?

DB: Voilà! Later on, they started to ask for more [drummers], and so now there may be four or five people who play. You see? In New York now guys make

> some money from this because there are lots of clubs.... They may propose a hundred dollars to you because there is a manager there, and he's the one who hires you. Now there are others who drink a lot, and it's their women, the young girls, young people who go there. So some young white guy will come up to me and say, "Hey! I want you to play for my girlfriend!" You say, "Okay, give me three hundred dollars." You play and because they are drunk, they give it to you.... That's how you *really* make money, but your contract says a hundred dollars. After that, I found that that was really not *my* work.... I'm done with that.

In response to the challenge of competing in the immigrant context, Djo Bi realized he had more options than conventional ballet-informed representations of Africa. Willing to stretch his wings and his musical boundaries, he tried new things that both allowed his creativity to flourish and diversified his sources of income. He played many styles, from African ballet to jazz, from reggae to rave. He collaborated with many different musicians, from young white Americans to Africans from all over the continent to African descendants from other parts of the diaspora. Burning Spear, a famous reggae singer from Jamaica; Gigi, a huge, world-music star from Ethiopia; and Mecca Bodega, according to its press kit an "explosive, world-class percussion band" featuring hammered dulcimer, brass, bass guitar, and a variety of percussion instruments. These were just some of Djo Bi's sonic endeavors. Mecca Bodega was particularly fulfilling because it gave him the space to begin composing his own pieces based on Guro and other Ivorian ballet rhythms.

Moving to Indiana

By 2006 Djo Bi had been living in New York for nine years and had established himself on the African music festival and camp circuit. In May of that year, he traveled to New Mexico to teach some sessions at Camp Bantu, an African music gathering founded by artists from the Congo and Zimbabwe. Harmony Harris, a Montessori teacher in Steamboat Springs, Colorado, was among the attendees that year; she described her experience:

> Maybe two hundred or more campers, probably a good fifty Africans. Not all of them are teaching drum and dance. Some are storytellers, some are merchants.... I thought it was just divine. It was just amazing!... People from the Congo and Zimbabwe started it. Also people from Guinea and Ghana who live in Boulder were there, and that year there were also people from Ivory Coast. What struck me [was] the—I don't know how to say—the connectedness. Okay, so if I can use a drug metaphor, it's like when people are on acid... there's this connectedness with everybody who there. It was like that but without the drugs.... [There was] this synchronicity to everything. There were chickens there that year.... In the morning they're all clucking in time;

everything's on time. People are shuffling their feet on time. You hear people talking, and there's just this rhythm to everything. The second day or so, when I started paying attention to the teachers, they're just blowing my mind for the simple fact of how much more of their brains they're using than we are in general—"Oh, I speak six international languages and eight tribal languages." And you play a couple instruments, and you sing and you dance. . . .

Feeling connected and vibrant, Harmony began to notice Djo Bi. I include this next passage in part for how it represents Djo Bi's extraordinary charisma.

It was maybe the third day of camp. There were about fifteen of us from [Steamboat Springs] . . . I'd watch these drummers play their hearts out all day. *All* day!! We'd all get together at meal times . . . and all the drummers from our town . . . had these man crushes on Djo Bi. "Oh, my God! Dr. Djo Bi—I took his class! He's so awesome! I love him! Aahh, Dr. Djo Bi! You remember when he went like that? You remember when he did this?" I mean they were just gushing, literally, over him. . . . Then the next night—as if we didn't drum and dance enough—at night there would be dance parties at this large communal room that . . . was the largest classroom space. There were . . . six of us girls sort of in a circle dancing, and Djo Bi and somebody else walked in, and we can see the door and it's . . . elevated by one step, and it's like he was backlit. I saw him when he walked in and it's like he was backlit—that's all I can say . . . he just stood out to me like nobody's business. We were all dancing, and he just came and joined our group. . . . And eventually he and I are dancing. And he's just giving some fun moves, and I'm following, and . . . I just thought he was really neat. And I saw him the next day. We were chatting and his accent was so thick!

Later some of Harmony's friends from Steamboat asked her to invite Djo Bi and some other African musicians and dancers to their town to conduct a workshop and perform.

So now I have a reason to communicate with him for the rest of camp. . . . We made plans for them to come in August, so I started talking on the phone a fair amount with Dr. Djo Bi and I started developing a friendship with him. And then I picked them up at the airport, took them to a camp they were participating in Boulder, and I brought them to Steamboat.

Harmony could not remember all the places she drove the drummers to, just that she was driving a lot. Her voice began to trail off as she struggled to remember details of the story, and then she admitted: "I had hearts in my eyes—I don't know, I was just driving. . . . That was all in 2006 and we moved here in 2007."

Once they had fallen in love and decided to move in together, they discussed where to go given that Djo Bi lived in New York and Harmony in Colorado. Djo Bi was weary of New York, and Harmony was ready to leave Steamboat Springs.

> We wanted to move someplace where there was drumming and dancing.... Somewhere in all these conversations I happened to say something about [having] family in Indiana.... I have a big family and more than sixty percent of them live in Indiana. He, having come from one village... you know, a small kind of place—big family, huge connections with relatives, and whatnot. Having lived in Europe for ten years... having had some pretty dark times in New York City for ten years, feeling homesick—hears that and thinks that sounds nice. "Maybe we should move to Indiana," he said. It was totally his idea because when I left in ninety-seven, I had no intention of returning to Indiana. Because... growing up here, it was really homogenous for me. Yet he said something about Indiana, and I'm just thinking, Oh, sweet little naïve person, you've never been to Indiana have you? So now I'm thinking God—where in Indiana can we live?... So we moved to Indiana. [We] considered Fort Wayne because of an old friend who had been teaching African dance there; Guinean dancer Moustapha Bangora was in Chicago and he would sometimes pass through Fort Wayne on his way to New York. So we thought there might be a bit of a community, a niche, there.

Indianapolis was an option, as Harmony had gone to high school in the suburb of Noblesville. "But I hadn't lived there in ten years. So... Broad Ripple? That's artsy..." In the ten years since she had left, Indianapolis had become home to a rather large African immigrant population, including several active Ivorian performers. But "It [was] not on my radar.... And even when we were in New York some guy was telling us about the huge convention of Africans that happens in Indianapolis."

Then there was Bloomington.

> I kind of always knew from the beginning it would be Bloomington... I had never really spent time in Bloomington, but it seemed like a neat place.... and the campus was so pretty. After having been in Colorado, one memory of mine was that people are often outside in Bloomington.... So we... moved here in... August. I left Steamboat in about... June or July and picked him up; we went to Santa Fe, Colorado. He did some classes, we traveled. Had some getting-to-know-you time.
>
> Once here in Bloomington, we stayed with my cousin for [about] a month.... Found a place to live. By... October.... we started looking for a place to teach, started classes.

In Bloomington the couple began offering African drum and dance classes, the former led by Djo Bi; the latter, by Harmony. Typically the classes were offered on the same evening, Djo Bi's *jembe* class for the first ninety minutes and then Harmony's dance class. Between classes the advanced drumming students would take a brief break and return to accompany the dance class led by Djo Bi. The rhythms for both classes came exclusively from Ivorian ballet: *kuku*, *zauli*, *bolohi, abodan*. To earn a living in the Midwest, Djo Bi returned to the familiar repertoire that he had first seen long ago on television in the classroom, that he had mastered on Abidjan stages, and that he had played across Europe and in dance classes in New York. The rhythms, the songs, the breaks, the dance routines—these became Djo Bi and Harmony's lifeline as they built up a base of students in Bloomington.

As their classes grew, the couple frequently changed location. The more students they had, the more space they needed and the more sound they produced. So, either because of needed space or noise complaints, they moved from a small school gymnasium to a youth center to a bed and breakfast to a yoga studio. Djo Bi joked, "When you're drumming badly nobody bothers you. It's when you're playing really *well*–that's when the cops come!" In 2007 they finally settled in the Lodge, a multipurpose second-story room in a downtown building rented for events such as art exhibitions and wedding receptions. The Lodge was conveniently situated and the right size, and it allowed just enough sound to escape into downtown Bloomington to attract curious pedestrians.

According to Harmony, by 2011 "more than 200 [students had] come through our doors." Getting students to commit longer term was hard, though. "I wish more of them would stay," she sighed. "It takes a while to get a foothold in the community when you're doing something completely different and it's not commercial—it's not like Zumba." I asked Harmony what she thought attracted students to their classes.

> I think people come for a lot of reasons—the exercise or dance or music. But I think they all stay for the same thing and that's just the vibe that's going on in there. . . . I don't know if they feel the same way about it that I do—that mind-body-spirit connection thing in the reciprocity between drummer and dancer—but I think there's something about that that keeps people coming back. It's not like a tango or a salsa class. . . That's a whole different vibe, a whole different level of interest. There is something really alive about this class that I think keeps them coming back. But I don't know what [initially] draws them in. The drums are like a pied piper; sometimes people show up because they hear the drums.

I spent many months regularly attending these classes as a dance student, and on many occasions exactly what Harmony described happened. The booming *dundun* and the lightning-fast cracks of *jembe* slaps were audible in the busy courthouse square, which was filled with outdoor restaurants and many people passing by on bicycle and foot. Often a curious face or two would peek around the corner of the second-floor landing, and some observers would stay long enough to ask for information about joining. Djo Bi's *jembe* was indeed like the pied piper, calling people in.

The Innovator

Again, it was not the ballet repertoire played with the conventional *dundun/jembe* instrumentation that most excited Djo Bi. He was drawn more to opportunities to experiment. For years he has expressed an interest in recording an album with me and his Guro friends Tra Bi from New York and Gao Bi from London "because" he says, "there are too many *jembe* players. We need something different. I want to sing with the guitar and bass." To complement his regular classes and occasional "traditional"—that is, ballet-style—performances in local schools, libraries, and parks during his five years in Bloomington, Djo Bi has performed in local nightclubs and bars with various configurations of his band Asafo. I have been fortunate on occasion to join the band on fretless bass, playing parts based on melodies that Djo Bi set to one of the ostinato patterns of an Ivorian ballet rhythm (PURL 10.1). In terms of instrumentation, the constants in an Asafo show are *jembes, dunduns,* and Djo Bi on vocals. Additional instrumentation varies from drum kit and congas to electric guitar, horns, backing vocals, and dancers. Along with Djo Bi's compositions, the band includes other material, such as jam band–style songs penned by one or another of the guitarists or songs by guest singer-songwriters in Grateful Dead style.

What Asafo shows is a side of Djo Bi as restless as it is innovative. No matter how good he is, Djo Bi is not content to be just another *jembe* drummer. In fact, he complains about drummers who overly focus on speed and technique. In a nationalistic move, he takes a swipe at Guineans, who he argues lack musical sensibilities:

> When you see someone who can play [*jembe*] like a machine gun—when [people] hear that, they want it. Machine gun [imitates its sound over and over]. It's not that [that I admire]. It's melody. It's not that. The *jembe* speaks! The lion, he roars! A *little*, that's all. Not every time! But now everyone wants [the machine gun]. That's all! When they do that, where do you go?

Spontaneously, Djo Bi launches into a vocal *jembe* imitation, singing mnemonic syllables. He sings a beautiful melody based on a characteristically complex rhythmic sequence (see figure 10.2).

Djo Bi's solo ends with another "machine gun roll" so as to contrast it with his beautiful drumming style, causing us both to laugh. "We're not at war!" he shouts. "You see? That's the problem. But it's going to change." You think?" I ask. "Why?" "Because people are tired of it. . . . I'm not going to say I'm the only one who will change it, but I am the only one composing who will change it."

Asafo: Djo Bi as Musical Chef

Djo Bi has continued developing his musical creativity and innovation in numerous incarnations of Asafo. In 2011 during a feedback interview, I asked him

"*Everyone Is a Cook, but He's a Chef!*" | 273

Figure 10.2 Djo Bi's mnemonic syllable pattern for a *jembe* solo.

about this aspect of his work. He described drawing on his ballet background and training as "taking" and his interpretations, his creative reformulations of his influences, as "giving." The taking makes his work "traditional"; composing is when he gives, which he argues makes him unique:

DR: What can you say in general about your approach when arranging and composing pieces for Asafo?

DB: It's very simple. There are many players, but few who can compose like I do. You know that my creations began when I was little. My father taught us, but I always had something more to bring to it. And now . . . I take African or Ivorian rhythms, which can come from any ethnic group. Now, I *take* . . . because I want to always remain traditional. So concerning my creation, when I *give* something to the bass guitar, for example, it's a *song* that I give. The bass then sings. When I give to the drum kit, the drum kit also sings. All that is based on the song. The song—that's to say that I divide the song.

In describing the melody the bass plays as a song, Djo Bi is perpetuating the West African tendency to conceptualize instruments as extensions of human beings and the sounds they make as their voices (Stone 2005). In Jula, one of the Mande languages spoken widely in Côte d'Ivoire, to "play" an instrument translates literally as making it speak (e.g., to play a xylophone is *ka bala fò*, or to speak *bala*). Djo Bi provides an example: his composition based on *abodan*, a dance from the Agni, an Akan subgroup from southeastern Côte d'Ivoire. This is familiar to me, as I performed its bass line at several Asafo shows. Djo Bi sings me the "song" he "gives" to the bass for *abodan* (see figure 10.3).

Djo Bi compositions are what he believes makes him stand out from more conventional ballet-style performers of Ivorian music and dance. "When I compose for Asafo, it's a little open," he says. "You know you will see many African groups who play [that] are different from Asafo. You yourself know, you have seen them. They have their *dundun* with their *jembe*. . . . I also do that." But of his work with Asafo, he says:

> That's creation. It's the imagination . . . with the bass, with the rhythm direct. [With a straight duple rhythm], I can take a song from the Congo, and I can bring it along there. That's what makes it so that all the drummers, whether it is Tra Bi [or] whoever it is . . . know when we play the ballet together, *everybody knows what it is* [my emphasis]. But when he comes and he plays with Asafo, he has to learn. Voilà, he has to learn. That's composition.

Djo Bi is affirming first the existence of ballet discourse—training and experience that allow immigrant performers to easily perform together—and second his innovation, the way his compositions build on and extend beyond ballet. As

Figure 10.3 Djo Bi's bass line for the rhythm *abodan*. The top line represents Djo Bi vocally marking out the underlying rhythm, and the second line represents the bass line; Djo Bi taught me this part using the mnemonic syllables indicated.

an example, he offers a rhythm from northern Côte d'Ivoire that he attributes to the Koyaka, though it is generally recognized as Senufo.

DB: When I take a rhythm from the North, it's already there. Now I go to Koyaka country . . . and I *complete* it a little. You see that it's *bolohi* that I am playing. . . . Everyone is a cook, but sometimes you say, "He's a chef!" That's how that happens. Voilà, my secret. And it's not written. I don't write it down. Tomorrow it's still there. Once I start, it comes directly and it's there forever. . . . It's like [a chef] preparing a sauce. . . . Which sauce are we going to cook today? Which meat are we going to use? It's sauce *gombo*, so we're going to put some eggplant in it. What meat are we going to put in it today? Maybe some agouti or maybe . . . grain sauce.

DR: I will need to write about this. There's "the tradition," there's "ballet," and then there's this, what you do–it's different!

DB: UH-HUH!

DR: It's a manifestation of all the same rhythms but in a totally different context.

DB: Voilà!

DR: You told me before that the kind of work you do with Asafo is your preferred style.

DB: It's my preferred style. Yes, that's true. Because it's a communication in an ethnic language. When you say "rhythm," it's like an ethnic language that speaks. When you say, "Guro," I speak Guro. When you say, "Yakuba," the Yakuba speak Yakuba. When you play *abodan*, it's like an ethnic language. When you play *kuku*, it's like you are speaking an ethnic language. When you play Guro, it's like you are speaking an ethnic language. It's like different languages, but we're the same thing. Our comportment is the same, but it's the language that changes. . . . When you have a piece of music, you can put it all in there together. We all speak French, but if I were here with Aristide, for example—he is an Abbé. . . . When I am in Guro country, there are no people around whom we call Abbé. But when we are all together in Abidjan, well, we all go eat in the same restaurant! Everyone eats the same food! And when you see them play, underneath the different rhythms it's the same beat!

Here Djo Bi extends the metaphor of "voice" to envelop the whole notion of music as a form of communication, with each form its own language. Ballet, understood this way, is discourse writ (or should I say "sung") large, a kind of metalanguage—a complex sauce featuring many ingredients or languages (*bolohi*, *abodan*, etc.).

"You are a master of metaphor!" I shout. Djo Bi laughs. "For us it's like that, so that the person comprehends what I'm talking about."

PART III
FINALE

11 Thoughts on the Way Out

ETHNOGRAPHIC RESEARCH AND WRITING contribute to an understanding of human experience from particular subjective viewpoints in particular contexts at particular moments in history. This book offers four individual viewpoints on the immigrant experience at a time of transition from the twentieth to the twenty-first century, a time of greatly accelerated mobility and intensified interconnectivity. It offers concrete portrayals of social interaction at the heart of the transnational movement of peoples, goods, and ideas that characterize this moment in the human story.

While the book is based on systematic research, its result is ultimately more art than science. These pages have explored the experience of being an immigrant—not just any immigrant but one who is responsible for, and whose livelihood at least partly depends on, symbolically representing whole communities based on discursive imaginaries—"African," "West African," "Ivorian"—that are contested on the basis of various historically informed discursive subjectivities. That my four consultants bear such a responsibility renders an intensive study of *their* subjectivities relevant to an understanding of larger communities, not in a microcosmic/macrocosmic way, not mathematically or algorithmically, but in a poetic way, as a poem through its particularity suggests something more generalizable. As poet Wayne Dodd once taught me, the more true to a particular experience a poem is, the more generalizable, or subjectively accessible, it is likely to be. My hope is that I have created accessible, humanized portrayals of performers acting as migrant laborers in transnational economic and discursive networks.

What do my consultants' stories, interrelated with their performances, tell us about the experience of immigration at this time in history? Certainly their participation in transnational economic interactions is mediated and made possible by ballet. Central to an understanding of both their stories and their shows, ballet is also a connective thread between the two. From the 1950s on, it has served as a mediator through which various actors—musicians and dancers, state politicians, concert producers, and reviewers—have created economic and discursive networks exploitable by skilled migrants. Critical preparation for lives and careers in the United States, experience in the Ivorian version of ballet—the professional staging of Ivorian music and dance traditions—bonds all performers this book has investigated. Like jazz musicians who master repertoire and aesthetic practices that enable even strangers to play together, Ivorian immigrants' experience in staged performance prepared them for North American stages and today enables them to meet American expectations for staged representations of "Africa."

However, this book has also shown that expectations can clash when discourses collide, revealing the layers of discursive transnational meaning that ballet elicits, from discourses shared across African national borders to those at turns connecting and colliding in North America. Performers make use of the term "ballet" in their discursive self-interpretations; this is epistemologically emic for Ivorians in America with whom I have studied, and it is deeply transnational. If the epistemologies of mobility—globalization, transnationalism, diaspora, flow—seem amorphous and abstract, "ballet" is concrete and specific, indexing practice and discourse that are transnational to the core. For Ivorian immigrant performers, then, transnational experience began not when they arrived in the United States but at home in Côte d'Ivoire in many dimensions of their lives, prominently including their experience learning ballet.

I have argued throughout that performance and individual life story are effective frames for understanding the mobile, transnational lives of my four consultants. Staged performance, being adaptable and mobile, as well as a site of heightened reflexivity full of polysemous potential, serves as a salient frame for the study of human actors in a highly mobile world. Vado, Samba, Sogbety, and Djo Bi are complex beings—contradictory, paradoxical individuals who are yet part of groups, nationalists who live transnational lives. Performance is a venue for the mediation, transcendence, and reification of difference. Take for example, the complex discourse that Vado performs in *Kekene*, simultaneously embodying his personal identity, his ethnicity, Ivorian nationalism, and international unity. In this space of heightened reflexivity, he performs a discourse through which he identifies as Ivorian and Mau, at the same time expressing a unity with others—ethnicities, nations, and races. Although he does not foreground his identity as a Muslim in his performances (or, for that matter, in his stories or, in my experience, his life), the fact that he is a Muslim who is so ardently propagating a discourse of universalism and unity should not be overlooked in our era of simplified discursive good/evil binaries that pit the West against Islam. In the fluid space of performance, such seemingly unresolvable differences are bridged.

Life story itself is a kind of performance, a genre that emerges not in daily life but in specially framed circumstances that are in some ways similar to the special framing of a staged performance. Ultimately created for the stage that this book represents, my consultants' life stories, like staged performances, are highly reflexive, fluid, transportable, and dynamic. Like works of fiction, they are specific, humanistic accounts of complex individuals making their way through particular contexts in complex worlds. As ethnographic stories, however, these accounts are made from actual experience; I have not taken a fiction writer's liberty to alter their plots according to my interests or to amplify their drama. I have merely done my best to write them well. As a form of ethnographic narrative, they are meant to expose readers to real-world issues through portrayals of recognizable human beings, with strengths and faults, with whom they can empathize.

Thus, this book is designed for readers to better understand a phenomenon—the dramatic increase in mobility in late twentieth/early twenty-first-century life—that is one of the most significant developments in this moment in history. Through their stories, we learn how and why four individuals became immigrant performers. We see them taking great risks to find better health care, to better support themselves and their families back home, to make a living from skills they have worked hard to craft, to teach the world about the things they deeply value.

Once in the United States, these men become members of a dispersed community for whom ballet serves as a primary form of affinity. Some strike out on their own, like pioneers of old heading west for lives less crowded with competitors or like immigrants in the industrial age seeking greater economic opportunity. Unlike early westward travelers, however, Ivorians like Sogbety and Djo Bi make homes in the American heartland but remain in constant communication with larger immigrant communities elsewhere in the United States and on other continents, including the homeland, through social media and mass communication interactions. What appear to be separate and stable islands in fact interconnect and are ever in motion. And through performances, the men find something of home as their dispersed community reconstitutes itself on, and because of, the ballet stage.

I have endeavored to humanize Vado, Samba, Sogbety, and Djo Bi, as well as the rest of the community of Ivorian immigrant performers, who too often are caught in homogenizing discourses based on simplistic binaries (see Mudimbe 1988). By choosing not to label them as members of a diaspora and instead looking for traces of diasporic sensibilities and discourses, I do not reduce them to categorical labels that discursively replicate and trap individuals in an unfamiliar epistemological house of mirrors. Thus, for example, I foreground Vado Diomande's own discourse about his life and work, which he calls both an expression of multicultural unity and traditional Ivorian dance, even as I find traces of what *I* interpret as diasporic sensibilities in the strong presence of African descendants from across the Atlantic diaspora both in his ballet performances and in his discussions of voudou in New York. Likewise, Samba defines his *Ayoka* show as an educational celebration of both "Ivory Coast" and "African culture," which he performs with Ivorians, Guineans, Liberians, and African Americans. I see this as evidencing a notably Pan-African and diasporic sensibility regarding the representation of Africa on stage. Similar arguments can be made about Sogbety's Lotus Festival performance, which interwove diasporic difference in the same ways that the national ballet originally interwove ethnic difference. In the North American context, then, ballet can be read as a manifestation of a diasporic sensibility.

An advantage of the "sensibilities" model is that it opens up analytical space for anyone, not just Ivorian immigrants, to employ discourse that exhibits diasporic sensibilities. If one side of the coin is that no one is essentialized and labeled, the other is that no one group "owns" any particular discourse. Diaspora, like cosmopolitanism, is an idea in our transnationally interconnected world that can be invoked by anyone for any strategic purpose, including to understand the world from particular subjective points of view. Seen from this perspective, Memphis in May had a laudable goal—to demonstrate African musical influences on American music.[1] This is reflective of a diasporic sensibility that has informed much scholarship on African music in the Americas. The script and overall production of the show, however—the way the performers told their story—was saturated with social evolutionary discourse. Mary Rau's decision to stage *Song of the South* with Ivorian Samba Diallo in the role of Uncle Remus reveals yet another diasporic sensibility—one in which peoples of African descent are sufficiently "one" in their shared African heritage to permit a late twentieth-century migrant laborer from West Africa to play a former slave born in the nineteenth-century American South. The dance magazine reviewer who critiqued Vado Diomande's color-blind performance of Ivorian traditional dance and multicultural unity exhibited yet another diasporic sensibility, this one based on an Afrocentric discourse. The performance stage is a prime arena for the simultaneous communication of often multiple discourses that do anything from mutual reinforcement to interweaving to frictive clashing.

This same argument applies to cosmopolitan sensibilities that, I assert, following Feld (2012) and others, are not the province of an elite class but are potentially available for people of many social positions and subjectivities in our fluid, interconnected world. Samba Diallo's Afrofit dance class; Sogbety Diomande's drumming and dancing with pop stars; Vado Diomande's stilt mask dances with a hip-hop-influenced New York City-tap dancer from French Guiana via Paris; and Djo Bi's club performances of his compositions mixing rock and ballet. All of these are examples of crafty and worldly individuals exhibiting cosmopolitan sensibilities as they transform experience into labor and form into commodity for a North American market hungry for diversity.

Djo Bi's wedding reveals both diasporic and cosmopolitan sensibilities by extending ballet discourse and practice not just to people of multiple ethnicities from multiple countries in Africa who live in multiple communities across the United States, Canada, and the United Kingdom, but also to immigrants from various parts of Asia. By interweaving standard Ivorian ballet form, including the iconic *jembe*, with other transnationally circulating items and their symbolic meanings (Kente cloth standing for "traditional Africa"; reggae reinforcing a discourse of feel-good multicultural unity), wedding participants infused the weekend with cosmopolitan sensibilities. Ballet itself is a form not just of nationalism but also of transnational interconnection and as such exhibits a cosmopolitan sensibility even as it reifies and transforms rural, ethnic practices. And ballet led all four—Vado, Samba, Sogbety, and Djo Bi—across the world via tours and eventual migrations across national borders. Ballet even led Djo Bi to live parts of his adult life on three continents.

Finally, all four are specialists who exhibit scholarly sensibilities in their work. As I do, Samba Diallo videotapes and studies dance styles and cultural meanings, from those of Ivorian immigrant *kuku* drummers to those of Senegalese immigrant *sabar* dancers. He publishes research in his quarterly educational newsletter and on his website.[2] Sogbety makes the lion's share of his income from educational residencies and programs and in 2013 won an Ohio Heritage Fellowship as an Ohio Arts Council Traditional Arts Master. Like Samba, he dreams of establishing his own school. Vado Diomande, via personal interactions, videotape, and dreams, researches musical and cultural traditions that inform his shows and school lecture/demonstrations. Dr. Djo Bi has participated in research projects since he was a late teen.

My consultants draw on ballet training to make a living in an international labor market and disseminate messages that are profoundly meaningful to them. On a personal level, however, they choose this work because it gives them life. "Born immersed" in the work that he loves, Vado uses dance to heal himself and his world. For Samba dance is a form of rejoicing "in his blood" that he uses to relieve stress and to create joy and reconnect with people for whom he longs and with places he can only remember. Sogbety performs because his mask spirit is "made by God" and comes from the heart. It connects him to his family and village and is his "key to life." Djo Bi sees drumming and dance as a celebration of joy and as a way to "remember who we are." These are the deepest sentiments that these four men express about their life's work, and it is these sentiments, and the beliefs that inform them, that most fundamentally motivated them to move across national and continental borders seeking work that both suffuses them with happiness and sustains them through hardship in their lives as immigrants in the United States.

Glossary

Abbé. Ethnic group of the Akan linguistic-cultural family in southeast Côte d'Ivoire.
Abidji/Adjoukrou. Ethnic group of the Akan linguistic-cultural family in southeast Côte d'Ivoire.
Abodan. Agni women's rejoicing dance.
Aboisso. Town in southeast Côte d'Ivoire.
Adjoss. Baule rejoicing dance.
Agboville. Town in southeast Côte d'Ivoire.
Agni. Ethnic group of the Akan linguistic-cultural family in southeast Côte d'Ivoire and southwest Ghana.
Akan. Linguistic-cultural family comprising dozens of ethnic groups in southeast Côte d'Ivoire and southwest Ghana.
Aluku. Guro rhythm/dance.
Appel. "Call" in French; a drummed signal that marks beginnings and endings of dances/rhythms and serves as a "break" to mark transition points in a dance/rhythm.
Arc musical. Musical bow played by various Ivorian ethnic groups.
Asafo. Band formed by Dr. Djo Bi Irie Simon, first in Europe and then in the United States.
Assinie. Resort town in southeast Côte d'Ivoire.
Attoungblan. Baule name for talking drums played by numerous Akan ethnic groups in Ghana and Côte d'Ivoire; Samba Diallo's dance troupe.
Ayoka. "Thank you" in Bete; annual show produced by Samba Diallo (*Ayoka*).
Azaguie. Town in southeast Côte d'Ivoire.
ɓaa. Generally, a drum played by the Mau and Dan people in Côte d'Ivoire.
ɓaaɗe. Multiheaded drum played by the Mau and Dan people in Côte d'Ivoire (sometimes referred to as *yado* in the United States).
ɓaa gen. "Foot of the drum" in Dan; rhythm/dance step.
ɓaanya. Mau drum played for a mask spirit (*nya*).
Badejo Arts. Group based in London led by Nigerian immigrant Peter Badejo.
Bala/balafon. Wooden xylophone played by the Mande people in West Africa.
Ballet de l'Armée. National performance ensemble formed by Guinean president Sekou Touré in the late 1950s.
Bamana. Ethnic group, primarily located in Mali, who speak Bamanankan (Bambara), the most common language in Mali.
Banco. Suburb of Abidjan.
Bangofla. Dr. Djo Bi's home village in Côte d'Ivoire.
Bangui. Palm wine.
Bata. Drum played by the Yoruba of Nigeria.
Baule. Major Akan-speaking ethnic group in Côte d'Ivoire.
Beoumi. Town in north central Côte d'Ivoire.
Berimbau. Brazilian musical bow.

Bete. Ethnic group of the Kwa linguistic-cultural family in west central Côte d'Ivoire.
Biatri. Upper-class suburb of Abidjan.
Bloc. Rhythmic flourish coordinated by the lead drummer and dancer marking the end of a break.
Bobo. Ethnic group in Burkina Faso.
Bolohi. Senufo panther mask/dance.
Bɔlɔnye. Senufo one-stringed harp.
Bondoukrou. Town and *départment* (akin to a US county) in northeast Côte d'Ivoire.
Bouaflé. City in central Côte d'Ivoire.
Bouaké. Côte d'Ivoire's second largest city.
Boundiali. Town in north central Côte d'Ivoire.
Break. Signal marking a transition in a dance/rhythm.
Bubu. Large, loose-fitting shirt.
Bugarabu. Cow skin drum originally from Senegal.
Burkinabé. Native of Burkina Faso.
Changement. "Change" in French; signal marking a transition in a dance/rhythm.
Cocody. Neighborhood (*quartier*) of Abidjan.
Coup. "Cut" in French; rhythmic flourish coordinated by the lead drummer and dancer marking the end of a break. Synonymous with **Bloc**.
Dabla. In Guro, poisonous thorn.
Daloa. City in west central Côte d'Ivoire.
Dan. Ethnic group in western Côte d'Ivoire (known as Yakuba) and eastern Liberia (known as Gio).
Danse. "Dance" in French.
Deux Plateau. Neighborhood (*quartier*) of Abidjan.
Dida. Ethnic group in south central Côte d'Ivoire.
Dogon. Ethnic group primarily in Mali.
Dundun. Largest of an ensemble of three drums (*sangba*, *kenkeni*, and *dundun*) commonly played with sticks by one drummer; the three-drum ensemble; Maninka dance/rhythm.
Dundunba. "Big dundun" in Maninka; dance/rhythm.
Ebrié. Ethnic group of the Akan linguistic-cultural family in southeast Côte d'Ivoire.
Échassier. "Stilt" in French.
Ecole de Danse et d'Echange Culturel (EDEC). School of Dance and Cultural Exchange, founded by Rose Marie Giraud in Abidjan.
Ensemble Djoliba. National performance ensemble formed by Guinean president Sekou Touré in the late 1950s.
Fan. In Dan and Mau, spiritual power or energy.
Ferkessedougou. Town in north central Côte d'Ivoire.
Festimask. Festival of Ivorian mask performance held to promote nationalism and tourism in Yamoussoukro, Côte d'Ivoire, in 1987.
File. In the Bamana language, wooden flute.
Flali. Guro rejoicing mask dance.
Gagnoa. City in west central Côte d'Ivoire.
Gbebge. Bete funeral dance.
Ge. Institution or school of *Ge*; individual spirits (*ge*), many of whom appear among humans as masked dancers.

geɓo. In Dan, spiritual realm parallel to and in fluid relationship with the corporeal realm.
ge gbleen. In Dan, stilt *ge*.
Getan. In Dan, *ge* music/dance.
Ginan. In Mau, spirit, probably etymologically related to the *djinn* in Islamic thought (in Dan, *yinan*).
Gla. Wè rejoicing mask.
Gohitafla. Town in the Guro region of west central Côte d'Ivoire.
Goli. Wan rejoicing mask.
Grand Bassam. City in southeast Côte d'Ivoire; from 1893 to 1896 the French colonial capital.
Gue Pelou. *Nya yan*, or Mau tall (stilt) mask spirit, from Toufinga, Côte d'Ivoire; sometimes referring to a spirit or god of the forest.
Guéré. Ethnic group of the Kru linguistic-cultural family in western Côte d'Ivoire. See also **Wè**.
Guirivoires. Dance and music ensemble formed by Rose Marie Giraud and modeled on the Ivorian national ballet.
Guro. Ethnic group of the southern Mande linguistic-cultural family in west central Côte d'Ivoire.
Institut des Arts et de l'Action Culturelle. Institute of the Arts and Cultural Action; part of the Ivorian national university system.
Issia. Town in west central Côte d'Ivoire.
Ivoire Spectacle. Ensemble directed by Seguenon Kone originally at the Hotel Wafou in Abidjan and now in New Orleans, Louisiana.
Jacquesville. Town in southeast Côte d'Ivoire.
Jegele. Senufo pentatonic wooden xylophone (often called a *balafon*).
Jeli. *Griot* in French; among the Mande of West Africa of the *nyamakala* caste system, an inherited role involving praise singing, oral history, instrument playing, and other social and ritual duties.
Jelibala. Wooden heptatonic xylophone played by Mande *jelis*.
Jembe. Goblet-shaped drum originally from the Maninka region near the Mali/Guinea border.
Jula. Ethnic group of the Mande linguistic-cultural family in northern Côte d'Ivoire; also a homogenizing label commonly used in Côte d'Ivoire for anyone from the north of the country and/or neighboring countries in the savanna or the Sahel region of West Africa.
Kada Club. Private ballet company, specializing in Guro music and dance, popular in Côte d'Ivoire in the 1980s.
Kalimba. Central African metalophone.
Katiola. Town in north central Côte d'Ivoire.
Kekene. "Oneness" in Mau; annual performance showcasing Vado Diomande's Kotchegna Dance Company in New York City.
Kenkeni. Smallest of three drums in the *dundun* drum set, which accompanies the *jembe*.
Kente. Famous cloth of the Akan linguistic-cultural family.
Koman. Mau mask spirit.
Kora. Twenty-one-stringed harp-lute commonly played by Mande *jelis*.
Korhogo. City in north central Côte d'Ivoire.

Kɔrɔ. "Bone" in the Mau language.
Kotchegna. Dance company formed by Vado Diomande originally in Abidjan (known as Ensemble Kotchegna) and later in New York City (Kotchegna Dance Company).
Koyaka. Ethnic group of the Mande linguistic-cultural family in central Côte d'Ivoire.
Kuku. Maninka harvest/rejoicing rhythm/dance.
Kutuku. Strong home-brewed Ivorian liquor.
Kwa. Branch of the Niger-Congo language family.
Les Ballets Africains. Ensemble formed by Fodeba Keita in 1952 and adopted by Guinean president Sekou Touré as a national ensemble in the late 1950s.
Makossa. Popular music style from Cameroon associated with Manu Dibango.
Malinke. See **Maninka**.
Man. City in western Côte d'Ivoire.
Mande. Linguistic-cultural family of ethnic groups in parts of Mali, Burkina Faso, Ghana, Côte d'Ivoire, Guinea, Senegal, Guinea Bissau, Liberia, Sierra Leone, and Gambia.
Mandenka. Ethnic group of the Mande linguistic-cultural family in Gambia.
Mandiani. Mande rhythm/dance.
Maninka. Ethnic group of the Mande linguistic-cultural family in parts of Guinea, Mali, and Côte d'Ivoire.
Maninkadon. Maninka dance.
Mau. Ethnic group of the Mande linguistic-cultural family in western Côte d'Ivoire.
Mauka. Language of the Mau.
Moré. Ethnic group in Burkina Faso.
N'goron. Senufo young girls' dance.
Nouchi, or Français de Moussa. Ivorian street French.
Nya. "Mask spirit" in Mau.
nya ba. "Big or great mask spirit" in Mau.
Nya yan. "Tall (stilt) mask spirit" in Mau.
Orchestre. "Band" in French.
Plateau. Commercial neighborhood (*quartier*) of downtown Abidjan.
Qur'an. Islamic holy book.
Rythme. "Rhythm" in French.
Sabar. Senegalese Wolof drumming/dance tradition.
Sangba. Medium-sized drum; one of three known collectively as a *dundun*, which accompanies the *jembe*.
San Pedro. Coastal port city in southwest Côte d'Ivoire.
Senufo. Gur-speaking ethnic group in northern Côte d'Ivoire and southern Mali.
Sikensi. Town in southeast Côte d'Ivoire.
Sinte. Rhythm/dance from the Boké region of Guinea.
Soli Wule. Guinean mask dance.
Soliya. Mande rhythm/dance.
Spectacle chorégraphique. Choreographed drama typically made up of interwoven dances/rhythms associated with particular ethnic groups.
Suéguéla. Town in western Côte d'Ivoire.
Suya. Indigenous people of the Amazonian rainforest in Brazil.

Tabaski. Islamic holiday honoring Ibrahim's willingness to sacrifice his son to obey the will of Allah (in Arabic, Eid al-Adha).
Tamtam Mandingue. Mande drum; ensemble formed by Guinean *jembe* drummer Mamady Keita in Belgium.
Tanke ge. "Dance/rejoicing mask spirit" in Dan.
Tématé. Wè/Dan girls' circumcision/initiation dance.
Tibloklalo. Dida dance/rhythm.
Timo. Guro funerary dance/rhythm.
Tindin. Mau rhythm common in *nya yan* mask spirit performances.
Topalon. Guro goblet-shaped drum.
Touba. City in northwest Côte d'Ivoire.
Toufinga. Mau village in northwest Côte d'Ivoire.
Toumodi. City in central Côte d'Ivoire.
Treichville. Working-class neighborhood (*quartier*) of Abidjan.
Tura. Ethnic group of the southern Mande linguistic-cultural family in western Côte d'Ivoire.
Union Theatre de Krindjabo (UTK). Theater troupe in Krindjabo, Côte d'Ivoire.
Ury. Guro funerary rhythm/dance.
Varietoscope. National team-based dance competition held annually in Côte d'Ivoire during the 1980s and 1990s.
Vavoua. City in west central Côte d'Ivoire.
Wambele. Senufo sacred mask dance.
Wan. Ethnic group of the Mande linguistic-cultural family in Côte d'Ivoire.
Wè. Ethnic group of the Kru linguistic-cultural family in western Côte d'Ivoire (comprising Guere and Wobe subgroups).
Wobe. Subgroup of the Wè ethnic group in the northern part of the Wè region.
Wolof. Dominant ethnic group of Senegal.
Yado. See ɓaaɗe.
Yakuba. See **Dan**.
Yopougon. Neighborhood (*quartier*) of Abidjan, home to many immigrants from western Côte d'Ivoire.
Yoruba. Major ethnic group in Nigeria.
Zambele. Guro rhythm/dance performed in Ivorian immigrant shows.
Zanloba. Guro rhythm/dance performed in Ivorian immigrant shows.
Zauli. Guro mask dance performed by the Ballet National de Côte d'Ivoire and favorite mask of President Félix Houphouët-Boigny.
Zenoula. Village in central Côte d'Ivoire.
Zikinin. Mau rhythm common in mask dances (in Dan, *zi-ki-ri*).
Zikri. Single-headed drum of the ɓaa type played by Mau and Dan.
Zo. Collective role of healer, diviner, mystical specialist, and sorcery combatant (in Dan, *zu*).
zu ge. *Ge* genre specializing in the work of a *zo* (*zu*).

Notes

Front Matter

1. Available at http://www.ethnomultimedia.org (accessed April 14, 2016).
2. The term *tribal mask* is a quote from a review of this performance in the Memphis daily paper *The Commercial Appeal* (Smith 1994). This image, in fact, does not represent a face mask but rather a kaolin face paint design commonly applied to the faces of young girl "jugglers" among the Dan (the girls do not actually juggle but rather are themselves juggled by muscular men). The misrepresentation is exacerbated by the modifier *tribal*, which evokes precisely the social evolutionary paradigm I find at the base of this show's concept.
3. The friction evident in the representation of contemporary residents of a huge West African city as social evolutionary forebears of Americans in the late twentieth century recalls Rainer Polak's discussions of the pluralization of meanings associated with the transnational spread of the *jembe*. Originally constructed completely of organic materials, the *jembe* head was fastened to its body with leather straps. The *jembe* known and played around the world featuring iron-ring construction is in fact a relatively recent creation, adapted for the stage by ballets in the mid-twentieth century. Polak writes, "For the Bamako drummers, the iron *djembe* represents the 'modern' *djembe*' and contrasts to the ancient model of a leather strap *djembe*; for Europeans and Americans the iron *djembe* is the 'traditional,' if not 'African,' *djembe* as opposed to industrially produced, lug-tensioned instruments" (2006, 178). This kind of irony is a common theme in ethnomusicological research on transnational musical culture (e.g. Stokes 2004; Kapchan 2007; Feld 1995).
4. In my first book (Reed 2003), I cited each direct quote from consultant interviews, linking the quotes to the original recordings from which they came. I made that decision because I believed my consultants' thoughts and words to be every bit as important and authoritative as published sources. For the present volume, however, I found constant citations of original recorded interviews to be disruptive to narrative flow and so have omitted them. Still, all direct quotes of consultants come from recorded interviews that will be deposited in the Indiana University Archives of Traditional Music. All translations are mine.
5. Musicologist Kofi Agawu asserts that African music scholars have been guilty of misrepresentations that simultaneously "Other" Africa while reproducing colonial power relations. Agawu's postcolonial critique asks us to "rethink the extent to which European influence has come to determine our construction of the "purest" of African musics" and to reformulate our understandings of African "creative activities not under the weight of a nostalgic look at the past but through a realistic look at the present" (Agawu 2003, xix).
6. Available at http://web.uvic.ca/ling/resources/ipa/charts/IPAlab/IPAlab.htm (accessed April 13, 2016).

1. Introduction

1. Here I evoke the metaphor of water as formulated in Gilroy's fluid, transnational model of African diaspora (Gilroy 1993).

2. By referring to the illusion of land being permanent and unchanging, I mean to evoke the core, unchanging part of Stuart Hall's model of human identities (Hall 2003).

3. Increased African immigration to the United States in recent decades can be partially attributed to the 1965 passage of the Hart-Celler Immigration and Nationality Act. Tolayan writes, "This Act, with amendments added in following years, rescinded the restrictive immigration quotas established in 1923–4, enlarged the number of immigrants and enabled non-European immigration to the USA on a global scale" (2012:6–7).

4. Notable exceptions are Eleni Bizas's book on Senegalese *sabar* dance in New York and Dakar (2014), Kay Shelemay's research on Ethiopian musicians in the United States (2011, 2006), Carol Muller's work on South Africans in the New Diaspora, particularly her jointly authored book with South African singer Sathima Bea Benjamin (2011); Sherry Canon's dissertation on African immigrant music in Los Angeles (2005), Vera Flaig's dissertation on the transnational spread of the *jembe* (2010), Henry Glassie's book on a Yoruba painter in Philadelphia (2010), select chapters (especially that by James Burns) in the edited volume *The New African Diaspora* (Okpewho and Nzegwu 2009), several publications by Ryan T. Skinner, including a compelling chapter on the expressive production of Malian space in Harlem (2008) and public practice research conducted via the Smithsonian African Immigrant Folklife Project that has resulted in events, CD releases, and publications of various kinds (see http://www.folklife.si.edu).

5. While rich theoretical work has resulted from analyses applying Appadurai's notions of globalized "flows" or "scapes" (Appadurai 1996), I chose not to invoke such metaphors because I find them diffuse and amorphous. Instead, I offer here a focus on ballet, as discourse and genre, as an ethnographically informed, concrete medium through which transnational connections are made.

6. Similar to Debra Klein's "global connections" (2007), I chose a simple, neutral term, "interconnection," to refer more specifically to the human interactions at the core of the cultural, social, and economic realities many call "globalization." Inda and Rosaldo define globalization as "the intensification of global interconnectedness, suggesting a world full of movement and mixture, contact and linkages, and persistent cultural interaction and exchange" (2008:4). This is the context I wish to consider in this book, but I argue against characterizing it as "global," which implies its extension equally, universally across the globe (cf. Turino 2003). Globalization, if we want to call it that, is not truly "global." Nonetheless, I occasionally use the word "globalization" in reference to the literature and discourse on the topic.

7. The Comaroffs' work on ethnicity as a capitalist asset in the global arena also provides insight on the processes of marketing elements of culture as commodity (Comaroff and Comaroff 2009).

8. Ethnomusicologist Mark Slobin also prefers the adjective *diasporic* over the noun *diaspora* (2012, 96; see also Slobin 2000).

9. Many theorists of diaspora have informed my approach, none more than Toloyan 2012, Hall 2003, Gilroy 1993, Monson 2000, Clifford 1994, Cohen 2008, Zelesa 2009, Braziel and Mannur 2003, Turino 2004, Slobin 2012, and Zheng 2010.

10. Black Africans (immigrants from African countries who self-identify as black) represent one of the fastest growing immigrant groups in the United States. Numbering just 64,000 in 1980, by 2009 they had increased by a factor of 16, to 1.1 million. Among the major reasons for this increase were the 1965 immigration reforms, which modified national origin quotas heavily favoring northern European countries and "created the current system in which most legal immigrants come through family reunification channels" (Capps et al. 2011:2)

11. Paul Gilroy's concept of "routes" (1993) pluralized diaspora conceptually so as to highlight the many historical encounters through which African diasporic identities have shifted and realigned.

12. See anthropologist Beth Buggenhagen's work on Senegalese Murid immigrants (2012) for a comparable study of transnational circulations of goods and meanings.

13. For an outstanding overview of research on diaspora in ethnomusicology see Slobin 2012.

14. For a sense of worldliness and connectedness rooted in African lifeworlds and subjectivities, Ryan Skinner (2015), drawing on Mbembe, suggests the term *Afropolitanism* (Mbembe 2010, 229, cited in Skinner 2015, 1–2). I find this a compelling notion, and yet, wary of reifying a *continentally* defined "-politanism," I have chosen to remain with the less confining yet admittedly more diffuse "cosmopolitan."

15. David Racanelli's work on Mande immigrant guitarists in New York City (2014) analyzes ways in which diasporic and cosmopolitan identities are alternately foregrounded in different musical and social settings in the city.

16. Ivorian "street French" is known by several names, including *nouchi* and *francais de Moussa* (Moussa being a common name in northern Côte d'Ivoire, which is stereotyped as being a less developed, less educated part of the country) (Reed 2012; Akindes 2002).

17. This approach is consistent with that of Henry Glassie in his recent book on Nigerian immigrant artist Prince Twins Seven Seven (2010).

18. In addition to Bauman's version of performance theory, approaches to the study of performance I most admire include Turino's adaptation of Percian semiotics (e.g., Turino 2014), and Ruth Stone's adaptation of Bauman in her focus on the performance event (Stone 2010).

19. Ryan Skinner, writing about Malian expressive constructions of a sense of "home" in New York City, conceptualizes performance as an interstitial "third space," a "social arena in which the demands of homeland and host country, native origins and foreign destinations, Africa and America could be produced and playfully mediated" (Skinner 2008, 279).

2. "Ballet" as Nexus of Discourses

1. Ernesto Cardenal, *Cosmic Canticle* (Willimantic, CT: Curbstone Press. 1993).

2. Schauert's research on Ghana's national ensembles analyzes the ways in which performers enact their own agency despite being molded by state policy to represent the nation. One of the personal goals that many ensemble members pursue when on international tours is "greener pastures." These tours represent opportunities to make more money, gain status, and defect in pursuit of financial gain. Among Ghanaians on tour, according to Schauert (2015), competition was so intense that performers complained of being victims of competitors' "juju" to physically hurt them (265).

3. Of Ecole Normale William Ponty, Charry writes that it was initially established in St. Louis, Senegal, in 1857 to "indoctrinate the sons of rulers into French culture." (Charry 2000:245) Its name was changed in 1918 to honor William Ponty, the governor of French West Africa from 1908 to 1915, and it was relocated to Gorée Island off the coast of Dakar at that time. After independence it became Ecole Normale Supérieure, located in Dakar (ibid.).

4. Though I find Keita's conceptualization of ballet very forward thinking for its time, I also see in it a somewhat false historical binary, here "ancient" and "modern," that is all too common. I recall a postcard I purchased in Côte d'Ivoire in the 1990s that juxtaposed two images: one of thatched-roof huts and another of the gleaming skyscrapers of downtown Abidjan's Plateau district, with the caption "Côte d'Ivoire: Yesterday and Today"; both photos were in color, of high quality, and obviously shot in contemporaneous times. So-called ancient and modern traditions *coexist* in contemporary Africa.

5. Of first-world audiences' expectations for African ballet Castaldi (2006) says, "The representation of the city in the work of the national ballet of Senegal would threaten the premises

of world dance that informed the display and performance of 'ethnic' art in the confines of high-art institutions in the first world.... While the city is an icon of modernity and the visible sign of globalization, the village stands in for the local and reassures white spectators of their superiority, their cosmopolitanism vis-à-vis the villagers, who are supposed to be bound to a narrow and naïve rural Africa.... The national ballet cashes in on these assumptions and is able to commodify 'purity' at a higher price than 'contaminated' representation of African dance would allow" (68–69).

6. Guinea alone among former French colonies in Africa refused to adopt the CFA currency, whose value was based on the French franc.

7. Kwabena Nketia is well known for developing the idea, in his landmark book *The Music of Africa* (1974), that the study of African music reveals both unity and diversity. In fact, the tensions between the general and the particular have long pervaded the study of African music (Waterman 1991).

8. George Dor has written a comprehensive history of African music and dance performance in North American universities, noting that such ensembles first appeared at UCLA and Columbia in 1964 (2014, 3). Both Dor (2014) and Locke (2004) have traced the historical predominance of Ghanaian traditions in the American academy.

9. For an overview of the long history of African performance in the United States, from its origins during slavery through its establishment as a staged tradition in the mid-twentieth century to its instantiations in university ensembles in the late twentieth and early twenty-first centuries, see Dor (2014, chap. 1).

10. A notable exception to the staged tradition of dancing in lines is Ghanaian Bernard Woma's troupe Saakumu. Woma deliberately maintains circular dance structures in his performances by locating instrumentalists (either the Dagara *gyil* xylophone or drums) in the center of the stage and choreographing dancers' movements in circles around them.

11. For a concise overview of the instability and conflict that plagued Côte d'Ivoire from 1999 through 2011, see http://www.bbc.com/news/world-africa-13287217.

12. In designating *kuku* as of Guinean origin, I am echoing my Ivorian consultants, who define *kuku* in such national terms. Defining a rhythm as "national" is undeniably foregrounding colonial and postcolonial epistemologies. *Kuku* comes from the northern Mande cultural region, which colonial and postcolonial national boundaries divided. That contemporary Ivorian musicians categorize a rhythm as Guinean speaks to the reality that many contemporary Africans have adopted such epistemologies, despite their colonialist roots, because of the now many-decades-long histories of national ensembles and the national music culture they produce.

13. Yet another reason for the appellation "city drum" could well be that the contemporary version of the jembe, with its iron ring construction, is in fact a rather new phenomenon introduced in Sahelian West African cities in the twentieth century (Polak 2006, 174ff) that rapidly spread throughout both urban and rural West Africa (not to mention much of the rest of the world). For a time, however, this louder drum with its tighter head and brighter timbre was associated with cities like Bamako, which again could account for the nickname.

14. Here he is referring to Guro drummers Dr. Djo Bi, Tra Bi Lizzie of New York City and dancer Bi Bo Ti from Syracuse, New York. The "Titos" he mentions, Papa Titos Sompa, is a good friend of Djo Bi's who lives in Ann Arbor, Michigan, but is from Congo-Brazzaville, Republic of Congo.

15. Eberhard Fischer distinguishes between two Zaulis: one, a sacred mask with animal horns and a beak (spoken in a low tone in the tonal Guro language) the other, an entertainment mask adopted by the national ballet (spoken in a normal tone). Though Fischer chooses to spell the latter *sauli* (2008, 249), I follow the conventions of my Ivorian interlocutors, who pronounce and spell the name *zauli*.

16. *Yado* is yet another flexible term that immigrants sometimes use to refer to both the multiheaded *baade* drum and its rhythms, but in Mau it most concretely refers to a net-strung gourd rattle, which the Dan call a *gle* (Reed 2003, 134–135), and to a dance featuring a rattle and drums.

17. I have chosen to use the Time Unit Box System (TUBS; see Koetting 1970) to represent transcribed rhythms because it effectively shows the layered relationships between rhythmic patterns (a key element of West African rhythmic structure) without superimposing foreign rhythmic concepts such as time signatures and bar lines.

18. See Gunderson and Barz (2000) for more on the central role of competition in East African music, including in stimulating innovation.

3. *Kekene*

1. Vado uses the French spelling of his ethnic group (*Mahou*), which is equivalent to *Mau*.

2. James Burns (2009), in his research on Ghanaian immigrant musicians in the United States, criticizes "intrusions of the Western super culture on African subcultural musics," specifically, the "attempt to restrict the performance of African music to Africans (or at least black people) dressed in tribal outfits" (140). He argues that such expectations tell of a racially based debate over "the power to control the visual aspect of African performance" (ibid.).

3. Lisa Diomande's thoughts, which support Vado's multiracial representational choices, bring to mind race in jazz history. As early as the 1930s, integrated jazz bands toured clubs throughout the Jim Crow South, and whites and blacks danced together in Harlem clubs. These examples are sometimes cited as evidence that societal change regarding race was foreshadowed in jazz before it became widely acceptable (Gioia 1999). Perhaps Vado is similarly ahead of his time in his representations of Africa on stage.

4. "If You Aren't Careful, You Don't Know Where You Will End Up!"

1. One interview occurred in Bloomington, Indiana, at Dr. Djo Bi's house.

2. In western Côte d'Ivoire among ethnic groups such as the Mau and their neighbors to the south, the Dan, only select families "own" masks, which they keep in sacred houses along with sacred paraphernalia. Historically, only members of these families perform masks and the various traditions associated with them, though in the past several decades outsiders have been joining in (Reed 2003, chap. 4).

3. In earlier research on this subject, I learned that the word *ge* is a complex, multifaceted combination of belief and practice, including the notion of a spirit that originates in the forest. Some consultants encouraged me to use *ge* in my publications rather than translate it as *mask* (Reed 2003, 68). In this work, however, which includes masks from various ethnic groups with names in their respective languages, it is simply impractical to use indigenous language for each ethnic group's mask traditions. I refer to the Mau *nya yan* as a "mask spirit" to emphasize the ontological nature of this phenomenon as it was taught to me. Fischer chooses to translate Dan *ge* as "mask spirit beings" for this same reason (Fischer 2014).

4. I use both Dan and Mau terms on occasion for two reasons: first, because stilt masks originated among the Dan and spread north to the Mau; second, because doing so allows readers to make linguistic and conceptual connections between this book and my earlier work on the subject (Reed 2014, 2009, 2008, 2005, 2005, 2003, 2001).

5. As I explain elsewhere, *zo* is found in variant forms (e.g., *zu* in Dan) in many Guinea forest region languages, particularly those of the southern Mande family, to indicate the role of indigenous religious healers/diviners/clairvoyants(2003, 189).

6. The word *sacrifice* can refer to any manner of giving to the mask spirits, from a symbolic offering of kola nuts in the United States to the killing of a cow in Toufinga.

7. Anthropologist Peter Geschiere writes that sorcery (which he translates as "witchcraft") also follows Cameroonian immigrants as they move abroad (2013, 52–64).

8. Vado's use of the term *voudou* here is a creative, metonymical reference to spiritual energy used for socially destructive ends among people of African descent and belief systems. Dan consultants would call such activity *duyaa* (Reed 2003, 193).

9. *Fathers of the mask* (*gedoemen*) is a term in the Dan language that Vado also uses to refer to elders who are the most powerful initiates in any sacred house associated with a particular *ge* spirit.

10. Van Beek and Blakely write that an old Dogon man once told Walter van Beek, "Dogon religion is a means for the old men to get meat" (1994, 11). Clearly there can be multiple interpretations of sacrifice.

11. My assumption, based on limited research and knowledge, is that it was a type of bone cancer that commonly attacks the jaw, perhaps osteosarcoma, multiple myeloma, Ewing sarcoma, or giant cell tumor. See http://www.livestrong.com/article/143839-jaw-bone-cancer-symptoms/ (accessed April 5, 2016).

12. In northern Mande languages, *kɔrɔ* means *bone*; it is unclear to me whether Vado was arguing that the word is polysemic—meaning bone or a bone disease depending on context—or was merely sharing the Mande word with me.

13. The conflict between Western and traditional medicine is dramatized in the BNCI's choreographed piece, "The Vampire," which Vado's troupe still performed occasionally during the period of this research.

14. See Sewell Chan (2006).

6. "I'm Happy Because I'm Different"

1. The term *Jula* is complex. While it can refer specifically to the northern Mande ethnic group whose homeland is in northern Côte d'Ivoire and southern Burkina Faso, more commonly it is a homogenizing label used by southern Ivorians to refer to all northerners, meaning those from the north of the country as well as Mali, Burkina, and so forth. As I write in *Dan Ge Performance*, "Simply put, when discussing the hundreds of thousands of various northern peoples or myriad nationalities and ethnicities living in southern Côte d'Ivoire, northerner = Jula = Muslim" (Reed 2003, 185).

2. Abidji and Adjoukrou are both classified as Kwa languages, which make up a loose set of languages spoken in southwest Ghana and southeast Côte d'Ivoire that are generally not mutually intelligible.

3. Tabaski is the West African name for the Islamic holiday Id al-adha, the celebration of Ibrahim's willingness to sacrifice his son to show obedience to God, who offered a lamb for sacrifice in his son's stead.

4. For more on local epistemologies of "tradition," "modern," and "popular" in Côte d'Ivoire, see Reed 2003 (especially chap. 3).

5. This company has since changed names twice, first to Parkway and then to Nypro Atlanta.

6. In Côte d'Ivoire it is customary to contribute (in French *cotiser*) to bereaved family members as they prepare for a funeral or even during the funeral ceremony. Such contributions offset the considerable cost of funerals, which, especially for non-Muslims, represent a ritual transition to the status of ancestor. Funerals are expensive, elaborate affairs with food, drink, and entertainment commensurate with the wealth and social power of the deceased.

7. For probably the best-known example of an African immigrant "becoming" a drummer and achieving great financial success and renown, see Eric Charry's introduction in Babatunde Olatunji's autobiography (2005).

7. "You Know You're in a Different Country"

1. *Yado* refers to a popular Mau dance in which this drum is played with a gourd rattle, also called *yado*. *Baanya* is a compound term referring to drumming for a mask spirit performance (*baa* = drum; *nya* = mask). *Baadè*, the Dan name of this drum, means mother drum (*baa* = drum; *dè* = mother).

2. http://www.sogbety.com/programs.html (accessed July 23, 2013).

8. "When You're in a New Context, You Try Things That Work in That Context"

1. See Reed 2003, especially chapter 3, for more on local epistemologies of "modern," "popular," and "traditional."

2. See http://www.youtube.com/watch?v=bmmFT_jkZUw&feature=related (accessed April 10, 2016).

9. "Open Village"

1. Stone describes the ways in which Kpelle people conceptualize the ritual space as protected by a "fence" separating initiates and noninitiates (2005, 66, 93).

2. The *gekia* accompanies and encourages the mask spirit, walking and/or dancing alongside it, ever available to fix any problems with the mask's costume, collect monetary donations, and serve as intermediary, repeating any words that the performing mask spirit speaks (Reed 2003, 183–184).

3. There are three "manifestations" of the same Gue Pelou spirit in the United States, each one associated respectively with Vado Diomande, Sogbety Diomande, and Moha Dosso.

10. "Everyone Is a Cook, but He's a Chef!"

1. In Guro naming, *Bi* means son and *Lou* means daughter, so Djo Bi is the son of Djo.

2. The denomination Djo Bi followed is known in Côte d'Ivoire as Eglise Protestante Evangélique (CMA), with CMA standing for Christian and Ministry Alliance. A popular Ivorian alternative to Catholicism, CMA has 285 parishes around the country. See http://www.eglisecma-ci.org/ (accessed April 11, 2016).

3. Djoniba Dance Center, a major locus of African and African diaspora drumming and dance instruction in Manhattan (see chapter 4).

11. Thoughts on the Way Out

1. Scholarly research on the African roots of African American music includes such important works as Herskovits' *The Myth of the Negro Past* (1941), Maultsby's "Africanisms in African American Music" (2005 [1992]), and Burnim's "The Black Gospel Music Tradition: A Complex of Ideology, Aesthetics, and Behavior (1985).

2. http://www.sambadiallo.com/ (last accessed April 7, 2016).

Bibliography

Agawu, Kofi. 2003. *Representing African Music: Postcolonial Notes, Queries, Positions*. New York: Routledge.
Akindes, Simon. 2002. "Playing It Loud and Straight: Reggae, Zouglou, Mapouka and Youth Insubordination in Côte d'Ivoire." In *Playing with Identities in Contemporary Music in Africa*. Edited by Mai Palmberg and Annemette Kirkegaard, 86–103. Uppsala: Nordiska Afrikainstitutet.
Appadurai, Arjun. 1996. *Modernity At Large: Cultural Dimensions of Globalization*. Minneapolis: University of Minnesota Press.
Arthur, John A., Joseph Takougang, and Thomas Owusu. eds. 2012. *Africans in Global Migration: Searching for Promised Lands*. Lanham, MD: Lexington.
Askew, Kelly M. 2002. *Performing the Nation: Swahili Music and Cultural Politics in Tanzania*. Chicago: University of Chicago Press.
Babiracki, Carol. 2008. "Between Life History and Performance: Sundari Devi and the Art of Allusion." *Ethnomusicology* 52 (1):1–30.
Barber, Karin. 1997 "Introduction." In *Readings in African Popular Culture*. Edited by Karin Barber, 1–11. Bloomington: Indiana University Press.
Barry, Dan. 2006. "A Word Recalls When Terror Was in the Mail." *New York Times*, Feb. 25. Accessed March 10, 2012. http://query.nytimes.com/gst/fullpage.html?res=9803EFDB1F3EF936A15751C0A9609C8B63.
Bauman, Richard. 2004. *A World of Others' Words: Cross Cultural Perspectives on Intertextuality*. Indianapolis: Wiley-Blackwell.
———. 1986. *Story, Performance, and Event: Contextual Studies of Oral Narrative*. Cambridge, UK: Cambridge University Press.
———. 1977. *Verbal Art as Performance*. Rowley, MA: Newbury House Publishers.
Berliner, Paul. 1979. *The Soul of Mbira: Music and Traditions of the Shona People of Zimbabwe*. Berkeley: University of California Press.
Bhabha, Homi. 1996 "Unsatisfied: Notes on Vernacular Cosmopolitanism." *Text and Nation: Cross-Disciplinary Essays on Cultural and National Identities*. Edited by Laura Garcia-Moreno and Peter C. Pfeiffer. Columbia, SC: Hamden House.
Bizas, Eleni. 2014. *Learning Senegalese Sabar: Dancers and Embodiment in New York and Dakar*. New York: Berghahn Books.
Bouttiaux, Anne-Marie. 2013. "Garants de continuité et perméables au changement. Les masques et leur dynamique en Afrique occidentale." In *La dynamique des masques en Afrique occidentale*. Edited by Anne-Marie Bouttiax, 9–26. Tervuren, Belgium: Musée royal de l'Afrique centrale.
Bravmann, Rene. 1983. *African Islam*. Washington, DC: Smithsonian Institution.
Braziel, Jana Evans, and Anita Mannur, eds. 2003. *Theorizing Diaspora: A Reader*. Indianapolis: Wiley-Blackwell.
Briggs, Charles L., and Richard Bauman. 1992."Genre, Intertextuality, and Social Power." *Journal of Linguistic Anthropology* 2 (2):131–172.

Buchanan, Donna A. 2006. *Performing Democracy: Bulgarian Music and Musicians in Transition.* Chicago: University of Chicago Press.

Buggenhagen, Beth. 2012. *Muslim Families in Global Senegal: Money Takes Care of Shame.* Bloomington: Indiana University Press.

Burnim, Mellonee. 1985. "The Black Gospel Music Tradition: A Complex of Ideology, Aesthetics and Behavior." In *More Than Dancing: Essays on Afro-American Music and Musicians.* Edited by Irene V. Jackson. Westport, CT: Greenwood Press.

Burns, James. 2009. "The West Is Cold: Experiences of Ghanaian Performers in New England and the United States." In *The New African Diaspora.* Edited by Isidore Okpewho and Nkiru Nzegwu, 127–145. Bloomington: Indiana University Press.

Butler, Judith. (1999) 2006. *Gender Trouble: Feminism and the Subversion of Identity.* New York: Routledge.

Canon, Sherri Dawn. 2005. "Music, Dance and Family Ties: Ghanaian and Senegalese Immigrants in Los Angeles." Ph.D. diss., University of Texas at Austin.

Capps, Randy, Kristen McCabe, and Michael Fix. 2011. *New Streams: Black African Migration to the United States.* Washington, DC: Movement Policy Institute.

Cardenal, Ernesto. 1993. *Cosmic Canticle.* Willimantic, CT: Curbstone Press.

Castaldi, Francesca. 2006. *Choreographies of African Identities: Négritude, Dance, and the National Ballet of Senegal.* Urbana: University of Illinois Press.

Chan, Sewell. 2006a. "A Wider Inquiry, as More People Get Antibiotics and 2nd Apartment Is to Be Checked." *New York Times*, Feb. 24.

———. 2006b. "New York City Man Has Inhalation Anthrax, Officials Say." *New York Times,* Feb. 23.

Chan, Sewell, and Colin Moynihan. 2006. "Federal Workers Decontaminate Anthrax Victim's Home." *New York Times*, March 3.

Charry, Eric. 2005. "Introduction." In *The Beat of My Drum: An* Autobiography, by Babatunde Olatunji. Philadelphia: Temple University Press.

———. 2000. *Mande Music: Traditional and Modern Music of the Maninka and Mandinka of Western Africa.* Chicago: University of Chicago Press.

———. 1996. "A Guide to the Jembe." *Percussive Notes* 34 (2):66–72.

Charry, Eric, Jan Jansen, and Camara Seydou. 2002. "The Mande Praise Song Kayra (Peace): Mande Global Perspectives." *Metamorphoses* 10 (1):300–321.

Clark, Gracia. 2010. *African Market Women: Seven Life Stories from Ghana.* Bloomington: Indiana University Press.

Clifford, James. 1997. *Routes: Travel and Translation in the Late Twentieth Century.* Cambridge: Harvard University Press.

———. 1994. "Diasporas." *Cultural Anthropology* 9 (3):302–338.

Coe, Cati. 2013. *The Scattered Family: Parenting, African Migrants, and Global Inequality.* Chicago: University of Chicago Press.

Cohen, David, Stephan Miescher, and Luise White. 2001. "Introduction." In *African Words, African Voices: Critical Practices in Oral History.* Edited by Luise White, David Cohen, and Stephan Miescher, 1–30. Bloomington: Indiana University Press.

Cohen, Joshua. 2008. "Stages in Transition: Les Ballets Africains and Independence 1959 to 1960." *Journal of Black Studies* 43 (10):11–48.

Cohen, Robin. 2008. *Global Diasporas: An Introduction.* New York: Routledge.

Comaroff, John L., and Jean Comaroff. 2009. *Ethnicity, Inc.* Chicago: University of Chicago Press.
Cooley, Timothy J. 2008. "Introduction." In *Shadows in the Field: New Perspectives for Fieldwork in Ethnomusicology.* 2nd ed. Edited by Gregory F. Barz and Timothy J. Cooley, 3–24. New York: Oxford University Press.
Craft, Katherine Williams. 2002. "Mask Dance Tells Story of Ivory Coast Music and Folklore." *The Morning Call* (Bethlehem, Pennsylvania), February 16.
Crapanzano, Vincent. 1980. *Tuhami: Portrait of a Moroccan.* Chicago: University of Chicago Press.
Cutter, Charles H. 1985. "The Genesis of a Nationalist Elite: The Role of the Popular Front in the French Soudan." In *Double Impact: France and Africa in the Age of Imperialism.* Edited by G. Wesley Johnson, 141–153. Westport, CT: Greenwood Press.
Davis, Peter. 1996. *In Darkest Hollywood: Exploring the Jungles of Cinema's South Africa.* Randberg, South Africa: Ravan Press.
D'Azevedo, Warren. (1973) 1991. *The Traditional Artist in African Societies.* Bloomington: Indiana University Press.
Dor, George Worlasi Kwasi. 2014. *West African Drumming and Dancing in North American Universities: An Ethnomusicological Perspective.* Oxford: University Press of Mississippi.
Dugger, Celia W. 2010. "South Africa Pushes to Make the Cup Its Own." *New York Times*, May 23. Accessed January 26, 2015. http://www.nytimes.com/2010/05/24/sports/soccer/24safrica.html?_r=2&.
Dutiro, Chartwell, and Keith Howard. 2007. *Zimbabwean Mbira Music on an International Stage: Chartwell Dituro's Life in Music.* Hampshire, UK: Ashgate Publishing.
Ebron, Paulla. 2002. *Performing Africa.* Princeton, NJ: Princeton University Press.
Erlmann, Veit. 1999. *Music, Modernity and the Global Imagination: South Africa and the West.* Oxford, UK: Oxford University Press.
Feld, Steven. 2012. *Jazz Cosmopolitanism in Accra: Five Musical Years in Ghana.* Durham, NC: Duke University Press.
———. 1995. "From Schizophonia to Schismogenesis: The Discourse and Practice of World Music and World Beat." In *The Traffic in Culture: Refiguring Art and Anthropology.* Edited by George Marcus and Fred R. Myers, 96–126. Berkeley: University of California Press.
Ferguson, James. 2006. *Global Shadows: Africa in the Neoliberal World Order.* Durham, NC: Duke University Press.
Fischer, Eberhard. 2014. *Four Dan Artists: The Sculptors Tame, Si, Tompeme, and Sön: Their Personalities and Work.* Chicago: University of Chicago Press.
———. 2008. *Guro: Masks, Performances, and Master Carvers in Ivory Coast.* Munich: Prestel Verlag.
Flaig, Vera. 2010. *The Politics of Representation and Transmission in the Globalization of Guinea's Djembé.* PhD diss., University of Michigan.
Gardinier, David E. 1985. "The French Impact on Education in Africa, 1817–1960." In *Double Impact: France and Africa in the Age of Imperialism.* Edited by G. Wesley Johnson, 333–344. Westport, CT: Greenwood Press.

Garuba, Harry, and Natasha Himmelman. 2012. "The Cited and the Uncited: Toward an Emancipatory Reading of Representations of Africa." In *Hollywood's Africa After 1994*. Edited by MaryEllen Higgins, 15–34. Athens: Ohio University Press.
Genzlinger, Neil. 2011. "The Week Ahead: April 10–April 16." *New York Times*, April 10.
Geschiere, Peter. 2013. *Witchcraft, Intimacy and Trust: Africa in Comparison*. Chicago: University of Chicago Press.
Gilman, Lisa. 2009. *The Dance of Politics: Gender, Performance, and Democratization in Malawi*. Philadelphia: Temple University Press.
Gilroy, Paul. 1993. *The Black Atlantic: Modernity and Double Consciousness*. Cambridge, MA: Harvard University Press.
Gioia, Ted. 1999. *The History of Jazz*. Oxford, UK: Oxford University Press.
Glass, Herbert. 2015. "About the Piece: Also Sprach Zarathustra." Los Angeles Philharmonic Association. Accessed May 12, 2015. http://www.laphil.com/philpedia/music/also-sprach-zarathustra-richard-strauss.
Glassie, Henry. 2010. *Prince Twins Seven-Seven: His Art, His Life in Nigeria, His Exile in America*. Bloomington: Indiana University Press.
Gomez, Michael A. 2006. *Diasporic Africa: A Reader*. New York: New York University Press.
Goodman, Jane. 2005. *Berber Culture on the World Stage: From Village to Video*. Bloomington: Indiana University Press.
Gourlay, Kenneth A. 1978. "Towards a Reassessment of the Ethnomusicologist's Role." *Ethnomusicology* 22 (1):1–35.
Gunderson, Frank D., and Gregory Barz. 2000. *Mashindano! Competitive Music Performance in East Africa*. Dar es Salaam: Mkuki na Nyota.
Hall, Stuart. 2003. "Cultural Identity and Diaspora." In *Theorizing Diaspora: A Reader*. Edited by Jana Evans Braziel and Anita Mannur, 233–246. Oxford, UK: Wiley-Blackwell.
Hazzard-Gordon, Katrina. 1985. "African-American Vernacular Dance: Core Culture and Meaning Operatives." *Journal of Black Studies* 15 (4):427–445.
Henderson, Clara. 2009. *Dance Discourse in the Music and Lives of Presbyterian Mvano Women in Southern Malawi*. Ph.D. diss., Indiana University.
Herskovits, Melville J. 1941. *The Myth of the Negro Past*. New York: Harper.
Herzfeld, Michael. 1997. *Cultural Intimacy: Social Poetics in the Nation-State*. New York: Routledge.
Inda, Jonathan, and Renato Rosaldo. 2008. "Tracking Global Flows." In *Anthropology of Globalization: A Reader*. Edited by Jonathan Inda and Renato Rosaldo, 3–46. Oxford, UK: Blackwell.
International Organization for Migration. 2015. "IOM Counts 3,771 Migrant Fatalities in Mediterranean in 2015." Accessed January 5, 2016. https://www.iom.int/news/iom-counts-3771-migrant-fatalities-mediterranean-2015.
Jackson, Michael. 1982. *Allegories of the Wilderness: Ethics and Ambiguity in Kuranko Narratives*. Bloomington: Indiana University Press.
Jacobson, Bernard. 2013. "Also Sprach Zarathustra, Op. 30 (1896)." Concert notes. Accessed January 24, 2014. http://americansymphony.org/also-sprach-zarathustra-op-30-1896.
Janelli, Roger, and Dawnshee Yim. 1993. *Making Capitalism: The Social and Cultural Construction of a South Korean Conglomerate*. Stanford, CA: Stanford University Press.

Johnson, Barbara. 1986. *Four Dan Sculptors: Continuity and Change*. San Francisco: Fine Arts Museum of San Francisco.
Kapchan, Deborah. 2007. *Traveling Spirit Masters: Moroccan Gnawa Trance and Music in the Global Marketplace*. Middletown, CT: Wesleyan University Press.
Karlsson, Jonas. 2001. "Fairy Tale." *New Yorker*, February 12.
Keíta, Fodéba. 1957. "La Danse Africaine et la Scéne." *Présence Africaine: Review Culturelle du Monde Noir*, 14–15 (Jun.–Sep.):202–209.
Kisliuk, Michelle. 1998. *Seize the Dance! BaAka Musical Life and the Ethnography of Performance*. New York: Oxford University Press.
Kisselgoff, Anna. 2001. "Like a Genie, So Elusive and Loose." *New York Times*, February 13.
Kiwan, Nadia, and Ulrike Hanna Meinhof. 2011. *Cultural Globalization and Music: African Artists in Transnational Networks*. London: Palgrave Macmillan.
Klein, Debra L. 2007. *Yoruba Bata Goes Global: Artists, Culture, Brokers and Fans*. Chicago: University of Chicago Press.
Koetting, James. 1970. "Analysis and Notation of West African Drum Ensemble Music." *Selected Reports, Institute of Ethnomusicology, UCLA* 1 (3):115–146.
Konadu-Agyemang, Kwadwo, Baaffour K. Takyi, and John A. Arthur, eds. 2006.*The New African Diaspora in North America: Trends, Community Building and Adaptation*. Lanham, MD: Lexington Books.
Kopytoff, Igor. 1987. "The Internal African Frontier: The Making of African Political Culture." In *The African Frontier: The Reproduction of Traditional African Societies*. Edited by Igor Kopytoff, 3–86. Bloomington: Indiana University Press.
Kratz, Corinne A. 2001. "Conversations and Lives." In *African Words, African Voices: Critical Practices in Oral History*. Edited by Luise White, David Cohen, and Stephan Miescher, 127–161. Bloomington: Indiana University Press.
Launay, Robert. 1992. *Beyond the Stream: Islam and Society in a West African Town*. Berkeley: University of California Press.
Lawless, Elaine. 1993. *Holy Women, Wholly Women: Sharing Ministries of Wholeness Through Life Stories and Reciprocal Ethnography*. Philadelphia: University of Pennsylvania Press.
Lewis, M. Paul, Gary F. Simons, and Charles D. Fennig, eds. 2016. "OLAC Resources in and about the Adioukrou Language. In *Ethnologue: Languages of the World*. 19th ed. Dallas: SIL International. Accessed January 22, 2015. http://www.ethnologue.com/language/adj/view/.
Lindfors, Bernth. 2014. *Early Africans Abroad: From the Hottentot Venus to Africa's First Olympians*. Bloomington: Indiana University Press.
Locke, David. 2004. "The African Ensemble in America: Contradictions and Possibilities." In *Performing Ethnomusicology: Teaching and Representation in World Music Ensembles*. Edited by Ted Solis, 168–188. Berkeley: University of California Press.
Marcus, George. 1995. "Ethnography in/of the World System: Emergence of Multi-Sited Ethnography." *Annual Review of Anthropology* 24:95–117.
Maultsby, Portia K. 2005. "Africanisms in African American Music." In *Africanisms in American Culture*. 2nd ed. Edited by Joseph E. Holloway, 326–355. Bloomington: Indiana University Press.
McDowell, John H. 2010. "Rethinking Folklorization in Ecuador: Multivocality in the Expressive Contact Zone." *Western Folklore* 69 (2):181–210.

McNaughton, Patrick. 2008. *A Bird Dance Near Saturday City: Sidi Ballo and the Art of West African Masquerade*. Bloomington: Indiana University Press.
Mecca Bodega. 2014. Press Kit. Accessed May 21, 2014. http://www.meccabodega.com/epk.
Miller, Christopher L. 1990. *Theories of Africans: Francophone Literature and Anthropology in Africa*. Chicago: University of Chicago Press.
Miller, Daniel, ed. 2009. *Anthropology and the Individual: A Material Culture Perspective*. London: Bloomsbury Academic.
Mitchell, Frank. 1978. *Blessingway Singer: The Autobiography of Frank Mitchell, 1881–1967*. Edited by Charlotte Frisbie and David McAllester. Tucson: University of Arizona Press.
Monson, Ingrid, ed. 2000. *The African Diaspora: A Musical Perspective*. New York: Routledge.
Mudimbe, V. Y. 1988. *The Invention of Africa: Gnosis, Philosophy, and the Order of Knowledge*. Bloomington: Indiana University Press.
Muller, Carol, and Sathima Bea Benjamin. 2011. *Musical Echoes: South African Women Thinking in Jazz*. Durham, NC: Duke University Press.
Nabokov, Peter. 1967. *Two Leggings: The Making of a Crow Warrior*. New York: Crowell.
Neal, Larry. 1968. "The Black Arts Movement." *Drama Review* 12 (Summer 1968):29–39. National Humanities Center Resource Toolbox: The Making of African American Identity 3, 1917–1968. Accessed April 23, 2016. http://nationalhumanitiescenter.org/pds/maai3/community/text8/blackartsmovement.pdf.
Nketia, Kwabena H. 1974. *The Music of Africa*. New York: W. W. Norton.
O'Connor, Bonnie. 1994. *Healing Traditions: Alternative Medicine and the Health Professions*. Philadelphia: University of Pennsylvania Press.
Okpewho, Isidore, and Nkiru Nzegwu, eds. 2009. *The New African Diaspora*. Bloomington: Indiana University Press.
Olatunji, Babatunde, with Michael Atkinson and Akinsola Akiwowo. 2005. *The Beat of My Drum: An Autobiography*. Philadelphia: Temple University Press.
Peacock, James L., and Dorothy C. Holland. 1993. "The Narrated Self: Life Stories in Process." *Ethos* 21 (4):367–383.
Perullo, Alex. 2011. *Live from Dar es Salaam: Popular Music and Tanzania's Music Economy*. Bloomington: Indiana University Press.
Polak, Rainer. 2012. "Urban Drumming: Traditional Celebration Music in a West African City (Bamako)." In *Hip Hop Africa: New African Music in a Globalizing World*. Edited by Eric Charry, 261–282. Bloomington: Indiana University Press.
———. 2006. "A Musical Instrument Travels around the World: Jenbe Playing in Bamako, West Africa and Beyond." In *Ethnomusicology: A Contemporary Reader*. Edited by Jennifer C. Post, 161–185. New York: Routledge.
Portelli, Alessandro. 1997. *The Battle of Valle Giulia: Oral History and the Art of Dialogue*. Madison: University of Wisconsin Press.
Racanelli, David. 2014. "Guitar Playing and Representation in the Changing Locations of New York City's African Music Scene." *Ethnomusicology* 58 (2):278–314.
Ramnarine, Tina K., ed. 2007. *Musical Performance in the Diaspora*. New York: Routledge.

Reed, Daniel, B. 2014. "Spirits from the Forest: Dan Masks in Performance and Everyday Life." In *Visions from the Forests: The Art of Liberia and Sierra Leone*. Edited by Jan-Lodewijk Grootaers, 82–91. Minneapolis: Minneapolis Institute of Arts.

———. 2012. "Promises of the Chameleon: Reggae Artist Tiken Jah Fakoly's Intertextual Contestation of Power in Côte d'Ivoire." In *Hip Hop Africa and Other Stories of New African Music in a Globalized World*. Edited by Eric Charry, 92–108. Bloomington: Indiana University Press.

———. 2011. "C'est le Wake Up! Africa: Two Case Studies of HIV/AIDS Edutainment Campaigns in Francophone Africa." In *The Culture of AIDS in Africa*. Edited by Gregory Barz and Judah Cohen. 180–192. London: Oxford University Press.

———. 2009. *Mask, Music and Dance Performance in Western Côte d'Ivoire, 1997*. Bloomington, IN: Ethnomusicological Video for Instruction and Analysis Digital Archive (EVIADA).

———. 2008. "Tradition and Identity in a Diversifying Context." In *The Garland Handbook of African Music*. Edited by Ruth M. Stone. 216–236. New York: Routledge.

———. 2005a. "The *Ge* Is in the Church and Our Parents Are 'Playing Muslim': Performance, Identity, and Resistance among the Dan in Postcolonial Côte d'Ivoire." *Ethnomusicology* 49 (3):347–367.

———. 2005b. "Masks and Music, Spirits and Sports: Gunyege in Performance." In *Imaging and Identity: African Art from the Lowe and Other South Florida Collections*. Edited by Marci Wittmer, 27–34. Miami, FL: University of Miami Lowe Art Museum.

———. 2004. "The Transformation into Spirit through a 'Constellation of Arts.'" In *See The Music, Hear The Dance: Rethinking Africa at the Baltimore Museum of Art*. Edited by Frederick Lamp. Munich: Prestel Verlag.

———. 2003. *Dan Ge Performance: Masks and Music in Contemporary Côte d'Ivoire*. Bloomington: Indiana University Press.

———. 2002. "Representation." In *Music and Culture of West Africa: The Straus Expedition*. Created by Gloria J. Gibson and Daniel B. Reed. Bloomington: Indiana University Press, CD-ROM.

———. 2001. "Pop Goes the Sacred: Dan Mask Performance and Popular Culture in Postcolonial Côte d'Ivoire." *Africa Today*, 48 (4):67–87.

———. 1993. "The Innovator and the Primitives: George Herzog in Historical Perspective." *Folklore Forum* 26 (1/2):69–92.

Rice, Timothy. 1994. *May It Fill Your Soul: Experiencing Bulgarian Music*. Chicago: University of Chicago Press.

Ruskin, Jesse D., and Timothy Rice. 2012. "The Individual in Musical Ethnography." *Ethnomusicology* 56 (2):299–327.

Said, Edward. 1978. *Orientalism*. New York: Pantheon Books.

Sany, Joseph. 2010. *Special Report 235: Education and Conflict in Côte d'Ivoire*. Washington, DC: United States Institute of Peace. Accessed May 13, 2015. http://www.protectingeducation.org/sites/default/files/documents/special_report_235.pdf.

Schauert, Paul. 2015. *Staging Ghana: Artistry and Nationalism in State Dance Ensembles*. Bloomington: Indiana University Press.

Seeger, Anthony. 2004. *Why Suya Sing: A Musical Anthropology of an Amazonian People*. Urbana-Champaign: University of Illinois Press.

Shay, Anthony. 2002. *Choreographic Politics: State Folk Dance Companies, Representation, and Power*. Middletown, CT: Wesleyan University Press.

Shelemay, Kay Kaufman. 2011. "Musical Communities: Rethinking the Collective in Music." *Journal of the American Musicological Society* 64 (2):349-390.
———. 2006. "Ethiopian Musical Invention in Diaspora: A Tale of Three Musicians." *Diaspora* 15 (2/3):303-320.
Shipley, Jesse. 2013. *Living the Hiplife: Celebrity and Entrepreneurship in Ghanaian Popular Music*. Durham, NC: Duke University Press.
Shostak, Marjorie. 1981. *Nisa: The Life and Words of a !Kung Woman*. New York: Vintage Books.
Shuman, Amy. 2011. "Life History Narratives and the Romanticization of Labor." Presentation at the American Folklore Society Annual Meeting, Bloomington, IN, October 13.
Skinner, Ryan Thomas. 2015. *Bamako Sound: The Afropolitan Ethics of Malian Music*. Minneapolis: University of Minnesota Press.
———. 2008. "Celebratory Spaces Between Homeland and Host: Politics, Culture and Performance in New York's Malian Community." *Migrations and Creative Expressions in Africa and the African Diaspora*. Edited by Toyin Falola, Niyi Afolabi and Aderonke Adesola Adesanya. 279-298. Durham, NC: Duke University Press.
Slobin, Mark. 2012. "The Destiny of 'Diaspora' in Ethnomusicology. *The Cultural Study of Music: A Critical Introduction.* 2nd ed. Edited by Martin Clayton, Trevor Herbert, and Richard Middleton, 96-106. New York: Routlege.
———. 2000. *Fiddler on the Move: Exploring the Klezmer World*. New York: Oxford University Press.
Smith, Whitney. 1994. "Hundreds Weave Ethnic, Musical Mosaic for Tattoo." *Commercial Appeal* (Memphis, TN), May 13.
Sterling, Marvin. 2010. *Babylon East: Performing Dancehall, Roots Reggae, and Rastafari in Japan*. Durham, NC: Duke University Press.
Stokes, Martin. 2004. "Music and the Global Order." *Annual Review of Anthropology* 33:47-72.
Stoller, Paul. 2002. *Money Has No Smell: The Africanization of New York City*. Chicago: University of Chicago Press.
Stone, Ruth M. (1981) 2010. *Let the Inside Be Sweet: The Interpretation of Music Event among the Kpelle of Liberia*. Bloomington, IN: Trickster Press.
———. 2005. *Music in West Africa: Experiencing Music, Expressing Culture*. Oxford, UK: Oxford University Press.
———. 2000. "Gbarbea Funeral." In *Five Windows into Africa*. Created by Patrick R. McNaughton, John H. Hanson, dele jẹgẹdẹ, Ruth M Stone, and N. Brian Winchester. Bloomington: Indiana University Press. CD-ROM.
———. 1994. "Bringing the Extraordinary into the Ordinary: Music Performance among the Kpelle of Liberia." In *Religion in Africa: Experience and Expression*. Edited by Thomas D. Blakely, Walter E. A. van Beek, and Dennis L. Thomson, 388-397. London: James Curry and Heinemann.
———. 1988. *Dried Millet Breaking: Time, Words and Song in the Woi Epic of the Kpelle*. Bloomington: Indiana University Press.
Stone, Verlon, and R. Stone. 1981. "Event, Feedback, and Analysis: Research Media in the Study of Music Events." *Ethnomusicology* 25 (2):215-225.
Stone-MacDonald, Angela, and Ruth Stone. 2013. "The Feedback Interview and Video Recording in African Research Settings." *Africa Today* 59 (4):2-22.

Tabmen, George W. W. 1971. *Gor and Gle: Ancient Structure of Government in the Dan (Gio) Tribe*. Mimeograph.
Talayesva, Don C., and Leo W. Simmons. 1942. *Sun Chief: The Autobiography of a Hopi Indian*. New Haven: Yale University Press.
Tang, Patricia. 2012. "The Rapper as Modern Griot: Reclaiming Ancient Traditions." In *Hip-Hop Africa: New African Music in a Globalizing World*. Edited by Eric Charry, 79–91. Bloomington: Indiana University Press.
———. 2007. *Masters of the Sabar: Wolof Griot Percussionists of Senegal*. Philadelphia: Temple University Press.
Taylor, Timothy. 1997. *Global Pop: World Music, World Markets*. New York: Routledge.
Thiongo, Ngugi wa. 1981. *Decolonizing the Mind: The Politics of Language in African Literature*. Oxford, UK: James Currey.
Titon, Jeff Todd. 1988. *Powerhouse for God: Speech, Chant, and Song in an Appalachian Baptist Church*. Austin: University of Texas Press.
Toloyan, Khachig. 2012. "Diaspora Studies: Past, Present and Promise." Oxford Diasporas Programme Working Paper 55, April. Oxford, UK: University of Oxford International Migration Institute.
Tsing, Anna Lowenhaupt. 2005. *Friction: An Ethnography of Global Connection*. Princeton: Princeton University Press.
Tuohy, Sue. 2001. "The Sonic Dimensions of Nationalism in Modern China: Musical Representation and Transformation." *Ethnomusicology* 45 (1):107–131.
Turino, Thomas. 2014. "Percian Theory for a Phenomenological Ethnomusicology." *Ethnomusicology* 58 (2):185–221.
———. 2008. *Music as Social Life: The Politics of Participation*. Chicago: University of Chicago Press.
———. 2004. "Introduction." In *Identity and the Arts in Diaspora Communities*. Edited by Thomas Turino and James Lea. Warren, MI: Harmonie Park Press.
———. 2003. "Are We Global Yet? Globalist Discourse, Cultural Formations and the Study of Zimbabwean Popular Music." *British Journal of Ethnomusicology* 12 (3):51–79.
———. 2000. *Nationalists, Cosmopolitans, and Popular Music in Zimbabwe*. Chicago: University of Chicago Press.
———. 1993. *Moving Away from Silence: Music of the Peruvian Altiplano and the Experiment of Urban Migration*. Chicago: University of Chicago Press.
Urban, Greg. 2001. *Metaculture: How Culture Moves through the World*. Minneapolis: University of Minnesota Press.
Urban, Greg, and Joel Sherzer. 1991. "Introduction: Indians, Nation-States, and Culture." In *Nation-States and Indians in Latin America*. Edited by Greg Urban and Joel Sherzer. Austin: University of Texas Press.
van Beek, Walter E. A., and Thomas D. Blakely. 1994. "Introduction." In *Religion in Africa: Experience and Expression*. Edited by Thomas D. Blakely, Walter E. A. van Beek, and Dennis L. Thomson, 1–20. London: James Curry and Heinemann.
Vertovec, Steven. 2001. "Transnationalism and Identity." *Journal of Ethnic and Migration Studies* 27 (4):573–582.
Wade, Peter. 2000. *Music, Race and Nation: Musica Tropical in Colombia*. Chicago: University of Chicago Press.

———. 1998. "Music, Blackness, and National Identity: Three Moments in Colombian History." *Popular Music* 17 (1):1–19.
Wallace, Jamie B. 2005. "American Perceptions of Africa Based on Media Representations." *Holler Africa*. London: Adonis and Abbey. Accessed February 10, 2014. http://www.hollerafrica.com/showArticle.php?artId=101&catId=&page=2.
Waltrous, Fleuretta. 2009. "Kotchegna Dance Company at the Miller Theatre." *Attitude: The Dancers' Magazine* 23 (2):32–34.
Waterman, Christopher A. 1991. "The Uneven Development of Africanist Ethnomusicology." In *Comparative Musicology and Anthropology of Music: Essays in the History of Ethnomusicology*. Edited by Bruno Nettl and Philip Bohlman, 169–186. Chicago: University of Chicago Press.
———. 1990. *Juju: A Social History and Ethnography of an African Popular Music*. Chicago: University of Chicago Press.
Watson, A. 2008. "Guinea Dance." In *Africa and the Americas: Culture, Politics, and History. A Multidisciplinary Encyclopedia*. Edited by R. M. Juang and N. A. Morrissette, 533–540. Santa Barbara, CA: ABC-CLIO.
Werbner, Pnina. 2006. "Vernacular Cosmopolitanism." *Theory, Culture, and Society* 23 (2–3):496–498.
White, Luise, Stephan Miescher, and David Cohen, eds. 2001. *African Words, African Voices: Critical Practices in Oral History*. Bloomington: Indiana University Press.
Wolf, Juan Eduardo. 2013. "Afro-Chile: Styling Blackness in the Music-Dance along Chile's Northern Border." Ph.D. diss., Indiana University.
Wood, Abigail. 2008. "E-Fieldwork." In *The New (Ethno)musicologies*. Edited by Henry Stobart. Lanham, MD: Scarecrow Press.
Zeleza, Paul Tiyambe. 2009. "Diaspora Dialogues: Engagements between Africa and Its Diasporas." In *The New Africa Diaspora*. Edited by Isidore Okpewho and Nkiru Nzegwu. Bloomington: Indiana University Press.
Zheng, Su. 2010. *Claiming Diaspora: Music, Transnationalism, and Cultural Politics in Asian/Chinese America*. New York: Oxford University Press.

Archival Sources

"Compagnie Nationale de Danse." Undated promotional brochure.
Kotchegna Dance Company. Undated promotional brochure.
Ministère de la Culture et de la Francophonie, Centre National des Arts et de la Culture. "Ballet National de Côte d'Ivoire." Undated archival document.

Index

Page numbers followed by "f" or "t" indicate material in figures or tables.

Abidjan USA, xxi, 3
Abidji ethnicity, 143–144
abodan rhythm/dance, 49, 53, 146–147, 271, 274–275 (274f)
Adje, Maurice, 149
adjoss rhythm/dance, 49, 53, 147
Africa: colonial model of, xx; Hollywood, stage depictions of, xviii, 5; interethnicity within, 106–108; performing, 240; remittances to, 118–121; seen as primitive villages, xvii–xix. *See also* immigrants from Africa
African Americans: affinity for masks by some, 221–222; Afrocentrism versus universalism among, 75, 83–89; and Guinean cultural collaboration, 67; interest in drumming among, 42–44, 87; and Memphis in May festival, xx; nationalism and transnationalism, 129–130, 136–139 (138t); persistent racism toward, xvii; recent immigrants as distinct from, 11t, 12–13; reverse passing by, 86
Agawu, Kofi, 291n5
Agni people, 49, 53, 149–150, 274
Akan linguistic/cultural group, 130, 227, 232–233, 236. *See also abodan* rhythm; Attoungblan
Akin, Louis, 109, 175
Alvin Ailey Dance Theater, 85, 92
amalgamation of traditions, 40–41
Américains noires, 13
Anthropology and the Individual (ed. Miller), 18
Appadurai, Arjun, 292n5
appel signals, 61
apprenticeships, 204
Arapurakal, Ranjit, 231
art history and individual-centered research, 18–19
Asafo band, 256, 272–274
Askew, Kelly, 36–37
Assamoah, Jean, 236
"assimilation and differentiation," 37
Atlanta, Georgia, 141–142; African dance in, 173–174; Atlanta Ballet Theater, 170; Fusion Production, 167; Ivorian population in, 67–68, 171–173; racism and conservatism in, 161; *Song of the South* dance recital, 164–166, 282. *See also Ayoka*; Diallo, Samba; Rau, Mary and Curran
Attitude magazine review, 75, 83, 86–87
Attoungblan dance troupe, 130–131 (137f, 138t). *See also Ayoka* (Samba Diallo)
Attoungblan drums, 132
atumpan, 130–131 (137f, 138t). *See also Ayoka* (Samba Diallo)
audience(s): benedictions to, 188–189; differences between African and North American, 63, 176; educating of, 40, 109; expectations of, 51, 87, 293–294n5; integrated into performance, 45, 140 (140f), 182, 189; Keita on tailoring performances to, 45–46; for *Kekene*, 75–76; for paid performances, 202; and performers "passing" as African, 86; performers themselves as, 229, 240; Samba tailoring performances to, 131–134, 139, 175; school children, 51, 212, 213–214; Sogbety tailoring performances to, 60, 183–184, 186, 191, 205; taking in different meanings, 26
authenticity of performances, 38, 75
author, role/approach of, xx, 19–24
Ayoka (Samba Diallo), 26, 133f; Atlanta 2010 performance, 129–130; blending of genres, ethnic elements, 129–130, 134–136; compared to *Kekene* series, 134–137; costs of producing, 169–170; as educational celebration, 281; genre/structure of, 134–136; instrumentation in, 134; inviting audience onstage, 140; Mary Rau underwriting support for, 169–170; meaning of *ayoka*, 131; non-narrative dance, 134; post-performance talk, 139–140; transnational but black performers, 136–137, 139. *See also* Attoungblan dance troupe; Diallo, Samba

baade, 47f; also called *yado, baanya*, 182, 214; *baade malon* dance, 175; drum pattern, 56, 57t; in Ivorian immigrant performances, 52;

309

ɓaade (continued)
"jembefied" version, 182; and Moha Dosso, 194; as mother drum, 182, 197; Sogbety on, 50, 183, 209–210, 214
ɓaa drums, 190
ɓaa gen ("foot of the drum"), 28
ɓaanya rhythm, 53
Badejo, Peter, 260–261
ballet, West African, 4–5, 37–41; blending of genres, ethnic elements, 129–130, 134; as both genre and discourse, 24–25; as challenge to European racism, 39, 85; competition and cooperation in, 64–68; cosmopolitan sensibility of, 283; creating networks of immigrants, 279, 281; distinctive features of, 44–45, 63; group identity with individual stars, 37; in languages foreign to performers, 28; as lingua franca for performers, 185; meaning of term, 253; as metalanguage, 275; as ready-made skill set, 5, 25, 33–35, 65, 116, 236; reinforcing ethnic values, rules, 109; as social field, affinity for Ivorians, xix, 240–242; as ticket to transnational market, 208–209; tours as gateways to global market, 35; as transnational community, 6, 183, 243–244; use of term "ballet," 280
Ballet de l'Armée, 41
Ballet National de Côte d'Ivoire. *See* BNCI
Bangora, Moustapha, 270
Baule people, 130, 146–147. *See also* Houphouët-Boigny, Félix
Bauman, Richard, 24–25, 293n18
Bedie, Henri Konan, 152
benedictions, 60, 89, 188, 221, 233, 236
Benjamin, Sathima Bea, 20, 292n4
Berliner, Paul, 18
Bete people, 237
Bhabha, Homi, 15
Bi Bo Ti, 50, 206, 208, 222, 230–231, 236–237, 262
Biemi, Gba Jacques, 124
Bizas, Eleni, 5, 85, 292n4
Black African immigrants in United States, 292n10
Black Arts Movement, 85
"Black is Beautiful" Movement, 42
Black Nationalism in America, 42
blending of genres, ethnic elements, 94; *Ayoka* yearly performances, 131–132; *Kekene* (Oneness) series, 87–88; Kotchegna Dance Company, 87–88, 110, 204
bloc (block) signal, 61
Bloomington, Indiana, 243. *See also* Lotus Festival

BNCI (Ballet National de Côte d'Ivoire): compared to Sikensi, 146; competition, distrust within, 64, 153; disallowing outside work, 110; Djo Bi and, 35, 249–250; dual missions of, 106; hiring professional drum makers/maintainers, 114, 116; hotels competing with, 251; and Houphouët-Boigny, 47–48, 68, 78, 106, 249; interethnic interactions in, 107; Memphis in May planning, 112; nationalism in, 77–79; providing life skills for immigrants, 105, 108–109; range of instruments in, 52; Samba's time in, 149–154; selection of Gue Pelou for, 100; Sogbety's time in, 200, 209; "The Vampire," 296n13; transnational influence on, 87–88; Vado as original member of, 75; Vado's audition for, 23–24, 93–95, 97, 99, 103, 188
Bobo people, 233
Bolohi mask spirit and associated rhythm/dance: in *Ayoka*, 135; and Djo Bi's improvisation, 275; at Djo Bi's wedding, 229, 238; Djo Bi teaching, 270–271; Guineans allowed to dance, 187; instruments for, 51, 134, 190, 209–210; as Ivorian ballet standard, 61, 188, 211; not reserved for initiates, 107; Sogbety dancing, 214, 219; tradition maintained in Côte d'Ivoire, 190. *See also* Senufo people
bɔlɔnye harps, 51, 190, 209–210
Bourdieu, Pierre, 6
Bouttiaux, Anne-Marie, 258
breaks, 61–64, 89, 129, 176, 182–183, 189. *See also* "compositions"; signals in dance/rhythm
Buffett, Jimmy, 222
Buggenhagen, Beth, 293n12
Burning Spear, 268
Burns, James, 292n4, 295n2 (ch3)
Burton, Marylese, 183, 187f, 189

Camara, Papa Ladji, 41–42, 49, 66, 87
Cameroon, 119, 136, 255
Canon, Sherry, 292n4
canonization of the repertoire, 52–61 (54t–55t, 57t–59t)
capital, cultural and social, 6, 34
Cardenal, Ernesto, 33
Castaldi, Francesca, 34–39, 44, 46, 293–294n5
cell phones to maintain community, 13, 25, 27, 118–119
changement, 61. *See also* breaks
Charry, Eric, 39, 40–44, 204, 293n3, 297n7
choreographed dramas, 60, 64
Christian, Fate, 213

Civil Rights Movement, 42, 84
Clark, Gracia, 21, 22
Clark, Raquel, 137, 138t
Clegg, Johnny, 149
Clifford, James, 10, 15
clothing: choice of Western or Ivorian, 239–240; kente cloth, 233, 234f
Cohen, Joshua, 86
Colombia, 37
colonization of the mind, 172–173
Comaroff, Jean, 292n7
Comaroff, John, 292n7
Commandant Tra, 247
competition in ballet: among friends, 141; within BNCI, 249–250; and cooperation, 64–65; creating mistrust, suspicion, 153, 169; between Guineans and Ivorians, 66–68; inspiring sorcery, voudou, juju, 92, 97–102, 293n3; in performance, 65–66, 107–108; presence of spirits in, 95
"compositions," 62–63, 230
Condé, Mamadou, 47–48, 87–88
"consultants": author's sharing drafts with, 21–22; primary and secondary, 20; use of term, 16–17
cooperation in ballet, 64–68
Copland, Aaron, xx
cosmopolitanism, 14–16, 282–283, 293n14
Côte d'Ivoire: distribution of immigrants from, 3; effects of civil war in, 222; military influence in, 247; opposing "backward" cultural expressions, 68; use of flag, maps in promotions, 132
Coulibaly, Daniel Ouezzin, 38
coup (cut) signal, 61
Crapanzano, Vincent, 18
cues/signals, 189
culture and social capital, 6

Dagobert, 155
Dagri, Paul, xv, 253
Dahoue, Mamadou, 113, 263, 266
dance: interdependent relationship with drummers, 65; learned through socialization, 229; as litmus test, 85; meaning of for African immigrants, 141. *See also* breaks
"Dance of Possession," 46
Dan Ge Performance (Reed), 19–20
Dan people and language: drums of, 197; and *Ge* stilt mask spirits, 90, 236; mask rhythms of, 194; traditional performances of, 233

"Dead Head" drum circle, 44
decolonizing the mind, 86
Dembele, Madou, 115
Dembele, Pablo, 89
Diabate, Kierno, 52, 66, 134–136, 138t, 182, 186–187 (187f)
Diallo, Samba, 3, 68, 140f, 142f; birth and childhood, 143–145; teen years, 147–148; religion, 144–145, 147–148; learning to dance, 145–147; Jeanne d'Arc de Treichville, 147–149; Varietoscope competition, 148–150; time in BNCI, 149–153; Memphis in May performance, 153–154; overstaying in Memphis, xv, 155–156; living in Maryland, 156; almost getting shot, moving to Atlanta, 156–157; working at Mary Rau's dance school, 157–158, 166; kicked out by cousin, 158–159; help from Mary and Curran Rau, 159–164, 169–170; death of mother, unable to go home, 162; playing Uncle Remus in dance recital, 164–166, 282; joining Fusion Production, 167; John Lewis assisting with INS, 167; work permit and green card, 168; becoming an American citizen, 140, 168–169, 178; Afrofit exercise program, xviii, 174, 282; and Atlanta's Ivorian community, 171–172; as a choreographer, 152, 175–177; future plans, 177–178; getting website design certificate, 177; inviting whites and blacks onstage, 140; living as an immigrant, 170–171; at Lotus Festival, 184; meeting author, xvi, 141–142; of mixed ethnicity, 131, 138t, 143–144, 147; and name *ayoka*, 130–131; promotional approach, 131–132, 191; on reasons for dancing, 141; as a scholar, 283; as a teacher, 173–175. *See also* Ayoka (Samba Diallo)
diaspora, 5, 7–8, 10, 14
diasporic, defined, 9
diasporic sensibilities, 281–282
Diomande, Kossa, 115, 119
Diomande, Lisa, 20, 80f; marriage to Vado, 125; on meaning of "cosmopolitan," 14–15; on meaning of "scholar," 8, 16; on race issues in booking, 81, 295n3; set design, 82; on Vado's personality, 91
Diomande, Sogbety, 133f, 216f; childhood interest in drums, dancing, 197–199; and his parents, 198; recruited by Vado for Kotchegna, 199–205; life in Abidjan, 200–202, 209; apprenticeship to play *jembe*, 203–204; at Memphis in May, 200, 205–206; recruited to Mask Dance Company, 206; getting visas, Social

Diomande, Sogbety (continued)
Security number, 206; adapting to cold of New York, 207; meeting, marrying Jennifer Vincent, 208; diversifying, 208–212; performing Gue Pelou, 211–212; performing at Disney's Animal Kingdom, 212; performing in schools, 212, 213; solo performance versus organizing shows, 216–217; performing in Mansfield, Ohio, 120, 213–215; Mansfield versus New York, 217–218; future aspirations, 222–224; bringing son from Africa, 223; adaptations of ballet form, 183, 219; on competition, jealousy, 65–66; on dancing Gue Pelou in Toufinga versus elsewhere, 219–220; going to United States, 119, 262; invited to NYC, overstaying, xv; on key to life, 224; on language in United States, 185; on life choices, 192; at Lotus Festival, 182–184, 191, 218f; Memphis in May, 200, 205–206; performing Bolohi rhythm/dance, 214, 219; performing with Jim Donovan, 219–220; performing with Jimmy Buffett, 222; performing with pop stars, 282; promotional approach, 191; responding to audience, 183; as a scholar, 283; self-identifying as West African, 185–186; on small-group ballet, 35; supporting family in Africa, 120; working for Africa, 223. *See also* West African Drum and Dance Company

Diomande, Tefini, 222–223

Diomande, Vado, 3, 47f, 80f, 92f, 281; identified as mask "proprietor" before birth, 94–95; audition for BNCI, 93–97, 99, 103, 188, 200; in BNCI, 77, 103, 105–106, 108–109, 116; village approval to take Gue Pelou, 101–102; jawbone issues from voudou attacks, 97–102, 111–112; returning to Toufinga to recuperate, 108; starting Kotchegna with Zagbo Martin, 108–109, 112, 114; running out of money, 110–111; Memphis in May opportunity, xvi–xvii, 112–113; to New York after Memphis, 113; bone grafts to repair jaw, 116–117; help from Gue Pelou, 112; hired by Djoniba as drum maker, 114–116; repairing, playing *jembes*, 114–116; teaching dance classes, 114–116; meeting Madou Dembele, 115; recruiting Sogbety, Moha, 119–120; Achilles injury, 117–118; marriage to Lisa, obtaining green card, 102, 125; touring, 121; bringing skins back from Africa, 122–123; contracting anthrax, possessions destroyed, 23, 121–124, 182; achieving success after regaining health, 121; remittances to Africa, 118–121; at Lotus Festival, 182; knee problems, 108, 125, 182; confidence regarding competition, 107–108; example of author notes on, 91–92; and Guinean dance, music, 47; language use of, 22–23; Memphis in May opportunity, xvi–xvii, 112–113; nationalism of, 77–78, 82; prayers, 91; requiring herbal/mystical medicine, 98–99; as a scholar, 283; shown dance steps in dreams, 103–104; touring, 121; on travels of mask spirits, 236; unity through diversity, 75–77, 82, 106; universalism of, 183; why he dances, 91; and the word *cosmopolitan*, 14–15; and the word *diaspora*, 7–8. *See also* Kotchegna Dance Company

"discourse," defined, 25

Djo Bi Irie Simon, 3, 41f, 244f; birth and childhood, 244–246; traveling with church, 246; move to Abidjan, joining Kada Club, 246–248; leaving church, 248–249; staying with Commandant Tra, 247–248; first contact with BNCI, 249–250; touring with Kada Club, 250; auditioning at hotel, 251–252; joining Zomblé Gonè Club, 252; joining Les Guirivoires, 252–254; changing age on birth certificate, 253–254; author in elder brother role, 253–254; leaving Les Guirivoires for Wafou, 254; rejoining Zamblé Gonè, 255; moving to France, 255–256; starting Asafo group, 256; trip to Turkey, 256; joining Georges Momboye in Paris, 257, 260; moving to Belgium, 257; museum mask research, 258–260; English tour with Badejo Arts, 260–262; Gao Bi reporting illegal visa, 261; and Mask Dance Company, xv, 208–209, 262–263; short marriage to Jennah, 263, 264–265; relationship with Lisa Vives, 263, 265; playing in subway, 265; meeting Yuichi Iida, 265; and Mecca Bodega, 266, 268; meeting Papa Titos Sompa, 266; diversifying repertoire, 266–268; meeting Harmony Harris, 268–269; moving to Bloomington, 270–271; at Lotus Festival, 182; teaching classes, 271; meeting author, 243, 271; as an innovator, 272–275 (273f, 274f); on ballet fostering interethnic friendships, 64; on *gbegbe*, 53, 62; on "mathematics of African dance," 62; playing as "in the village," 209; as a scholar, 283; training in ballet, 35; wearing kente cloth, 233, 234f. *See also* "Open Village" wedding

Djo Bi Vié, 244

Djo Lou Gouana Martine, 244

Djoniba Dance and Drum Centre, 85, 92, 113–114

Dodd, Wayne, 279
Donovan, Jim, 213, 219
Dor, George, 294n8
Dosso, Moha, 20, 191; in *Ayoka,* 136–137, 138t; becoming director of Kotchegna, 119, 206; at Djo Bi's wedding, 232, 241–242; fire tricks, 241–242; legally returning to U.S., 206; living in Ohio, Indiana, 120; at Lotus Festival, 46, 187t; at Memphis in May festival, 112, 119–120, 200, 205; nationality/race/ethnicity, 138t; performing Gue Pelou, 46, 120, 188, 194; and Samba's citizenship, 169; training, 120; Vado on, 120–121
dramas, choreographed, 60, 64
Dr. Djo Bi. *See* Djo Bi Irie Simon
dreams as communication from mask spirits, 103–104
drum circle culture, 87, 257
Drums of Passion (Olatunji), 42, 44, 116
dundunba rhythm, 53
dundun drums, 87, 182–183; required for ballet, 35; *tématé* on, 56; *tindin* on, 51–53, 54t–55t, 56, 134, 235–236; types of, 40; in United States, 41. *See also* jembe/dundun pairing

Ebron, Paulla, 5, 120
Ecole Normale William Ponty, 38, 293n3
economic production and aesthetic practice, 5
Edwards, Brent Hayes, 86
ensemble, 39
Ensemble Djoliba, 41
Ensemble Kotchegna, 51, 103
Ermey, Peter, 188
Etchue Wuehoun group, 149
"Ethiopian Musical Invention in Diaspora" (Shelemay), 20
ethnography: focused on individuals, 17–19; life story form of, 21–24, 279–281; as poetic form, 279; research methods for this book, 27–28; Society for Ethnomusicology, 194; value of long-term research, 105
"Evolution of African Music into Modern American Music, The," xiii, xviii

Faby, Feu Soumahoro, 147
fan (life force), 221–222
"Fanfare for the Common Man" (Copland), xx
Fangalo, Gayle, 135
Faustin, Dagbo, 103
Feld, Steven, xix, 15, 20, 282
Ferguson, James, 237

Ferguson, Missouri, xvii
Festimask, 106
Fischer, Eberhard, 294n15, 295n3 (ch4)
Flaig, Vera, 43–45, 63, 292n4
fluidity among performers, groups, 110
"folklorization," 36
Foua Bi, Jacques, 248
"frictions" in global connections, xvii
Frisbie, Charlotte, 18

Gao Bi, 230–231, 236, 251, 254, 261–262, 272
Garuba, Harry, xviii
Gaudens, Max Quao, 148, 151
gbegbe rhythm, 53, 54t, 62, 176, 188, 237
GDE (Ghana Dance Ensemble), 39–40
ge gbleen (Dan stilt mask spirit genre), 49, 94
genre, defined, 25
Gershwin, George, xx
Geschiere, Peter, 12, 119, 296n7
Ge stilt mask spirits, 90, 220–221. *See also* stilt mask spirit(s) (*nya yan*)
getan repertoire, 89–90
"Ge ya yi kan" song, 233
Ghana: drumming and dance in America, 43; Ghana Dance Ensemble, 34, 39–40, 105; hiplife artists, 6–7
Gigi, 268
Gilroy, Paul, 292n11
ginan/yinan (spirits), 46, 95, 101, 103, 188. *See also* stilt mask spirit(s) (*nya yan*)
Giraud, Rose Marie, 150, 252–254
Giuggia, Michelle, 137, 138t
Glassie, Henry, 18–19, 292n4
"global capitalism," 12
"global connections," 5
"globalization," 292n6
Gohoun, Euphrasie, 89
Golden Sounds, 136
goli rhythm, 149
Goodman, Jane, 24
Goré, Eric Bli Bi, 228f, 230–231
Gougoua, Richard, 231, 238
gourd rattles with beaded nets, 134
Gourlay, Kenneth, 17–18
Gue Pelou mask spirit and associated rhythm/dance, 96f, 135, 228f; in *Ayoka* performances, 129, 134; can dance with any music, 221; at Djo Bi's wedding, 233–236, 238; Ivorian performances of, 61, 188, 190, 211; at Lotus Festival, 181, 187–189; Moha Dosso performing, 46, 188, 194, 211; with New York jazz musicians, 211–

Gue Pelou mask spirit (*continued*) 212; objections to mask leaving, 100–101, 119; origin of, 94; rhythms of, 53, 56–61 (58t, 59t); rules for performance, 188–189, 221; sacred housing for, 188, 220, 227, 228f, 233; Sogbety performing, 188, 211; speaks, sings Dan exclusively, 90, 94, 107, 189; standardized performance sequence, 60; in "The History of Mahou Masks," 89; Vado performing, 94, 188, 211

Guinea/Guinean people: competition with Ivorians, 65, 66–68, 77, 114–115; Djo Bi on music of, 272; as early ballet style in United States, 39, 41–42, 46–47, 210; Maninka/Malinké ethnicity, 88–89, 129; popularizing *jembe* and *dundun*, xix, 50–51; Samba on, 175; and Sekou Touré, 43–44, 48, 68, 257; shared culture with Ivorians, 186–187; Sogbety on, 185; Soli Wule rhythm and mask spirit, 53, 188. *See also* Bangora, Moustapha; Diabaté, Kierno; Keita, Fodeba; Keita, Mamady; Koivogui, Hamidou; *kuku* rhythm; LBA (Les Ballets Africains); Mande people

Guro people: differences among, 252; flutes, 190; as "real players" of zauli, 210; weddings among, 232, 236–237. *See also* Zauli mask spirit and associated rhythm/dance

Hall, Stuart, 292n2
Harris, Harmony, 20, 63, 188, 227, 236, 238 (238f), 243, 268–271. *See also* "Open Village" wedding
Hart, Mickey, 43
Hazzard-Gordon, Katrina, 85
"heightened reflexivity" of performance, 24, 78, 280
heterogeneous identities, 12–13
Himmelman, Natasha, xviii
hiplife artists, 6–7
"History of Mahou Masks, The" (Vado Diomande), 60, 76–77, 82–83, 88, 109, 295n1(ch3). *See also Kekene* (Oneness) series
Holland, Dorothy C., 21
Houphouët-Boigny, Félix: of Baule ethnicity, 130; and BNCI, 47–48, 68, 78, 105–106, 249; death of, 152; and Ecole Ponty, 38; financial support from, 106; installing televisions in schools, 249; and "Ivorian Miracle," 143; pro-Western, anticommunist, 68; Zauli favorite mask of, 78
human–spirit dream communication, 103–105
"Hunt, The" ballet drama, 109
hybrid nature of folklore, 38–39

"I Call Your Name" (Clegg), 149
identity labels, 12–13
"I Got Rhythm" (Gershwin), xx
Iida, Yuichi, 233, 265
immigrants from Africa: growth of, 4; knowing their place of origin, 13; maintaining community through performance, 186; terms for, 12–13; as transnational, 3, 5
Inda, Jonathan, 292n6
informal performance: at Lotus Festival, 184; at "Open Village" wedding, 229–232, 239–242
"informant"/"*informateur*," 16
"interconnection," 292n6
interviews, language of, 22–23
IPA (International Phonetic Alphabet), xxvii
island, performance as tip of, 4
"Ivorian Miracle," 143, 152, 201
Ivorian National Ballet, 25
Ivorian nationalism: in ballet, 46–49; and competition with Guineans, 65, 66–68, 77, 114–115; and *gbegbe* rhythm, 53; in Kotchegna Dance Company, 78

Janelli, Roger, 16
Jang, Joe, 265
Jazz Cosmopolitanism in Accra (Feld), 20
jealousy among performers, 65–67, 102, 261. *See also* sorcery by competitors
Jeanne d'Arc de Treichville, 148–149
jegele xylophone, 52, 239, 254
jelibala, 134, 181, 182–183
jeliya, 5
jembe, xviii–xix, 37, 41f; ballet version of, 45–46; as a city drum, 190, 203; "explosion" of 1990s, 257; fame bringing jealousy, 65–66; *kuku* rhythm, 53–56 (54t, 55t), 188; and LBA, 40–44; Papa Diarra, 129; patterns for, 53–56 (55t). *See also jembe/dundun* pairing
jembe/dundun pairing, 46–47; in Asafo, 272; in Ayoka, 135; as ballet standard, 51–53, 54t–55t, 134, 182, 204; collaboration with Jimmy Buffett, 222; communicating power, 82; Djo Bi on, 274; at Djo Bi's wedding, 239, 241; early examples of, 205; introduced by Guineans, 50–51, 66; maintaining community through, 186; in New York, 211; not in BNCI, Mask Dance, 209; in place of "authentic" instruments, 210; transposing mask rhythms for, 236
jembefication, 44, 49–52; of *baade*, 182; drawbacks of, 190; growth of, 46–47; in *Kekene*,

87–88; at Lotus Festival, 189–190; and Mask Dance Company, 209; in New York City, 210
Jim Crow South, 295n3 (ch3)
Jimson, 150
Joanne (friend of Samba), 155–157
Jula, 176, 296n1; language, 183, 201, 203, 273–274; people, 143–144, 146, 204

Kablan, Patrice, 149–150
Kafundo, Justin, 124
Kamaté, Yahyah, 212, 230, 239
Keita, Fodeba, 38–40, 45–46
Keita, Mamady, 43, 68, 257
Keita, Modiba, 38
Kekene (Oneness) series, 26, 79f; *Attitude*'s review of, 75–76; blending of genres, ethnic elements, 87–88; as both traditional and multiethnic, 80–81; as choreographed drama, 60, 88; compared to *Ayoka*, 134–137; discourse on stage, 82; Girlane Zetra (TC) introduction to IV, 76; *jembe/dundun* instrumentation for, 87; life story as performance in, 280; meaning of title, 77; program notes, 82; racial diversity of performers, 75, 83–84 (84t). *See also* "History of Mahou Masks, The" (Vado Diomande)
Kennesaw, Georgia, 157, 160–166, 177
kente cloth, 233, 234f
Kimoun, Robi, 256
King, Martin Luther, Jr., 84
Kiwan, Nadia, 5–6
Klein, Debra, 5, 35, 292n6
"ko fli do" (Excuse me) ritual, 235
Koivogui, Hamidou, 66, 136, 138t, 186–187 (187f), 232, 235–236
"kola" payment, 202
Kone, Seguenon: at Disney's Animal Kingdom, 212; Djo Bi on, 64; and Jimmy Buffett, 222; playing *jegele* xylophone, 52, 110, 238–239, 254; trying to help Djo Bi, 255, 262
Kopytoff, Igor, 106
Kotchegna Dance Company: accused of bringing bad luck, 102; allowing moonlighting, 110; blending of genres, ethnic elements, 87–88, 110, 204; BNCI experience helping, 103; choreographed dramas in, 60; first overseas tour, 109; "History of Mahou Masks" for, 109; instrumentation, 87; meaning of name, 77; Memphis in May festival, 205; "modernizing" traditional performance, 204–205; Moha Dosso as director, 119, 206; promotional materials for, 78, 81–83; race/ethnicity of performers in, 81, 83–87 (84t); reverse passing in, 86; traditional yet multicultural, 80–81, 89; types of drums used in, 204–205; universalism and nationalism in, 78–79, 82, 83; U.S. shows, 121, 124; Vado starting New York version of, 206; yearly Lincoln Center performances, 215. *See also* Diomande, Sogbety; Diomande, Vado; *Kekene* (Oneness) series
Kourouma, Moussa, 47, 251–252
Kratz, Corrine A., 21
kuku rhythm (Maninka), 46, 53–56 (55t), 134–135, 188, 270, 275, 294n12

Lawless, Elaine, 21
LBA (Les Ballets Africains), 38–39, 40, 48, 63, 68, 86, 257
Les Ballets de Fodeba Keita, 38
Lewis, John, 167–168
Lizzie, Tra Bi, 20; backing out of Mansfield show, 214; Djo Bi and, 62, 230, 235, 272, 274; as Guro in United States, 50; in *Kekene IV*, 84t; marriage, 263; in Mask Dance Company, 206–207, 209–210, 262–263; performing in clubs, 267; playing as "in the village," 209
Lotus Festival, 193f, 194, 218f, 281–282; author as master of ceremonies, 181; Bloomington, Indiana setting, 181; genre/structure of, 187–189; Gue Pelou performance at, 46, 47f, 60, 181–184, 188–189; instrumentation, 189–190; nationality/ethnicity of performers, 186–187 (187f); Samba teaching dance at, 142f; Sogbety performance at, 182–184, 191, 218f; visuals, 191. *See also* West African Drum and Dance Company
Loua, Zan Lou, 247

Mande people, 49–50, 77, 237; influence on Ivorian ballet, 38, 40, 49–50, 66, 135, 210–211; instruments of, 38; *jeli* caste, 134, 137, 182–183; Jula, 201, 204, 273–274; Mandification, 37, 44; Maninka/Malinké ethnicity, 88–89, 129, 134, 182; music/dance culture, 210. *See also* jembefication; Toufinga
Mansfield, Ohio, 120, 186, 194, 213–219, 223, 243
Mansfield, Pennsylvania, 121–122
"Marriage, The" (Sogbety Diomande), 60
Mask Dance Company, xv; Djo Bi and, 208–209, 262–263; founded by Bley Zaguehi, 120–121, 206; jembefication in, 209–210; reason for name, 210; Sogbety and, 206, 208–210
mask spirits. *See* stilt mask spirit(s) (*nya yan*)

Matias, Zewenin, 246
Maultsby, Portia, 9
Mau mask spirits (*nya*), 46, 76, 93–95, 129–130, 188, 221. *See also* "History of Mahou Masks, The" (Vado Diomande); stilt mask spirit(s) (*nya yan*)
Mau people, 88, 109, 233. *See also* Mau mask spirits
May It Fill Your Soul (Rice), 18
McAllister, David, 18
McDowell, John, 36
McNaughton, Patrick, 18–19
Mecca Bodega, 266, 268
Meinhof, Ulrike, 5–6
Meiway, 150
Memphis in May Festival, xv, xiii–xviii; African Americans and, xx; BNCI at, 112; colonialist discourse in, xx, 39; Kotchegna Dance Company, 205; Moha Dosso, 112, 119–120, 200, 205; Samba in, 153–154; Sogbety in, 200, 205–206; Vado in, xvi–xvii, 112–113
"Michelle Nigeria," 137, 138t
migrant crisis worldwide, xxi
military-style training, 105
Miller, Daniel, 18
Mitchell, Frank, 18
Momboye, Georges, 257
Mongueï, Fanzie, 155–157
Monson, Ingrid, 14
Morning Call, The, review, 78–79
movement, human, 5
Muller, Carol, 20
Murray, Pia, 88
"musical community," 25–26
Musical Echoes (Muller and Benjamin), 20
musical labor, 6
Muslims, xxi, 144–145, 147–148, 195–196, 280

National Dance Company (Ghana), 34
nationalism: friction between Guineans and Ivorians, 77; Kotchegna troupe and, 77–78, 82; mixing with universalism, 78–79, 82, 83, 132; Samba, 130; Vado Diomande, 77–78, 82
(nation)-state ensembles, 36–37
Nea, Jules Hié, 47
Neal, Larry, 85
"New African Diaspora," 4; arts and individual experience in, 14; characteristics of, 11–13; daily communication worldwide, 26; versus old, 11t; performing a, 11, 26; use of term, 7, 9
New York City, 42, 85
New Yorker Gue Pelou article, 121

New York Times Gue Pelou article, 121
n'goron rhythm/dance, 53, 88
Ngugi wa Thiongo, 86, 172
Nguyen, Jason, 9, 16
Nisa (Shostak), 18
Nketia, Kwabena, 40, 43, 294n7
Nkrumah, Kwame, 39–40
Nobakov, Peter, 18
Nya (Mau mask spirit), 46, 76, 93–95, 129–130, 188, 221. *See also* "History of Mahou Masks, The" (Vado Diomande); stilt mask spirit(s) (*nya yan*)
nya ba (Great Mask Spirit), 221

O'Connor, Bonnie, 125
Olatunji, Michael Babatunde, 42–44, 115–116
Olatunji Center for African Culture, 42
online media examples guide, ix–xii
"Open Village" wedding, 41 (41f), 53, 96f, 282–283; ethnic groups among attendees, 227; formal performance, 232–237; informal performance I, 229–232; informal performance II, 239–242; "sacred" housing for Gue Pelou, 227, 228f; United Nations Band, 237–239
orchestres, 39

Pan-African symbolism, 83
panther mask. *See* Bolohi mask spirit and associated rhythm/dance
Papa Diarra, 20, 129, 132, 135–136, 183, 189, 233; pictured, 96f, 138t, 187f, 228f
participant-observation methods, 27
pattern "pa tun pe de," 56, 59t
Peacock, James L., 21
Pennsic festivals, 213
performance, 24–26; informal, 229, 240–241; of nationalism, 36; pay for, 26, 202; reinforcing community, 25; as tip of island, 4; as transnational labor, 5. *See also* "Open Village" wedding
performing "for those who know," 240, 241
Perullo, Alex, 6
Polak, Rainer, 35, 44, 63, 291n3
"politics of con/disjunction," xix
Portelli, Alessandro, 22
Powerhouse for God (Titon), 18
"preballet" instrumentation, 56
presence of spirits (*yinan; ginan*), 95
Prince Twins Seven-Seven, 19
PURL references, ix–xii; [2.1–2.6], 46; [3.1], 76; [3.2], 88; [3.3], 89; [5.1], 129; [5.2, 5.3], 135; [5.4],

139; [7.1a], 181; [7.1b, 7.4], 188; [7.2, 7.3], 182, 189; [9.1], 230; [9.2, 9.3], 231; [9.4, 9.5], 232; [9.6], 233; [9.7, 9.8], 236; [9.9], 237; [9.10, 9.11, 9.12], 238; [9.13], 53, 239; [9.14], 241; [10.1], 272

Racanelli, David, 293n15
Radin, Paul, 21
Randall, Multhee, 135, 137
Rau, Mary and Curran, 140, 157–167 (160f), 169, 282
reconstruction, nationalism as, 37
reflexivity, 17–18, 22, 24, 78, 280
rehearsals for annual concerts, 232
religion in Côte d'Ivoire: Christianity, 144–145, 147; Islam, 144–145, 147; mixed marriages, 144–145
remittances, 12–13, 118–121
reverse passing, 86
"rhythm/dance," 28, 63–64, 275
Rice, Tim, 18
rock music and ballet, 213, 282
Rosaire de Treichville, 150
Rosaldo, Renato, 292n6
Rose (acquaintance of Mary Rau), 157–158
Rose, Jennah, 261, 263, 264

Saakumu, 294n10
sabar drums, 37, 211
Said, Edward, xviii
samaba dance, 204
Samba. *See* Diallo, Samba
Schauert, Paul, 34, 40, 105, 110, 209, 293n2
"scholars," Ivorian artists as, 8, 16–17
Seaman, Melanie, xvi, 20, 213–215
secular masks, 107
Seeger, Tony, 104
self-identification, 12–13
Senegal, 34, 211
sensibilities, diasporic and cosmopolitan, 9, 16
Senufo people: 274; *bɔlɔnye* harps, 190; *jegele* xylophone, 52, 239; *n'goron* rhythm/dance, 53, 88; rhythm/dances intermixed in Kotchegna, 87; Wambele mask reserved for initiates, 107. *See also* Bolohi mask spirit and associated rhythm/dance; Kone, Seguenon
Shakira, 136
Shao, Oliver, 5
Shelemay, Kay Kaufman, 20, 25–26
Shepperson, George, 10
Sherzer, Joel, 36
Shipley, Jesse, 6

Shostak, Marjorie, 18
signals in dance/rhythm, 61–64, 189. *See also* breaks
Sikensi, Côte d'Ivoire, 143, 146
Simmons, Leo W., 18
sinte rhythm, 135
Skinner, Ryan T., 292n4, 293nn14, 19
slap signals, 61, 129, 189
slavery as unifying experience, 12
Slobin, Mark, 292n8
Smyrna Cultural Center, 129
Society for Ethnomusicology, 194
Sogbety. *See* Diomande, Sogbety
"Sogbety Diomande's West African Celebration," 194
Soli Wule rhythm and mask spirit, 53, 135, 188
Sompa, Papa Titos, 231, 233, 239, 266
Song of the South (Disney), 164–166, 282
sorcery by competitors, 92, 97, 99–100, 112, 123
Soul of Mbira (Berliner), 18
Soumahoro, Abou, 155, 223
spirit visitation in dreams, 13, 15
state ensembles, 36–37
Sterling, Marvin, 86
stilt mask spirit(s) (*nya yan*): in Abidjan, 202–203; African Americans responding to, 222; appearing in dreams, 101; interethnic performances breaking "rules," 134; mask families, 94–95; mask itself not same as mask spirit, 120, 259; origin of, 90, 94; preparations for performance, 188; Samba on importance of, 177; secular, 107; sonic manifestations of, 190; U.S. versus home village performances, 219–220. *See also* Gue Pelou; Mau masks
Stone, Ruth, xv, 97, 293n18, 297n1 (ch9)
"street French," 293n16
"submerged voices," 21
Sun Chief (Talayesva and Simmons), 18

Talayesva, Don C., 18
Tamango, 121, 282
Tang, Patty, 87
Tanzanian popular music, 6
tap dancer, 121, 282
Taylor, Timothy, 51
Tchimou, Robi, 255
témate rhythm/dance, 53, 56, 63, 107, 188, 209, 257
tempo changes, 129
"third space," 293n19
tibloklalo rhythm/dance, 53

time, clock versus social, 201–202
tindin rhythm/dance, 53–60 (57t–59t), 181, 183, 188, 233, 236
Titon, Jeff Todd, 18
Toa, Clarice, 65, 183, 187f, 189
Toloyan, Khachig, 10, 292n3
topalon (Guro drum), 204, 256
Touba region, 195
Toufinga, 195–196; authority from proximity to Dan region, 56; Gue Pelou's departure from, 100–102, 188, 221; *jembe* in, 50; Sogbety on, 185, 192, 201–202, 219–220; Vado as "Big Man" in, 108, 119–121; Vado scouted by BNCI, 93, 95, 100, 200
Touré, Sekou, 39, 41, 43, 48, 68, 85
Tra Bi. *See* Lizzie, Tra Bi
"transcultural capital," 5
"transnational": defined, 13; immigrants as, 3; marketplace as, xix, 5; state ensemble as, 36–37; West African ballet as, 44–49
Treichville, Côte d'Ivoire, 143
True, Christy, 160, 227, 229, 242
Tsing, Anna, xvii
Tuhami: Portrait of a Moroccan (Crapanzano), 18
Tuohy, Sue, 36
Turino, Thomas, 14, 36, 232
Two Leggings (Nobakov), 18
"typical" music and dance, 146

unifying diversity, 37, 40
unifying experience, 12
United Nations Band, 237–239
United States: as Now to Africa's Past, xvii; proposals to ban all Muslims, xxi; spread of *jembe* in, 41–44; spread of *jembe* to, 41–44
unity in/through diversity, 40, 75–78, 82, 129–132, 294n7
Urban, Greg, 36, 220
ury rhythm, 53. *See also gbegbe* rhythm

Vado. *See* Diomande, Vado
Valentine, Von, 137, 138t
"Vampire, The" (Vado Diomande), 60, 109
van Beek, Walter, 296n10
Varietoscope competition, 148–150
Verbal Art as Performance (Bauman), 24
"vernacular cosmopolitanism," 15
Vertovec, Steven, 13
Vincent, Jennifer, 192–194, 208

visas: faked, 260–262; obtaining of, 206, 208, 222–223, 255; overstaying of, xv, 35
Vives, Lisa, 263, 265
voice metaphor, 273–275
"voudou," 97, 99

Wade, Peter, 37
Wafou, Hotel, 251–252
"Waka Waka (This Time for Africa)" (Shakira), 136
Webster, Tia, 135, 138t, 169
wedding. *See* "Open Village" wedding
Werbner, Pnina, 15
West African Drum and Dance Company, 183–186
West African health care paradigm, 92–93
white performers: complaints about, 139; in Kotchegna dance troupe, 80
Wolofization, 37
Woma, Bernard, 294n10

Yankey, Emmanuel, xv
Yapo, Adépo, xv
yinan/ginan (spirits), 46, 95, 101, 103, 188. *See also* stilt mask spirit(s) (*nya yan*)
Yoruba bata, 5, 35
Young Audiences, 212, 213

Zagbo, Martin, 52, 108–109, 237–238
Zaguehi, Bley, 120, 206, 209, 262–263
zambele/flaly rhythm/dance, 53
"Zangalewa" (Golden Sounds), 136
zanloba rhythm/dance, 53
Zauli Lou Kambo, 245
Zauli mask spirit and associated rhythm/dance, 135, 188, 190, 209–210, 229, 238, 247, 252, 270; dancing to *kuku* in *Ayoka*, 135; Djo Bi recording of, 257; favorite mask of Houphouët-Boigny, 78; as Ivorian ballet standard, 61–63, 188, 211; and jembefication, 51–52; legend of, 53; in Lotus Festival, 188; not reserved for initiates, 107; PURL [9.10], 238; requirements for dance, 50; in "The Marriage" choreographed drama, 60
Zekalo, Blaise, 20, 187f, 228, 230, 235
Zeleza, Paul Tiyambe, 11, 14
Zetrea, Girlane, 76
Zie, Coulibali, 154–155
zikinin rhythm, 53, 60, 233, 236

DANIEL B. REED is Associate Professor in the Department of Folklore and Ethnomusicology and affiliated faculty for African Studies and the Center for the Study of Global Change at Indiana University. He is the author of *Dan Ge Performance: Masks and Music in Contemporary Côte d'Ivoire* (IUP, 2003), co-winner of the Amaury Talbot Prize from the Royal Anthropological Institute of London. He is also co-author, with Gloria Gibson, of the CD-ROM *Music and Culture of West Africa: The Straus Expedition*, and author of numerous articles, media publications, and museum catalog entries on Ivorian music and mask performance.

www.ingramcontent.com/pod-product-compliance
Lightning Source LLC
Chambersburg PA
CBHW070259240426
43661CB00057B/2590